Klemens H. Fischer

The Evolution of the EU Treaties

From the Treaties of Rome to the Conference on the Future of Europe

Including BREXIT and the Windsor Framework

HART

Nomos

The Deutsche Nationalbibliothek lists this publication in the Deutsche Nationalbibliografie; detailed bibliographic data are available on the Internet at http://dnb.d-nb.de

ISBN: HB (Nomos) 978-3-7560-1293-0
ePDF (Nomos) 978-3-7489-4077-7

British Library Cataloguing-in-Publication Data
A catalogue record for this book is available from the British Library.

ISBN: HB (Hart) 978-1-5099-8014-7

Library of Congress Cataloging-in-Publication Data
Fischer, Klemens H.
The Evolution of the EU Treaties
From the Treaties of Rome to the Conference on the Future of Europe.
Including BREXIT and the Windsor Framework
Klemens H. Fischer
422 pp.
Includes bibliographic references and index.

ISBN 978-1-5099-8014-7 (hardcover Hart)

Online Version
Nomos eLibrary

1st Edition 2024

For Kirsten

The journey has been enjoyable
and well worth making – once.
WSC,
28 Hyde Park Gate,
January 24, 1965

... even a third time.
KHF,
Florence-London-Tōkyō
December 2023

General Remarks and Acknowledgements

Mieux vaut se disputer autour d'une table
que sur un champ de bataille.

Jean Monnet

Every generation claims a *dies ater* or an *annus horribilis* for its era, with the respective intensity being very much adapted to the prevailing Zeitgeist and circumstances. The year 2022, however, can justifiably be classified as an objectively dark year, the beginning of which marks a caesura in Europe. The Russian attack on Ukraine on 24 February 2022 constitutes a Zeitenwende that will be comparable to both the Great War and the Second World War. The Founding Fathers of the European Community, which steadily, if not always harmoniously, evolved into the European Union, had in mind the goal of preventing a third Great War by integrating the defeated Axis powers. From its outset in the early 1950s, European integration has always been economically based and dominated, but by its nature it represented a comprehensive peace project unparalleled in history.

The European Union was awarded the Nobel Peace Prize in 2013, a decision that did not meet with understanding or even approval everywhere. This partial ambivalence may have many facets, from general EU scepticism to specific rejection. However, one major reason may be that the peace aspect of the European Union has been all but forgotten in favour of an almost exclusively economic orientation.

Even before the Russian-Ukrainian catastrophe, the European Union's ideal world was already dramatically shaken when the United Kingdom declared her withdrawal and both the EU and the United Kingdom had to learn to live with the consequences of Brexit. Whatever one's view on Brexit, it was the result of a process in which none of the parties involved could convince the other of their respective positions and eventually there was insufficient basis for a sustainable compromise.

Most conflicts are based on a lack of both an understanding of the subject matter and a willingness to explore and understand the opposing view and to find a compromise for the good of all. In this book, I have tried to trace the development of individual EU policies from their beginnings to the present. It is a journey with detours, surprises, disagreements, and unexpected stops. Above all, however, it is a journey that was ultimately borne by all participants in mutual agreement and compromise.

European integration will continue in one way or another, it will be shaped by endogenous and exogenous processes, it will continue to be a mirror of its time.

We will see in the course of this volume that the reforms of the Treaties came in several waves, originating in the realisation that the Community/Union had to be prepared for the coming and almost foreseeable challenges of each era. The sooner the Heads of State and Government came to this realisation, the better the reforms. Reforms that came under fire did not necessarily meet the multiple challenges. The wisdom of the ancient Romans, expressed in the dictum *sine ira et studio*, is presumably most appropriate.

This book is intended to contribute to the understanding of the development up to the present state and thus also to be a basis for future development.

At this point I would like to thank my long-time publisher NOMOS, who also made this book possible. Above all, I am indebted to the staff at NOMOS, who needed a lot of patience this time. I would also like to thank the staff at Hart Publishing, with whom I was privileged to work for the first time.

My very personal thanks go to my wife, Kirsten B. Fischer, PhD. Not only did she have to accompany one of my books for the third time, but this time she especially motivated me not to give up. My special thanks go to all my friends who took the time to discuss the individual sections of the book with me and who supported me with advice, input and, above all, time, and in the end even remained my friends.

Ceterum censeo ... it is the author's duty to take the blame for everything that went wrong and ask for leniency - that is what I humbly ask of every reader.

Florence-London-Tōkyō, 2024 Prof. Dr. Klemens H. Fischer

Table of Contents

List of Abbreviations

AA/	as amended by
ACP	African, Caribbean and Pacific Group of States
aka	also known as
BSE	Bovine spongiform encephalopathy
CAP	Common Agricultural Policy
CARICOM	Caribbean Community of States
cf.	see
CFEU	Conference on the Future of Europe
CFSP	Common Foreign and Security Policy
CSDP	Common Security and Defence Policy
CIS	Commonwealth of Independent States
COMECON	Council for Mutual Economic Assistance
CoR	Committee of the Regions
CPSU	Communist Party of the Soviet Union
DUP	Democratic Unionist Party
EAEC	European Atomic Energy Community
EAGGF	European Agricultural Guidance and Guarantee Fund
EC	European Community
ECB	European Central Bank
ECHO	European Community Humanitarian Office
ECHR	European Convention/ Court of Human Rights
ECJ	European Court of Justice
ECSC	European Coal and Steel Community
ECU	European Currency Unit
EDC	European Defence Community
EEA	European Economic Area
EEAS	European External Action Service
EEC	European Economic Community
EESC	European Economic and Social Committee

EFTA	European Free Trade Association
eg.	for example
EMU	European Monetary Union
EPC	European Political Community/ Cooperation
EPU	European Political Union
ERDF	European Regional Development Fund
ERP	European Recovery Program
ESCB	European System of Central Banks
ESF	European Social Fund
ETUC	European Trade Union Confederation
EU	European Union
FPÖ	Freiheitlich Partei Österreichs
GATT	General Agreement on Tariffs and Trade
GDP	Gross Domestic Product
GDR	German Democratic Republic
i.a.	inter alia
i.c.	in concreto
IBRD	International Bank for Reconstruction and Development
IGC	Intergovernmental Conference
IPCR	Integrated Political Crisis Response mechanism
ITO	International Trade Organisation
KPD	Kommunistische Partei Deutschlands
MLF	Multilateral Nuclear Force
NATO	North Atlantic Treaty Organization
OEEC	Organisation for European Economic Cooperation
OJ	Official Journal
OJ C	Official Journal C series
OJ L	Official Journal L series
ÖVP	Österreichische Volkspartei
PES	Party of European Socialists
PSC	Political and Security Committee
QMV	Qualified majority voting
SEA	Single European Act

SED	Sozialistische Einheitspartei Deutschlands
SPD	Sozialdemokratische Partei Deutschlands
SPÖ	Sozialdemokratische Partei Österreichs
TCEU	Treaty on the Constitution for Europe
TECSC	Treaty on the European Coal and Steel Community
TEC	Treaty on the European Community
TEDC	Treaty on the European Defence Community
TEEC	Treaty on the European Economic Community
TEU	Treaty on the European Union
TFEU	Treaty on the Functioning of the European Union
ToA	Treaty of Amsterdam
ToL	Treaty of Lisbon
ToM	Treaty of Maastricht
ToN	Treaty of Nice
TREVI	Terrorisme, Radicalisme, Extrémisme, Violance Internationale
UK	United Kingdom
UN	United Nations
UNESCO	United Nations Educational, Scientific and Cultural Organization
USA	United States of America
USSR	Union of Soviet Socialist Republics
VAT	Value Added Tax
VCLT	Vienna Convention on the Law of Treaties
WA	Withdrawal Agreement
WEU	Western European Union

Notes: Internet links as of 31 March 2024

I. The Historical Development of European Law

The unity of Europe was a dream of few,
became a hope for many, and
is today a necessity for all.

Konrad Adenauer

The development of the European integration can only be understood if the circumstances surrounding the founding of the European Coal and Steel Community are explored and even that would fall short. To arrive at an overall picture, we have to look back even further into the history of Europe and make a comparison between the post-war order of 1918 and the post-war order of 1945.

The steps taken after the end of World War I, which today are considered inappropriate, can be identified - at least in part - as contributory causes to the outbreak of World War II and give the politicians who drafted the postwar order in 1945 an even better report card than they are entitled to anyway. On both the winning and losing sides of World War II, politicians, economists, and military leaders had realised that isolating the defeated countries would be the wrong approach to achieve a stable new order; moreover, they all faced with the Soviet Union a newly emerged superpower, unwilling to give up her - recently established - hegemonic power.[1]

The formation of blocs in the West, in the East, and among the nonaligned[2] was the logical consequence. Isolating the defeated nations of Germany and Japan was therefore out of the question, as these two states

1 It should not be forgotten that the USSR after World War I had entered into a somewhat strange partnership with Germany, especially in military matters. The reason for this Russo-German rapprochement was the mutual desire to establish relations on a political, military, and economic level; Germany in particular wanted her tank and air force officers to be trained on Soviet territory, as this would not have been allowed on German soil due to the Treaty of Versailles. The Treaty of Rapallo - together with its secret side agreements - sealed Russo-German relations in 1922, being consolidated and expanded in 1926 by the Treaty of Berlin.

2 The only non-aligned state on European soil was to remain Yugoslavia, which maintained close relations with the Soviet Union and was herself communist in orientation but was able to avoid having to join COMECON or the Warsaw Pact.

would have created a vacuum that would almost inevitably have been filled by one of the two blocs - and most certainly not by peaceful means. It may not have been easy for the Western states that were defeated and occupied by the Third Reich in the first half of the war or brought to the brink of defeat to make a sincere peace and integrate Germany as an equal partner in the post-war order. Pragmatism and political foresight - especially in France - triumphed over short-term revanchist considerations.[3]

The foundation of the Coal and Steel Community was the - legal and institutionalised - manifestation of this idea. However, the reaction to the global political situation was also to play an essential, almost determining role in the further history of European integration. The tighter the Iron Curtain and the more tense the East-West confrontation became, the more the Member States of the Community closed ranks. The various waves of enlargement of the Community and the founding of the European Union - as the umbrella of a Community that expanded above all in terms of content - must also be viewed from this perspective. The call for a foreign

3 Pragmatism in combination with extraordinary flexibility were also evident as early as 1940, when Winston Churchill proposed a union of France and Britain to keep at least La France d'outre-mer alive. This proposal was not aimed as a love marriage, but intended to prevent the French fleet, at a time when France was on the brink of military defeat, from falling into the hands of Nazi Germany. Eventually, the proposed common citizenship, a common parliament, a unified cabinet and common institutions for foreign, defence, economic, and financial policy came to nothing. Great Britain nevertheless defied Hitler and was able to end the war victoriously, France rose from the ashes of the Vichy regime and played a decisive role in the defeat of the Third Reich. But it was not only Messrs Churchill and de Gaulle who were involved in this Anglo-French alliance. A certain Mr Jean Monnet also appears in this rather remarkable story. This idea, which was due to the war situation, was not to remain the last attempt at such an alliance between the two countries. On 10 September 1956, French Prime Minister Guy Mollet boarded a plane bound for London. In his luggage he had a no less unusual proposal. "When the French Prime Minister, Monsieur Mollet, was recently in London, he railed with the Prime Minister the possibility of a union between the United Kingdom and France" (cf. http://www.theguardian.com/world/2007/jan/15/france.eu). This quotation from a now declassified document from the time of PM Antony Eden's government shows that the later almost bitter love-hate relationship between France and the United Kingdom may have been the story of a rejected love. It could also have been simply another facet of pragmatic politics. No source suggests that France signed the Treaties of Rome only because she did not enter into an alliance with Britain. Similarly, there is no source evidence that France intended to involve Britain in the integration process of the European Communities through this alliance. Whatever may have been behind the French advances, one conclusion may be legitimate: The politicians who had just survived the horrors of the Second World War were aiming for alliances, not divisions.

minister of the European Union articulated in 2003 only becomes understandable when the events surrounding 11 September 2001 and the resulting wars in Afghanistan and Iraq are considered, just as only the overall view of the political situation in the first half of the 1950s provides an answer to the question of why the European Defence Community ultimately failed in 1954.

Synoptic approaches are faced with the challenge to adequately assess all the relevant circumstances in depth and detail. This may be due, among other things, to the fact that both the selection of these circumstances and their categorisation are subjective. However, they not only allow for criticism, but even encourage it. An absolute portrayal of historical events - in the sense of an all-encompassing portrayal - almost rules itself out. Nevertheless, it is only the historical view that makes it possible to understand the course of events in all its facets. Contrary to all declarations of intent, the synoptic and parallel overall portrayal of European history, as called for by Jorge Semprún on the occasion of the informal meeting of EU Ministers for Culture in Weimar in early autumn 1999,[4] has not yet begun, let alone been written. History is still experienced and written from a national or even regional perspective, without considering the fact that Europe only becomes and is rich through its diversity, that a multifaceted representation of its development is therefore a direct outflow of this diversity and at the same time manifests Europe's diversity. The development of European primary law is not only a matter of legal considerations; these lead to the formulation of ideas, demands, and compromises. Legal texts are in general the statutory outflow of political, economic, and military considerations, which in turn are the reaction to events, processes or developments. They are interdependent and must be understood as a holistic work.

Spanning the arc from the first European Treaty, the Treaty establishing the European Coal and Steel Community, to the Treaty of Lisbon, and including the Conference on the Future of Europe as well as Brexit, is an exercise that presents a particular challenge for both the reader and the author. The aim of this book is to span this huge arc in such a way that the decisive steps of change can be traced before they are finally submerged in the annals of the respective archives. However, such a book can neither be planned nor implemented as a substitute for the relevant commentaries on

4 Mr Semprún admitted on this occasion that this kind of historical portrayal would also be subjective, but that it was precisely this subjective portrayal that was an outflow of diversity.

the individual policies of the European Union; this would require several volumes, which in turn would prevent the intended easy access.

The aim and content is a synoptic presentation of the individual stages of development in two respects. On the one hand, from a broader politico-historical point of view, and on the other hand, from the perspective of the deliberations of the intergovernmental conferences that led to the very texts of the Treaties. In the first part, the politico-historical section, the circumstances and background of the genesis of the individual treaties are discussed and placed in the overall picture of the respective political environment. In the second part, which presents the genesis of the individual policies, the politico-historical context is brought together with the concrete negotiating situations in order to give as accurate a picture as possible of the actual course of negotiations and the reasons for certain treaty changes. This synoptic perspective makes certain treaty changes, whose logic threatens to become increasingly obscure to the user after a certain time, both comprehensible and traceable. In the synoptic presentation of the analysis, this edition not only deals with primary law that was once in force or is still in force, but also refers to those provisions that were contained in the failed Constitutional Treaty and nevertheless found their way into the realm of the Union's treaty system by way of the Treaty of Lisbon.

I.1. Establishing the European Coal and Steel Community – 1945-1951 – Overcoming War Resentment[5]

Le talent travaille, le génie crée.
Robert Schuman

When the surrender of the German Wehrmacht came into effect on 8 May 1945, the guns fell silent on the European theatre of World War II.[6] Not only had it been a total war, but the destruction - both physical and psychological - had reached almost total proportions.[7] In contrast to World War I, not only the frontline theatres of war, but above all the hinterland of the warring parties had been exposed to the effects of enemy fire. Only the United States of America - apart from some attacks by German submarines and warships - had not suffered any damage or territorial encroachment by the enemy (with the exception of the attack on Pearl Harbour, which is not part of the American mainland). The European and Asian warring parties had not only paid a heavy blood toll but were also faced with severely damaged infrastructures and territorial damage.[8] Only twenty-seven years after the peace negotiations in Versailles, the European political landscape had to be reordered from scratch.

However, the situation in 1945 was in many respects not comparable to that of November 1918. The end of World War I also marked the end of centuries-old monarchies; in particular, the successor states of the defunct Habsburg monarchy emerged and were to give the European political landscape a completely new face. Austria remained as the core country of the Habsburg monarchy and became a federal republic, Hungary, the Czech Republic, and Slovakia turned their backs on the monarchical system of government, but new monarchies emerged in the Balkans - or rather, former monarchies restored themselves as independent states. The

5 Full text of the Treaty establishing the European Coal and Steel Community: https://eur-lex.europa.eu/legal-content/EN/TXT/?uri=LEGISSUM%3Axy0022.

6 The Imperial Japanese troops only surrendered in the Pacific theatre of war - as a direct result of the two atomic bombs dropped on Hiroshima and Nagasaki - on 2 September 1945, one day after the sixth anniversary of the outbreak of World War II.

7 When Reich Propaganda Minister Goebbels called for total war, hardly anyone in the Berlin Sportpalast may have been aware of the direction in which this "total" was to develop.

8 Only the neutral states of Switzerland, Sweden, Spain, and Portugal had survived the war almost unscathed.

Tsarist Empire had already collapsed in 1917 and the Soviet Union had established herself on its former territory. Moreover, Poland had reappeared on the political map as an independent state. In south-east Europe and in the neighbouring Asian and African territories, the Ottoman Empire had totally disintegrated. However, the peace negotiations were not to achieve the desired result; the situation at the end of the war was too emotional, and the urge for reparations and territorial claims overshadowed the original goal of a peace order. As early as in 1918, the last year of the Great War, the American President Woodrow Wilson had formulated his 14-points plan,[9] which was to become the basis of the European post-war order. The aim of this programme was to make the European landscape safe for democracy, as it were, after the end of the monarchies that ruled without popular participation, and at the same time to install a lasting, stable peace order. A central concern was the preservation of the peoples' right to self-determination, which necessarily required a high degree of sensitivity in the drawing of borders.[10] Parallel to a European post-war order, a global organisation was to help avoid armed conflict to a large extent. The newly created League of Nations was destined to be the referring platform; a platform for stabilisation and conflict resolution, a platform for open diplomacy, a platform for democratically legitimised foreign policy.[11] However, the American advance was to quickly lose momentum and give way to mutual territorial claims and demands for reparations. The United States of America withdrew - disillusioned or even frustrated - when the Versailles peace negotiations developed contrary to her intention. The successor states of the defeated war parties were soon confronted with ethnic minorities on their territory who made demands that these young governments found difficult to deal with; in Germany, politicians, military, and other groups felt virtually humiliated by the Treaty of Versailles and sought change; Austria had to come to terms with being reduced from a once gigantic empire to a comparatively small heartland. The League of Nations, which was based on the principle of unanimity, was not the instrument that had been hoped for. The victorious but weakened power Russia which had in the meantime transformed into the communist Soviet Union, was confronted with massive economic, political, and military difficulties.

9 https://www.theworldwar.org/learn/peace/fourteen-points.

10 The treatment of the different ethnic groups should be just as important as the treatment of historically grown entities.

11 All this contrasts with the destabilising settlement of armed conflicts and the secret diplomacy of non-democratically legitimised absolutist ruling dynasties.

These problems led to a self-perception as an isolated quasi-loser. Germany in particular saw herself increasingly isolated and not integrated as an equal partner in the post-war order. To cut a long story short, the post-war order of 1919 was doomed to failure.

Even before the end of World War II was in sight, the future of Germany - and thus of Europe - was to become the subject of controversial debates among the Allies at the Teheran Conference (28 November to 1 December 1943); at most, agreement was reached on the westward shift of Poland's future border. At the Yalta Conference (4 to 11 February 1945), however, the Allies agreed on the division of Germany - and Austria - into four occupation zones and reached an understanding on reparation payments. Parallel to these decisions, the initiative was also taken to establish the United Nations, which was to be a kind of successor organisation to the League of Nations, albeit with a significantly different framework. After the end of all military hostilities and the - provisional - occupation of the former territory of the Third Reich, the decisive conference to shape the post-war order took place in Potsdam (17 July to 2 August 1945). In negotiations that were as tough as they were marked by mutual mistrust, the victorious powers agreed on the final definition of the four occupation zones in Germany and Austria, the establishment of the Allied Control Council in Berlin and Vienna respectively, the procedure for denazification and demilitarisation, the amount and type of reparations, the westward transfer of Poland's border, the reaction to the ethnic expulsions, and the establishment of an Allied Council of Foreign Ministers. These decisions represented the minimum consensus of the Allies, the recognition of the Oder-Neisse line as Poland's new western border and the expulsion of Germans - and Austrians - from the Eastern European states were made definitive.[12] According to the will of the victorious powers, Germany and Austria were to be divided into four occupation zones, but otherwise both

12 These expulsions were essentially based on the so-called Beneš Decrees in what was then Czechoslovakia and the so-called Avnoj Decrees in what is now Slovenia. The Beneš Decrees in particular were to lead to renewed and extremely emotional debates in Germany and Austria on the one hand and in the Czech Republic on the other on the occasion of the Czech Republic's imminent accession to the EU in May 2004. The Czech Republic - supported by the Commission, namely Commissioner Verheugen, who was responsible for enlargement - successfully refused to repeal these decrees before accession. The reasoning for the refusal adhered closely to the legal opinion that these decrees did not fall under the acquis communautaire as will be discussed later.

were to be regarded each as a single economic area and as an independent state. The political situation in the Eastern European states liberated by the Soviet troops was not necessarily pro-Soviet at this time. On the contrary, in some states there were already a number of non-communist parties participating in the respective governments and that way able to exert their political influence. However, the Soviet Union's hegemonic aspirations soon became clear, for example in January 1947, when she intervened massively in the election campaign in Poland and supported the communist-oriented and dominated Democratic Bloc. The year before, the Communist Party had already become the strongest party in Czechoslovakia. The interventions in favour of the communist parties were the Soviet Union's reaction to what she saw as the unfavourable election results in Hungary in November 1945, when the communist party gained a mere 16.9% of the vote and only narrowly remained in government.[13] In Romania, there was blatant electoral fraud in 1947, suppression of the opposition, and the forced abdication of the king. Only Yugoslavia was able to escape the influence of the Soviet Union, as Marshal Tito, although allied with Stalin, otherwise took a fairly independent path. In the referring German occupation zone, the Soviet Union, as the occupying power, enforced land reform[14] and united the Communist Party of Germany (KPD) and the Socialist Party of Germany (SPD) in the newly founded Socialist Unity Party of Germany (SED) in order to permanently prevent the coexistence of two - large and competing - left-wing parties.

The emerging confrontation between the two systems became increasingly apparent, but in contrast to the end of World War I and the political course under Mr Clemenceau, France of all countries was now to play the leading role in the future integration of Germany.[15] However, before these

13 The elections in Bulgaria in 1945, sometimes referred to as "pseudo-elections", had led both to the result desired by the Soviet Union and to the suppression of any opposition that began immediately afterwards.

14 This land reform, which essentially involved the expropriation and redistribution without compensation of plots of land larger than 100 ha, was to occupy the Federal German courts again in the course of reunification.

15 However, this assessment must also be viewed critically from the point of view that the French Foreign Minister at the time, Aristide Briand, was already vehemently in favour of a united Europe in 1919 after World War I and characterised the system to be aimed for as a "régime d'union fédérale européenne". His plan for Europe was about a united Europe that had to be created on the basis of urgent and vital needs; moreover, this project had to be based on mutual trust. One could even call Mr Briand the Founding Father of a common foreign and security policy, because he

French initiatives could have an impact, the Organisation for European Economic Cooperation (OEEC)[16] and the Council of Europe[17] were founded in 1948 and in 1949 respectively. Alongside these economically and politically oriented organisations, the first military alliances were established, inter alia the mutual assistance pact between the Benelux countries, France and Great Britain in 1948, which also became known as the Brussels Pact.[18] Although Winston Churchill, in his Zurich speech of 19 September 1946,[19] was the first to call for a new foundation of Europe, which would at any rate have to be supported by a partnership between France and Germany, it was the Frenchman Jean Monnet who synthesised the ideas and visions circulating at the time in the plan he developed for the French Foreign Minister Robert Schuman, and both broadened and condensed them to an unimagined extent.[20]

---

demanded that such a newly established Europe should, if necessary, also cooperate with other states or even groups of states if they also had an interest in the universal development of peace. In any case, he argued, it was essential to create greater unity in Europe. At the time, in contrast, French policy, which was supported by other interests, did not allow for such thoughts and was heading towards the isolation of Germany.

16 The original OEEC later transformed into the Organisation for Economic Co-operation and Development (OECD).

17 The fact that the Ministerial Committee of the Council of Europe, in contrast to the Consultative Assembly of the OEEC, to which each Member State sent representatives, was to be the centre of gravity, was due to a reservation on the part of Great Britain, which, while increasingly turning its interest to the European continent, clearly saw her main interest in the Commonwealth and in transatlantic relations. Furthermore, the idea of a European executive that could have limited or even curtailed national sovereignties was both alien and unacceptable to the British, an attitude that still manifests itself - occasionally and to varying degrees – until today and eventually led to Brexit.

18 The accession of Germany and Italy in 1954 transformed the Brussels Pact into the Western European Union.

19 cf. http://www.coe.int/t/dgal/dit/ilcd/Archives/selection/Churchill/ZurichSpeech_en.asp .

20 In the further development and condensation of these conceptual outlines, Mr Monnet benefited from the fact that he had already wielded considerable political influence in the interwar period as Deputy Secretary General of the League of Nations from 1919 to 1923 and, above all, had clearly seen the failure of the policies of that time.
However, the plan devised by Monnet cannot necessarily be considered original in all its features. In 1713, during the peace negotiations of Utrecht, the French Abbé de Saint Pierre published a "mémoire pour rendre la paix perpétuelle en Europe" based, among other considerations, on the idea that a permanent alliance of princes should be established in order to maintain the European balance of powers. In

Monnet's initiative, which was to go down in history as the Schuman Plan, was on the one hand a reaction to the circumstances after World War II - the already de facto division of Germany and the increasingly tense East-West relationship - but on the other hand it drew lessons from the treatment of Germany after World War I. The Schuman Plan was a novel response to this. Ultimately, there were two options to choose from, either integration or isolation of Germany. The relationship between the Eastern and Western hemispheres had become clearer but nonetheless more complex with both the rise to power of communist parties in the future Eastern bloc countries and the Truman Doctrine. The Truman Doctrine of 12 March 1947, which stated that American aid would be given to all countries resisting communist influence, was the most logical reaction to the Stalin doctrine that communism and capitalism were incompatible.[21] At

addition, Mr de Saint Pierre proposed that the observance of this alliance should be supervised by a "European Senate", which should have both legislative and executive powers. In addition to French ideas, not least by Mr Rousseau, who praised Mr de Saint Pierre's proposals but did not consider them feasible, it was also German philosophers who advocated a European federation, for example Mr Kant in his memorandum "Ewiger Friede" (Perpetual Peace). At the time of the Congress of Vienna, it was again the French who took up these ideas, namely Messrs Saint Simon and Thierry in their memorandum "de la réorganisation de la société européenne ou de la nécessité et des moyens de rassembler les peuples de l'Europe en un seul corps politique en conservant à chacun son indépendance nationale" of 1814. In addition to Mr Briand's initiative mentioned above, the Paneuropa movement founded by the Austrian nobleman Count Coudenhove-Kalergi should also be mentioned here. The Paneuropa movement aimed to create a United States of Europe - excluding the Soviet Union and Great Britain, as they did not conform to the system and formed their own spheres - structured according to the principles of the rule of law. For a detailed collection of sources, which can be seen as a precursor to the idea of European integration, cf. in particular Ziegerhofer et al., Die „Vereinigten Staaten von Europa".

21 The Truman Doctrine also represents a turn away from the Monroe Doctrine, developed in 1823, which had itself been directed against the interventionist efforts of the Holy Alliance under the slogan "America the Americans". Whereas the Monroe Doctrine stood for a course of isolationism, the Truman Doctrine stood for a course of direct interventionism.
The Monroe Doctrine comprised (a) neutrality and (b) a policy of non-interference by the USA in European affairs and, in return, banned any interference by Europeans on the American continent. It was intended to exclude colonisation by European powers in particular. The "no-colonisation principle" of the Monroe Doctrine was expanded in the years between 1845 and 1869/70 to the "no-transfer principle", which prohibited non-American powers from ceding colonies on the American continent to other powers without the consent of the USA; in addition, the Monroe Doctrine subsequently prohibited the acquisition of American land by non-American powers

the Moscow Foreign Ministers' Conference in March and April 1947, held shortly after the release of the Truman Doctrine, the differences became abundantly clear. The development of the German occupation zones was unbalanced by the Marshall Plan in that the Soviet Union had almost nothing to offer in the economic field.[22] The USA had offered Poland, the Czechoslovak Socialist Republic (CSSR) and Hungary - as well as the Soviet Union (!) - participation in the Marshall Plan, but under pressure from Moscow these three states refused - needless to say, the Soviet Union (Union of Soviet Socialist Republics - USSR) did not accept the offer either. Participation was by definition out of the question for the Soviet zone both in Germany and in Austria. With the establishment of the North Atlantic Treaty Organisation (NATO) on 4 April 1949, the military dividing lines had in any case been clearly drawn.[23] In 1947, the UK and the USA had already combined their two German occupation zones to form the United

without the consent of the USA. Finally, the Monroe Doctrine was not, after all, a dogma whose content and scope is taxatively determined, but rather the doctrine was defined by its interpretation at the respective time; however, all of these interpretations had the basic tendency in common that the doctrine should be interpreted as a protective doctrine for the prosperity and security of the people of the USA.

The policy of isolationism - i.e. the economic and foreign policy isolation of a country from all other countries, whereby a sufficiently large domestic market, economic self-sufficiency, and freedom from international obligations must be given as a prerequisite for the long-term success of this policy - was first abandoned by the USA through her entry into World War I in 1917 and finally through her entry into World War II.

The Truman Doctrine, which clearly distinguished between two different forms of society - one characterised by freedom and one by totalitarianism - laid a universal claim and thus stood at the beginning of the US containment policy towards the USSR and thereby formed a cornerstone of the Cold War. The aim of the containment policy was to prevent or contain the spread of communism and Stalinism. The containment policy according to the Truman Doctrine found its direct continuation in the Eisenhower Doctrine. The rather defensive orientation of containment was thereby amended in favour of the aggressive roll-back principle.

22 The European Recovery Program (= ERP) - aka Marshall Plan - was an integral part of the implementation of the Truman Doctrine. It included comprehensive US foreign aid to restore the (western) European economy in pursuit of the two goals of (a) expanding the political sphere of influence for protection against Russia and (b) building up a sales market for US industry, which had been fully developed during the war.

23 The Brussels Pact fell into insignificance virtually overnight with the founding of NATO and led only a shadowy existence since then. Even the later quasi-incorporation of the Western European Union, which emerged from the Brussels Pact, into the European Union should hardly change this downgrading.

Economic Territory, and in 1948, France and her zone also joined this grouping, resulting in a unified trizone in western Germany, in which the German mark was introduced as a means of payment in the same year.[24]

With these steps, the integration of the western part of Germany had already been advanced almost irreversibly. Nevertheless, France's memory of Germany's rapid strengthening after World War I was still present. Accordingly, Monnet's core idea aimed at integrating Germany into the Western economic sphere and, through this integration, preventing a military conflict between Germany and the Western European states in the long term. The armies of the time were based not least - apart from manpower - on the striking power and mass of the tank and artillery forces deployed. Coal and steel were indispensable for both weapons systems. Mr Monnet's almost ingenious approach was, on the one hand, to prevent Germany from being able to freely dispose of these two components and, on the other hand, to prevent one-sided discriminatory control so as not to provide any possible revanchist forces with a basis for argument. Accordingly, not only the industrial areas in the Rhineland and Westphalia would have to be subject to such control, but also the industrial area in Lorraine.

Such a control, if it did not aim to be discriminatory or to subject France or Germany to an international organisation, would have to be exercised jointly by the two states concerned. Jean Monnet, however, went a decisive step beyond the approach of joint control. Such joint control authorities always contain the national approach, which in the final consequence would lead to a blockade of the authority if it were based on the principle of unanimity. In his eyes, the only way out was a common supranational administration that would supervise these communitarised key industries.

Between 16 April and 5 May 1950, a total of nine versions of the Monnet draft were drawn up, to which a counter-draft was submitted on 6 May 1950. On 9 May 1950, the French government's declaration on a joint Franco-German heavy industry was published, which was henceforth referred to as the Schuman Plan. In the run-up to the publication of the Schuman Plan, positive reactions had already been obtained from Germany, Italy, the Benelux countries, and the United States of America. On 3 June 1950, the governments of the Benelux countries, Germany, Italy, and France agreed to open negotiations on the Schuman Plan in the so-called

24 Although the introduction of the Deutsche Mark was highly symbolic, the fight against inflation and the prevention of the proliferation of the black market were at the forefront of the introducing decision.

Six-Power Declaration.[25] Although invited, the United Kingdom declined to participate in the Schuman Plan negotiations; nevertheless, talks between the French and British governments on the UK possibly joining the Schuman Plan continued into the late autumn of 1950.[26] The United Kingdom felt that it could not enter into direct negotiations on such a treaty; her preferred method would have been a conference of ministers from interested countries to consider and resolve the question of the most effective and expeditious method of negotiating the problem under discussion.[27] Neither France nor the other signatories of the Six-Power Declaration saw any reason or even need to change their chosen method, but rather saw the United Kingdom's hesitation as an attempt to prevent the supranational character of the Community a priori or, if necessary, to let the project fail through negotiations on the procedure.[28]

The actual negotiations essentially went through three stages, namely two major negotiating rounds and a final drafting phase.

The first round of negotiations lasted from 20 June to 10 August 1950 and began with an almost week-long debate on principles, at the end of

---

25 *The French, German, Belgian, Italian, Luxembourg and Dutch Governments, in their determination to carry out a common action for peace and European solidarity and for economic and social progress, have set themselves the immediate objective of merging coal and steel production and setting up a High Authority whose decisions will be binding on France, Germany, Belgium, Italy, Luxembourg, the Netherlands and other countries which may join them in the future.*
Negotiations will begin on the basis of the French proposal of 9 May this year, at a date to be proposed in the immediate future by the French Government, with a view to working out the terms of a treaty which will be submitted to the Parliaments concerned for ratification.

26 At the same time as the Six-Power Declaration of 3 June 1950, the British government published a communiqué in which it praised the French initiative and affirmed that it had supported it from the outset but did not want to take part in the forthcoming negotiations (https://www.cvce.eu/en/obj/british_communique_on_the_schuman_plan_3_june_1950-en-edf2e199-794a-4ea5-b8ad-9d0fd6576ad1.html). In the end, the British government had not found a way to follow the procedure stipulated by France to draft a treaty within the framework of the announced negotiations.

27 In the communiqué referred to earlier, the UK concluded that if the French government was prepared to revise its position in order to reach an agreement on the procedure for opening negotiations, the UK would be prepared to participate in such negotiations.

28 Even after the conclusion of the first phase of negotiations and a new invitation to participate, the United Kingdom insisted on a change of method and - after this unsuccessful final attempt - did not sit down at the negotiating table.

which Mr Monnet tabled a written draft treaty to the other delegations.[29] After a week-long break during which the negotiators reflected on this draft and consulted their respective governments, they met again on 3 July 1950 and discussed the French text, which was eventually accepted as the basis, until 10 August. The institutional questions were in the centre of attention in this first phase and were to remain so in the second phase of negotiations from 31 August to 6 October 1950. Despite all agreements, reservations, and proposed amendments, the original framework remained intact. In the third and final phase from 10 October 1950 to 11 April 1951, the text was finalised step by step in the editorial process.

From 12 to 18 April 1951, the Ministerial Conference on the Schuman Plan and the establishment of the Coal and Steel Community took place, culminating in the adoption of the Treaty establishing the European Coal and Steel Community (ECSC Treaty) on 18 April 1951.

With the signing of the ECSC Treaty by the founding states, the first step towards a communitarisation of Europe had been taken. In contrast to all international organisations that had been established up to then, this was the first supranational organisation to which the Member States had transferred sovereign rights; an organisation which, through the High Authority, had a body that was responsible not to the Member States but to the community and could decide independently within the framework of the Treaty; an organisation that had a Council of Ministers in which decisions could be taken not only unanimously but also by majority voting, so that

29 This draft had already been prepared in detail by France before the start of the negotiations but had not been presented at the outset for - at least - two reasons. On the one hand, the impression that the negotiations would be prejudiced was to be avoided, and on the other hand, the results of the discussions and the various national submissions were to be incorporated. France was thus able to impose her special mark on the Treaty - and subsequently on all other Treaties to come - from the very outset. France also used this method in later years, particularly when the Treaty of Nice was negotiated under the French EU Presidency in the second half of 2000. At the Biarritz European Council, the delegations were confronted with a composite draft of articles, which the French Presidency declared would reflect the positions of the Member States and would therefore be ready for adoption. Although this method did not necessarily meet with the general approval of the delegations, France replicated the method at the European Council in Nice in December 2000. The approach of the President of the Convention, Giscard d'Estaing, who - almost single-handedly - formulated at least substantial parts of the Draft Constitutional Treaty bypassing the Convention and simply presented it to the Convention on his own initiative, even exceeding the mandate of the Convention, must also be classified accordingly.

a Member State could even be bound against its will; an organisation that has its own Court of Justice, to which the Member States do not have to expressly subject themselves in order to establish its jurisdiction, but do so ex contractu.

The ECSC Treaty entered into force on 23 July 1952 and its four institutions - the Council, the Assembly, the High Authority, and the Court of Justice - began their work that same year. It was only fair that Jean Monnet was appointed the first President of the High Authority.

I.2. Establishing the European Economic Community and the European Atomic Energy Community - 1951-1957 - In the Shadow of the Cold War[30]

Mieux vaut mener à bonne fin des résolutions imparfaites que d'en chercher toujours de parfaites qu'on ne trouvera jamais.

Charles de Gaulle

Before the entry into force of the ECSC Treaty on 23 July 1952, the founding states of the Coal and Steel Community had already signed the Treaty on the European Defence Community (EDC) on 27 May 1952. This community was also the brainchild of a French initiative. The EDC was undeniably a reaction to the events in Europe as well as in the Far East. On the European theatre, the debate about rearming Germany was ostensibly on the agenda, but the underlying question was how to react to the permanently intensifying crises between the Eastern and Western hemispheres and the flare-up of proxy wars. France, at any rate, had thrown almost all resentments against the former wartime enemy Germany overboard and thus made a radical cut in her historical understanding of Franco-German relations.[31] France no longer regarded Germany as a potential adversary or even aggressor, but as an ally in the face of a greater danger. A unilateral rearmament of Germany, however, was out of the question from France's point of view as well and, moreover, would have been diametrically opposed to the idea of the ECSC. Such a German rearmament could therefore only take place within the framework of an alliance. With this in mind, France proposed the formation of a European armed force, which would be composed of units from different nations, but under a common command, with a structure based on that of the ECSC.[32] The negotiations resulted in the EDC Treaty, which was ratified by Germany, the Netherlands and

30 Full text of the Treaty establishing the European Economic Community: https://eur-lex.europa.eu/legal-content/EN/TXT/?uri=CELEX:11957E; Full text of the Treaty establishing the European Atomic Energy Community: https://eur-lex.europa.eu/legal-content/EN/TXT/?uri=OJ:C:2016:203:TOC.

31 Ultimately, it was not only World Wars I and II that had shaped this relationship - with France emerging victorious in both of these wars - but also - and above all - the Franco-German War of 1870/1871, which had ended with the defeat of France and the coronation of the first German Emperor at Versailles.

32 In particular, the institutional setting of the EDC was strongly reminiscent of that of the ECSC.

Belgium in 1953 and subsequently by Luxembourg in 1954 but rejected by France in 1954. The Assemblé National had not been able to bring itself to give its consent and thus allowed the military alliance to fail within the framework of the European Community that was just coming into being.[33] France and Germany, however, attributed such great importance to a military option for European integration that, after the failure of the EDC, they sought another solution that pursued the same goal. In extremely tough negotiations, Germany was granted the right to have its own armed forces, was put on equal footing with the other contracting parties, and the occupation statute was repealed. However, the integration of the German armed forces did not take place by way of the - ultimately - failed EDC, but through Germany's acceptance into the system of the Brussels Pact, which was uno actu transformed into the Western European Union (WEU), and its integration into NATO.

However, these developments in the military realm were not only driven by developments in Europe, as mentioned above. Although the end of World War II had led to the defeat of the National Socialist claim to power in Europe and the Imperial Japanese hegemonic ambitions in the Far East, new frontlines emerged almost simultaneously, which on the one hand filled the power vacuum that had arisen in the short term, and on the other hand were the direct result of independence aspirations in the former colonies and the ever-increasing expansion of communist influence.

After the end of hostilities in the Far East, crisis-like developments had already occurred in Korea and Vietnam. The outbreak of military hostilities between communist and non-communist forces in Korea foreshadowed a new dimension of the East-West conflict.[34] The attack of communist troops from North Korean territory into the South on 24 June 1950 marked the begin of the Korean war. The USA landed troops as early as 25 June 1950. The conflict lasted about three years, with the chances of victory constantly changing. The armistice concluded in 1953 ended this war but left behind a divided country that could still not be reunited seventy years later. Korea was not the only trouble spot in this greater region, however.

33 At that time, no one anticipated that this failure would not only be a short-term setback but would instead turn into a lasting dispute or disagreement in the community and later in the Union.

34 Korea was occupied by American and Russian troops after World War II. The consequence was the emergence of two regimes with diametrically opposed political orientations. A comparison with German conditions and similar developments could not necessarily be ruled out as unrealistic in the late 1940s and early 1950s.

The end of World War II marked the beginning of the final collapse of the colonial empires. The age of decolonisation and the formation of new states partially overwhelmed the political decision-makers in the European state chancelleries. Around 1900, the international community[35] counted only about fifty sovereign nations. With the exception of the German Empire, the colonial powers were able to maintain their positions after World War I, although certain concessions had to be made; in any case, the central leadership of the respective Motherland remained intact. After World War II, however, anti-colonialist efforts found an almost ideal breeding ground in the anti-colonial attitude of the USA on the one hand and the anti-imperialist attitude of the Soviet Union on the other. Moreover, the formation of blocs as a result of the Cold War[36] had made a significant contribution to the intensification of antagonisms in the colonies and to the flare-up of independence movements.[37] The era of decolonisation not only led to the

35 A term that only emerged and became meaningful with the founding of the UN.

36 The term Cold War was introduced by Bernard Baruch in his speech on 16 April 1947 ("Let us not be deceived - we are in the midst of a Cold War today"), cf. http://www.politico.com/story/2010/04/bernard-baruch-coins-term-cold-war-april-16-1947-035862.

37 Germany lost her colonies after 1919, whereas Italy lost her possessions in the course of and after World War II. The independence movements that arose in the Middle East, North Africa, and India after 1919 were suppressed more or less without bloodshed by the colonial powers. The view prior to the outbreak of World War I that the respective colonies should not be involved in the war, since the colonial population's experience of the colonial powers waging war among themselves could have negative effects on their quasi-loyalty, was substantiated, as was the fear that the necessity of involving units recruited from the colonial population could not only strengthen the self-image of this very population, but possibly even turn it against the respective colonial power. Thus, after 1919, India already demanded concessions from Great Britain for her support in World War I, but the reforms were not sufficient to justify the renewed blood toll of Indian troops in World War II - around two million Indian soldiers served under the Union Jack. In 1947, India was finally given independence. With Indonesia's declaration of independence by President Sukarno after the withdrawal of the Japanese occupation troops, an essential cornerstone of the Dutch economy collapsed. France - in contrast to Great Britain, which had managed to find a way of indirectly binding her former colonies in the Commonwealth - refused decolonisation, but after her defeat at the Battle of Dien Bien Phu on 7 May 1954, she was forced to give up her colonial claim to Indochina and - like the Netherlands - lost part of her economic base. The example of Ethiopia, which had never been under colonial rule, spread across the African continent and led to further African self-government with Egypt's independence in 1922 (On the Algerian War, cf. Stora, Histoire de la guerre d'Algérie, 1954-1962; on the Battle of Dien Bien Phu in its political and military significance, cf. i.a. Windrow, The Last Valley; on the

formation of a large number of new states, but also to a massive decline in the economic influence of the - now former - colonial powers; as a direct consequence, their economies had to be restructured.

Another step towards concentrating political attention on Europe had been the Soviet Union's first nuclear weapons test in 1949. The USA had lost her monopoly on the nuclear weapon as the Soviet Union had overcome a strategic deficit. The unilateral nuclear shield over Western Europe had effectively been neutralised by a nuclear counter-response, and the USA - together with her Western European allies - had to develop a new strategy to counter possible aggression by communist forces. Due to the option of a nuclear weapon strike on both sides, the USA decided to station troops in Europe, but was limited in the number of readily available troops due to her involvement in the Far East, just as the European colonial powers were constrained due to the respective wars of independence.

It was precisely against this complex and increasingly confusing scenario that Stalin proposed the neutralisation of Germany in a note of 10 March 1952. As a consequence of the Coal and Steel Community, Stalin feared that the situation in Germany could elude the Soviets and so offered - more or less - immediate reunification as the price for German neutrality.[38] The

overall account of the Vietnam War, cf. i.a. Karnow, Vietnam). After World War II, the independence movement grew rapidly and led to the independence of more and more states. France's rule over Algeria began to totter already in 1954, however, the war of independence lasted until 1962.

38 Among other things, this Stalin note stated that (a) Germany would be restored as a unified state, (b) all occupying troops would be withdrawn from Germany no later than one year after the peace treaty came into force, (c) the German population must be guaranteed democratic rights, (d) Germany must not in future join any alliance or coalition directed against any state that had participated with its armed forces in the war against Germany.
Germany, however, immediately rejected Stalin's offer. With good reason, Stalin's proposal was not seen as a path to neutrality, but as a neutralisation; Germany was afraid of being isolated and did not want to endanger the integration process. Austria's path to neutrality must be assessed quite differently. Austria, war-weary and not integrated into the ECSC process, tried to steer towards as independent a development and future as possible - although her participation in the ERP had been accepted. The permanent neutrality, which the Austrian National Parliament sovereignly decided on 26 October 1955 after the withdrawal of the last Allied occupation soldier and which is guaranteed under international law, was on the one hand an expression of this will for independence, but on the other hand also the fear that an alliance with a supranational character would lead back to dependency; moreover, the ban on annexation to Germany stood in the way according to the legal assessment of the time anyways; nevertheless, the pressure of the USSR must by no means be denied. Over

Soviet Union obviously rated the dynamics of (West) European integration higher than the West European states themselves, which had suffered two setbacks on the road to integration in immediate sequence. With the failure of the EDC, the efforts to found the European Political Community (EPC) had also come to an abrupt end. On 10 September 1952, the Council of the European Coal and Steel Community in Luxembourg had decided to establish a European Political Community. This Luxembourg resolution was based, among other things, on Article 38 of the Treaty establishing the European Defence Community (TEDC), the aim of which was to entrust the Assembly of this Community with the task of deliberating on the constitution of a new Assembly, elected on a democratic basis, which could form part of a future federal or confederal community, based on the principle of the separation of powers and, in particular, with a bicameral system.[39] The foreign ministers of the European Coal and Steel

---

the years, Austria's permanent neutrality was to become a myth, but it almost stood in the way of accession to the EC in 1995, although this obstacle was removed at the very last minute by a protocol declaration (on Austria's post-war history and the path to neutrality cf. i.a. Rauchensteiner, Der Sonderfall).

39 Article 38 TEDC (https://aei.pitt.edu/5201/1/5201.pdf)
1. Within the period provided for in Section 2 of this Article, the Assembly shall study:
(a) the creation of an Assembly of the European Defense Community elected on a democratic basis;
(b) the powers which might be granted to such an Assembly; and
(c) the modifications which should be made in the provisions of the present Treaty relating to the other institutions of the Community, particularly with a view to safeguarding an appropriate representation of the States.
In its work, the Assembly will particularly bear in mind the following principles: The definitive organization which will take the place of the present transitional organization should be conceived so as to be capable of constituting one of the elements of an ultimate Federal or confederal structure, based upon the principle of the separation of powers and including, particularly, a bicameral representative system.
The Assembly shall also study problems to which the co-existence of different organizations for European cooperation, now in being or to be created in the future, give rise, in order to ensure that these organizations are coordinated within the framework of the federal or confederal structure.
2. The proposals of the Assembly shall be submitted to the Council within six months from the date on which the Assembly shall have assumed its functions. These proposals will then be forwarded, together with the opinion of the Council, by the President of the Assembly to the Governments of the Member States, which, within three months from the date of the receipt of these proposals, shall call a conference for the purpose of examining them.
This article had been added to the TEDC on an Italian initiative.

Community asked the Members of the Assembly of the European Coal and Steel Community to prepare a draft treaty on the establishment of a European Political Community.[40] The Constitutional Committee set up to discuss the Luxembourg resolution adopted a working programme on 27 October 1952 and a preliminary draft for a Pact for the Union of European States as early as 4 November of the same year. On 10 January 1953, the Ad Hoc Assembly adopted a draft statute for the European Political Community and from 29 January to 10 March 1953, editorial work on the draft took place. The foreign ministers of the ECSC forwarded the draft to their governments, but France, in particular Foreign Minister Bidault, raised substantial objections. The Conference of Foreign Ministers in Paris therefore decided on 13 May 1953 to transfer the pending - and presumably final - decision to an intergovernmental conference to be held in Rome from 12 June to 1 July 1953. This conference did not take place due to the outbreak of a profound governmental crisis in France. Nevertheless, the Member States of the ECSC tried to sustain the momentum and reaffirmed their will to establish the European Political Community at the conferences of foreign ministers in Paris on 22 May 1953 and Baden-Baden on 8 August 1953 respectively. The new proposals for a Community statute, drafted by a deputies' conference, were submitted to another Conference of Foreign Ministers in The Hague on 26 to 28 November 1953. A conference of foreign ministers on the European Political Community, which was planned for 30 March 1954 - and set to adopt the final decision - was postponed at France's request without a new meeting date being proposed. Due to the failure of the EDC in the French parliament, no new date was set for the decision on a European Political Community. Both projects had failed because of France, of all countries, which was up to that time the motor of integration.[41] However, the integrationist forces in Western Europe had

40 A comparison with the Convention of 2002/2003 and the demands of the European Parliament to be included in the Intergovernmental Conference as an equal partner not only arises here but seems - from a historical point of view - to be more than justified.

41 Monnet's original idea had been to conclude a framework treaty on European integration, which would make it possible to clarify detailed questions and also the question of extending the cooperation of the Member States at a later date and - above all – to allow for a maximum of flexibility. However, the decision of the Founding Fathers to conclude a detailed Treaty on the ECSC went in a different direction, which led, among other things, to the result that for the time being the ECSC and only later other integration treaties were concluded. Whether Monnet's approach could have prevented the crises surrounding the EDC and the EPC and resulted in

not finally ground to a halt. In 1955, the Benelux countries sent an undated memorandum to the Member States of the ECSC in which they proposed nothing less than the fusion of national economies in a single European market.[42] This memorandum already contained elaborated objectives and included, among other things, the demand to extend the common foundations for economic development inter alia to the fields of transport, energy, and the use of nuclear energy for peaceful purposes.[43] According to the Benelux countries, this community was to be based on a common market to be achieved through the gradual removal of quantitative restrictions and customs duties.[44] However, the Benelux countries did not confine themselves to economic and institutional proposals; they also extended the catalogue to social issues and considered it essential to gradually harmonise the existing regulations in the individual countries, especially those relating to the duration of work, the remuneration of overtime[45] and the duration and remuneration of holidays.[46] The ECSC Member States decided to convene the Messina Conference as a result of this memorandum, which had been circulated at a meeting of the foreign ministers of the ECSC.

The Messina Conference took place on 1 and 2 June 1955 and resulted in the establishment of a group of government experts, chaired by the then Belgian Foreign Minister Paul-Henri Spaak, to examine the necessary conditions for implementing the proposals of the Benelux Memorandum, laid down in a resolution adopted by the Ministers of Foreign Affairs of

---

a less formal approach - in particular not the establishment of three independent treaties - is debatable. However, the idea was taken up again by the Maastricht Treaty and the concept of enhanced cooperation.

42 France too - despite her fatal role in the failure of the EDC and EPC - had become active again before the Benelux Memorandum by issuing a unilateral note.

43 As English was no official language of the ECSC, the memorandum was tabled in French and German only (https://www.cvce.eu/obj/memorandum_des_pays_benelux_aux_six_pays_de_la_ceca_18_mai_1955-fr-69a6f717-1c7b-4491-a820-54540fa93ec7.html).

44 In Benelux's view, the establishment of a European economic community necessarily presupposed the creation of a common authority which would have to be given the autonomous and independent powers necessary to achieve the objectives set.

45 i.c. Night work, work on Sundays and public holidays.

46 These considerations can be regarded as an early blueprint for the so-called Social Europe, as it was vehemently demanded by Austria at the Intergovernmental Conference (IGC) 2007 at the latest.

the Member States of the ECSC.[47] In essence, the Messina Conference had endorsed the proposals of the Benelux states; however, the penultimate passage of the resolution clearly shows that the coal and steel states had not yet given up the attempt, on the one hand, to integrate the United Kingdom and, on the other hand, to extend the number of Member States in principle.

The committee set up by the foreign ministers met from 9 July 1955 to 21 April 1956 and presented them with a report that proposed nothing less than the establishment of two additional communities, one economically oriented and one energy oriented.[48] The Committee argued, among other things, that a sectoral expansion of the ECSC Treaty or a sectoral integration of new policy areas into the ECSC Treaty would not lead anywhere. Rather, a customs union cum common market would have to be established on the one hand and a community with the aim of a common development of the peaceful use of nuclear energy on the other. With these proposals, the Spaak Group accommodated the two large Member States, France, and Germany, with regard to their - in part very different - interests. Germany had already recognised at a very early stage the advantages of a Common Market with Internal Market-like features for its expanding, almost booming industry; France, on the other hand, had been advocating nuclear energy for some time, fearing a looming energy crisis.[49] On the basis of

47 https://www.cvce.eu/obj/resolution_adopted_by_the_foreign_ministers_of_the_ecsc_member_states_messina_1_to_3_june_1955-en-d1086bae-0c13-4a00-8608-73c75ce54fad.html.

48 The social agenda that the Benelux had originally pursued almost completely receded into the background.

49 France was to be proved right in her suspicions, as the Suez Crisis of 1956 showed in the long term. On 23 July 1952, revolutionary Egyptian officers had deposed King Farouk and brought Gamal Abdul Nasser to power, who quickly aligned himself with the Eastern Bloc. Massive arms shipments from the Eastern Bloc to Egypt in 1955 led the USA to refuse loans for the construction of the Aswan Dam in 1956, whereupon Mr Nasser nationalised the Suez Canal, thus setting an affront against the United Kingdom and France, the main shareholders of the Suez Canal Company. As a result, Egypt imposed a blockade of the Strait of Tiran at the opening of the Gulf of Aqaba to the Red Sea, as well as a closure of the Suez Canal both to Israeli ships and ships bound for Israel. In addition, Egypt, Syria, and Jordan formed an alliance that finally led Israel - in secret agreement with the United Kingdom and France, which landed troops at the Suez Canal at the same time - to launch a pre-emptive strike against the Gaza Strip and the Sinai Peninsula on 29 October 1956, crossing the Suez Canal by up to 16 km in the course of the eight-day military conflict. Only a simultaneous ultimatum by the USA and the USSR forced Israel to gradually withdraw. The Suez Crisis not only led to the downfall of the Eden government in the United Kingdom

the Spaak Group's feasibility study, the first intergovernmental conference in the history of European integration was set up, chaired by Spaak himself. After tough and hard negotiations, which lasted from June 1956 to February 1957, this conference was successfully concluded. In October 1956, the project had been briefly endangered, almost doomed to failure, when the United Kingdom had presented a proposal for a free trade zone, thus giving those states an opportunity to leave the protracted negotiations that did not intend to come closer to the French attempts to declare in particular her social laws to be the community standard. The relationship between France and Germany, which was suffering from increasing tensions, was largely eased by the signing of the Saar Agreement on 27 October 1956, enabling the incorporation of the Saarland into the Federal Republic of Germany, but the uprising in Hungary and the Suez crisis put yet another strain on the negotiations. It was precisely these crisis developments and German solidarity for France, as well as the successful conclusion of the Saar Agreement, that contributed significantly to France agreeing to a clearly determined roadmap for the Common Market in bilateral negotiations in Paris on 6 November 1956 and at the same time waiving her right to veto the implementation of the second stage of this market.[50] France, however, had not abandoned all her demands and - as a result of the dramatic situation of her overseas territories - demanded an association of these overseas territories and former colonies in February 1957.[51] The background to this demand was the desire for a price and sales guarantee for products from these territories in the Common Market, as well as the raising of investment funds for the development of these territories, in which the Member States of the Community would participate, but would be denied access to the markets of the overseas territories as well as co-determination rights. In the end, France obtained free access for the products concerned - though without a price guarantee - and a commitment to invest, with the resources

and ushered in the final stage of the independence aspirations of the British and French colonies, it also plunged the industrial nations into the first energy crisis. The Suez crisis had made the vulnerability of European industry evident were it to continue to rely - almost exclusively - on crude oil. The dependence of Russian fossil fuels may tell us something about the short memory of states – and their representatives.

50 France was able to "save face" by successfully claiming an emergency clause that would allow her to take unilateral safeguard measures if, one year after the entry into force of the Common Market, there was no tendency for German labour costs to converge with those in France.

51 This requirement also included comparable regions of Belgium and the Netherlands.

to come from a Community fund and after consultation with the parties concerned. After the failure of her free trade initiative, the United Kingdom withdrew from the negotiations and went her own way, which would not take on quasi-integrationalist features again until 1960 with the founding of European Free Trade Association (EFTA).

On 25 March 1957, the founding treaties of the European Economic Community (EEC) and the European Atomic Energy Community (EAEC) were signed in Rome by the six founding states of the ECSC. After the Benelux states were the last to deposit their instruments of ratification in Rome on 13 December 1957, the EEC Treaty and the EAEC Treaty entered into force on 1 January 1958.[52]

52 As with the ECSC, a total of four institutions was envisaged for the EEC and the EAEC. Perhaps also from the experience of the ECSC, the founding states did not, however, comply with the demand of the Benelux Memorandum for a strong executive at Community level and endowed the EEC Commission and the EAEC Commission with fewer powers than the High Authority of the ECSC. In particular, the EEC Commission was embedded more strongly than its counterparts in the ECSC and the EAEC in an institutional interaction with the Council under primary law.

I.3. The Merger Treaty – 1957-1965 – In the Face of Failure[53]

Compromise is the art of dividing up a cake
in such a way so that everyone thinks
they have the biggest piece.
Paul-Henry Spaak

The conclusion of the negotiations on the Treaties of Rome should actually have triggered a new dynamic to accelerate the integration motor even more; the opposite occurred. The following eight years turned out to be an era of stagnation, almost of premature failure. In any case, this period was marked by individuals who at least intended to steer integration in a direction other than that which was becoming apparent.

The United Kingdom had once again not been able to impose her ideas on the six founding states, but she was not willing to give up her idea of free trade in goods without supranational obligations and in June 1957 began to discuss the establishment of a European free trade area with the Scandinavian and Nordic countries. The British won the support of the Council of Ministers of the OEEC, which, on the basis of its own proposal of 18 July 1956, advocated at its meeting of 16 to 17 October 1957 a free trade area to which all OEEC members and the EEC should belong. In addition to the establishment of the Benelux Economic Union between Belgium, the Netherlands, and Luxembourg on 3 February 1958,[54] intense negotiations took place between the OEEC Member States and the Member States of the Communities on the establishment of a European free trade area. France and Germany, however, saw this as merely an attempt by the British to achieve their goal by other means and - presumably - to undermine the new Paris-Berlin axis. Accordingly, they vehemently opposed such developments. On 14 November, France's veto caused a European wide free trade area to fail. On 15 December 1958, the OEEC Council of Ministers noted the disagreement in the Council of Ministers, which saw the British

53 Full text of the Merger Treaty: https://eur-lex.europa.eu/legal-content/EN/TXT/?uri=CELEX:11965F/TXT.

54 This agreement, which came into force on 1 November 1960, is in direct succession to the Monetary Agreement of 21 October 1953 and the Customs Agreement of 5 September 1954. The aim of the Benelux Union was to ensure the free movement of persons, goods, capital and services. To a certain extent, this agreement can be considered a harbinger of enhanced cooperation.

initiative finally fail. This experience was remembered by France and the United Kingdom for decades to come.

Despite this obvious setback, the United Kingdom left no stone unturned to achieve at least a downsized solution at another negotiating table. At a ministerial conference on 20 to 21 July 1959, she was able to secure a positive decision by the Stockholm Conference of the seven OEEC states that did not want to join the EEC to form EFTA;[55] negotiations began shortly afterwards in Stockholm on 8 September 1958. After negotiations that were as short as they were intense, the Treaty establishing EFTA was finalised on 4 January 1960 and entered into force already on 3 May 1960. Thus, in the western half of Europe, the EEC had a competitor that was neither equal nor fully comparable, but the EEC could no longer claim a free trade monopoly.

Meanwhile, the international political situation had by no means become less tense and the Cold War was smouldering along subcutaneously, as it were. Mr Khrushchev's demand for an apology for Western reconnaissance flights carried out over the Soviet Union airspace brought the Paris Conference on Détente of 16 to 17 May 1960 quite unexpectedly to a grinding halt. During his visit to the USA the year before, the Soviet leader had not been opposed to an agreement on peaceful coexistence with the USA, but away from the European theatre, the two superpowers had left no stone unturned to expand their respective spheres of influence. In Europe itself, the Soviet leadership feared that the influence of the USA could become overwhelming and that they would face further uprisings in the territories under their control.

The Mansholt Plan for reforming the Common Agricultural Policy (CAP) of 7 July 1960 led to controversial debates in the Member States, but these quickly disappeared from the agenda after the French President Charles de Gaulle, at his meeting with Mr Adenauer at Ramboullet Castle on 29 and 30 July 1960, presented his ideas for a permanent conference of the Heads of Government of the EEC Member States, as well as a secretariat and coordination commission for the areas of defence, foreign policy, economy, and culture. After France had successfully thwarted what she regarded as an attack by the United Kingdom, she again wanted to take the initiative in European integration. France saw her role in world politics slowly diminishing, since she had already suffered her first devastating

55 i.e. United Kingdom, Denmark, Norway, Sweden, Austria, Switzerland, and Portugal.

defeat in Indochina, was also entangled in a violent war of independence in Algeria, and concluded that she had to at least remain the leader in Europe. With Charles de Gaulle - as a result of the coup in Algiers in May 1958 - a representative of France had taken the helm of the state who had set himself the goal of setting France's hegemonic aspirations on a different course, or at least of reviving them politically and economically. Immediately after the political summer recess in 1960, Mr de Gaulle again took the initiative and on 5 September called for the political organisation of Europe through regular consultations of the governments, without, however, accepting further supranational institutions other than for purely technical questions. Additionally, he demanded the staging of a Europe-wide referendum. Initially, Mr de Gaulle was to be successful in this attempt as the Heads of State and Government of the Community decided at the Paris Conference on 10 to 11 February 1961 to cooperate more closely on political issues and to establish a "Political Union of the Six".[56] The Frenchman Christian Fouchet was appointed head of the commission that was responsible for drawing up proposals to this end. At the same time, however, the Netherlands - much to the annoyance of the French - brought the United Kingdom back into play when they demanded that the British be admitted to the Communities. Shortly afterwards, Germany reacted by announcing through her Foreign Minister von Brentano that a direct link between EEC and EFTA was out of the question and that at best individual accessions of EFTA members to the EEC could be considered. Accordingly, on 9 August 1961, the United Kingdom applied for EEC membership with negotiations beginning on 11 November 1961.

However, this British advance was to be overtaken by another historic event: on 13 August the border between West and East Berlin was closed and the German Democratic Republic (GDR) authorities began building the Berlin Wall. The 22nd Party Congress of the Communist Party of the Soviet Union (CPSC) from 17 to 31 October 1961, which culminated in the condemnation of Stalin, did nothing to ease this crisis. (West) Germany was confronted with a challenge she could not handle on her own and was therefore immediately supported by the USA. Thus, in the eyes of other EEC Member States, American influence in Germany gradually increased to an extent that could possibly oppose the integrationalist forces - at least in connection with the potential EEC accession of the United Kingdom, which by the very nature of things formed a close alliance with the USA.

56 This decision was reaffirmed by the so called Godesberg Decision on 18 July 1961.

That December was to bring further unpleasent surprises. Although the responsible parliamentary committee presented a positive report including recommendations in favour of a European Political Union on 12 December, Mr Fouchet failed with his first plan in the EEC's Council of Foreign Ministers. His plan was based on the ideas of Mr de Gaulle, on the model of a Europe of Fatherlands, and on the concept of a classical international federation of states, which accordingly did not contain any supranational elements. The other Member States could not and did not want to follow this concept, as they wanted to push ahead with the supranational integration approach. However, the Parliament stuck to its roadmap and adopted its recommendation on the establishment of the European Political Union (EPU) on 21 December. Despite all these divergences within the Community, the three EFTA states Austria, Sweden, and Switzerland had submitted applications for association on 15 December.[57]

The French line of confrontation of 1961 was to be hardened in 1962, when the second Fouchet Plan was rejected on 18 January as well. Mr Fouchet had revised his plan but based it even to a greater extent on Mr de Gaulle's concepts. Mr de Gaulle stepped up the pace by firmly rejecting any kind of integration on 5 February and advocating a Union of States. The Netherlands finally escalated the situation when she demanded the immediate participation of the United Kingdom in the negotiations on the EPU and her accession; surprisingly, the Dutch were supported only by Belgium. Although the concrete content of the EPU treaty had already been put beyond dispute, the foreign ministers' negotiations on the EPU were suspended on 17 April. Mr de Gaulle felt disavowed and declared on 15 May 1962 that there could be no Europe other than a Europe of States and therefore the concept of supranationality was to be rejected in the strictest terms. With this in mind, Mr de Gaulle saw no contradiction in his bilateral negotiations with the more integrationalist Germany since these were essentially negotiations between sovereign states. Mr de Gaulle increasingly outed himself as an opponent of British accession to the EEC. He had already expressed this at a bilateral meeting with the British PM Harold Macmillan in Paris on 2 and 3 June 1962. Due to the increasingly apparent differences between Paris and London, the British accession negotiations

57 The USSR reacted negatively to the Austrian application and considered any association of Austria with the EEC to be clearly contrary to the Austrian State Treaty and the status of permanent neutrality. However, Austria did not withdraw the application despite continued pressure from Moscow.

were adjourned on 5 August 1962. While Messrs. Adenauer and de Gaulle intended to intensify Franco-German cooperation and resume negotiations on the EPU, the USA - together with her NATO allies - was confronted with the Cuban Missile Crisis, which was to bring the world to the brink of nuclear war. However, from 22 to 28 October 1962, all eyes turned to military and security issues rather than economic ones; questions of whether to turn to supranationality or intergovernmentalism were abruptly pushed to the background.

US Secretary of Defence McNamara completely reoriented the strategy towards the Soviet Union and propagated the concept of flexible response from December 1962 onwards; US President Kennedy and British PM Macmillan agreed on military-nuclear cooperation and invited France to become a member of a Multilateral Nuclear Force (MLF). Mr de Gaulle, instead of reacting with reluctance, rather rejected such a force; France's nuclear forces were to be exclusively under French command. Uno actu, Mr de Gaulle vetoed the UK's entry to the EEC. The EEC reacted to this French move by suspending accession negotiations not only with the UK but also with Denmark, Ireland, and Norway; on 29 January 1963 negotiations with the British were called off. Meanwhile, Mr de Gaulle, continuing with his concept, signed the so-called Elysee Treaty with Mr Adenauer at a bilateral meeting in Paris on 21 to 22 January 1963, which included agreements on regular consultations on all political issues of common interest. That very treaty was immediately strongly criticised by Luxembourg and Belgium as a deviation from the common path of integration. In June, the Council of Europe tried to take the initiative and decided in the Committee of Ministers to discuss the political problems of European unification due to the crisis of integration efforts on a permanent basis. It was not until January 1964 - this time on Germany's initiative - that another attempt was to be made to push ahead with integration. On 9 January, Chancellor Erhard announced a political initiative to reshape Europe, emphasising friendship with both the USA and France. Mr de Gaulle held off for the time being, but on 23 July 1964 he stated that an independent Europe was an absolute necessity. In Mr de Gaulle's opinion, Germany's European policy proposals were unacceptable; moreover, he accused Germany of being dependent on the USA. On 1 December 1964, a new never-ending story in European integration was to unfold. The EEC's Association Agreement with Turkey on the establishment of a customs union with subsequent accession to the Community came into force. But not only the relationship with Turkey was to remain controversial and delicate for decades. After the Permanent Representatives Committee had discussed Austria's application to the Communities in detail on the basis of an avis from the Commission, which had suggested that formal negotiations should begin immediately, negotiations with Austria were opened on 19 March 1965.[58]

Despite all the centrifugal forces weighing on the Community, the Member States were able to agree on at least one fundamental innovation. On 8 April 1965, the Member States signed the so-called Merger Treaty, under which the Council and the Commission (aka High Authority) were merged and made competent for all three Communities. The Communities on the one hand and the Member States on the other were neither willing nor able to do more than this administrative-technical step. Despite all the willingness to adopt a European perspective, two concepts were irreconcilably opposed. Europe had to decide between a supranational and an intergovernmental approach. Moreover, the communities had to decide whether to open up to new members or to remain a community of six in the long run. Despite the almost programmatic title of the Merger Treaty, integration was already about to be put to the next test.

58 In total, there should be no more than six rounds of negotiations.

I.4. The Single European Act – 1965-1986 – Consolidation[59]

I am extraordinarily patient,
provided I get my own way in the end.
Margaret Thatcher

President de Gaulle had not given up his campaign against more integration on a supranational basis, just as he had not given up his campaign against the accession of the United Kingdom. Moreover, he was suspicious of all attempts by the USA to gain more political influence in Europe. To top it off - in the eyes of his critics - he announced on 17 June 1965 that the German question had to be settled by an agreement between Western and Eastern Europe, since it was ultimately a European matter. However, the real éclat happened on 30 June 1965 and was to lead to the temporary but total paralysis of the Community. France rejected the Commission's reform proposals for the financing of the agricultural market and stayed away from the meetings for seven months. The agricultural question was only a pretext for a deep-rooted French concern. On 1 January 1966, the transition from unanimity to qualified majority voting (QMV) in the Council of Ministers, as provided for in the Treaty, would have come into force, and with it the right of veto. France tried to prevent this by simply not being present.

De Gaulle saw himself on the winning track. He had successfully pushed back the American-Canadian project of the Multilateral Force until President Lyndon B. Johnson had had to abandon it,[60] the British efforts to join had been boycotted, and thus, the USA and the United Kingdom had been kept away from the continent. In the end, however, Mr de Gaulle also benefited from the tactically unwise approach - in historical retrospect - of Commission President Hallstein in connection with his proposals for reforming the budgetary procedure.[61] The German Chancellor Erhard tried

59 Full text of the Single European Act: https://eur-lex.europa.eu/legal-content/EN/TXT/?uri=OJ:L:1987:169:TOC.

60 Mr de Gaulle mockingly remarked that the Multilateral Force had probably been more of a Multilateral Farce.

61 Mr Hallstein had explained his plans first to the Parliament before presenting them to the Council, thus creating a fait accompli that the Member States would not agree to. Both the content and the presentation were rejected by the Council. Mr Hallstein's package proposal did contain a goody for each Member State, but the Council was paralysed precisely because no one dared to speak out in order not to lose their advantage. This entanglement ultimately led to total immobility in the Council.

to smooth the waves with his government declaration of 10 November 1965, in which he stated that Germany's European policy was not directed against the USA, but that statement reassured no one. It was not until the Luxembourg compromise of 29 January 1966 that France was persuaded to take her seat again. The compromise provided that majority decisions under the respective treaty provisions would not be enforced if the vital interests of an overruled Member State were affected; de facto, the principle of unanimity in the Council continued to apply.[62] Mr de Gaulle was not fully satisfied, and not only declared on 6 March 1966 France's withdrawal from the military structure of NATO but, together with the Soviet President Podgorny, called for a policy of détente and rapprochement in Europe in the Moscow Declaration of 30 June 1966. The United Kingdom did not consider the end of her accession efforts but had to face another French veto on 27 November 1967. However, the era of Mr de Gaulle was nearing its end. After the Prague Spring was brutally crushed in 1968 and the Soviets oriented their policy according to the Brezhnev Doctrine, the Western world had moved closer together again. What is more, the Commission scored a surprising coup with the Mansholt Plan for agricultural reform. Mr de Gaulle also faced major problems in domestic politics,[63] but an absolute majority for the Gaullists in the June 1968 election only delayed the political end. On 28 April 1969, Mr de Gaulle finally resigned. His successor was Georges Pompidou.

After the era of stagnation, indeed almost of disintegration, there was a clear need to move swiftly towards consolidation. In December 1969, the Heads of State and Government agreed at their meeting in The Hague on the completion of the Internal Market, enlargement, deepening the Communities, in particular to resume accession negotiations with Denmark, Ireland, Norway, and the United Kingdom, and to gradually introduce an Economic and Monetary Union (EMU) by 1980. The Council of Ministers was subsequently able to adopt an agreement on agricultural financing, the introduction of own resources for the Community, and extended budgetary powers for the Parliament. The Community seized the momentum and on 6 March 1970, under the chairmanship of Luxembourg's Prime Minister Pierre Werner, set up a committee to draw up a draft for an EMU. The

62 This compromise was first violated on 18 May 1982 - also on the occasion of an agricultural question.

63 The student riots in Nanterre in 1967 and the violent street battles in Paris in May 1968 had led him to dissolve the National Assembly.

so-called Werner Plan was presented on 8 October 1970, but failed at first in 1971 due to the collapse of the Bretton Woods system[64] and the resort to national crisis management. In addition to the EMU issue, the Member States had also moved towards closer political cooperation and had dealt with fundamental questions of procedures and principles at the Viterbo Conference in May 1970. The follow-up took place in Luxembourg in October 1971, where the Member States agreed on the Davignon Report as the basis for a Common Foreign Policy within the framework of the European Political Cooperation (EPC).[65]

On 22 January 1972, British persistence was to prove its worth. The Communities concluded the accession negotiations with the United Kingdom, Denmark, Ireland, and Norway.[66] However, the real pinnacle of integration after years of stagnation was the decision of the Paris European Council on 20 October 1972 to develop the Community into the European Union, to complete the establishment of the EMU by 1980, and to include new areas of activity into the integration agenda.[67]

In addition to intensive work on these major reform steps, the Community also expanded its external outreach by transferring exclusive competence for foreign trade policy to the Commission as of 1 January 1973, thereby achieving a more united stance vis-à-vis potential negotiating partners. The so called German question also gained momentum when the Basis-of-Relations Treaty between the Federal Republic of Germany (FRG) and the GDR entered into force on 21 June 1973. Before the end of the year, the Copenhagen European Council was able to adopt a document on European Identity on 15 December,[68] according to which Europe was to adopt a common line on all essential issues.

---

64 The Bretton Woods Agreement of 1944 was a monetary agreement based on the following principles: (i) fixed exchange rates (against the US dollar or gold), (ii) exchange rate changes above 10% only after approval by the International Monetary Fund (IMF), (iii) convertibility of members' currencies, (iv) financing of the IMF by Member States. The Bretton Woods Conference established (a) the Bretton Woods Agreement, (b) the IMF, (c) the International Bank for Reconstruction and Development (IBRD), and (d) the International Trade Organisation (ITO).

65 As early as 19 November of the same year, the first meeting of foreign ministers within the framework of the EPC took place in Munich.

66 In the end, Norway did not join because of a failed referendum.

67 i.e. cohesion, environment, and energy policy.

68 Full text of the declaration: https://www.cvce.eu/obj/declaration_on_european_identity_copenhagen_14_december_1973-en-02798dc9-9c69-4b7d-b2c9-f03a8db7da32.html.

France did not make a significant comeback until 1974 when, on the initiative of President Valéry Giscard d'Estaing, the formal establishment of the European Council was decided in Paris on 14 September. This put the quasi-informal meetings of the Heads of State and Government on an official foundation. At the first such meeting, held in Paris on 9 to 10 December 1974, the European Council decided that QMV applications should be extended and that direct elections to the European Parliament should be introduced in 1978. At the same time, the Belgian PM Tindemans was instructed to prepare a report on the transformation of the Community into a European Union. Mr Tindemans presented his report on 29 December 1975 as Report on the European Union, which also included the option of a two-speed Europe for the future development of integration.

In the following years, work was carried out behind the scenes on the drafting of the Tindemans Report, the accession of Greece was pushed through,[69] and further foreign policy engagement was pursued. Nevertheless, the internal activities in particular hardly generated any tangible results, as was evident from the so-called Three Wise Men Report of 29 October 1979, commissioned by the European Council, which identified the lack of will to integrate on the part of the Member States as the main reason for the stagnation of the Community. This crisis was intensified when the United Kingdom demanded a renegotiation of her contributions to the Community on the occasion of the Dublin European Council on 29 November 1979, as she considered herself to have been overcharged by the terms of accession. The United Kingdom had come back powerfully, with the first female Prime Minister who was to occupy a position in Europe comparable to that of Mr de Gaulle for years to come. Margaret Thatcher was as britophile as Mr de Gaulle had once been francophile, she shared Mr de Gaulle's Eurosceptic attitude - and she was just as convinced of herself as the Frenchman ever was.[70] But not only the United Kingdom gave the Community a formidable headache. The European Parliament, directly elected for the first time, rejected the draft budget for 1980 presented by

69 The Act of Accession was signed on 28 May 1979.

70 In her autobiography, she even speculated that the Labour government she replaced might have been the last ever (cf. Thatcher: The Downing Street Years, p 12). Whether the phrase "I want my money back" attributed to her belongs to the realm of fairy tales or was actually uttered is difficult to verify, but the fact is that the Community introduced the notorious British rebate. In her book on Strategies for a Changing World, Ms Thatcher makes no reference to this, but refers succinctly to the fact that she secured rebates in the mid-1980s (cf. Thatcher: Statecraft, p 390).

the Commission on 13 December 1979, requiring it to be redrafted. The economic situation in Europe was to deter the Community in 1980 in any case from dealing more intensively with the European Union project at political level. The European economy was hit harder by the iron and steel crisis than by the oil shocks of 1973 and 1979. On 6 October 1980, the Commission requested the Council's approval for the imposition of production quotas. The Luxembourg European Council of December 1980 felt compelled to focus on the overall economic situation. However, developments were taking place outside the Community which - in the long term - were to lead to even more far-reaching changes. The independent trade union Solidarnośċ, founded on 31 August 1980, was not only to herald the end of communism in Poland, but it also became the nucleus of an erosion that affected the entire hegemonic realm of the USSR. Despite all the economic problems, the European state chancelleries made renewed attempts towards more integration. The next initiative in this series originated from the foreign ministers of Italy and Germany, who advocated a strengthening of the EPC, known as the Genscher-Colombo Initiative after its initiators. Both had realised that Europe's capacity to act would have to be strengthened quickly and effectively if economic progress was not to completely marginalise foreign policy aspirations. Their concept thus aimed at more integration, more coherent action, and strengthening of the community. After thorough preliminary negotiations, the London European Council adopted the Genscher-Colombo Plan for improving the EPC and creating a European Union.[71] Messrs. Genscher and Colombo even stepped up the pace and submitted a joint draft of the German and Italian governments on the Single European Act (SEA) and a Declaration on Economic Integration to the European Parliament as early as 19 November 1981.[72] The London European Council took note of both documents about a week later, but without taking any substantial further steps.

On 29 and 30 March 1982, on the occasion of the 25th anniversary of the Treaties of Rome, the President of the Commission, Gaston Thorn, and his counterpart in the European Parliament, Pieter Dankert, took the

71 Due to PM Thatcher's obstructionism, no progress could be made at the previous Maastricht and Luxembourg European Councils, neither in the field of agriculture and fisheries nor in issues concerning the social and economic situation of the Community.

72 https://www.cvce.eu/en/recherche/unit-content/-/unit/02bb76df-d066-4c08-a58a-d4686a3e68ff/511084a1-fac4-44e0-82b1-a7a101b2d913/Resources#5e817e60-b68a-41b4-9d75-6509220a94ee_en&overlay.

opportunity to strongly criticise the weakness and the obvious stagnation of the Community. The President of the Council of Foreign Ministers, Leo Tindemans, agreed with this criticism, but the Member States could not be persuaded to take decisive steps, especially in foreign policy matters, despite the Community's undeniable inefficiency in that very sector. In this situation, the European Parliament emerged for the first time as a pioneer of integration. After a committee on institutional reform had already been set up in July on the initiative of the Italian MEP Alterio Spinelli, the Parliament presented guidelines for the reform of the Treaties and the establishment of the European Union on 6 July 1982. The Member States, however, apparently had other concerns for the time being. Throughout the Community, the desire for the accession of Portugal and Greece, which had each managed to shake off dictatorship, became increasingly urgent, while the United Kingdom was confronted with an Argentine invasion of the Falkland Islands and defeated Argentina in a military strike that was as swift as it was hard-fought. After almost a year of stagnation, the Stuttgart European Council was able to adopt the Solemn Declaration on European Union on 19 June 1983, based on the draft SEA. Parliament followed suit and presented a Draft Treaty establishing the European Union on 14 February 1984. France also joined in when, in June of the same year, the French Head of State addressed the European Parliament in favour of the development of a Union and negotiations between the Member States to this end. Together with German Chancellor Helmut Kohl, who assumed power in October 1982, President Mitterrand was not only to revive the Franco-German axis, but to become the driving force behind the transition from the Community to the Union. The European Council subsequently took the initiative again, set up the Dooge and Adonnino Committees[73] at the end of June 1984, approved the interim reports of the two committees in December 1984, and convened the Intergovernmental Conference on the Revision of the Treaties of Rome at its meeting of 28 and 29 June 1985.[74]

---

73 The former was to deal with institutional issues, the latter with the issue of a so-called Europe of Citizens. The Dooge Report became the starting point for the deliberations on the SEA.

74 In the meantime, three events had occurred which were destined to have a considerable influence on the development of integration. Firstly, on 7 January 1985, Jacques Delors, a French politician with Jesuit training and a socialist background, had taken over the office of Commission President and would become the leading figure of the coming years, secondly, on 12 June, the accession treaties with Spain and

After a surprisingly short but highly intense intergovernmental conference, the final draft of the SEA was presented on 27 January 1986. On 17 February, the foreign ministers of Germany, France, Ireland, the Benelux countries, Portugal, Spain, and the United Kingdom signed the SEA; Denmark, Italy and Greece followed on 28 February.[75]

The SEA came into force on 1 July 1987, marking the first and fundamental amendment to the Treaties of Rome, thus establishing a well-balanced consolidation after years of stagnation and at the same time paving the way for a European Union.

Portugal were signed, and thirdly, on 14 June, the Schengen Agreement was signed by Germany, France and the Benelux countries.

75 In Denmark, the SEA initially failed in parliament, but in a referendum on 27 February 1986, the Danish voted in favour of the SEA, as did the Irish on 26 May 1987.

I.5. The Treaty of Maastricht – 1986-1991 – Towards the End of the Cold War[76]

You cannot achieve unity by
stepping on each other's toes.
François Mitterrand

Having taken a major step towards closer integration through the SEA, the Community tried again to score points on foreign policy terrain. A great success for the Community was the invitation to the President of the Commission, Jacques Delors, to participate at the G-7 Summit in Tōkyō. This was the first time that the Commission's outstanding role was recognised outside the Community's realm which clearly strengthened its position in international bilateral and multilateral negotiations. In the same year, the USA and the EC were able to settle their trade dispute, which had lasted several years and in which both sides had accused each other of massive protectionism. The Community felt compelled to symbolically document its newly established self-confidence by adopting a resolution of the Council and the representatives of the governments of the Member States meeting within the Council on 13 November 1986 on the introduction of appropriate uniform signs at the external and internal borders of the Community. This act, symbolic both ways, should not obscure the fact that the United Kingdom may have just about come to terms with the SEA, but did not appear to be at all willing to allow further integration. Although PM Thatcher had to accept the release of the Delors I package, an action programme for the implementation of the SEA, and participate in its implementation according to the principle of pacta sunt servanda, she was not prepared to go any further.

In the meantime, a new generation had assumed power in the Soviet Union, especially Mikhail Gorbachev, the Soviet leader who was to make a decisive contribution to the end of the Cold War, but also, unintentionally, to the demise of the USSR. In his speech of 10 April 1987, Gorbachev presented his idea of a Common House of Europe[77] and thus called on the

76 Full text of the Treaty of Maastricht: https://eur-lex.europa.eu/legal-content/EN/TXT/?uri=OJ:C:1992:191:TOC.

77 A Common Economic Area between the EU and Russia, proposed years later by President Vladimir Putin, was - at least prima facie - in the same tradition but was eventually rejected by the West.

US government, which under President Ronald Reagan, who had been in office since 1981, had switched to a more offensive policy against the communist hemisphere fairly soon after his inauguration. The foreign policy stance of the USSR was still difficult to assess at this time, in particular whether the liberal forces around Gorbachev or the orthodox forces of the old nomenklatura would prevail. This uncertainty became apparent in two successive Russian reactions: in May 1988, Moscow informed Austria that EC membership was incompatible with Austria's State Treaty and that the USSR, as one of the four signatory powers, would veto it; in June of the same year, the EC and its communist counterpart, the Council for Mutual Economic Assistance (COMECON), signed a cooperation agreement. Mr Gorbachev faced growing internal resistance when in 1988 he ended the no longer winnable war in Afghanistan after nine years by withdrawing Red Army troops and was confronted with criticism for - allegedly - abandoning Soviet interests. However, the Community found itself rather incapable of acting in the face of these foreign policy upheavals, as it still lacked - despite the EPC - a basis for common and coherent action in foreign policy matters. Yet even internally, the situation had not developed for the best, and the Copenhagen European Council in December 1987 had to postpone the decision on the Delors I package until mid-February 1988 before reaching an agreement.[78] The Commission changed its tactics due to opposition in some Member States. In the so-called Ceccini Report, which was presented on 29 March 1988, the Commission showed the costs of not implementing the Single Market.[79] In this period of general uncertainty, PM Thatcher gave an incendiary speech to the Collège d'Europe in Bruges on 20 September 1988, in which she not only castigated the EC bureaucracy and criticised the acceleration of the integration process, but above all simply rejected the project of a European Union. Europe's insecurity was to be heightened by Gorbachev's speech to the UN General Assembly on 7 December 1988, when he announced the unilateral withdrawal of 240,000 Red Army troops from the Eastern European satellite states. World politics was clearly not steered or even controlled by Brussels; the initiative lay with

78 Mr Delors had caused no less irritation in some Member States with this package than he had with his first major effort, the White Paper on the Completion of the Internal Market of June 1985. However, his persistence was to lead him to success also in this case.

79 The Ceccini Report predicted price reductions of up to 6 %, around 1.8 million new jobs, and additional growth of 4.5 % once the Internal Market was completed.

the state chancelleries in Moscow, Washington, London, Paris, and - due to the German question - Bonn.

Jacques Delors took advantage of this weakness in foreign policy and the obvious gap in competence to push ahead with the internal shaping of the Community. At the same time, Mr Gorbachev accelerated the surrender of the USSR's claim to total control of the Eastern Bloc when - in a turn away from the Brezhnev Doctrine - he proclaimed the so-called Sinatra Doctrine[80] in Strasbourg on 6 July 1989: In a Common House of Europe, there should no longer be concerted armed interventions by the Warsaw Pact, but rather the Member States of this alliance had a right to an independent course. Mr Gorbachev's new course led to the rather rapid disintegration of the Soviet hegemonic empire. On 11 September 1989, after the dismantling of Hungary's border fortifications with Austria, a mass exodus of GDR citizens started, who entered the FRG by this route without Hungarian soldiers or the Red Army's troops intervening. Neither Moscow nor East Berlin could stem the tide. The communist leadership of the SED regime, loyal to the party line in nearly blind obedience until the end, capitulated and decided on 9 November 1989 to open the GDR's borders to the FRG and West Berlin. The Berlin Wall, the symbol of separation, had fallen. US President George Bush sr., who had succeeded President Reagan in office, supported the West German government under Helmut Kohl, after French support had also been assured. In order to demonstrate the unity of the Paris-Bonn axis, Messrs. Mitterrand and Kohl called on the EC Member States in their speeches to the European Parliament on 22 November 1989 not only to accept the drastic foreign policy changes in Eastern Europe, but also to actively participate in shaping them, and at the same time to intensify their efforts to shape the internal structure of the EC - above all its necessary integration and the realisation of the Internal Market.

At that moment, the EC was confronted with a further bundle of challenges that seemed capable of shaking the foundations of integration as well as the entire post-war order: The Soviet empire was on the verge of collapse, new applications for EC membership were imminent,[81] even a German reunification came within reach. The momentum of the Internal Market, which increasingly touched on monetary policy, social policy, migration and asylum policy, as well as cross-border crime, the increasingly

80 The term Sinatra Doctrine was coined in reference to the song "My Way".

81 Finland, Austria, Sweden, and – as history repeats itself – Norway.

criticised democratic deficit of the Community, and the ineffectiveness of national economic and social policy measures due to economic globalisation, led Commission, Parliament, and some Member States to consider a deepening of the Community as essential. However, they met with bitter opposition from the United Kingdom on the one hand and the desire of some EFTA states to join on the other. The resulting dogmatic dispute between enlargement and deepening was to be the determining factor for the following years.

Messrs. Mitterrand and Kohl once again took the initiative and on 18 April 1990 called for the opening of an intergovernmental conference to establish a political union, parallel to an intergovernmental conference on the establishment of an Economic and Monetary Union (EMU). They argued that in addition to strengthening the democratic legitimacy of the Community and the efficiency of its institutions, the establishment of a Common Foreign and Security Policy (CFSP) was indispensable. The Dublin European Council followed this initiative on 28 April, instructed the EC Foreign Ministers to draw up respective recommendations for reform and decided at its meeting in Dublin on 25 and 26 June to set up two intergovernmental conferences, the results of which were to be ratified by the end of 1992. For the time being, however, the Community could hardly come to terms with this plan, as it was once again engulfed by highly dramatic geopolitical events. After both the Soviet Union and the United Kingdom had agreed to the reunification of Germany, which came into force on 3 October 1990, and after the collapse of the USSR's satellite system on the Community's eastern borders, an unexpected crisis was unfolding in the Middle East when Iraqi troops invaded Kuwait in a surprise coup on 2 August 1990, triggering the First Iraq War.[82] A process of disintegration also began in Yugoslavia, which was to end in a ferocious civil war only about a year later.

Things did, however, start to get moving on the inner-European issues when PM Thatcher resigned as leader of the Tory party and as Prime Minister on 22 November 1990 and handed over to John Major, who in turn took office as Prime Minister on 29 November 1990. At the extraordinary meeting of the Rome European Council on 27 to 28 October 1990, Ms Thatcher had to take note of the fact that her resistance to a stronger

82 "First" refers to the armed intervention of the US-led coalition to liberate Kuwait. In an alternative numbering, "first" refers to the war between Iraq and Iran from 1980 to 1988.

integration of Europe and to the concept of a European Union had been overruled by the other Member States. The Rome European Council reaffirmed the will to transform the Community into a Union, to give the European Parliament more legislative rights, and to introduce European citizenship. PM Thatcher was also unable to block the introduction of a single currency and an independent European Central Bank from being approved as objectives.

Messrs. Kohl and Mitterrand did not let the momentum pass and kept the initiative. In order to structure the framework of the intergovernmental conferences as broadly as possible, they proposed in a joint note to the Italian EC Presidency that the extension of Community competences should in any case also cover the areas of environment, health, social affairs, energy, research and development, and consumer protection. Furthermore, questions concerning migration, asylum, and organised crime should no longer be dealt with at intergovernmental level, but by the ministers for justice and home affairs. And again, the European Council followed their lead. At its meeting in Rome on 14 and 15 December 1990, it set up two parallel intergovernmental conferences on the issues defined in Dublin. The list of objectives for these intergovernmental conferences had grown considerably and already indicated that these conferences would set European integration on new tracks. In addition to strengthening the political dimension of the Community and strengthening the European identity, the European Council also listed institutional reform to eliminate the democratic deficit as a further declared objective. The catalogue of proposals by Messrs. Kohl and Mitterrand was also included and should subsequently be expanded.

The intergovernmental conferences met in quick succession starting on 15 December 1990, but were faced as early as February 1991 with further ideas from France and Germany, which proposed, among other things, to make all areas of foreign relations the subject of a CFSP - the establishment of which no one doubted or even fought any longer. It was not until March 1991 that the Commission intervened in the process with quite a publicity effect - though Mr Delors had always been actively involved in all Franco-German steps in the background - and held an inter-institutional conference together with Council and Parliament to discuss the possibilities of extending Parliament's scope for co-shaping EC decisions. Two days later, on 7 March, the Commission presented a proposal for the CFSP, which provided for unanimity in security policy decisions, but also for a mutual assistance obligation of the Member States.

While the Community was preparing for its future, the Warsaw Pact unceremoniously dissolved on 1 July 1991. The Western military alliance NATO had lost its adversary overnight. The response of the reactionary forces in Russia was not long in coming. On 19 August 1991, a self-proclaimed emergency committee in Moscow staged a coup and had Mr Gorbachev interned on Crimea while he was on holiday. Although the coup collapsed after three days, the end of the USSR had come. The CPSU - after Mr Gorbachev's resignation as General Secretary of the party - was banned in almost all the republics of the USSR or dissolved itself. Even the founding of the Commonwealth of Independent States (CIS) by the presidents of eleven former Soviet republics (including Russia) on 21 December 1991 could not stop the collapse, nor could the political end of Mr Gorbachev, whose policy approach of perestroika and glasnost had made the break from communism possible in the first place. He resigned from all his posts on 25 December 1991.

In the meantime, the Community was able to concentrate fully on its internal affairs. Luxembourg, which held the presidency in the first half of the IGC, was able to hand over a well-advanced basis for negotiations to the incoming presidency of the Netherlands. The Luxembourg European Council had followed the Franco-German proposal for harmonisation of asylum, immigration, and foreign nationals' policy in June 1991 so that the EC presidency Luxembourg was able to reach an agreement on a draft treaty.

During the seventh round of the IGC 1991, however, a crisis was to occur quite unexpectedly when the majority of the Member States rejected the adapted Dutch draft treaty. The Netherlands had gone a decisive step further and proposed a single treaty instead of the three-pillar model. Henceforth, the IGC 1991 worked again on the basis of the Luxembourg draft which was accepted by all Member States. However, detailed questions concerning the structure of the Union, the voting modalities in the CFSP, and the extension of Parliament's rights remained unanswered. Parliament saw the danger of not being sufficiently satisfied in its eyes and threatened in a resolution of 10 October 1991 not to approve the outcome of the conference if its demands were not fully met.[83] The Netherlands submitted a revised

83 The European Parliament threatened without a legal basis, since neither a Treaty amendment nor a new Treaty requires parliamentary approval, as the Parliament itself is only established by the Treaty. Nevertheless, the Parliament still maintains this unfounded claim.

draft on 8 November, which was again very similar to the Luxembourg draft. In the last preparatory meeting before the decisive European Council, the Dutch Presidency was able to tick off essential elements, but the CFSP in particular was still the subject of controversial discussion.

At the Maastricht European Council on 9 and 10 December 1991, the intergovernmental conference was nevertheless successfully concluded and the Treaty on the Establishment of the European Union (= TEU) aka Treaty of Maastricht (= ToM) was adopted. The breakthrough had only been possible after concessions had been made to the United Kingdom, which had resisted any extension of the Community's competences to fiscal and social matters until the very end and had demanded an opt-out from the Monetary Union. Denmark was granted the same opt-out after the first referendum in June 1992 had failed.

Finally, an agreement on this new Treaty was reached - despite all opposition from within and the political upheaval on the external borders. An economically oriented community had turned into a political union.

I.6. The Treaty of Amsterdam – 1992-1996 – An Attempt at Correction[84]

If there is one thing Britain should learn from the last 50 years, it is this: Europe can only get more important for us.

Tony Blair

The year 1992 was supposed to begin favourably for the Community on its way to a Union with the signing of the Maastricht Treaty on 7 February 1992. Already five days later, however, old frontlines resurfaced when the Commission presented the Delors II package for a five-year budget plan. The aim of this medium-term financial plan was to increase the Community budget in order to be able to finance the implementation of the Union Treaty, the promotion of competitiveness, and the improvement of cohesion. The European Parliament also caused disquiet. Although it approved the TEU, it called on all Member State parliaments to draw up further proposals for reform and improvement and to submit them to the national governments.[85]

Apart from these internal issues, the Community took decisive steps in foreign policy in the first half of 1992, including the establishment of the European Community Humanitarian Office (ECHO) on 1 March 1992. The launch of this office set new standards in the field of foreign policy and development aid, as it not only had financial aid at its disposal for the benefit of Eastern European countries and developing countries, but also extensive stocks to enable it to act immediately in case of need. Furthermore, following tough negotiations, the Agreement on the European Economic Area (EEA) between the Community and the seven EFTA States was concluded and entered into force on 1 January 1994.[86]

---

84 Full text of the Treaty of Amsterdam: https://eur-lex.europa.eu/legal-content/EN/TXT/?uri=OJ:C:1997:340:TOC.

85 As noted above, these are at best symbolic actions.

86 The enthusiasm of some of the EFTA states concerned was extremely modest, since they had sought direct accession to the Communities. The Commission - and above all its President Jacques Delors - were rather sceptical about enlargement, even in the case of rich states; Mr Delors' credo was deepening before enlarging. Mr Delors saw the internal coherence of the Community endangered by an overly rapid and sizeable enlargement, but in the end had to bow to pressure and conduct accession negotiations with Austria, Finland, Norway, and Sweden.

The successful conclusion of the TEU had - not least due to the CFSP component - triggered a jolt towards increased defence policy measures by the Member States. Messrs. Mitterrand and Kohl agreed in La Rochelle[87] on 22 May 1992 to establish a Franco-German army corps with a projected strength of 40,000 to 50,000 men. A few weeks later, the WEU ministers met in Petersberg near Bonn for one of the last meetings that was to be of significance for this alliance. In the so-called Petersberg Declaration, the ministers agreed that the WEU was of considerable strategic importance for European security, but that this necessarily required its enlargement to include all Member States of the EC; NATO accession of all EC Member States should also be sought in the medium term.

After these positive steps, which pretended relative unity, the Community reached the limits of its consensus at the Lisbon European Council at the end of June 1992. Despite many attempts to push through his financial proposal, the President of the Commission had to acknowledge the preliminary failure of the Delors II package.[88] The next crisis was already on the horizon over the summer months. The British pound came under increasing pressure, forcing the UK government to withdraw from the European Monetary System on 17 September.[89] The Birmingham European Council from 5 to 6 October dropped its original agenda and focused on the EMS crisis . However, it did find an appropriate opportunity to discuss the further course of action regarding the TEU and decided to make the Community more transparent and to strengthen the competences of the subordinate administrative levels vis-à-vis the central units[90] within the framework of subsidiarity. While this meeting was still concluded without any tangible result, the extraordinary Edinburgh European Council 1992 was a success after all. The UK Presidency,

87 A deliberately chosen symbolic location, La Rochelle was home to German submarine forces during World War II. Both the city of La Rochelle and the harbour facilities in La Pallice remained under German command until the surrender on 8 May 1945. Both escaped destruction because the German commander of the fortress, Vice-Admiral Ernst Schirlitz, had agreed with the French Frigate Captain Hubert Meyer to refrain from any destruction if there was no Allied attack. Through this "Convention of La Rochelle", La Rochelle was surrendered intact by the German forces.

88 Mr Delors, however, was to improve the Commission's record once again with the successful conclusion of the so-called Blair House Agreement on 20 November 1992. With this agreement, the EC and the USA had reached an accord on the reduction of subsidies for agricultural exports, thus ending the ongoing blockade in the GATT negotiations.

89 Italy followed this unilateral London move and contributed to further turbulence in the exchange rate mechanism.

90 i.c. countries, regions, cities, and municipalities.

which had itself provoked some of the turbulence, was able to break the deadlock in the Community by acting as an honest broker in an almost unparalleled manner. Denmark was granted several of the requested opt-outs from the TEU,[91] the Delors II package was adopted, the - long overdue - growth initiative was approved, and the start of accession negotiations with Finland, Norway, Austria, and Sweden was set for 1 January 1993. The Edinburgh European Council also resolved the question of the seats of the Community institutions, which had been smouldering under the surface, the enlargement of the European Parliament to 567 members, and finally even the allocation of these seats to the Member States.

The year 1993 was to begin with a taste of success for the Community. On 1 January 1993 the Single Market finally entered into force and with it the free movement of goods, persons, capital, and services. After accession negotiations with Finland, Austria, and Sweden had officially started on 1 February, Norway followed suit on 5 April and joined the ongoing negotiations. Due to the acquis screening in the course of the EEA negotiations, the time frame was set at about one year, with special emphasis on the issue of agriculture which was not part of the EEA acquis. The negotiations proceeded swiftly at the beginning but came to a standstill towards the end of the year, as the applicants were not prepared to make any concessions on various issues, while the Commission was equally unwavering in its position, whereby it could count on the support of several Member States. The Community, however, seemed to have few concerns, notably with regard to the accession negotiations, because despite the ongoing negotiations, the Copenhagen European Council decided in June 1993 that the - temporarily - associated states of Central and Eastern Europe would be admitted as members of the Community as soon as they fulfilled the necessary political and economic conditions. The European Council had thus initiated a politically irreversible process that would lead eleven years later to the biggest wave of enlargement, the so-called Big Bang.

Despite these positive signals within the EC, an emerging crisis in Eastern Europe almost led to a civil war in Russia, probably resulting inmassive foreign and security policy repercussions for the Community. In Russia, Boris Yeltsin had taken over the legacy of Mikhail Gorbachev and tried to continue the democratisation initiative of his predecessor. The G-7 summit in Tōkyō decided on 9 July 1993 on a comprehensive programme to support the transformation of the Russian economy in the form of a stabilisation fund.

91 The opt-outs refer to EMU, CFSP defence concepts, secondary residence issues, and European citizenship.

However, the old Soviet nomenklatura, consisting of CPSU members, high-ranking generals of the Red Army, and senior officers of the KGB, were not willing to accept the changes and attempted a second coup. On 3 October, the coup broke out, but was brutally crushed by army units loyal to the government under massive deployment of armoured units. Despite more than a hundred fatalities, the situation quickly calmed down and in December of the same year, the first democratic elections were held in Russia, in which Mr Yeltsin - surprisingly only by an extremely narrow margin - emerged as the winner. The Community reacted unexpectedly quickly and gave all political support to the democratic forces in Russia.[92]

Shortly after the entry into force of the EEA Agreement,[93] the accession negotiations with Finland, Austria, Sweden, and Norway were also heading for the finishing line. At a jumbo summit that began on 25 February 1994, the negotiations were to be concluded. However, the final rounds did not turn out to be the expected "walk in the park". Sweden and Finland reached an agreement with the Community in the early hours of 1 March, but Austria and Norway still saw the Community's demands as an unacceptable set of conditions. It was not until the morning of 3 March that the Community and Austria, which had already openly threatened to break off the negotiations, reached an agreement. Negotiations with Norway were suspended until 15 March due to irreconcilable differences on fisheries issues. Finland, Austria, and Sweden joined the Community on 1 January 1995, Norway finally concluded the negotiations too but failed a second time in a referendum.

No sooner had the Community had a little distance from one mega-negotiation than it initiated the next series of rounds through the decision of the Corfu European Council in June 1994. On the Greek island, the European Council established the so called Reflection Group which was to prepare the IGC for the revision of the Treaties in 1996. Although the Heads of State and Government had not yet been able to agree on a new Commission President at this meeting, the Delors era had irrevocably come to an end. On 15 July, after protracted arguments, the Heads of State and Government agreed on the Luxembourg prime minister, Jacques Santer. Personally of the highest integ-

92 Mr Yeltsin put the trust that the community had vested in him to the test the very next year when he ordered the invasion of Chechnya and thus attempted to abruptly end the independence of the Caucasus region that had been unilaterally proclaimed in 1991. Only a few months earlier, at the G-7 summit in Naples, Russia had been accepted into this group, which from then on met as the G-8.

93 Full text: https://eur-lex.europa.eu/legal-content/EN/TXT/PDF/?uri=CELEX:21994A0103(01).

rity, he nevertheless remained a compromise in the office of Commission President, who also did not necessarily show a lucky hand in the selection of the Commission members.[94] Mr Santer himself, however, acted quite successfully in the background - albeit sub-optimally in terms of his media image - and managed to reach a broad consensus on the question of the eastern enlargement of the Union at a meeting with nine Central European states[95] in Alpbach, Austria, on 22 August 1994. It is worth mentioning that he was still President-designate of the Commission at that time. It was not only in the Commission, however, that an era came to an end. In the same year, Jacques Chirac replaced the terminally ill François Mitterrand as French President, thus ushering in a renaissance of the conservatives in France. His first acts in office were to show that Mr Chirac was not willing to pursue a consensual foreign policy at all costs, but rather saw himself in the tradition of President de Gaulle. In the face of national and international opposition, he resumed the nuclear bomb tests on Mururoa Island, thus sending clear signals across the Atlantic. The fact that President Chirac unilaterally suspended the Schengen Agreement after a wave of bombings in France also brought him blatant criticism.

Almost hidden from public view, the Reflection Group worked on the revision of the Treaties. It was not until the meeting of the EU Foreign Ministers in Messina on 2 to 3 June 1995 that the work of the Reflection Group was officially discussed for the first time. The Foreign Ministers had met in Messina to hold a ceremonial act to mark the 40th anniversary of the Messina Conference, but the focus was on the consultations in preparation for the IGC 1996.[96] The Foreign Ministers mandated the Reflection Group to draw up concrete proposals for the revision of the Treaties. The Cannes European Council in June confirmed this mandate, yet in fact devoted more time to foreign policy issues by adopting several financial packages for the Mediterranean region, the Central and Eastern European states, and the African, Caribbean and Pacific Group of States (ACP). It also set security policy accents when it called for a four-month ceasefire in the still raging war in

94 The Santer era ended with the resignation of the Commission on 14 January 1999 after a dispute between the European Parliament and the French Commissioner Edith Cresson. Due to the protracted struggle between the Parliament and the Commission, the latter acted as a lame duck for quite some time and could hardly give any impetus to further integration.

95 i.c. Germany, Italy, Liechtenstein, Austria, Czech Republic, Switzerland, Slovakia, Slovenia, and Hungary.

96 These consultations took place in neighbouring picturesque Taormina.

Bosnia and instructed the EU mediator for Yugoslavia, the Swede Carl Bildt, to continue and, if necessary, intensify his efforts to find a peaceful solution.

The joint declaration of the Italian Foreign Minister Susanna Agnelli and her German counterpart Klaus Kinkel, which they had issued on the occasion of their meeting in Porto Ercole on 15 July 1995, burst into the almost united position of the Member States. They called for a substantial deepening of integration, the strengthening of the Parliament and the Commission, the expansion of QMV usage, and a forceful advancement of the CFSP. Despite this unilateral advance, which did not meet with the full approval of all Member States, Germany and Italy had thus staked their claim to a decisive role in the forthcoming intergovernmental conference. The Mallorca European Council at the end of September 1995 reacted in a generally accommodating manner and essentially spoke out in favour of the reforms urged by Germany and Italy.[97] So as not to be completely left out, the Presidents of the European Parliament, Klaus Hänsch, and the Commission, Jacques Santer, felt obliged to present their proposals at least outside the conference rooms. In Strasbourg on 15 November - just in time for the final presentation of the Reflection Group to the next European Council - they demanded an accelerated deepening of integration, a radical reduction of bureaucracy, and, most importantly, a simplification of the decision-making process.[98] The Madrid European Council in December 1995 was to be of particular importance, as not only the IGC 1996 was on its agenda. After the Union had signed the New Transatlantic Agenda[99] with US President Bill Clinton and President Chirac had announced that France would in future cooperate more closely militarily with NATO again, the Heads of State and Government were able to deal with the supposedly essential question of what Europe's common currency should be called. Each proposal was scrutinised meticulously for possible national favouritism before they agreed on the

97 On the fringes of this summit, France's nuclear tests were debated quite controversially with Mr Chirac making it unmistakably clear that he would not deviate from his line.

98 This requirement was only to be fulfilled by the Lisbon Treaty.

99 The New Transatlantic Agenda (full text: https://ec.europa.eu/commission/presscorner/detail/en/PRES_95_356) is complementary to the Transatlantic Declaration of 1990 (full text: https://www.europarl.europa.eu/cmsdata/124320/trans_declaration_90_en.pdf) and includes (a) the expansion of cooperation in the areas of (i) securing peace and strengthening democracy worldwide, (ii) combating organised crime, drug trafficking, and terrorism, (iii) expanding global trade relations, and (iv) science and culture, and, called for by the United States, (b) the declaration that NATO is the central element and indispensable link between the United States and Europe.

artificial name Euro.[100] Less controversial was the introduction of the currency in the euro countries as of 1 January 1999.[101] In the background, however, the increasingly heated situation in Northern Ireland was also debated, with US President Clinton immediately offering to act as mediator.

The following year was dominated by the intergovernmental conference on the revision of the Treaties. The preparatory group that accompanied the negotiations[102] made great progress and agreed on more and more elements, in particular the extension of the scope of QMV. However, midway through the IGC, two landslide election results burst in, which were to change the political landscape of the Union for several years. After eighteen years of political decline, the Labour Party, under its new leader Tony Blair, won a majority in the elections. In France, Mr Chirac had miscalculated by calling elections and was then forced to govern with the Socialist Lionel Jospin in a so-called "cohabitation". Mr Blair soon faced massive foreign policy challenges such as the handover of Hong Kong and the Northern Ireland conflict, while Mr Jospin had only one domestic challenger in President Chirac. Mr Blair, however, left his political mark on Europe more distinctly than Mr Jospin ever accomplished.[103] Mr Blair mastered his tasks and was able to install a new centrist policy with his political programme, the so called Third Way, which also gained considerable influence within the European Union, at least until Mr Blair's involvement in the second Gulf War alongside the USA.

---

100 Even the term ECU was rejected, as it turned out that a very early French coin bore this name. The ecu d'or (the term ecu is derived from the word heraldic shield) was the first French gold coin introduced by King Louis IX. The ecu as a French currency unit was introduced under Louis XIII in 1641 and minted until 1793. In the context of European integration, the term ECU was used as an abbreviation for "European Currency Unit" until the introduction of the euro.

101 From today's perspective, the most remarkable aspect is that Germany, of all countries, demanded at the Madrid Summit that, in addition to the strict convergence criteria of the ToM, an even more rigid Stability Pact should be concluded in order to reduce the national debt even further, but failed with this demand. This failure was to be bitterly avenged during the financial crisis of the 2010s.

102 This group was called "Amis de la Présidence". However, the IGC 2000 already abandoned this designation and set up a high-ranking group of government representatives. On the one hand, the latter designation had a clearly more official character and sounded more serious; on the other hand, the "Groupe des Amis" comprised by no means only friends of the presidency.

103 The outcome of the IGC 1996, the Treaty of Amsterdam, could even be described as a Blairite Treaty, with PM Blair's share comprising the positive aspects of the Treaty. The failure to achieve comprehensive overall reform is clearly attributable to Germany, as shown below.

The Heads of State and Government had agreed on creating a Union that was closer to its citizens and more capable of acting externally. At the same time, however, the EC pillar would have to be reformed. In the view of some Member States, the best way to increase the capacity to act internally and externally would be to limit or even reduce the size of the Commission, whereby a new method of composition would have to be agreed upon. In addition to this rather technocratic issue, however, substantive revisions were to be undertaken, especially the expansion of the cases of application of QMV.

However, the outcome of the IGC 1996 fell short of expectations in every respect. At the very last minute, the IGC had to withdraw essential reforms that had already been agreed upon in order to bring the conference to a successful conclusion. Throughout the negotiations, the German delegation not only faced considerable domestic political pressure from the Länder, but some ministries stonewalled, too. From their point of view, too much extension of QMV would have restricted their respective sovereignty even more than the ToM already did. At the final summit in Amsterdam on 16 and 17 June 1997, Chancellor Kohl eventually pulled the emergency brake in the early hours of the morning and succeeded in having several new QMV applications withdrawn, especially in the area of asylum.[104]

What remained was the understanding that the Treaty of Amsterdam (ToA) could only be a transitional solution, since it had not been able to solve the essential questions satisfactorily and could at best be described as suboptimal. The notorious Amsterdam-left-overs remained on the table,[105] which were to lead the following intergovernmental conference to a crucial test. However, the transitory nature of this Treaty revision was to have less of a negative effect on the further development of the European Union than initially feared. It had become clear to the Member States that they would have to undertake a new attempt to make the necessary revisions. However, the attempt at a correction had failed for the time being.

104 This traumatic experience of the German veto came as all the more of a shock as Germany - and Helmut Kohl in particular - had always been regarded as the unwavering engine of integration. This failure, too, was to take its revenge some two decades later, above all on Germany.

105 i.e. (a) weighting of votes in the Council, (b) size and composition of the Commission, (c) extension of QMV cases.

I.7. The Treaty of Nice – 1997-2000 – Corrections[106]

> *Tonight, I realised for the first time, that this Europe of ours will be blown apart with horrido, if our country does not show European leadership.*
>
> Joschka Fischer

Although the shock of the Union's Amsterdam failure was still lingering, foreign policy events were to dominate the agenda in the following two and a half years, as were internal European issues far removed from discussions on institutional reform. The Algerian civil war and the increasing terrorist attacks on Western embassies and tourists contributed to the Union's intensified foreign policy activities, as did the equally dramatic situation in Afghanistan since the Taliban regime had come to power in 1996. The EU learned to make constantly better use of the instruments of the CFSP, although here too the failure of the Amsterdam Treaty was becoming apparent. Within the Union, the Blair government came under considerable pressure when the Northern Ireland conflict threatened to escalate again after the Omagh bombing, notwithstanding intensive peace negotiations. In addition, the Yugoslav conflict had escalated on the Union's borders and led to massive military involvement by NATO. This was done without UN approval but was politically unavoidable due to the genocide-like massacres of the civilian population. It was the first international action under the R2P (Responsibility to Protect) framework. The first ray of hope in terms of integration policy was the introduction of the euro on 1 January 1999. The citizens of the euro countries had accepted the currency changeover faster than the political elites had expected. Even before the end of the switchover period, twelve national currencies were abandoned almost without comment and made way for the single currency.[107]

106 Full text of the Treaty of Nice: https://eur-lex.europa.eu/legal-content/EN/TXT/?uri=OJ:C:2001:080:TOC. Consolidated version of the TEU: https://eur-lex.europa.eu/legal-content/EN/TXT/?uri=OJ:C:2002:325:TOC. Consolidated version of the TEC: https://eur-lex.europa.eu/legal-content/EN/TXT/?uri=OJ:C:2002:325:TOC. For a detailed account of the IGC 2000, cf. Fischer, Der Vertrag von Nizza.

107 The euphoria of consumers was to fade just as quickly when waves of inflation in the euro countries threatened to blur the originally positive image of the new currency. Only the Eurosceptics found unreserved favour in the new currency, as it once again provided them with arguments against European integration.

However, the unalloyed joy did not last long. On the night of 16 March 1999, the Santer Commission resigned as a whole. President Santer was faced with the decision of either persuading the French Commissioner Edith Cresson to resign or being formally forced out of office by the European Parliament. In a dramatic meeting, the College of the Commission decided to resign collectively after Ms Cresson refused to resign of her own accord.[108]

The Heads of State and Government felt compelled to quickly find a potent replacement for Mr Santer and believed they had found it in Romano Prodi, who exercised his office with great commitment and an enormous leap of faith. This crisis-ridden development in the EU institutions had become the first test of European policy for the new German Chancellor Gerhard Schröder, who held the rotating presidency of the European Council. The European Council in Helsinki under the subsequent Finnish Presidency on 11 December 1999 succeeded in paving the way for an IGC to revise (the revision of) the Treaties. It drew on the outcome of the Cologne European Council in June 1999, which had decided to convene an IGC the following year to overcome the Amsterdam leftovers and allow for the enlargement of the Union by ten or more states.[109]

The IGC on institutional reform began on 14 February 2000. Despite the Portuguese Presidency's attempt to conceal any negative vibrations, it quickly became apparent that fault lines were rapidly emerging on the substantive issues. Above all, some Member States complained that the catalogue of topics was too limited. If the Union was to be fundamentally reformed, this had to be done thoroughly and comprehensively. However, the IGC 2000 was not to be the only issue the Union had to deal with. Alongside the raging mad cow disease (Bovine spongiform encephalopathy - BSE) epidemic and the last twitches of the regime in the Federal Republic of Yugoslavia, the Union was confronted with a completely unexpected

---

108 She was supported in this by some of her colleagues who did not want to hand over any member of the College to Parliament; whether Parliament would have actually carried out its threat of a vote of no confidence in the Commission will never be known.

109 This particular task was assigned to the IGC 2000 as the principal agenda, since the accession negotiations with the so-called Luxembourg Group (Estonia, Poland, Slovenia, the Czech Republic, Hungary, and Cyprus), which had been underway since 1998, indicated that enlargement would take place in the foreseeable future. On 15 February 2000, negotiations with the second group, the so-called Helsinki Group (Romania, Bulgaria, Slovakia, Latvia, Lithuania, Malta), were launched.

threat of rift. In the autumn of 1999, federal elections had been held in Austria, a process that in the past had not necessarily caused shock waves abroad. After months of coalition negotiations between the two incumbent coalition parties, the Social Democratic Party of Austria (SPÖ) and the conservative Austrian People's Party (ÖVP), there was still no result, and Austria continued to be governed - without causing a stir - by the old government in accordance with the constitution. However, this transitional arrangement ended with the completely surprising coalition agreement between the ÖVP and the right-wing Freedom Party of Austria (FPÖ). The new Austrian coalition government was sworn in on 4 February 2000. This attracted the attention of some Union leaders who saw the FPÖ as a party that was too far leaning to the right and therefore unacceptable as a governing party within the realm of the EU. The network of prime ministers introduced under the Austrian EU presidency in 1998 was applied for the first time and worked smoothly - to Austria's detriment. As there was no adequate legal basis in the Treaties, the other EU Member States joined forces on the basis of international law and imposed sanctions on Austria, underlining, however, that this would have no effect on Austria's membership in the EU.[110] The Austrian federal government under Chancellor Wolfgang Schüssel declared the EU to be the scope of "business as usual" and continued to work without restrictions in all bodies of the Union. The sanctions of the Fourteen nevertheless had a direct impact on the ongoing IGC, as it was thanks to Austria's initiative, supported in particular by Belgium, that the sanctions procedure was taken up and revised within the framework of EU primary law, integrating above all rule of law principles.[111]

However, the Portuguese Presidency focused on the tasks at hand and, in tough and thorough meetings of the Group of Government Representatives (which preceded the Foreign Ministers and the European Council),

110 Apart from some ministers refusing to shake hands with their Austrian counterparts or trying not to appear in joint photos, not much changed on the surface. Initial attempts to show one's opinion of the new Austrian government by demonstratively taking off one's headphones when an Austrian minister took the floor in the Council of Ministers were quickly dropped, as otherwise - due to a lack of sufficient language skills and knowledge of the content of the speech - one could no longer follow the debate.

111 The sanctions against Austria were lifted before the end of the IGC 2000, not least after the report of the Wise Men, which had thoroughly reviewed the political situation in Austria. Even in retrospect, it will hardly be possible to clarify which Member States took the decisive initiative for the sanctions and with what enthusiasm the individual Member States were involved.

reached agreement on a growing number of issues, with the exception of the core issues, the notorious Amsterdam "left-overs". After all, Portugal complied with the wish of the majority of Member States to extend the agenda of the conference.[112]

Europe had hardly any free resources to take care of anything other than itself, although the geopolitical situation was becoming increasingly critical due to the escalating Middle East conflict.[113] On 1 July 2000, France took over the rotating EU presidency and with it came President Chirac's chairmanship of the European Council. The period of extensive discussions came to an end and the Presidency stepped up the pace by presenting concrete draft texts. However, it had also become clear to the French that not everything would be settled in Nice, at least not once and for all. The spectre of new "left-overs", this time " Nice-left-overs", loomed. This very danger, which would have clearly documented the failure of the conference, was quickly dispelled when Mr Chirac spoke at the Biarritz European Council in mid-October of a necessary post-Nice process, which of course in no way would be comparable to the notorious left-overs but being rather an expression of the fact that European integration is a constantly evolving process.

The Nice European Council was nevertheless to be memorable and, above all, excessively long. The final negotiations lasted from 7 December until dawn on 11 December 2000.[114] The opening up of the agenda had proved its worth in the final hours of the negotiations, as the Presidency had managed to put together packages in which all Member States could find themselves, as they were able to successfully push through their own demands.

Despite all negative comments on the Nice agreement, the Amsterdam-left-overs had been resolved and, thanks to the enlargement protocol, the

---

112 While this was again met with scepticism due to fears of not reaching a conclusion at the Nice European Council in December 2000, it also opened up the possibility for the Presidency to present additional compromises.

113 In July 2000, the Camp David peace talks between President Clinton as mediator, Israeli Prime Minister Ehud Barak, and Palestinian leader Yasser Arafat failed. Europe had reason to look down with considerable scorn on the USA only in the autumn of that year, when the USA could not determine for weeks who had been elected as new president: Clinton's former running mate Al Gore or his challenger, Texas Governor George Bush jr. The latter was only declared the winner by a final decision of the Supreme Court on 12 December 2000.

114 Both the mood in the IGC and the weather conditions were a good reason to speak of dawn rather than sunrise when Mr Chirac closed the conference at around 6 am.

Union was able not only to conclude the ongoing accession negotiations but also to carry out enlargement within a new institutional framework. Furthermore, the Nice European Council adopted the Declaration on the Future of the Union, which launched the post-Nice process.

Corrections were made to the Treaties, but the Member States had not yet found new paths for the Union.

I.8. The Convention on the Future of Europe - 2001-2003 - A Novel Approach[115]

That is what I have been telling you for sixteen years.

Helmut Kohl

The excitement about the correction was limited, as the Treaty of Nice (ToN) had already been declared dead before the EU foreign ministers had signed it on 26 February 2001. Undeniably, the ToN had not been a creative success. The criticism nevertheless made it abundantly clear that this Union, which was on the verge of its most extensive enlargement, needed new approaches if it was to continue to have a raison d'être and a guarantee of existence. The post-Nice process should provide the platform for this. The demand for a broader legitimisation of the European Union was articulated by all, and the involvement of the European and national parliaments in the preparatory process of a future Treaty revision seemed politically inevitable. The Swedish government confined itself to technical preparations and exploratory rounds during its EU Presidency in the first half of 2001, but the Belgian Presidency significantly accelerated the process. Weeks before the Laeken European Council in December 2001, the Member States had already informally agreed to respond in particular to the wishes of the Parliament and to hold a convention to prepare the next IGC, in which parliamentarians should be prominently represented.

Before this summit took place, an event was to shake not only the USA but the whole world to its political and ideological foundations. On 11 September 2001, two planes hijacked and piloted by terrorists crashed into the World Trade Center in New York and another into the nerve centre of American defence in Washington, the Pentagon. Not only the USA was affected, but the security policy of all states also had to be questioned. Suddenly, the urge for a robust CFSP grew in the Union and EU leaders agreed that only a strong and united Europe would be able to respond adequately to this new challenge.

115 Full text of the Draft Treaty establishing A Constitution For Europe: https://eur-lex.europa.eu/legal-content/EN/TXT/?uri=OJ:C:2003:169:TOC. For a detailed account of the Convention on the Future of Europe cf. Fischer, Der Konvent.

These considerations were reflected in the Laeken Declaration of 15 December 2001[116] and in the preceding debates in the Member States on greater proximity and transparency. At Laeken, the European Council set up a Convention, chaired by former French President Giscard d'Estaing, to provide answers to the main questions related to future developments for the Thessaloniki European Council in June 2003.[117] In order to respond adequately to the forthcoming enlargement and to involve the future Member States in the process, they were invited to participate in the work of the Convention on an equal footing.

The Convention opened its deliberations on 26 February 2002 and explored the different visions of the Convention members in the first phase, which was dedicated to gathering all opinions. In the following phase, which lasted from 12 September 2002 to 7 February 2003 and was called reflection phase, the Convention discussed concrete issues and possible solutions, in particular in the working groups set up. In the final phase - the proposal phase - the Convention drew up a complete text for a new and single Treaty establishing a Constitution for Europe.

However, even during the Convention, the Union could not focus exclusively on its own future. After the USA, together with the United Kingdom, had waged war in Afghanistan both in response to the terrorist attacks of 11 September 2001, and the involvement of the Taliban regime and its refusal to hand over the mastermind of the attacks, the Saudi Osama Bin Laden, the situation in the Middle East had also escalated. On 20 March 2003, the USA, leading the so-called "Coalition of the Willing", attacked Iraq without UN approval. The European Union and its Member States suddenly faced a division. The majority of the Member States and the accession countries had opposed going to war alongside the USA. The United Kingdom led those European states that would join the USA. France in particular reacted vehemently against the members of the Coalition of the Willing and criticised above all the accession countries that had joined this coalition. The American Secretary of Defence Donald Rumsfeld added fuel to the fire when he referred to the European states that had joined the USA as the New Europe to which the future - and thus also the unres-

116 Full text of the Laeken Declaration: (full text of the Laeken Declaration: https://www.consilium.europa.eu/media/20950/68827.pdf).

117 In particular with regard to (a) a better division and definition of the Union's competences, (b) the simplification of the Union's instruments, (c) the issues of democracy, transparency, and efficiency, (d) potential paths towards a constitution for European citizens.

tricted sympathy of the USA - belonged. Not only was the transatlantic relationship seriously disrupted, the Heads of State and Government also had to admit how incompetent Europe really was in foreign policy issues. Neither the foreign ministers nor the Heads of State and Government had succeeded in bringing about a coherent European position. France as a Permanent Member of the UN Security Council and Germany as a rotating member of this body at that time were unable to prevent the invasion of Iraq by the USA and the United Kingdom. Additionally, the Union had not only failed to prevent the war but had not even managed to find a unified European position. At the extraordinary meeting of the European Council in Athens on 16 April 2003, the Heads of State and Government agreed that the only way to solve this problem was to establish a European Union Minister for Foreign Affairs. The Convention immediately took up this decision and included it in its proposal for a Constitutional Treaty.

Despite various obstacles, the Convention, in particular its chairman Giscard d'Estaing, wanted to present a complete text proposal at the European Council in Thessaloniki on 20 June 2003, but this effort massively failed. The Convention was only able to adopt and to submit a fragment. The final document, which was drafted in the subsequent improvement phase until 4 July 2003, contained completely new approaches to the shaping of primary law. The formerly separate treaties TEU and TEC had become a single treaty, which at the same time abandoned the pillar structure of the ToM. The Parliament's demand had prevailed and the EU Charter of Fundamental Rights, which had been solemnly adopted at the Nice European Council in December 2000, had found its way into primary law. However, the Convention text also provoked the most heated controversies. For some Member States, the new areas of application for QMV did not go far enough, others saw their red lines already greatly overstepped. The question of whether or not to include an explicit concept of God in the future constitution divided the Member States, as the strictly secular-oriented states did not want to allow such a mention. The group of small and medium-sized Member States felt unfairly disadvantaged by the planned reduction in the size of the Commission - and especially by the proposed method of rotating Member States in the College of Commissioners. At least two Member States already announced in Thessaloniki that they would not agree to the new voting procedure in the Council under any circumstances and would insist on the Nice regime. To make matters worse, Giscard d'Estaing, supported mainly by Chancellor Schröder and the incoming Italian Council Presidency, particular Prime Minister Silvio Berlusconi, demanded that the next IGC adopt the Convention proposal tel quel and only make necessary technical adjustments. This was all the more surprising as it was not even clear whether the Convention proposal had really been adopted by consensus.[118]

However, to call the Convention a failure would be too harsh a judgement, despite all the dissent about its outcome. The Convention not only sought new ways; it broke completely new ground. It had provided the future intergovernmental conference with a template against which it would have to be measured. In any case, the door had been opened for a radical reform of the European Union.

118 On the question of the existence of a consensus on the Convention proposal, cf. Fischer, Konvent, p 96.

I.9. The Treaty establishing a Constitution for Europe – 2003-2004 – An Attempt at a Radical Reform[119]

Warmly welcome to our family.

Anders Fogh Rasmussen

The IGC on a Constitutional Treaty was ill-starred from the very outset. After the already rising tide had just been smoothed at the European Council in Thessaloniki in June 2003, for the time being there was absolute calm. Prime Minister Berlusconi, who should have realised by this time at the latest that the Italian Council Presidency was in for a Sisyphean task, accepted the Draft Constitutional Treaty from Giscard d'Estaing in a pompous ceremony in Rome on 18 July 2003 and guaranteed the successful conclusion of the forthcoming IGC in December 2003, since Italy would not accept any changes to the content of the draft. Accordingly, Berlusconi decreed that the conference should be called IGC 2003, anything else would be illusory.[120] With these statements, however, Berlusconi had not only incurred the wrath or at least the incomprehension of the other Member States. His first appearance in the European Parliament as EU President turned into a scandal when during the debate he suggested to a critical German MEP that he could play the role of a concentration camp warden in a movie just being shot in Italy. The IGC and official Brussels then went into summer recess. The fact that there was a whole bundle of unanswered questions on the table did not seem to irritate anyone.

In the meantime, Austria had rallied the so-called group of like-minded states, which was not willing to accept the Convention's draft tel quel.[121]

119 Full text of the Treaty establishing a Constitution for Europe: https://eur-lex.europa.eu/legal-content/EN/TXT/?uri=OJ:C:2003:169:TOC. For a detailed account of the IGC 2004 cf. Fischer, Der Verfassungsvertrag.

120 Mr Berlusconi was to be wrong twice: firstly, substantial changes were made to the content of the draft, and secondly, it was only the Irish who brought the IGC to a conclusion that would go down in the annals of the Union as the IGC 2004.

121 At the outset, the group consisted of Austria, Finland, Malta, Hungary, Slovenia, the Czech Republic, and Lithuania. Towards the end of the IGC, the number of states had risen to thirteen. Both Austria's Chancellor Schüssel and his Foreign Minister Ferrero-Waldner emphasised from the beginning that this was not obstructionism but a constructive contribution to the IGC. Considering that essential compromise proposals emanated from this group, which ultimately led to a successful conclusion of the conference, the criticism of the peers expressed at the beginning seems unjustified in view of the final result.

In particular, the reorganisation of the size and composition of the Commission was not acceptable in the eyes of these states. Furthermore, the establishment of a permanent President of the European Council was just as critically questioned by this group as the proposed institution of the European Council. However, the big Member States had agreed that there should be no changes to the content of the Convention draft. In this they were supported by the Parliament, which otherwise ran the risk of losing the ground gained by the draft, in particular regarding the budgetary procedure. Nevertheless, all positions could be considered moderate and negotiable, except those of Poland and Spain with regard to the voting system in the Council. Spain and Poland had been disproportionately served in the weighting of votes in the Council at the IGC 2000 and strictly refused to deviate from this voting system in favour of the double majority of the Convention draft.

Italy, however, had apparently ignored all these reservations and complications and only started the actual negotiations on 4 October 2003. The group of like-minded managed to thwart the Presidency's approach already in this first round of negotiations by successfully opposing the proposed Legislative Council, which was subsequently deleted from the draft. This cleared the way for substantive negotiations. Italy - and Mr Berlusconi in particular - had not been prepared for this. On closer examination, the Convention's proposal turned out to be largely outside the scope of consensus. In November 2003, Italy tried to save what could be saved and convened a conclave of foreign ministers in Naples. There, many open positions could be clarified, but the hard-core issues - Commission, decision-making process, budgetary procedure, voting procedure in the Council - remained unresolved.

The European Council meeting in Brussels in December 2003, which was supposed to be a triumph for Mr Berlusconi, ended in disaster. Poland[122] and Spain persistently blocked, but the other conferees were not ready to give in. Moreover, they were not prepared to negotiate on the other unresolved issues until Poland and Spain had given in. At noon on 13 December 2003, the Presidency had to admit its failure by ending the European Council without a result in the IGC.

The Irish presidency, which took over the chair on 1 January 2004, had a difficult legacy to take on. PM Ahern, however, was to find the right means

122 The Polish Prime Minister Miller gained notoriety with his statement "Nice or Death".

to get the negotiations back on track through perseverance and calm. He trave lled to all capitals and held exploratory talks. Unlike his predecessor, he did not promise anything to the respective negotiating partners and did not hold big press conferences. In addition, Ireland had to consider the accession of ten new Member States on 1 May 2004, as well as the Commission's proposals for the Financial Perspective 2007 to 2013 and the publication of the Cohesion Report. Already preoccupied with their own agenda, the Presidency and the Union were thrown into severe turmoil by the terrorist attack in Madrid in March 2004. But even this unforeseen and most tragic event could not shake Irish stoicism. Mr Ahern set facts quickly and efficiently by having the EU interior ministers prepare a draft action plan at an ad hoc meeting to be presented to the European Council for discussion only a few days later.

It was not until 24 March, the eve of the Brussels European Council, that the Presidency issued its interim report on the state of the IGC and concluded that, following the exploratory talks, the will of the Member States to resume the conference could be established. Ireland accepted the risk of having to face the ultimate failure even of this new beginning. It was clear to all concerned that the Union would be plunged into a serious institutional crisis if no agreement was reached at the European Council meeting in Brussels in June 2004.[123] In his interim report, Mr Ahern warned very clearly of the consequences of failure and appealed to the goodwill of all Member States not to let the integration of Europe fail over the question of the voting procedure in the Council. With this interim report, Ireland brought new momentum to a deadlocked situation and was able to maintain this momentum until the end.

The Irish roadmap was not even affected by the negative referendum on the Cyprus issue on 24 April 2004. Undeterred, Mr Ahern completed the Tour de Capital[124] and continued to explore the options for a settlement. The almost catastrophic turnout in the European Parliament elections of 10 to 13 June 2004, in which only 45.5% of eligible voters participated, was skilfully used by the Irish Presidency to demonstrate that only a successful conclusion of the IGC 2004 could provide a new and directional impetus to

123 As early as December 2003, some Heads of State and Government had spoken in frustration of the possibility of dissolving the Union and reducing it to a core Europe in which only those states willing to fully integrate would participate.

124 Until the coming into force of the Treaty of Lisbon, the EU President visited the Heads of State and Government in their respective capitals ahead of a European Council meeting to discuss the meeting's agenda.

both Union and integration. To Ireland's advantage, Spain - with the change of government from the conservative PM José Maria Aznar to the socialist PM José Luis Rodríguez Zapatero - had moved away from her rigid stance. PM Ahern presented a list of unresolved issues to the European Council in Brussels in June 2004, including the definition of qualified majority voting, the number of seats in the European Parliament and the size and composition of the Commission. Already on the first night of the summit, Mr Ahern resorted to the ultima ratio and held so-called confessional talks. The new polish PM Belka was confronted with the fact that his country was totally isolated. In the late hours of 18 June 2004, PM Ahern presented a final compromise text, making it clear that the package would not be reopened. He thus confronted the conference with a take-it-or-leave-it decision. The compromise was such that there would be neither clear winners nor losers. Poland, too, concluded that it had resisted long enough and agreed to the deal.

At the IGC 2004, the Union had agreed on a new basis for primary law which, compared to the results of the IGC 1996 and the IGC 2000, represented a radical reform and not just an attempt at reform. Until the planned entry into force of the new treaty on 1 November 2006, there was still a long and rocky road ahead of this reform project, which had only come about after all Heads of State and Government had admitted to themselves that only a radical step could ensure the continuation of integration, otherwise a failure of the successful process that had lasted for over fifty years could not be ruled out. But everything turned out differently than planned in Europe's state chancelleries.

I.10. The Treaty of Lisbon - 2004-2007 - At the Precipice[125]

The EU has overcome
its institutional crisis.

José Socrates

When Europe is in a celebratory mood, there seems to be no stopping it and every cliché is served. So it was with the ceremonial signing of the Treaty establishing a Constitution for Europe. Not the real hero of the negotiations, Irish Prime Minister Ahern, but the unsuccessful former chief negotiator, Italy's Prime Minister Berlusconi, was to take the limelight. On 29 October 2004, the "Cavaliere" invited to Rome and put the spotlight on the historic venue of the Sala Degli Orazi e Curiazi at Campidoglio. The location was as well chosen as the message: The circle is closed, the Heads of State and Government of the European Union[126] sign the Constitutional Treaty (= TCEU) at the same place where the Treaty establishing the European Economic Community was signed!

In contrast to this early milestone in the history of the European integration, the Constitutional Treaty was not even to come into force.

Some Member States were very keen to complete the ratification process as quickly as possible: Lithuania and Hungary before the end of 2004, Italy, Greece, Spain (after the required referendum had turned out positively), Slovenia, Slovakia, Romania, Bulgaria, and Austria by May 2005. These states had immediately set their parliamentary procedures in motion and ratified the TCEU. In Germany, both the Bundestag and the Bundesrat approved the Treaty in May 2005, but a constitutional complaint suspended the procedure.

On 29 May 2005, the rejoicing over the new Treaty came to an abrupt end. France's President Chirac had called a referendum at his own discretion, and the result was a clear 55% against the Treaty. President Chirac had clearly miscalculated when he called the referendum. Nevertheless, he was in a predicament that made it difficult for him to hold this non-compulsory

125 Full text of the Treaty of Lisbon: https://eur-lex.europa.eu/legal-content/EN/TXT/?uri=OJ:C:2007:306:TOC. Consolidated version of the TEU: https://eur-lex.europa.eu/legal-content/EN/TXT/?uri=OJ:C:2008:115:TOC. Consolidated version of the TFEU: https://eur-lex.europa.eu/legal-content/EN/TXT/?uri=OJ:C:2008:115:TOC. For a detailed account of the IGC 2007 cf. Fischer, Der Vertrag von Lissabon.

126 With the exception of Croatia, which was only present, the representatives of the candidate countries Bulgaria, Romania and Turkey also signed.

referendum. In the run-up to this referendum, one of the arguments in France was that a referendum had already been held when the Maastricht Treaty was adopted and that one was therefore in line with tradition. How a tradition can be derived from a one-off event - especially since neither the Treaty of Amsterdam nor the Treaty of Nice had been subjected to a referendum - is hard to argue stringently, but if it had been a success, it would have been a success all along the line. In reality, this strategy proved to be a disaster. Shortly afterwards, on 1 June 2005, a Dutch referendum also crash-landed: 61.6% of the votes cast rejected the Constitutional Treaty. Some reasons for these popular failures can be found in xenophobia. Long before the Front National's success in the 2010s under Marine Le Pen, her father and founder of the Front National, Jean-Marie Le Pen, had rocked French politics when he tried to win the 2002 presidential election inter alia with xenophobic slogans, only to be eventually defeated by Mr Chirac. Under these circumstances, it may seem strange that President Chirac justified his campaign for the Treaty by saying that it was a precondition for the next enlargement; in particular, the rapid admission of Turkey, which Chirac particularly favoured, would only be possible this way. The situation was much more precarious in the Netherlands, where a religiously motivated murder of a Dutch film director critical of Islam shortly before the referendum intensified an already latent xenophobic mood. The accusation that the Treaty was neoliberal also contributed to the rejection. Another element may have been added, which regularly occurs in so-called mid-term elections: the electorate uses such elections, which it does not consider that relevant, to settle accounts with the government. All this could have been easily known in Paris and The Hague - if only one had wanted to. The art of elegantly denying reality was to reach unimagined levels in 2005.

Luxembourg's PM Jean Claude Juncker, otherwise considered a great tactician, proved to be just as great a master in the art of denial of reality. In addition to the disaster of the Constitutional Treaty, for which he was not responsible but nevertheless had to manage, the final negotiations on the Financial Perspective for the years 2007 to 2013 had to be concluded as scheduled at the European Council in June 2005. Juncker seemed to miss what everyone saw coming, and he failed miserably because of the veto of Tony Blair, who considered the planned agricultural expenditure to be completely excessive. At the end of the first semester of 2005, the Union and its Member States were faced with a shambles: The Constitutional Treaty had failed and the future budget had to be renegotiated. In a further spike of denial of reality, the European Council concluded that the work on the budget had made considerable progress through joint preparation and that an overview had been gained on the constitutional project, thus maintaining the line that the ambitious European project was more valid than ever. There was no trace of realism in the conclusions of the European Council.

The realists in the European Council knew at this point that it was only a question of when and not if: the Constitutional Treaty "patient" was in a coma and slowly but surely drifting away. The realists were sure that neither France nor the Netherlands could be morally pressured if all other Member States ratified. The humanists among the realists began to remember Cicero.[127]

However, PM Blair took office as President with unequalled verve, thus laying the foundation for a successful British EU Presidency in the second half of 2005. Consequently, the European Council on 15 and 16 December 2005 not only took note of a thorough stock-taking of the constitutional project, but the budget issue was also resolved and concluded to everyone's satisfaction.[128]

It was therefore up to Austria to find a quick way out of the impasse of the constitutional project. From 26 to 28 January 2006, the kick-off conference "Sound of Europe" took place in Salzburg. Federal Chancellor Schüssel, who, together with his congenial Foreign Minister Ursula Plassnik, played a decisive role in the planning and subsequent implementation of this Presidency, served up all the clichés that lent themselves to this conference: Salzburg, Mozart, Sound of Music. Only Salzburg remained what it was during the conference, Mozart became Cerha,[129] and the Sound of Music became the Sound of Europe. True to this convergence, the conference quickly became an atonal and confrontational event, which clearly showed - at least with regard to the Netherlands - that the Constitutional Treaty could no longer be saved. The Austrian EU Presidency launched a further consultation on this issue with a so-called subsidiarity conference in April 2006, at which representatives of local and regional authorities were also able to express their views. The Presidency's report on the information and communication activities of the Member States during the period of

127 i.c.: 'Quo usque tandem ...', Cicero, Cataline Orations 1.

128 In retrospect, this was the penultimate grand service that PM Blair had been able to render to the Union before leaving Downing Street N° 10.

129 Friedrich Cerha is one of the most prominent composers of the 20th and 21st centuries, but his music cannot necessarily be described as tonal.

reflection was not only the first tangible result of the Schüssel-Plassnik duo's shuttle diplomacy, but also included the exit scenario offered by the European Commission.[130] The diffuse overall picture was summarised in this report in a legendary formulation: *Perceptions vary greatly from one Member State to another.* There was hardly anything more to add to this profound analysis. Federal Chancellor Schüssel finally succeeded in paving the way for the realists by having the European Council adopt the so-called twin-track approach, which aimed, on the one hand, to make the best possible use of the options offered by the existing Treaties and, on the other hand, to develop a new approach which, under the German Presidency in the first half of 2007, was to lead to an assessment of the state of the deliberations on the Constitutional Treaty and possible future developments. These results should serve as a basis for decisions on the continuation of the reform process, concrete steps should then be initiated in the second half of 2008 at the latest.[131]

Germany took over the presidency in this critical situation, probably also in the hope that the political conditions in the Member States would remain stable so that the project could get back on track with its trusted partners. This hope was dashed when Chancellor Angela Merkel's Austrian counterpart, Wolfgang Schüssel, surprisingly lost the elections and she was unexpectedly confronted with a social democratic chancellor. Elections were also due in France, which ultimately led to the replacement of President Chirac, as he was no longer a candidate, Belgium was already in a massive election campaign, and it was foreseeable that Tony Blair would give in to pressure from his party and hand over the office of Prime Minister to Gordon Brown. Nevertheless, Germany swam along on the wave of success,[132] albeit somewhat insensitively,[133] and was able to score another

130 This scenario was euphemistically called Plan D ("The Commission's contribution to the period of reflection and beyond: Plan D for Democracy, Dialogue and Debate", European Commission: COM(2005)494 of 13 October 2005, https://eur-lex.europa.eu/legal-content/EN/TXT/PDF/?uri=CELEX:52005DC0494&qid=1674048711236&from=EN).

131 Accordingly, the "sandwich chair" Finland, positioned between Austria and Germany, kept a low profile with public appearances on this topic.

132 Both the EU-Russia Summit (at this point still an absolute showcase) and the G8 Summit went well for German Chancellor Merkel in the media.

133 The celebrations of the 50th anniversary of the Treaties of Rome took place not in Rome but in Berlin and were crowned with the Berlin Declaration. Italy's enthusiasm was limited, and she had to be content with the consolation prize of a plenary session of the Committee of the Regions.

hit with the well-placed Berlin Declaration.[134] The declaration concluded by stating that "we must always renew the political shape of Europe in keeping with the times. That is why today, 50 years after the signing of the Treaties of Rome, we are united in our aim of placing the European Union on a renewed common basis before the European Parliament elections in 2009. For we know, Europe is our common future." Thus, even the last supporter of the constitutional project realised that it had been abandoned and that new paths had to be taken.

The Member States quickly split into a group of maximalists and a group of minimalists.[135] The basic position of the maximalists included the following - very narrow - scope for negotiation:

- Keeping the Treaty on the Constitution for Europe (TCEU) in structure and content, in particular (i) the voting modalities (double majority), (ii) the provisions on the size and composition of the Commission, (iii) the extension of qualified majority voting, (iv) the dissolution of the pillar structure, and (v) the granting of legal personality to the EU.
- Abandoning the designation "Constitutional Treaty" negotiable
- Abandoning the designation "Foreign Minister" negotiable
- Withdrawal of the text of the Charter of Fundamental Rights from the corpus, but simultaneous legal anchoring by binding reference in the text of the Treaty
- Abandoning parts of Part I to be considered negotiable (especially symbols).

The group of minimalists (France, the Netherlands, the United Kingdom, the Czech Republic, and Poland) did not form a homogeneous bloc and accordingly held very different positions. France was basically in favour of keeping the content of the TCEU, but demanded a change in the external form, in particular the abandonment of the title "Constitutional Treaty". The new President Sarkozy sought - as already announced in the election campaign - a traditional amendment treaty in the form of a covering treaty. On the issues of (i) voting modalities, (ii) size and composition of the European Commission, and (iii) extension of qualified majority voting, France took a similar position to the maximalist group, as well as on the

134 https://web.archive.org/web/20070927204801/http://eu2007.de/de/News/download_docs/Maerz/0324-RAA/English.pdf.

135 Fischer (2010), 37-39.

issue of the Minister of Foreign Affairs, the Charter of Fundamental Rights, and parts of Part I.

In comparison, the situation in the Netherlands was more complex. In addition to a new orientation of the Treaty with regard to name, scope, and treaty character, the Netherlands explicitly demanded that the terms "constitutional treaty" and "foreign minister" be abandoned. While the position of the Netherlands was still in line with that of France, a new element was introduced with the demand for the inclusion of national parliaments in the Treaty, which should have the right to block legislative proposals of the Commission.[136] With a view to future enlargements, the Netherlands also demanded that strict criteria for the accession of new Member States be anchored in the Treaty in order to raise the relevant threshold.[137] An additional demand concerned the deletion of the explicit reference to the primacy of EU law over national law.[138]

The United Kingdom was a delicate case for two reasons: From a content point of view, as the UK had made very clear the red lines, she would not cross,[139] and from a political point of view, as the term of office of PM Tony Blair was coming to an end. In principle, the United Kingdom took a similar position to France and the Netherlands, particularly with regard to avoiding a referendum at all costs. The four clearly and irrevocably defined red lines concerning (i) a separate treatment of the Common Foreign and Security Policy from the other parts of the Treaty,[140] (ii) the removal of the Charter of Fundamental Rights,[141] (iii) the abandonment of the text regarding the primacy of EU law over national law, and (iv) the abandonment of the establishment of the legal personality of the EU. The political dimension was closely intertwined with the substantive demands. Mr Blair's successor,

---

136 This Dutch demand was called the red card for national parliaments, following FIFA's football rules.

137 With this demand, the Netherlands was in good company, as several Member States were sympathetic.

138 The demands concerning the participation of national parliaments, enlargement criteria and legal precedence emerged from the national debate in the Netherlands. Prime Minister Balkenende assumed that another referendum could be avoided if these three demands were met.

139 The United Kingdom's particular antipathy towards the Schengen provisions was not yet explicitly communicated at this point, but in the course of the negotiations it was argued all the more strongly and uncompromisingly.

140 i.c. keeping the principle of unanimity, no possibility of interference by the European Parliament, no jurisdiction of the European Court of Justice.

141 Either this Charter should in principle not be legally binding or it should be provided with an opt-out for the United Kingdom.

Gordon Brown, was already known to be extremely Eurosceptic and, in the event of a referendum, would almost certainly be defeated and thus have to call new elections, which he would also lose. From New Labour's point of view, this had to be avoided at all costs for reasons of party tactics. In domestic terms, New Labour's demands were in line with those of the opposition Tories and the Liberals. In terms of foreign policy, the United Kingdom feared above all a communitarised CFSP and the granting of legal personality to the Union with respect to her permanent seat on the Security Council in the United Nations.

However, the main sticking point - at that stage - was Poland. The Polish position is the easiest to describe: no matter what the Treaty says, the voting modalities would have to be restored to the status quo ante in favour of Poland, i.e. from the double majority system back to the Nice regime.[142] All the preliminary negotiations only went so far, and the stand-alone position vis-à-vis the other Member States only seemed to fortify Poland's position.

In the run-up to the summit in June, the final state in the group of minimalists, the Czech Republic, had sat on the running board of the Polish wagon and expressed her unwavering loyalty to the Polish demand.

Almost unimpressed by these developments, the German Council Presidency presented a non-paper at the European Council meeting on 20 and 21 June 2007, which for the first time set out in detail what the framework for a future IGC might look like:

- The so-called constitutional concept would have to be abandoned.
- The TEU and the TEC would remain in force and be amended on the basis of the outcome of an IGC, which would be called a Reform Treaty.
- The TEAEC and the existing protocols would be adapted to the Reform Treaty through appropriate protocols.
- The structure of the TEU should be revised to reflect the results of the IGC 2004 that would eventually be incorporated.
- The structure of the TEC should be essentially maintained, changes would be necessary due to transfers to the TEU and the results of the IGC 2004 to be incorporated.

In retrospect, German Chancellor Merkel had risked a lot and made her own fate dependent on the success of this tactic. After hours of negotiations on the second day, some of which were not necessarily friendly, it became

142 In a startlingly regular fit of suicidal ideation, the Polish leadership announced that this demand would be worth dying for.

clear that Poland would be isolated with her demands. Poland, however, continued to insist on her positions, in particular, the question of her weight in the votes led to a bizarre, almost Kafkaesque volte-face. Poland argued that if she had not suffered so many deaths in World War II, she actually would have a population of around 66 million today - and she wanted to have that weight now.

The intention, however, was to keep Poland on board and so negotiations resumed. What really happened in the last hours before the showdown will probably remain forever hidden in the mists of the distant past. The German EU Presidency will, of course, appear in the official history books as the one that brought about and secured success. However, there is much to be said for the thesis that PM Blair (who thus made his last active contribution to the success of European integration) and President Sarkozy (who made his first contribution) had defeated Poland in a fierce battle with Lech Kaczyńsky, with the simultaneous media battle between Warsaw and Berlin already being fought at a very low niveau.

Nevertheless, at the last second Germany resorted to a means that was completely unforeseeable for Poland. Poland was given the choice of either going along with the IGC or the conference would be convened with a majority vote. In Warsaw, all EU commentaries were scoured until the sobering realisation was reached that this move was legitimate.[143] In the early hours of 23 June 2007, the European Council was able to adopt the negotiating mandate for an IGC to reform the Treaties.

Winners look different would have been an appropriate headline. In any case, there was no real winner: the supporters of the constitutional idea were clearly defeated; those who wanted to maintain the status quo of the distribution of competences had to accept majority decisions in the area of justice and home affairs; Poland announced that it now wanted to push through her demands even more strongly.

However, one decision of this European Council was supported by all Member States: the motto of the Union "United in Diversity" provided for in the Constitutional Treaty was not to be included in the Reform Treaty.[144]

Once again, it was up to Portugal to chair a landmark intergovernmental conference - and at the same time to put aside any other ambitions for her own presidency in the second half of 2007.

143 Only later did Poland realise that she would have ample opportunity to place her own positions prominently during the upcoming IGC.

144 cf. Fischer (2010), p 46.

The IGC 2007 was at any rate to be conducted quite differently from previous conferences of this kind. The diverging positions of the Member States, which had resurfaced as expected after the European Council, were to be reduced to a minimum. The almost ingenious way to achieve this was to entrust the negotiations to the Council's group of legal experts. The genius of this is not so much that a working group should try its hand at the technical aspects, but in the chair itself. This particular Council working group is traditionally chaired by the Council's Legal Service and not by the respective Presidency. The Council's then Legal Adviser and Director General of the Legal Service, Jean-Claude Piris, was to become the true key figure for success. Mr Piris, gifted with a brilliant legal mind, political skill, and a self-confidence that was by no means underdeveloped, never left any doubt as to who would ultimately decide in this group. He saw himself as the guardian of the mandate of the European Council. With incredible skill, Mr Piris solved both the minor problems (e.g. inaccuracies in the mandate) and the difficult ones (e.g. when it was unclear whether it was a necessary adjustment or a deviation from the telos of the mandate) in consultation with the group. Even if Mr Piris had to bow to the special wishes of the United Kingdom for political reasons,[145] he has otherwise remained true to his line.[146]

Portugal approached the political negotiations in a rather relaxed manner but decided to negotiate in camera. This tactic, with which Portugal had already been extremely successful at the IGC 2000, was to prove itself again. The Portuguese Chair was able to avert many a deviation from the mandate without losing face. In the case of Poland, however, this method did not seem to work either. In addition to the challenges posed by certain key players, there was an election campaign in Poland and the EU issue was dragged into it, according to the motto that one should not show any weakness towards Brussels. But Portugal mastered this too with flying colours.

Towards the end of summer 2007, the opponents of the reformed Constitutional Treaty slowly but surely brought their guns into position and

145 These special requests, which were already close to à la carte membership, seemed too little ten years later and resulted in the BREXIT debate.

146 With almost somnambulistic certainty, Mr Piris had enforced a principle in the negotiations that was to cause headaches for some delegations. Only English and French were permitted as language rules, but only the French version of the text served as a working basis. This stipulation was instrumental in ensuring that the negotiations progressed very quickly.

prepared for the final negotiations. Poland, the Czech Republic, and above all Italy were seen as blocking candidates after the United Kingdom had already pushed through all her wishes.

The penultimate act took place on 10 October 2007 when the Portuguese Presidency presented its mid-term review to the European Parliament in Strasbourg. The speakers in the Parliament, Elmar Brok and Andrew Duff, were cautiously enthusiastic, but both knew that the Parliament's demands were reaching their limits. Only five days later, on 15 October 2007, the Presidency had the last opportunity to prepare the ground for the final negotiations. At the regular meeting of EU foreign ministers, the Reform Treaty was at the centre of the debate. Poland made a fatal negotiating mistake when demanding that the Ioannina clause be elevated to the rank of primary law and insisting on the appointment of a Permanent Advocate General. Since this second demand by Poland was not directly related to the IGC, it opened up the possibility of a trade-off for Portugal, but the Presidency withheld it for the time being - leaving Poland on a long leash.

The list of open political questions was long and discussed in detail, but it was clear to the European Council from the outset that it would not find a final deal at this meeting. However, it was to be made clear to the delegations that success was only within reach if all participants made painful concessions - thus isolating the three dissenters.

On the eve of the informal summit, the Portuguese Presidency may have felt reminded of Cicero's accusatory incipit in the Senate session of 8 November 63 BC: "Quo usque tandem abutere, Catilina, patientia nostra?".[147]

The concluding summit in Lisbon, which was supposed to give the Reform Treaty a more resounding name, took place on 18 and 19 October 2007. The Portuguese Presidency had done an almost perfect preparatory job by recognising that the majority of the open points were not enforceable, but only conceding this behind closed doors. The Member States concerned were thus able to save face, as their concessions could be presented as necessary for unity.

That way, Portugal had isolated those Member States that continued to block. Poland, the Czech Republic, and Italy - following the example of the World Security Council - were referred to as veto powers, but they could no longer exercise real power without being blamed for the ultimate failure of the negotiations.

---

147 When, o Catiline, do you intend to cease abusing our patience?

Poland's concerns were nevertheless solved with elaborate manoeuvres, in that the Ioannina clause was not directly incorporated into primary law, but an elegant back door was finally opened by a declaration on a Council decision that was to enter into force uno actu with the Reform Treaty. Appeased by the addition of a permanent Advocate General, Poland had relented and no longer closed her eyes to the other compromises. Portugal had discovered a back door in another delicate case, as the Czech Republic could be pacified by a declaration of the Commission to be annexed to the Treaties along the lines of the Czech demand.

Italy's demand for an additional seat in the European Parliament was met in a way that was as elegant as it was unusual. The maximum number of MEPs was not to be exceeded, no Member State wanted to have its seats reduced, so the number of 750 was unalterably fixed. The Portuguese Presidency resorted to an unconventional trick in that the composition of the European Parliament was now 750 MEPs and the President. The seat thus - virtually - added was allocated to Italy.[148]

Portugal had squared the circle and got all the Member States, the European Commission, and the European Parliament on board. On 19 October 2007, shortly after 1 a.m., Portugal was able to declare the IGC successfully concluded.

The Portuguese Presidency ended with yet another success. After the proclamation of the EU Charter of Fundamental Rights on 12 December 2007 in Strasbourg by the Presidents of the Council, the European Parliament, and the European Commission, the Reform Treaty was signed on 13 December 2007 in Lisbon. This marathon session[149] was concluded on 14 December 2007 with the European Council meeting in Brussels. The Reform Treaty, now called the Treaty of Lisbon, was mentioned rather tersely in the conclusions of this European Council: "The European Council welcomes the agreement reached by the IGC on 18 October 2007 on the Treaty of Lisbon and its subsequent signature on 13 December 2007, as well as the proclamation of the Charter of Fundamental Rights on 12 December

148 This semantic trick does not change the fact that the President is of course also a Member of the European Parliament.

149 This marathon turned into a logistical nightmare for European air traffic control, as the entire entourage of Heads of State and Government first had to travel to Lisbon and from there fly directly on to Brussels, with a slot to Strasbourg added for some participants.

2007. It calls for the swift completion of national ratification procedures so that the Treaty can enter into force on 1 January 2009".[150]

Those who had expected the Union and the Member States to return to essential tasks may have been right, but the question of essentiality can be judged in different ways. The Union was on the brink of the precipice, for without the Lisbon Treaty it would have had to remain in the Nice regime.

The question now was whether the EU was finally moving away from the precipice or heading further towards it.

150 http://data.consilium.europa.eu/doc/document/ST-16616-2007-INIT/en/pdf.

I.11. Economic Crisis, War, and Global Terror - 2008-2015 – One Step Closer to the Precipice

Let us never negotiate out of fear.
But let us never fear to negotiate.
John F. Kennedy

During the negotiations on the Lisbon Treaty, the world around the European Union had changed dramatically - without the Union taking much notice. The blow of the rejection of the Constitutional Treaty was too severe, the shock of the failure of this project too intense, the opportunity for further self-occupation too tempting. The following events are intended to serve as examples; they are neither representative nor complete, but they represent highlights of further developments. The shortcomings that emerged at the beginning of these examples would later lead to greater turbulence.

The first signs of a dramatically developing global wave of terrorism were evident by mid-2009 at the latest, when Russia, of all places, was hit hard by a terrorist attack by Chechen separatists. In Beslan, 1.128 hostages were taken. This terrorist attack was only violently ended days later. About a month afterwards, locals and tourists died in well-disguised suicide attacks on the Red Sea.

The curtain was to rise on the first act of the Ukrainian drama at the EU's external border. The so-called Orange Revolution in November 2004 hounded President Yanukovych, who had been declared the winner of the election and had only won through massive electoral fraud against his opponent Mr Yushchenko, out of office. The initial wave of support from the European Union was considerable, but early statements about possible EU accession (and also NATO accession) were quickly withdrawn.[151] The first Russian-Ukrainian gas crisis at the turn of 2005/2006 had a significant impact, as the Union did not want to jeopardise Russian gas supplies, but the inability of the Orange revolutionaries to implement reform promises weighed even more heavily.

Developments in China did not go unnoticed, but Beijing did not have to expect a particularly harsh reaction from the Union against the anti-secession

151 Almost two years later, during the visit of the EU Commissioner for External Relations, Benita Ferrero-Waldner, and the Chairwoman of the Foreign Affairs Council, Ursula Plassnik, there was no longer any talk of accession, but only of the European Neighbourhood Policy and the instruments associated with it.

law of 14 March 2005, which made it virtually impossible for Taiwan to legally withdraw from the Chinese federation. Undeterred, China continued on its path and, after this relatively moderate measure, resorted to more massive means, including the seizure of uninhabited island groups.

A small and rather unknown magazine triggered a mass reaction in the Islamic world. The Muhammad cartoons that appeared in Jyllands-Posten on 3 September 2005 were to be the beginning of a never-ending wave of protest that culminated tragically in the murderous attack on the magazine Charlie Hebdo in Paris on 15 January 2015.

No stone was left unturned on the Western Balkans during this period. On 3 June 2006, Montenegro declared her independence and seceded from Serbia, on 1 January 2007 Bulgaria and Romania became EU members, the accession of Albania and Croatia to NATO was vigorously pursued and finally decided in April 2008. Kosovo also seceded and declared independence in early February 2008.

In the middle of the decisive phase of the IGC 2007, however, an event occurred that was to affect not only the Union but the entire world economy on an unexpected scale. On 9 August 2007, interest rates on interbank loans suddenly skyrocketed - the beginning of the financial and economic crisis, triggered by obviously non-performing subprime.

The particular piquancy, though, lay in the domestic sphere of the Union. This time, the leaders were so confident that the Treaty would be ratified that they paid no attention to the dissenting voices emerging in Ireland. Instead, they turned to other Member States they considered more problematic.

All this combined resulted in a highly explosive mixture that was to preoccupy the Union for many years to come.

This concentration of events should have been sufficient to shift attention from purely internal to external considerations. But far from it! No sooner had the Treaty of Lisbon been signed and sealed as the "real" issues were at stake: personnel decisions that were to result from the Treaty. On the one hand, the President of the European Council had to be appointed, on the other hand, the High Representative of the Union for Foreign Affairs and Security Policy. Everyone who was (and had been) considered important was mentioned, discussed, discarded, and taken up again.

The ratification of the Lisbon Treaty began as something of a sideshow and was stalled as early as May when German President Horst Köhler complied with the German Supreme Court's request not to sign the instrument of ratification before its ruling was issued. The next blow came from Ireland, when a majority of 53.4% rejected the adoption in a referendum. As expected,

Polish President Lech Kaczyńsky did not miss this opportunity and refused to sign the instrument of ratification, arguing that the Treaty had failed because of the Irish referendum. This allowed him to take revenge on the winner of the national elections, Donald Tusk, but at the same time he had bound himself to a final Irish result.

Irish Prime Minister Brian Cowen, underestimated by some, achieved a result at the European Council in December 2008 that he could never have achieved during the IGC.[152]

The European Council gave the necessary legal guarantees on the three points requested by Ireland: (i) the Treaty of Lisbon would not affect national fiscal policy in any way; (ii) the security and defence policy of the Member States would be preserved in its entirety and thus also Ireland's traditional policy of neutrality and the relevant obligations of other Member States; (iii) the provisions of the Irish Constitution concerning the right to life, education, and family would not be affected in any way by the fact that the Treaty of Lisbon gives legal status to the Charter of Fundamental Rights of the European Union, nor by the provisions of this Treaty concerning justice and home affairs.[153] In addition to these conditions, the European Council made a further volte-face. The reduction to a number of Commissioners smaller than the number of Member States had already been indirectly questioned during the Lisbon negotiations, but the fact that the European Council would even go back on the reform of the Treaty of Nice in this respect is more than astonishing. The European Council agreed that - provided the Treaty of Lisbon enters into force - a decision would be taken in accordance with the necessary legal procedures, according to which one nominee of each Member State would continue to be a member of the Commission.[154]

Under these dramatic circumstances, the collapse of Lehman Brothers on 15 September 2008 recedes almost completely into the background, although this collapse was to lead to a chain reaction a short time later that could have been foreseen, too. Overnight, a banking crisis developed into a sovereign debt crisis of unimaginable proportions.

The Union was nonetheless able to score a major foreign policy success during this period when French President Sarkozy, who held the rotating

152 http://data.consilium.europa.eu/doc/document/ST-17271-2008-INIT/en/pdf.

153 cf Fischer (2010), p 88.

154 At its meeting on 18 and 19 June 2009, the European Council adopted the necessary provisions (Fischer (2010), pp 88f). On 12 March 2013, the European Council adopted the Decision on the number of Members of the European Commission (2013/272/EU), OJ L 165/98 of 18 June 2013.

presidency of the European Council at the time, played a major role in bringing the Russian-Georgian war to an end. The two parties of the conflict signed the peace plan brokered by Sarkozy in mid-August 2008, which led to a frozen conflict but prevented further bloodshed.[155] Not far away, the situation came to a head anew, the gas conflict between Russia and Ukraine boiled up again and was to reach another climax at the turn of the year 2008/2009. At that time, no one wanted to believe that it was a kind of war by proxy that would ultimately lead to an all-out war.[156]

On the "home front", the year 2009 was understandably focused on the engagement with the Lisbon Treaty.[157] In the end, everything developed positively for the Treaty. The German Supreme Court ruled in favour of the Lisbon Treaty on 30 June but criticised the accompanying law, which was accordingly amended by the German Bundestag. In Ireland, the anti-EU alliance disintegrated and failed miserably both in the European Parliament elections in June 2009 and in the second referendum on the Lisbon Treaty on 2 October, when 67.1% of the votes cast were in favour of accepting the Treaty. Poland, in particular the President, now also bowed to the majority. After Austria, the Czech Republic, and Germany had found a face-saving solution regarding the Beneš Decrees[158] by agreeing that Protocol No. 30 on the application of the Charter of Fundamental Rights of the European Union to Poland and to the United Kingdom should also be applicable to the Czech

155 Occasionally, this intervention is used as an argument against the establishment of the Permanent President of the European Council and the High Representative, as Mr Sarkozy has shown what courageous intervention can achieve. This argument can only be agreed with insofar as it was the person Sarkozy who made the success possible, not the function.

156 Here, too, caution is required when claiming in retrospect that a bolder engagement of the European Union would have prevented the war in the Donbas or the occupation of Crimea in 2014. This would have required not only a realistic threat potential of the Union towards Russia, but also the acceptance of the Ukrainian side.

157 And so the election of Kirill I as Orthodox Patriarch of Moscow and all Rus on 1 February 2009 went almost unnoticed. On closer inspection, it was foreseeable that Kirill I would play a prominent role in the Russian-Ukrainian dispute.

158 The Beneš Decrees comprise the 143 presidential decrees issued by the Czechoslovak government-in-exile in London until the appointment of the provisional National Assembly on 21 October 1945 and later approved by the provisional Czechoslovak National Assembly in March 1946. The following decrees are of particular importance in the - extremely controversial - debate on the Beneš Decrees:

- Decree No. 5 of 19 May 1945: Decree of the President concerning the invalidity of some transactions involving property rights from the time of loss of freedom and concerning the National Administration of property assets of Germans, Hungarians, traitors and collaborators and of certain organizations and associations

Republic, this hurdle was also taken and the European Council was able to take note of the adoption of the Treaty of Lisbon by all Member States at the end of October 2009. Although the conclusions were drafted in very cautious language, they once again showed both the tensions that had existed up to the adoption and the challenges that the Union would now have to face.[159]

The reference to the High Representative in these conclusions should not be misinterpreted, because this new function as defined in the Lisbon Treaty had to be filled first, as well as that of the new - permanent - President of the European Council. The Heads of State and Government were well aware of how far-reaching these two personnel decisions would be, because these two positions - and the first office bearers - would shape the face of the Union to the outside world for years to come.

The two large party families had originally agreed that the President should go to the Socialist side (after the Commission President had already been taken by the Conservatives), and the High Representative to the Conservatives. This preliminary decision, however, was to fail because of the Socialists' personnel, since the only imaginable candidate would have been the former British Prime Minister Blair. However, his own party group, which could not or would not forgive him for his alliance with the United States, was particularly divided over his candidacy. Moreover, some opponents argued that he came from a Member State that did not belong to the Euro Council. His running mate would have been the Austrian Foreign Minister Ursula

- Decree No. 12 of 21 June 1945: Decree of the President concerning the confiscation and expedited allotment of agricultural property of Germans and Hungarians, as well as traitors and enemies of the Czech and Slovak nation
- Decree No. 28 of 28 July 1945: Decree of the President concerning the settlement of Czech, Slovak or other Slavic farmers on the agricultural land of Germans, Hungarians and other enemies of the state
- Decree No. 71 of 19 September 1945: Decree of the President concerning the work duty of persons that had lost Czechoslovak citizenship

Added to this was Law No. 115/1946 concerning the legality of actions related to the fight for renewed freedom of the Czechs and Slovaks and the exemption of certain crimes from the statute of limitations.

On 14 October 2022, the Commission had issued "Summary Findings of the Commission Services - The Czechoslovak Presidential Decrees in the Light of the Acquis Communautaire" (https://www.mzv.cz/file/14078/evropska_komise_findingsfinal_eng.pdf). During the IGC 2007, the Czech Republic had already expressed concerns that an incorporation of the EU Charter of Fundamental Rights would make it possible to combat the decrees, especially as a legal basis for recourse claims.

Cf. Fischer (2010), p 90, footnote 212.

159 http://data.consilium.europa.eu/doc/document/ST-15265-2009-INIT/en/pdf.

Plassnik, who was also the subject of much debate. In the end, everything turned out differently and the Socialists renounced the post of president, whereupon the carousel of candidates was set in motion again. The Heads of State and Government surprisingly quickly agreed on two candidates, on the one hand on the incumbent Belgian Prime Minister Herman van Rompuy as President of the European Council, and on the other hand on Lady Catherine Ashton as High Representative of the Union for Foreign Affairs and Security Policy. In favour of the latter was the fact that she was already an acting member of the Commission and therefore did not have to be confirmed by the European Parliament. The Heads of State and Government desperately wanted to avoid such a hearing so as to avoid giving the Parliament further appearances. In favour of the former was his experience and the fact that he had managed to deal with the extremely complicated situation in Belgium quite discreetly and even to stabilise it. On 19 November 2009, the informal European Council, chaired by Swedish Prime Minister Fredrik Reinfeldt, agreed on this personnel package, and the Lisbon Treaty entered into force on 1 December 2009. This was the last meeting of the Heads of State and Government to be chaired by the rotating Council Presidency. The European Council on 10 and 11 December 2009 was already chaired by Herman van Rompuy.

The first major crisis seemed to have been overcome after the Treaty of Lisbon entered into force before the end of 2009. The events at the external borders of the Union, which almost came to a head at the beginning of 2010, on the one hand, and the domestic crises developing at the same time, were to push the Union and its Member States in a completely different direction. The Union began to tumble from one crisis to the next.

In December 2010, the self-immolation of a Tunisian street vendor was to become the trigger for what was soon to be known in the West as the Arab Spring aka "Arabellion" in the Maghreb and Mashreq region. France, of all countries, despite her close relations with the Tunisian regime, apparently did not have the slightest idea of the volcano on which the Tunisian president was riding. The Parisian reaction that one could gladly and immediately send police to help contain these small uprisings was fortunately not to be realised. The president could no longer be kept in office and was barely able to escape into exile - together with his family and his amassed gold reserves. Not much further east, fate was not so merciful to another dictator. Muammar Al Gaddafi lost his army, his office, and his life after the USA and the EU Member States, surprised and humiliated by the events in Tunisia, massively supported the opposition militarily. The tide continued to wash eastwards, sweeping away Egyptian President Mubarak, who suddenly found himself in prison. A brief uprising in Bahrain was quickly crushed with Saudi help (interestingly to note, this opposition was not supported by the West). Jordan and Iraq, which was still in crisis anyway, were not involved, Iran, which was also not involved, probably benefited from being completely isolated. The interventions of the Western group of states were rather modest in their impact, the Arab Spring ebbed away as quickly as it had come. With the counter-revolution of the conservative group in Egypt supported by the army - and at times also by the West - driving the Muslim Brotherhood, which had democratically come to power after the fall of the old regime, out of office again, the Arab Spring finally ended. The Arab Spring collapsed in North Africa on 8 June 2014 at the latest, when the former field marshal Abd al Fattah al Sisi, was sworn in as president at the Egyptian constitutional court. What remained is a relatively stable Tunisia (whose success is largely due to the high level of education of the population and perhaps also to the fact that there was no significant external intervention), a practically failed state of Libya, a high percentage of which was temporarily occupied by the Islamic State movement (referred to as "Daish" by the Arab speaking world) that emerged in the course of the Arab Spring, and on whose territory anarchy reigns in various areas, a still-stable Morocco, and an equally stable Algeria (both of which rest their stability on a massive deployment of security forces), a restabilised Egypt, a torn Yemen in which Saudi Arabia and Iran are waging a brutal proxy war, a Jordan that is holding up surprisingly well, and a Lebanon that continues to be destabilised. European attempts to establish a common foreign and security policy in this crisis ridden zone essentially failed, but the real catastrophe broke out in Syria, whose civil war was to plunge the Union into a crisis at the turn of the year 2015/2016.

As already mentioned, the Union's eastern neighbourhood developed in a direction that was neither desired nor expected. After the Russian-Georgian war came to a halt in 2008 - in no small part thanks to the EU's intervention -, Ukraine was unable to regain her peace. The Orange Revolution imploded, not least due to its own inability to deliver what it had promised to the Ukrainian people, and the Orange Revolution's trigger, Viktor Yanukovych, was able to make an unexpected comeback. Ukraine became the scene of a proxy war between the Union and Russia. The escalation was prompted by the question of whether Ukraine should turn to the Russian-led Eurasian Union project or accept the European Union's offer of association. Although the association had been agreed in Brussels in February 2013, President Yanukovych refused to sign the referring document at the Vilnius summit on 28 to 29 November 2013, as the pressure from Russia had become too intense. Still on 30 November 2013, the Ukrainian opposition gathered on the central Kiev Maidan square and managed to topple Yanukovych in February 2014 for a second time. Ukraine was finally turning towards the European Union. Should the Ukrainian leadership have believed that the Union or NATO would reward this renewed u-turn with accession negotiations, this can only be explained by a fundamental misjudgement of the situation. After the new Ukrainian government pushed a law through the Verkhovna Rada that would have discriminated against the Russian language in Ukraine, Vladimir Putin reacted in a way that was completely unforeseen by the West. Mr Putin's geopolitical understanding could not allow Ukraine to deny Russia medium- to long-term access to Crimea and thus to the naval port of Sevastopol, which was - and still is - vital for the Russian Black Sea Fleet. Taking advantage of the unstable situation in Ukraine - especially the language law and the claim based on it that Russians are no longer safe in Ukraine – Mr Putin annexed Crimea without further ado. In the Donbas, the secessionists rose up and brought the regular Ukrainian army to the brink of collapse. This time, however, the European Union had learned from the mistakes of the Arab Spring and was now holding back on promises. At the same time, however, the Union demonstrated for the first time that it could very well use its means to act in unison against a military intervention that is illegal even under the most generous interpretation of international law. The sanctions against Russia adopted by the Union have been a first and very strong sign of life of a developing common foreign and security policy. But here, too, the theatre of war in Syria plays a role that still needs to be clarified.

However, these two chains of events affecting the Union from the outside were by no means the only catastrophes to befall Europe. Right at the beginning of the implementation of the Lisbon Treaty, the Union had to accept the bitter lesson of marching divided and being defeated as a whole.

As provided for in the Lisbon Treaty, the European Union tried to obtain the High Representative's right to speak at the United Nations but failed at the first attempt in an unexpectedly embarrassing manner.[160] The European Union has [...] only the position of an observer at the United Nations and can therefore only speak at the end of sessions. For this reason, the EU Presidency-in-office always took the floor on behalf of the EU. The High Representative's own right to speak was intended both to illustrate the EU's self-image as a global political actor and, of course, to strengthen the High Representative's

160 The following paragraph is taken from Fischer (2011), p. 44.

position. The first office holder, Lady Ashton, had already cancelled a mission to the United Nations at short notice in mid-August 2010 because she had been denied the right to speak in a special session on the flood disaster in Pakistan. In order to avoid such situations in the long term, the EU Member States had proposed or rather demanded in a corresponding draft resolution that the President of the European Council or the High Representative should speak on behalf of the EU during the sessions of the United Nations General Assembly. These two EU representatives should also be given the right to (i) make proposals, (ii) table amendments, and (iii) respond directly to contributions to the debate. However, the Europeans had apparently not prepared the vote on 14 September 2010 thoroughly enough. Suriname's motion to postpone the vote on resolution A/64/L.67 of 31 August 2010, tabled on behalf of the Caribbean Community of States (CARICOM), was adopted by 76 votes to 71. Even states such as Canada, Australia, and New Zealand abstained from voting, thus contributing significantly to the failure of the EU resolution. The EU diplomats had thus not succeeded in time in overcoming the well-known objections to the right of EU representatives to speak (i.c. (i) preferential treatment of the EU compared to other regional organisations such as the Arab Union, CARICOM or the African Union, (ii) interference in the functioning of the United Nations and the interaction of the UN Member States, (iii) increased weight of the EU within the General Assembly). It was only in a second, coordinated attempt that the Union was able to wipe this foreign policy slate clean.

This example also shows the steep learning curve of the Union. The failure in the first attempt was unsparingly analysed and the consequences drawn from it. Accordingly, the second attempt was a success, this time under the motto "United we march, united we win".

At the same time, since 2010 the Union has had to make every effort it could economically, financially, and probably also domestically to keep Greece, which was practically insolvent at the time, afloat. The rapidly changing governments in Greece, a referendum on a no longer upright EU proposal to consolidate the budget and continuous strikes by the - in reality indescribably suffering - Greek population did little to stabilise the situation. The accusation of inconsistency on the part of the Union, however, misses the point: the decision to keep Greece in the Eurozone was evidence of the ability to come to a conclusion quickly and not to let political decisions be imposed by the global stock markets. This is not the place to discuss the economic question of the reasonableness and correctness of this decision. Nor is this the place to discuss whether the way in which the - admittedly - radical austerity measures were implemented was the right one. It is the political question that is the crucial one. And this question is: Is the European Union in a position to respond to a massive crisis in a timely manner after considering all possible alternatives and is it in a position to sustain this decision - with the necessary adaptations - in the long term? The answer can be answered in the affirmative today. The aid for Greece may have been a piecemeal solution to close the ever new gaps, but the Union did not break up and the Eurozone survived.

In addition to these support measures, which are intermediary per se, the Union has also succeeded in creating a permanent response to the economic and financial crisis with the so-called Fiscal Compact.[161] This treaty was ratified on 2 March 2012 by all EU Member States - with the exception of the Czech Republic and the United Kingdom - and represents the only adequate legal response to the euro crisis. The adoption of such an act should not be a reason for special mention, as the Union regularly adopts legal acts. Nevertheless, this act deserves special attention. It is the rare example of states admitting that they have to take measures that will not only have short-term effects but will change their sovereignty in the medium to long term for the good of the whole. The Fiscal Compact definitely contains such elements, as it massively restricts the right of Member States regarding their future budgetary policy. The second reason for mentioning it is the way the treaty came about. Germany ultimately demanded that the Fiscal Compact be anchored in the Union's primary law, which would have required an IGC and the amendment of the Treaties. This path would have meant implementation within a time horizon of at best three years from the start of negotiations and would also have been associated with the uncertainty that ratification would fail in a Member State. In the end, Germany could be convinced of an elegant solution, which was no less legally binding and had the advantage of prompt implementation. The Fiscal Compact was concluded as a treaty under international law between the Member States (with the two exceptions mentioned), with the contracting parties committing - in an abbreviated form - to transpose its content into EU secondary law. Although this example should not set a precedent, because in principle the path of the community method shall be followed, pragmatism triumphed here over dogmatism in favour of the overriding goal of lasting stabilisation.

161 The Fiscal Compact is part of the Treaty on Stability, Coordination and Governance in the Economic and Monetary Union, i.c. Title III Article 3 to 8 (https://eur-lex.europa.eu/legal-content/EN/TXT/PDF/?uri=CELEX:42012A0302(01)).

Nevertheless, the Union continued to face two unresolved crises that threatened to jeopardise the project of European integration. The civil war in Syria with all its horrors and catastrophes, with its endless brutality and contempt for humanity, with its innocent victims and its brazen victors, is not the actual subject of this study. It is the consequences of this conflict that brought the Union nearly to its heels. The Syrian conflict triggered an enormous wave of refugees. Together with the simultaneous influx of refugees from Afghanistan and Pakistan on the one hand and those from Africa on the other, the refugee wave from Syria led to the temporary collapse of the Schengen system. Greece, completely overwhelmed by the sudden influx, saw no other option than to divert the arriving masses towards the Balkans, from where they tried to march on to Austria and, above all, Germany. On 31 August 2015, the now legendary sentence "We can do it" was uttered at the German chancellor's summer press conference.[162] A few days later, first hundreds, then thousands set off from Hungary towards the West. After a column of around 200,000 refugees moved from Budapest towards Vienna and was briefly brought to a standstill at the Austrian border, the Austrian authorities had to capitulate as the pressure became untenable. In a late-night phone call from 4 to 5 September 2015, Angela Merkel informed Austrian Chancellor Werner Faymann that Germany would not close its borders but open them and accept the flow of refugees. As a result, Austria felt more or less compelled to open her borders.

It will always be a matter of interpretation whether Chancellor Angela Merkel's statement that Germany would unilaterally suspend the Dublin procedure triggered the enormous influx of refugees across the Balkans towards Germany, but it is indisputable that the pull was intensified as a result. Equally incomprehensible is the fact that the European Council did not convene a special meeting and find a coordinated European solution. During the financial crisis, the European Council had impressively demonstrated its crisis resilience and solution capacity. This time it was not given any chance. The initially almost exuberant welcoming culture gradually gave way to a certain scepticism and ultimately pushed the main host countries Germany, Austria, and Sweden to their limits. The other Member States invoked the Schengen Code or openly declared that they did not want to accept refugees, with some even distinguishing between Christian and Muslim refugees. After months of negotiations, the Union was still unable to agree on a common line. However, the inability to find a solution was and is on no account a means to

162 https://www.swr.de/swr1/bw/programm/fuenf-jahre-wir-schaffen-das-100.html.

stop the flow of refugees. Since then, this flow has ebbed gradually, but it has never dried up. And the European Union, even in early 2024, has still not found a unified asylum policy as an answer to this perennial dilemma.

This led to the second conflicting situation, which arose from the Syrian conflict. Russia had gained a key role in ending the war in Syria. But this in turn brought the Ukraine conflict into play, due to which the Union imposed sanctions on Russia. Vladimir Putin was fully aware of the Russian key position in Syria and was able to use military force because of Russia's domestic legal and political conditions. This geopolitical approach, which the West had deemed no longer permissible, was certainly an option for Mr Putin, as he had demonstrated in Crimea and the Donbas. The use of ground troops to end the war in Syria was out of the question for the West in the short and medium term, while Russia did not hesitate to resort to this means if necessary. Only Russia's intervention on the side of the Assad regime made a settlement of the conflict - and the survival of the Assad regime - basically possible. For the Union, this raised the question of which weighed more heavily: Refugee flows that can no longer be managed and put intra-European solidarity to the test, or a Ukraine whose support is gradually being reduced, at least to a level that Russia can live with. The answer that the EU finally came up with was neither fish nor fowl and eventually led to the catastrophe in Ukraine and had by no means ended the civil war in Syria.

As if all these challenges had not already been enough, British Prime Minister David Cameron had blatantly accepted the threat of the United Kingdom leaving the European Union in order to discipline his own party, appease some recalcitrant backbenchers, and give the Tories another election victory. A possible UK exit had since hovered over Europe like a sword of Damocles, undermining economic and political stability.

I.12. Brexit and the Conference on the Future of Europe – 2016-2021 – Into the Abyss and Back Again

Success is the temporary victory of
one part of personality over another.
Martin Suter

Prime Minister David Cameron promised before the 2015 House of Commons elections to negotiate a new relationship between the Union and the United Kingdom that would give the British the best of both worlds. Considering the then relationship, it was already an à la carte membership anyway, as the UK had a myriad of opt-ins and opt-outs. But this was not enough for the Eurosceptic British. Already on the occasion of the European Council in December 2015, the Heads of State and Government had agreed to find mutually satisfactory solutions in the following four areas of concern at its February 2016 meeting: (i) competitiveness, (ii) economic governance, (iii) sovereignty, (iv) social benefits and free movement. The weeks leading up to the February 2016 Summit were marked by the most intensive negotiations, in which the - on the whole rather hapless - President of the European Council, Donald Tusk, did his utmost to bring the other Member States, the European Commission, and above all the European Parliament to a common, extremely UK-friendly line.

Mr Tusk had set out four negotiating baskets: (i) Economic governance, where (a) a decision by the Heads of State and Government would set out principles to ensure mutual respect between Member States participating in the further deepening of Economic and Monetary Union and those that do not, paving the way for further integration within the euro area while preserving the rights and responsibilities of non-participating Member States, (b) a second decision would establish a mechanism which, while providing the necessary assurances on the concerns of non-euro area Member States that it cannot constitute a veto or delay urgent decisions, should support compliance with the above mentioned principles, (ii) Competitiveness, whereby a decision of the Heads of State and Government, together with a more detailed statement by the European Council and a statement by the Commission, would confirm the commitment to strengthen efforts to improve competitiveness by i.a. regularly assessing progress in simplifying legislation and reducing burden on business so that red tape is cut, (iii) Sovereignty, whereas a decision of the Heads of State and Government recognises that the United Kingdom, given its particular situation, is not committed to further political integration under the Treaties, while reinforcing respect for subsidiarity, (iv) Social benefits and free movement, whereby the existing Treaties would be fully respected, in particular the principles of free movement and non-discrimination, but the UK's concerns should be addressed by building on the clarification of the interpretation of the existing rules, including a statement by the Commission on a number of issues related to better combating the abuse of free movement.[163] At the European Council on 18 and 19 February 2016, Mr Cameron obtained, based on Mr Tusk's proposal, even further concessions that partly called the future European integration into question. Without going into the technical details, the question of future integration should be highlighted as an example: What meaning does the dictum of the "ever closer Union of the peoples of Europe"[164] still have if a Member State is allowed to opt out of it but remains a full member? The Heads of State and Government Package Agreement - which is strictly speaking an agreement under international law between the Member States and not a decision of the European Council - as well as the draft Council decision on the Banking Union and several declarations by the European Commission committing to come forward with proposals to amend existing EU legislation in the areas of free movement and access to social benefits for EU workers should enter into force as soon as the UK had notified the Council of the decision to remain in the EU after the in-out referendum.[165]

Four months after this historic European Council, the referendum in the United Kingdom on remaining in the European Union took place on 23 June 2016. The campaign went as expected, the blows from both sides increasingly hitting below the belt, especially the Brexeteers, above all the hardliner Boris Johnson, known as a notorious fighter with the truth, distinguished themself with adventurous promises. The EU-critical Tories spread the view that only after withdrawal would they be able to negotiate with the Union on equal footing and so get the best for the United Kingdom only bilaterally.

The official European Union stayed completely out of the referendum campaign in order - supposedly - not to offer the Tories any platform for

163 Cf. https://www.consilium.europa.eu/en/press/press-releases/2016/02/02/letter-tusk-proposal-new-settlement-uk/.

164 TEU Preamble N° 13.

165 Cf. https://cms.law/en/deu/insight/brexit.

attack. In the end, simple slogans won out over long-winded declarations, populism over factual reality, EU critics over EU supporters. Like a boomerang, the migration crisis of summer 2015 came back as a direct hit in the Remainers' line of defence. The Brexeteers put up a huge column of refugees with the catchy slogan "Breaking Point".[166] The extent to which the Brexeteers' victory was due to this election poster is, of course, impossible to quantify, but the consensus was that it dealt a death blow to the Remainer campaign.[167]

No sooner had the result of the Brexit referendum been officially confirmed than David Cameron announced his resignation as of October of the same year. Some commentators cast him as the proverbial captain leaving the sinking ship. However, two points stand against such a view: on the one hand, the ship had sunk the moment the referendum had gone in favour of withdrawal; on the other hand, it would have been simply implausible to let a prime minister negotiate the withdrawal who had spoken out in favour of the UK remaining in the European Union. The first time [David Cameron] left the confines of Downing Street after the result was to visit Buckingham Palace [to discuss with the Queen] what had happened.[168] According to his memoirs, he contacted his closest ally, Michael Gove, then Nicola Sturgeon, the Scottish First Minister, knowing that the Scottish National Party would try to exploit the result in their favour, and subsequently the other First Ministers; only then did he inform the European leaders and the American President Obama. It is not only the sequence of these phone calls that is interesting, but the message that David Cameron said he repeated word for word on each call: 'I had a strategy to keep Britain in the EU. I executed the strategy. It didn't work. I'm sorry.'[169] British understatement in its purest form - Mr Cameron must have been aware with the announcement of the referendum result that his time in Downing Street would be forever linked to the losing bet against an EU exit. In defeat, however, he showed that he could not only display a stiff

166 The full text of the poster read: "BREAKING POINT – The EU has failed us all – We must break free of the EU and take back control of our borders – Leave the European Union – ON 23rd JUNE", cf. https://www.semanticscholar.org/paper/%E2%80%9CRuled-Britannia%E2%80%9D%3A-Metaphorical-Construction-of-the-Ross-Bhatia/0f9d9a594755639d1f1c1bd1fc658b00ddeabfeb/figure/1.

167 On the background and course of the Brexit campaign cf esp. Oliver, Craig: Unleashing Demons.

168 Cameron, David: For the Record, p 685.

169 Cameron, p 686

upperlip, but that he would muster all the dignity he could. His successor in office, Theresa May, was more than able to hold a candle to him in this respect - quite the opposite of Boris Johnson, who even as prime minister should remain true only to himself.

The Union leaders reacted almost immediately to the UK's irreversible departure and convened a special meeting in Bratislava to which the British Prime Minister was no longer invited. The narrative vis-à-vis the United Kingdom also changed abruptly. One had indeed just lost the Member State that had the best global network, a functioning and battle-hardened army, nuclear forces, both a stable economy and currency, and, last but not least, a permanent seat on the World Security Council, but those who want to voluntarily withdraw from paradise in the eyes of the European integrationists were by no means to be stopped, they are rather to blame and to be pitied themselves.[170]

At their special meeting, the remaining 27 Heads of State and Government adopted the Bratislava Declaration and the Bratislava Roadmap.[171] In the declaration, they invoked the irreversibility of the European integration process and their determination to make the EU-27 a success. What this statement implies about the six decades until the Bratislava Summit was left open by the summit participants. Overall, the undertone of the declaration is more despondent than offensive, more apologetic than self-convinced, more disillusioned than filled with clear visions for the future. The roadmap did not sound too enlightening either, not only in the section "General diagnosis and objectives". The areas of main challenges identified by the summit participants ((i) migration and external borders, (ii) internal and external security, (iii) economic and social development and youth) and the planned measures read like the task catalogue of a newly founded organisation. The shock of the negative UK referendum had a deeper impact on the remaining EU Member States than they officially were willing to admit.

The dilemma they found themselves in was due to circumstances and some decisions of their own. Brussels had made far-reaching concessions

170 Movie addicted readers might be reminded on a famous quote from the 1998 movie “Lock, Stock and Two Smoking Barrels”: *‘Too late, too late’ will be the cry when the man with the bargains has passed you by* (https://www.technia.com/blog/plm-too-late-too-late-will-be-the-cry/).

171 https://www.consilium.europa.eu/media/21250/160916-bratislava-declaration-and-roadmapen16.pdf.

to the UK that would have made membership à la carte possible. Nevertheless, these concessions had not been enough in the end. What if another Member State were to follow this path and demand even more far-reaching concessions with reference to the failed referendum? Equally heavy on the Union's shoulders was the ongoing migration crisis. The refugee agreement with Turkey, concluded in particular on Germany's initiative, was highly explosive, as it gave Turkey the opportunity to put pressure on the EU by threatening to reopen the borders to refugees whenever Ankara saw fit.[172] Turkey was already in a state of emergency after an amateurish coup attempt on 15 to 16 July 2016 against the president and the ruling AKP party failed within five days. President Recep Tayyip Erdoğan used this coup, which he himself described as a 'gift from God' to reshape country and punish enemies,[173] to radically clean up his political opponents, and the army's purging could not have been more comprehensive.

The year 2016, however, had another election on the agenda that was to permanently shake world politics and shape it for more than one term of office. On 8 November, Donald Trump won the US presidential election and set out to make America great again in January 2017.

Contrary to the government's view, the House of Commons had maintained that the Article 50 proceedings could only be triggered with its consent because it was not a Crown prerogative case. On 3 November 2016, the High Court had endorsed this view and was later confirmed by the UK Supreme Court. The Daily Mail then ran the slogan "Enemies of the People", claiming that the judges were attempting to frustrate the Brexit.[174] After the House of Commons finally agreed, PM May was able to trigger Article 50 TEU in a letter to European Council President Donald Tusk on 29 March 2017. At that point, no one had any idea how controversial and emotional these negotiations would become. At times, they were hyped up as a duel between the EU chief negotiator Michel Barnier[175] and the UK

172 Seven years later, Mr Erdoğan showed, on the occasion of the NATO membership applications of Sweden and Finland, which levers he is willing to use to achieve his goals, which come very close to blackmail.

173 https://www.euractiv.com/section/global-europe/news/erdogan-says-coup-was-gift-from-god-to-re-shape-country-punish-enemies/.

174 https://www.dailymail.co.uk/news/article-3903436/Enemies-people-Fury-touch-judges-defied-17-4m-Brexit-voters-trigger-constitutional-crisis.html.

175 Michel Barnier published his highly personal memoirs on the negotiations in 2021 under the lurid title 'My Secret Brexit Diary'. In addition to extremely illuminating passages on the course of the negotiations, the reader is also allowed to participate

Prime Minister Boris Johnson, which certainly corresponded to the self-assessment of the two top politicians, but not necessarily to the negotiating reality in the UK, where the Speaker of the House of Commons, John Bercow, whose particular way of calling the House to order was to gain global notoriety, was to become the most prominent opponent of the own government. Unfortunately, the self-sacrificing fight of PM Theresa May is often forgotten, who had to battle both Brussels and a hostile House of Commons.[176] Both the EU and the UK, however, took their leave from the international stage for about three years, almost completely absorbed in the Brexit negotiations and more or less ignoring the world around them. On 17 January 2017, PM May declared in her Lancaster House speech that the UK would leave the Single Market in any case and that it would be better for the UK to leave the EU without a deal than with a bad deal for Britain.[177] Already on 22 May 2017, the Council (in its Article 50 formation) authorised the start of the Brexit negotiations[178] and endorsed the negotiating guidelines proposed by the European Commission on 3 May.[179]

---

in Mr Barnier's most personal impressions and opinions of his British counterparts, which as a rule do not turn out too friendly and sometimes almost slide into the grotesque. At the same time, Mr Barnier shows the burden he has had to suffer when, for example, he takes us on his summer holiday and tells us: 'Monday, 8 August 2016: First names - From the terrace of a Sicilian villa where I am spending a few days' (sic!) holiday with my wife Isabelle and a few friends, I begin to put together my team'. (Barnier, Brexit, p 17). Even Christmas is cancelled for him by the Brexit negotiations, which he shares with us - without seeking sympathy: 'Monday, 23 December 2019: Citizens' rights - Christmas Eve. Steve Barclay has been trying to reach me for two days and we finally manage to speak.' (Barnier, Brexit p 295). Whatever was said against Michel Barnier - not least on the basis of his memoirs and the writing style cultivated there - he was certainly the perfect choice. He dominated the negotiations on the EU side due to his calmness, composure, and incredible expertise. Above all, he never exceeded the limits of his mandate; rather, he clearly showed not only the UK, but above all the EU, where the boundaries lay and thus contributed significantly to a negotiation outcome that may be considered a perfect example of a Nash equilibrium. Boris Johnson's tactical games never worked against him, perhaps because he apparently considered them unworthy of any reaction.

176 Theresa May had definitely behaved ladylike, her successor could not hold a candle to her in this respect. It may be seen as an irony of history that the only Sir at the table was Mr Barnier.

177 https://www.gov.uk/government/speeches/the-governments-negotiating-objectives-for-exiting-the-eu-pm-speech.

178 https://www.consilium.europa.eu/en/press/press-releases/2017/05/22/brexit-negotiating-directives/.

179 https://ec.europa.eu/commission/presscorner/detail/fr/MEMO_17_1183.

The so-called Bratislava Roadmap had envisaged that the goals set for the process would be implemented by the 60th anniversary of the Treaties of Rome on 25 March 2017. During the Spring European Council on 29 April 2017, the intention had been to review the progress on implementation. However, the Heads of State and Government concentrated mainly on the Brexit negotiations and came to the conclusion that the roadmap adopted had already been implemented in the various sub-items. The Bratislava process was quickly consigned to oblivion.

President Trump made good on one of his campaign promises on 1 June by announcing the US withdrawal from the Paris Climate Agreement. This withdrawal from an international treaty was to be followed by others, such as the withdrawal from United Nations Educational, Scientific and Cultural Organization (= UNESCO) on 12 October of the same year and from the Iranian Nuclear Agreement on 8 May 2018. Mr Trump's various actions would have given the EU the opportunity to position itself as the more reliable partner on the world stage and fill the gap left by the US in international relations. Unfortunately, the EU was too self-referential in these years and the subsequent US President Joe Biden filled the gap faster than expected.

Still under the impression of the gruesome London Bridge bomb attack on 3 June, snap elections were held in the UK on 8 June, although the government would still have had three years to serve. Theresa May had intended to get a new and hopefully strong mandate for the Brexit negotiations but was dealt a bitter defeat. The result of the election was a hung parliament that made it impossible for the Tories to dominate. Theresa May had to enter into a confidence-and-supply deal with the Northern Irish loyalist Democratic Unionist Party (= DUP), which was likely to make her government vulnerable to blackmail. The negotiations themselves took place from 17 July onwards in camera, as it were. PM May first presented her ideas for a future EC-EU relationship to the public at a speech in Florence on 22 September 2017.[180] On 8 December, in an overnight dash to Brussels, Ms May achieved a breakthrough in negotiations that had been deadlocked in the weeks before. Both sides published a joint report

180 https://www.gov.uk/government/speeches/pms-florence-speech-a-new-era-of-cooperation-and-partnership-between-the-uk-and-the-eu.

indicating that sufficient progress had now been made on the key issues to continue negotiating successfully in the New Year.[181]

Russia reacted late, but massively, to the US sanctions imposed in the wake of the Ukraine crisis and its aftermath, expelling a record 755 US diplomats on 1 September. The NATO accession of Montenegro on 5 June, which brought the Alliance to 29 members, did not particularly please Russia, as it only added to Moscow's paranoia that the Western military alliance wanted to encircle Russia. However, 2017 ended with a big bright spot. God's mills grind slowly but thoroughly. After almost two decades, the victims of the Srebrenica massacre found justice when Ratko Mladić was found guilty of genocide by the International Criminal Court in The Hague.

On the other side of the world, China decided to contribute another instalment to the 'Back to the Future' series. On 11 March 2018, the government approved a constitutional amendment that removed term limits on office, while granting Xi Jinping 'President for Life' status. This reversed all such reform moves since Mao's death and put Xi on a par with the founder of communist China. As if that were not enough, the geopolitical centre of gravity shifted further towards the Far East. After long preliminary negotiations, a North Korea-US summit was held in Singapore on 12 June, which was to have far-reaching consequences. The EU also tried to move in this direction and was able to conclude the Japan-EU Economic Partnership Agreement on 17 June, which had been stalled until the end due to the agreement of the respective agricultural sectors, especially in the rice-growing sector. This breakthrough created the largest global bilateral trade alliance, encompassing an open trade area with almost a third of the world's GDP.

In Europe itself, however, it was mainly the approaching Brexit that played the unrestrained first violin. In Brussels, Member States vacillated between a hard line, close to punitive action, and a moderate path, the outermost line of which was to maintain the integrity of the Single Market. Not least thanks to the steadfast stance of Michel Barnier, the second group prevailed in the long run, which the London negotiators mistakenly interpreted as weakness. The Remainer faction slowly became aware that the withdrawal process was almost irreversible and tried to regain the

181 https://commission.europa.eu/publications/joint-report-negotiators-european-union-and-united-kingdom-government-progress-during-phase-1_en.

initiative by demanding a second referendum on the Brexit deal to be concluded. After all, they brought over 700,000 protesters onto London's streets on 20 October. In vain, as it later turned out. These protests were preceded by desperate attempts by PM May to wrap up the Brexit negotiations in favour of the UK. In the process, however, she had to make more and more concessions to Brussels. In a speech at Mansion House on 2 March,[182] she gave a few hints on these compromises, as the UK had to make concessions in the key areas of free movement, budget cuts, the role of the ECJ, trade, and fishing rights. Two weeks later, on 19 March, the UK and the EU published a draft agreement that was not really worth the name, as large parts of the so-called agreement were colour-coded and whole sections were marked with the comment "no agreement has yet been found".[183] Nonetheless, PM May tried not to let go of the reins of action and called her cabinet to a meeting in Chequers. On 6 July, she unveiled her so-called Chequers plan,[184] which was essentially based on the principle of managed divergence from EU rules. To the great annoyance of the hardline Brexeteers, the Brexit according to these ideas turned out to be a soft Brexit with a common rulebook with the EU over goods. In protest to this plan, Brexit minister David Davis left the cabinet on 8 July, followed by foreign secretary Boris Johnson on 9 July. Sixteen more ministers were to leave by the end of the year. Theresa May's situation deteriorated visibly and after the summer break she had to accept another blow. EU leaders rejected the Chequers plan at a summit in Salzburg, Austria, on 21 September, saying it was merely an attempt to cherry-pick EU rules. To Ms May's displeasure, however, it did not stop at these general remarks. The President of the European Council, Donald Tusk, rejected parts of the plan as "not going to work" and, moreover, they would be likely to "undermine the single market". She was particularly hard hit by Mr Barnier's dismissal of the Irish border part of the proposal as illegal. However, she could still count on a section of the British press calling the Salzburg summit an ambush against Ms

182 https://www.gov.uk/government/speeches/pm-speech-on-our-future-economic-partnership-with-the-european-union.

183 https://assets.publishing.service.gov.uk/government/uploads/system/uploads/attachment_data/file/691366/20180319_DRAFT_WITHDRAWAL_AGREEMENT.pdf.

184 https://www.gov.uk/government/publications/the-future-relationship-between-the-united-kingdom-and-the-european-union/the-future-relationship-between-the-united-kingdom-and-the-european-union-html-version.

May.[185] Despite all the prophecies of doom, the EU and the UK reached an agreement on the terms of the UK's withdrawal on 25 November, which was adopted by the European Council (Article 50 formation). PM May, however, must have been aware that this deal was doomed to fail after she had to agree to an all-UK customs union with the EU in order to resolve the controversial Irish border "backstop" in Ireland's favour.[186] Before the end of the year, Theresa May had to endure another humiliation. On 13 December, she survived a confidence vote on her Tory leadership, but had to promise to resign before the next election. A vote in the House of Commons could no longer take place in December 2018 because of the expected strong opposition.

The year 2018 ended in uncertainty about the future of Europe, while in the Far East, not only did the sun rise, but the shift of the geopolitical centre of gravity to this region became increasingly manifest.

For the secular, liberal Western world, it was an interesting but not necessarily earth-shattering event when, on the day before the Orthodox Christmas, 5 January 2019, His Beatitude Bartholomew I of Constantinople issued a formal decree granting independence to the Orthodox Church of Ukraine from the Russian Orthodox Church. This step was preceded towards the end of 2018 by the subordination of the Ukrainian Orthodox Church under the ecclesiastical jurisdiction of the Ecumenical Patriarchate of Constantinople by a unification council that convened in Kyiv on 15 December 2018. The Ecumenical Patriarch Bartholomew I granted a tomos of autocephaly, which is in essence a decree of ecclesial independence, to the Ukrainian Orthodox Church on 5 January 2019.[187] With this ecclesiastical move, two formerly competing Ukrainian Orthodox Churches were united. The Ukrainian Orthodox Church of the Kyiv Patriarchate and the Ukrainian Autocephalous Orthodox Church are from then on under the leadership of the incumbent primate and Metropolitan of Kyiv and All Ukraine. Thus the break with the Russian Orthodox Church and the Patriarch of Moscow and All Rus had become a fact. It was only three years later

185 https://www.theguardian.com/politics/2018/sep/20/may-in-fight-to-save-chequers-brexit-plan-after-salzburg-ambush. The Economist was not quite so unambiguously supportive of PM May, but not uncritical of EU leaders either (cf. https://www.economist.com/europe/2018/09/21/eu-leaders-are-united-on-brexit-but-divided-on-migration).

186 https://www.consilium.europa.eu/en/meetings/european-council/2018/11/25/.

187 https://orthodoxyindialogue.com/2019/01/16/tomos-of-autocephaly-the-full-text/.

that the West became aware of its far-reaching significance, particularly the intolerable humiliation it meant for Russia.

June 2019 was set to be a crucial month both for the EU and globally. The German Manfred Weber had entered the EP elections in May as the EPP's top candidate with the declared goal of becoming Commission President. He had the support of the EP, which interpreted the EU Treaty in such a way that the European Council could propose the candidate, but was bound by the EP's election result, especially with regard to the top candidate. Mr Weber and the EP, however, had counted the chickens before they hatched. Manfred Weber had not been the European Council's first choice even before the ballot, and after a significant setback for the conservatives in Germany, he had lost even more ground. But above all, French President Macron had reservations about Mr Weber as Commission President. Theresa May's last European Council after her resignation as Tory leader on 7 June was therefore a source of tension. The Heads of State and Government had been unable to reach agreement on the personnel package at their regular meeting on 20 and 21 June and therefore had to travel to Brussels again for a special meeting on 30 June. It quickly became apparent that Manfred Weber would not make it, but the political balance gave the Party of European Socialist's (= PES) candidate Frans Timmermans from the Netherlands just as little chance. Hours and hours passed, one candidate after another was considered and rejected. Outside the European Council building, the EP roared - albeit cautiously - having again failed to get its way with its demand for a mere formal nod to its candidate. Like a magician conjuring a white rabbit out of a hat, Emmanuel Macron was very late in presenting his personnel package, which included German Defence Minister Ursula von der Leyen as Commission President, whom no one had on their radar. Frans Timmermans was to be given the post of Commission Vice-President, the Spaniard Josep Borell was to take over the post of High Representative of the Union for Foreign Affairs and Security Policy, the French Christine Lagarde was to move into the European Central Bank as President, and the Belgian Jean Michel was to head the European Councils as permanent President. Much to their disappointment, the former Eastern bloc countries were once again not on the list.

Silence and confusion spread, as not even Germany had had von der Leyen on her books. On closer inspection, however, more and more Heads of State and Government were able to find a certain charm in the list. The gender balance was assured, as was the distribution among the party families, large and smaller Member States would be served, and last but not least, the EP had not been yielded to. A tidbit on the side was that the German chancellor would have to abstain from the vote due to the Berlin coalition requirements. Thus, white smoke rose unexpectedly. Ursula von der Leyen's path into the inner sanctum of the Berlaymont building was anything but paved, however, as massive resistance spread in the EP. The EP saw itself badly duped and forced von der Leyen to make a myriad of electoral promises, such as completing the banking union, reforming the European electoral system, granting the EP the right of initiative for EU laws, averting climate catastrophe through a CO_2 levy, ending inhumanity on the Mediterranean through a radical reform of refugee policy in line with EU states, and - last but not least - holding a conference on the future of Europe. Nevertheless, it was only enough for a very narrow election result. In a secret ballot in Strasbourg, 383 MPs voted for Ms von der Leyen, with the necessary absolute majority being 374. A total of 327 parliamentarians voted against her. After all Commissioners had been confirmed by the EP, the new Commission took up its work extremely belatedly on 1 December 2019.

In the shadow of these crucial EU personnel debates, the Brexit drama gathered momentum, especially in the UK. The events literally came thick and fast. PM May's deal lost the first meaningful vote in the House of Commons by 432 to 202, so - on a mandate from the House of Commons - Ms May had to seek alternative arrangements to the Irish backstop in Brussels on 30 January. But even this improved deal failed to get a majority. After the UK attorney-general ruled that the new deal did not guarantee that the UK could unilaterally leave the backstop, the government lost the second meaningful vote by 149 votes. The humiliation continued when Theresa May had to go to Brussels on 20 March at the request of the House of Commons and asked for a delay of the Brexit from 29 March to 30 June. As early as 21 March, the EU's prompt response came: the UK would either leave the EU on 22 May with a deal or on 12 April without one. A few days later, on 29 March, the government lost the third meaningful vote by a margin of 58 votes. It was clear to everyone that this government would not find a majority for this deal in this House of Commons. The danger of a withdrawal without an agreement, i.e. a hard Brexit sought by the Brexeteers anyways, loomed large. Theresa May was to have a final success, however, when EU leaders agreed at a special summit on 10 to 11 April to a flexible extension of the exit date to 31 October, with the UK free to leave the EU earlier if it passes the deal. The British request for an extension of the deadline fell on deaf ears with the EU negotiators, as the view had meanwhile become widespread in Brussels that the EU should under no circumstances be blamed for a hard Brexit. This played into the hands of future Prime Minister Johnson, who immediately after assuming office came up with new demands, such as on 19 August to ditch the Irish backstop from the withdrawal agreement, and set a target date of 31 October 2019, with or without a deal. Mr Johnson played high stakes and tried with all his might to keep the House of Commons out of the further Brexit process, even sending it into a forced recess in the meantime, which was later declared inadmissible by the Supreme Court. This prorogation of Parliament was to be effective from 9 to 12 September 2019 and last until the State Opening of Parliament on 14 October 2019; effectively, the House was suspended between 10 September and 24 September. On 4 September, Parliament, which finally resumed sitting, passed the so-called Penn Bill, which more or less made it impossible for the government to go through with a no-deal Brexit.[188] PM Johnson went down in history when he made a full-throated promise on 5 September in a speech to a police training college that he would rather be dead in a ditch than ask for another Brexit extension.[189] Boris Johnson, however, continued to pursue his course and sent the next deal variant to Brussels on 3 October, in which the Irish backstop was no longer included. The Commission rejected this draft in its entirety. On 8 October, the withdrawal negotiations collapsed completely, and Council President Tusk accused Mr Johnson of playing a "stupid blame game". Mr Tusk may have been objectively correct, but PM Johnson should have in fact been accused of gaslighting. The Brexit negotiations actually only focused on the Irish question and Mr Johnson tried to convince the EU through not necessarily subtle methods that it was responsible for a new hard border between Northern Ireland and Ireland because it was uncompromisingly going its way and would also risk the Irish peace for the single market. After all, Mr Johnson managed to negotiate the backstop not with the EU but directly with the Irish PM. On 17 October, a new UK-EU deal was announced, which saw the UK make concessions over Northern Ireland. Stealthily, quietly, and silently, PM Johnson had to ask for another

188 https://www.instituteforgovernment.org.uk/article/explainer/benn-act-eu-withdrawal-no2-act.

189 https://www.theguardian.com/politics/2019/sep/05/boris-johnson-rather-be-dead-in-ditch-than-agree-brexit-extension.

Brexit extension in Brussels after the House of Commons decided on 19 October not to vote on the deal until the laws implementing Brexit were in place. On 29 October, the EU granted a "flextension" until 31 January 2020. To make matters worse, Boris Johnson and his Tories won the snap elections on 12 December with an 80-seat majority.

At midnight CET (11 pm UK time) on 31 January 2020, the United Kingdom said goodbye to the European Union. At the time, nobody could have guessed that it would not only be a political farewell, but also a physical one that would last for months.

On 23 January, the Chinese city of Wuhan was quarantined after an outbreak of alleged bird flu. The world took little notice, as such outbreaks were nothing new and always collapsed relatively quickly. This time, however, everything was to be different, and the world was never again to be the same as it was before the emerging pandemic.

The European Council reacted surprisingly quickly and activated IPCR, the Integrated Political Crisis Response mechanism, which is the EU framework for coordination of cross-sectoral crises, on 28 January 2020. After several Council formations and also the European Council had met in videoconference format, the Heads of State and Government agreed on 17 March to reinforce the external borders by applying a coordinated temporary restriction of non-essential travel to the EU for a period of 30 days, at the same time as the border posts within the EU came down. Soon there was talk of a lockdown, which was also implemented. The world had literally come to a standstill, doings and dealings came to a standstill, and social contacts reduced to almost zero.

There was no blueprint on how to proceed, as the last major pandemic had taken place about a hundred years ago. The Spanish flu was now only a faint light deep in the cave of the past with little to compare it to.[190] One factor was crucial, however. Human mobility had become incomparably faster. Whereas the Spanish flu had taken weeks to be transported by US troop carriers to the Western Front in France, a tourist in the 21st century needed only about seven hours to cover the same distance. In addition to this increase in speed, travel in the 21st century is not a luxury, but almost part of everyday life. These two factors led to an explosive expansion. However, as with the banking crisis, the European Council showed in

190 On the origins, the course, and the effects of the Spanish flu cf. esp. Spinney, Laura: Pale Rider – The Spanish Flu of 1918 and how it changed the World, London 2017.

this crisis that it is able to act relatively quickly. The border closures were and are heavily criticised, but it was perhaps the only - quite analogue - option to break the chain of contagion.[191] As straightforward as this step may have been, the consequences were difficult to manage. The simple question arose of how the world's population would continue to live, how sustenance would be ensured, how the sick would be treated. It quickly became apparent that no one was even remotely adequately prepared for such a challenge. Hospitals had not enough ventilators, there were too few intensive care units, and medical masks were practically non-existent. It was to take bitter revenge that health care, an essential component of so-called services of general interest, had been commercialised. Providing intensive care beds is just as expensive as maintaining personal protective equipment and has a correspondingly negative impact on the respective balance sheets. However, no political party was able to capitalise on this failure, as the same precarious situation existed in all states, whether they were led by left or conservative governments. The European Commission tried to take over the steering wheel, but due to a lack of competence, both in terms of the Treaty and in terms of content, the Member States remained the masters of the situation.

For months, people had to be content with the hope of not contracting COVID, as no vaccine was available. But this crisis was also to become an eloquent example of what science is capable of doing when the research funds flow sufficiently. After several months of the pandemic and too many deaths, the EU was able to grant provisional authorisation for the first vaccine developed by BioNTech and Pfizer.[192] The Member States gave the mandate to purchase vaccines to the Commission, which was completely overwhelmed by it for at least two reasons - at any rate in the first phase. On the one hand, the Member States had difficulty agreeing on a key for the individual vaccines, and on top of that there was the question of distribution among the individual states. Moreover, it became apparent that the Commission, although a well-oiled administrative apparatus, had no experience in acting and negotiating as a buyer on the free market. All in all, the EU was not among the first to be supplied, but only after the USA, Israel, and, of all countries, the UK, which in retrospect was to serve

191 On the question of breaking chains of contagion and the usual course of epidemics and pandemics, cf. esp. Kucharski, Adam: The Rules of Contagion, London 2020.

192 On the scientific and commercial background of the development of the first COVID vaccines, cf. esp. Zuckerman, Gregory: A Shot to Safe the World, New York 2021.

the Brexeteers a brilliant justification for their endeavours. In all countries, there were also bitter debates about who should be vaccinated and when.

In addition to the general impact on the healthcare sector, COVID triggered a very different spark that would have lasting geopolitical consequences. The Western world was suddenly confronted with its dependence on Far Eastern and Asian supplies. India, the world's largest producer of pills, decided to serve its own market first before exporting. This was a serious blow, but it could be overcome, especially in the USA, which was almost self-sufficient. However, the supply chain disruptions in the electronics sector, especially in semiconductors, could not be compensated that easily. The European car industry in particular was in danger of coming to a complete standstill. In addition to these primarily economic effects, which by their very nature are capable of having a lasting impact on security and defence policy, the EU suddenly came under massive pressure from the states of the Western Balkans, which felt abandoned and intensified their contacts with Russia and China. The EU did everything in its power to counter these accusations. During the EU-Western Balkans Zagreb Summit on 6 May 2020, the Union assured this group of states of its commitment to collaboration in the fight against COVID-19. Resentment remained, however, and some accused the EU of giving preferential treatment to its own nationals. The alleged help from China and Russia quickly turned out to be pure propaganda, as the vaccines from these two states could in no way compete with those of Western companies and the masks supplied turned out to be completely ineffective in some cases.

This, however, revealed the third weak point, which was to have the most long-term ramifications apart from the medical ones. The EU's financial resources were far from sufficient to cushion the immediate and future damage and effects of the pandemic. The dam bursting into unrestrained borrowing could no longer be stopped.

Amid global chaos and the interim easing of travel restrictions incumbent US President Donald Trump lost the election on 3 November 2020 to his challenger Joe Biden.

In retrospect, 2021 turned out to be the year of the calm before the storm, although there were some unmistakable signs on the horizon. The year started with the entry into force of the African Continental Free Trade Area, which on paper should have led to an improvement in trade and living conditions, but which did not manifest itself in the short or medium term. However, the focus quickly turned to the USA. President Trump had called the result a stolen election immediately after the polls closed and left open whether he would allow a smooth transition of office. On 6 January, the world froze as Trump supporters stormed the Capitol and disrupted the certification of the 2020 presidential elections. Although this process was completed after hours of hope and trepidation and Joe Biden's victory became official, the impossible had happened and the US had lost her democratic innocence. The credibility of the democratic Western liberal system was in question, even though Joe Biden took the oath of office on 20 January and was sworn in as the 46th President of the United States of America. Only briefly did the EU gain attention when it - most embarrassingly - invoked on 29 January Article 16 Northern Ireland Protocol of the Withdrawal Agreement following a row over COVID-19 vaccine supplies. After massive protests, the EU had to turn tail and withdraw this decision. The damage was done nonetheless and the Brexeteers were provided with new ammunition. Adding to the embarrassment was the Commission's statement that it had acted "in error".[193]

The bad news did not stop there. On 20 March, Turkish President Erdoğan declared his country's withdrawal from the Istanbul Convention. The expected robust reaction from the EU was not forthcoming. This blatant breach of human and especially women's rights was not enough for Brussels to break off accession negotiations with Turkey, at least until this withdrawal decision was reversed. Only a few days later, Russia warned NATO not to deploy any troops on Ukraine territory after the West became nervous over reports of a large Russian military build-up on her Western borders to Ukraine. It is questionable whether such an out-of-area deployment would have been permitted under the NATO Treaty. It is equally questionable whether ignoring Russian warnings would have prevented the 2022 invasion. However, more mistrust towards President Putin would certainly have been appropriate. Brexit played almost no role in 2021 after the dramatic events of the previous year, the Council (in its General Affairs formation) reiterated support for the Northern Ireland Protocol on 21 September, in particular underlining that this protocol would not be renegotiated.[194]

After the exhaustive Brexit negotiations, the EU had to repeatedly postpone the start of the Conference on the Future of Europe because of

193 https://www.theguardian.com/world/2021/jan/29/eu-controls-on-vaccine-exports-to-northern-ireland-trigger-diplomatic-row.

194 https://www.consilium.europa.eu/en/meetings/gac/2021/09/21/.

COVID. Moreover, the vast majority of Member States strictly rejected an automatism in the form of a subsequent IGC, which was merely supposed to cast the demands of the conference into a new Treaty. The Parliament was able to celebrate an interim success when the joint declaration was finally signed by the Parliament, the Council and the Commission on 10 March 2021. The executive board, composed of representatives of the three signatories, met for the first time at the end of March. On 9 May, after a year's delay, the ceremonial opening session of the Conference took place on Europe Day in Strasbourg. Throughout the rest of the year, meetings of the Conference Plenary and the European Citizens' Panel took place. The conference participants, at least those representing the EP, civil society, national parliaments, and directly accredited citizens, had high hopes for the coming year, when the Conference was to be concluded and the proposals for the future of Europe adopted.

And so ended the year that was to become the last year before the Zeitenwende.

I.13. The Day After Tomorrow – 2022-2024 – Back at the Precipice

If you are going through hell,
keep going.
Winston Churchill

The year 2022 will go down in the history of the European continent as annus horribilis. In her quest to keep Ukraine at least as a buffer state, Russia chose the unrestricted military option and was no longer content with both the annexation of Crimea, which is illegal under international law, and more or less direct participation in the separatist uprisings in the Donbas. The German Chancellor Olaf Scholz described the invasion of Russian forces into Ukraine in the early hours of February 24 as a turning point.[195] As striking as this categorization may be, it raises the legitimate question of what exactly is meant by it. The simplest explanation is that there is a time before and a time after the attack. This is a purely mechanical answer that acknowledges the event as such but does not include any analysis as to its content. It is certainly neither the place nor sufficient space to analyze the Russo-Ukrainian War. One thing is undeniable, however: the deployment of regular armed forces alone does not constitute the turning of the tide. Already the military annexation of Crimea has been this turning point if one classifies the military conflict in the Western Balkans in the course of the dissolution of Yugoslavia as a pure civil war. The classification as a turning point can rather be justified by the fact that the EU (i) finds itself directly at its external border in a situation that can be classified as war under international law and (ii) can no longer remain neutral. The EU finds itself in the precarious situation that, while it is willing to take all support measures that are not yet considered close to war or even an act of war, it recognizes that this will probably not be enough for Ukraine to win this war. The EU has been extremely sympathetic to Ukraine, and in its wake Georgia and Moldova, politically, even granting candidate status to Ukraine and Georgia in a very short time after the application for membership. However, some EU Member States already had to be massively pressured to take these

195 Chancellor Scholz elaborated on his speech to the German Bundestag in an article in Foreign Affairs magazine (https://www.foreignaffairs.com/germany/olaf-scholz-global-zeitenwende-how-avoid-new-cold-war). For the original text of the speech cf. https://www.bundesregierung.de/resource/blob/992814/2131062/78d39dda6647d7f835bbe76713d30c31/bundeskanzler-olaf-scholz-reden-zur-zeitenwende-download-bpa-data.pdf.

steps. Italy, for example, reacted in August 2023 to Ukraine's blunt demand to open accession negotiations already in the fall of the same year with an equally open rejection of a swift enlargement.[196] Austria had been pointing out since mid-2022 that Ukraine's situation was unique but that the EU should by no means forget the Western Balkans and the years of profound changes in the states of this region. The package deal that Austria demanded between Ukraine and Bosnia and Herzegovina eventually bore fruit, and this state was also granted candidate status in December 2022. The pivotal point here is the fact that a further criterion has been included in the enlargement process. It is no longer just about the de facto state of a country and the fulfilment of the political and technical criteria set out in the Treaty, but also about the fact of being attacked by Russia or being threatened by such an attack. At present, it is difficult to predict how the debate in the Council will develop, in particular whether there will be a clear paradigm shift in the EU's enlargement policy from a meritocratic to a foreign and security policy aka geopolitical approach. If the Union does not decide in favour of one approach or the other, this will inevitably lead to a two-speed enlargement process. This development will confront the EU with a number of challenges, including (i) what incentive will candidate states have to fulfil the technical criteria if political pressure is deemed sufficient, (ii) what impact will the accession of states that insufficiently fulfil the economic criteria have on the economic cohesion of the EU, (iii) does this give a potential aggressor at least indirect power to co-decide on future EU members? Ultimately, the question arises as to whether a merit-based approach can ever be reintroduced if the pendulum now swings in the direction of a geopolitical justification of the enlargement process.

The sanctions imposed on Russia by the EU, in conjunction with its allies and befriended states, also represent a turning point. They have reached a level that hardly allows for escalation, even if there is great disappointment that Russia has been hit less hard than hoped.

Further evidence of the actual existence of a turning point is the EU's reorientation of its Common Security and Defence Policy. Even the four remaining neutral Member States, Austria, Cyprus, Ireland, and Malta, are pushing their political and legal limits.

A less pleasant part of this turning point is the prominent dominance of the U.S., China, and Russia, next to which the EU and its Member States are rather

196 https://www.euractiv.com/section/politics/news/italian-eu-minister-calls-for-reflection-period-before-more-enlargement/?_ga=2.110127621.1865349995.1692688603-787985968.1678955334.

overshadowed. The consequences of the 2008 financial crisis, the 2015 wave of refugees, and the 2020 pandemic are having such an economic impact that the world's richest economic area is not in a position to take the reins in hand.

The Zeitenwende invoked by Mr Scholz can also be seen in the example of Brexit and its consequences, especially the development of the United Kingdom after her exit from the EU, based on the examples of the Russo-Ukrainian War and AUKUS. History's verdict on PM Johnson remains to be seen, but he will definitely score a credit regarding Ukraine. Without the UK's immediate willingness to side with Ukraine and to forge an alliance of supporters, Ukraine might not have been able to resist the onslaught of Russian forces so successfully. The UK may have seen better times[197] and Brexit definitely did not immediately become the success story Brexeteers had hoped for. This can be demonstrated as tragically as clearly through the example of the NHS. The promise that the NHS would receive millions after leaving, which would no longer have to be transferred to Brussels,[198] turned out to be as untenable as the promise of flourishing landscapes in the former GDR after reunification. Yet the UK has shown herself to be resilient enough to survive without the EU and to continue as a player in international relations. The way in which the UK, on the one hand, almost literally booted out France, while at the same time establishing herself as a military power in the Pacific, can arguably be considered a diplomatic masterpiece. AUKUS marks the UK's return to the grand stage of military powers. Neither France nor the EU could counter this move and had to watch how not only France's image was damaged. Those who always expected or hoped that the UK would apply for readmission to the EU will be proved wrong.[199] How tenacious the British are willing and are able to

197 The English journalist Peter Foster, who accompanied the Brexit negotiations for the Daily Telegraph and subsequently continued to work on this topic for the Financial Times, pointed out as early as 2015 'how insignificant [the United Kingdom] risks becoming" (Foster, Peter: Facing Facts - Is Britain's Power Diminishing?, 2015), addressing the negative consequences of BREXIT in his most recent book (Foster, 2023).

198 Cf. https://www.independent.co.uk/news/uk/politics/brexit-eu-referendum-nigel-farage-nhs-350-million-pounds-live-health-service-u-turn-a7102831.html.

199 The Rt Hon Penny Mordaunt MP published a remarkable book together with Chris Lewis on a post-Brexit United Kingdom. The two authors take completely diametrically opposed positions on Brexit, but they take a common approach to a future Britain by focusing on the British character. They argue for a radical modernisation without throwing overboard the country's typical characteristics. One point in particular unites them both, however: the loud call for optimism and the rejection of timidity in the face of manifold challenges (MORDAUNT, Penny/ LEWIS, Chris:

negotiate, they proved already in the first years after the withdrawal. As early as September 2022, the Council had to discuss in detail the state of relations between the EU and the UK and the implementation of the Withdrawal Agreement, in particular the Protocol on Ireland/Northern Ireland, following the UK government's decision in June 2022 to bring forward legislation that would repeal key elements of the Protocol and its response to the infringement procedure launched by the Commission on 15 September 2022. Nevertheless, the EU showed itself more willing to compromise than to be intransigent, and so the Council reaffirmed the EU's readiness to discuss constructively a negotiated solution within the Protocol.[200] As the British side showed no inclination to offer any compromises at an early stage, the EU was forced to reach a provisional agreement on a regulation on autonomous measures. This regulation was to set out those rules and procedures that would allow the EU to exercise its right to enforce and implement the Withdrawal Agreement and the Trade and Cooperation Agreement, and included a package of measures, notably (i) remedial, rebalancing, and compensatory measures, (ii) temporary suspension of relevant preferential treatment of certain products, (iii) refusal, revocation, suspension, limitation or conditioning of air carriers' authorisations or permissions and their operation, and (iv) measures restricting trade and investment. Any such measures would have to be proportionate to the objectives sought and effective in bringing the UK into compliance with the relevant agreements. The measures must also comply with the specific criteria set out in those agreements.[201] Intensive negotiations continued until March 2023, when the Council green-lighted the Windsor Framework on 21 March, which was negotiated on 27 February. This agreement preserved peace on the internal Irish border without either side losing face. The United Kingdom had successfully secured a renegotiation and the EU was able to claim that the Windsor Framework was merely an implementation of the Withdrawal Agreement.

The United Kingdom's decision to leave the European Union is legitimate. The European Union is not a coercive community or even a dungeon of nations, as the Habsburg Monarchy was called at its end by the breakaway constituent states. The Union is made up of sovereign states that can join this community voluntarily and leave it again accordingly. Thus, it is not Brexit per

---

Greater - Britain after the Storm, London 2021). It is perhaps precisely this (functional) optimism that the EU sometimes lacks or has almost lost after so many crises.

200 Cf. https://www.consilium.europa.eu/en/meetings/gac/2022/09/20/.

201 Cf. https://www.consilium.europa.eu/en/meetings/gac/2023/03/21/.

se that is to be questioned, nor the previous attempt by the United Kingdom to achieve à la carte membership for herself, because this attempt is also legitimate in itself. The decisive question is rather whether the Union, with these far-reaching - and ultimately insufficient - concessions, has not already given up its constitutive element and is in danger of becoming a loose association of states in which each member only participates where it expects individual advantages. At the same time, the Union must ask itself whether the United Kingdom's criticism of European integration should be dismissed out of hand or whether it would not be advisable to give careful consideration to preventing further withdrawals.

The Conference on the Future of Europe would have been a most appropriate occasion to reflect on this. After one year, the conference ended on 9 May 2022, in the midst of the turmoil caused by the Russo-Ukrainian War, where it had begun, in Strasbourg, the seat of the European Parliament. Hundreds of proposals had been received, few of which necessitated Treaty change. In total, the final report comprised 49 categories of proposals, broken down into 326 measures. The Council published a technical evaluation of the proposals and measures of the conference as early as June 2022, which will be updated on an ongoing basis.[202] This evaluation is of particular interest as it shows that almost 95% of the conference proposals could be implemented within the current Treaty framework. The Council had therefore decided to focus its work on the overwhelming majority of proposals that could be implemented within the existing EU Treaties, in order to respond quickly to citizens' suggestions. Ultimately, it will come down to a showdown between the EP and the European Council on the question of holding an intergovernmental conference, which will essentially be about extending the rights of the EP. However, this approach means that it could take years to implement, with implementation through Treaty change also still dependent on all Member States agreeing to the outcomes of such an IGC.

In 2024 and the years to come, the European Union will probably face its greatest test to date. Both internal and external conflicts are affecting the very substance of the self-image of European integration. This precarious situation is all the more complex because the endogenous and exogenous challenges cannot be considered in isolation from each other, let alone solved. They are mutually dependent and must therefore be addressed as a package. The migration wave of 2015 had already shown that the previous homogeneity of

202 https://data.consilium.europa.eu/doc/document/ST-10033-2022-ADD-1-REV-1/en/pdf.

the Union has been shaken by enlargement: A structure that had grown over some fifty years was met by the ideas of new members; fifteen states of the ancien régime clashed with just as many states of the two most recent waves of enlargement, which had themselves only shaken off one regime and were not prepared to take orders, as it were, from a new one; a relatively rich Europe was met by a relatively poorer Europe, which expected solidarity with itself but was not fully willing to share the modest prosperity it had achieved in the meantime.

After the Soviet Union imploded, the European Union absorbed the resulting Intermediate Europe[203] in two enlargement steps, bringing its borders right up to Russia. Currently, Intermediate Europe still consists of Belarus, Ukraine, Moldova and Georgia. The dispute over these states and territories has long been underway. In the face of the Russian challenge, Ukraine, Moldova, and Georgia have decided to turn westwards. In February 2022, Russia chose the military option to re-establish her defunct hegemony.[204] Europe will have to give an answer as to what offer it is willing or able to make to these states. It is in the nature of Intermediate Europe, which includes not only the three states mentioned above but also those of the Western Balkans, that it will disappear. If the Union does not act promptly and decisively, it will not be able to hold on to these states in the long term and could lose them to the Russian hegemonic sphere.

The Union will have an urgent need to find an answer as to how to implement the values it preaches, both internally and externally, or whether it will have to abandon them in the medium to long term.

Every generation has the right and also the duty to reinterpret and reshape the idea of European integration, otherwise the European project, which was conceived as a process from the very beginning, will ossify. If it can no longer react flexibly enough to internal developments, the rigid shell will burst, and the European project will fail.

It is not the Treaties that hold Europe together, not its legal acts, not its common currency. It is the belief in an idea. An idea to which all citizens of the European Union owe the fact that they have been able to live on a war-free continent since 1945. It is the faith in this very idea, and thus in itself, that the Union must rediscover and live. The idea of the Founding Fathers was to solve cross-border challenges in a joint effort and to expand this approach of a

203 On the concept and definition of Intermediate Europe, cf. Fischer (2016), esp. p. 65.

204 On the background and the geopolitical and international legal classification of the Russian-Ukrainian war cf. Fischer (2022).

common solution by growing together. The Founding Fathers, guided by the experience of two world wars, had recognised that Europe can only exist together in the long term and that the whole (= Union) is more than the sum of its parts (= Member States).

II. The Evolution of EU Policies

It is no part of my case
that I am always right.

Winston Churchill

Today's EU primary law, i.e. the Treaty on European Union and the Treaty on the Functioning of the European Union, is the result of numerous covering treaties, the Lisbon Treaty being the most recent in this series, which together with the Maastricht Treaty and the Lisbon Treaty[205] has had the most significant impact on primary law.

In the following synoptic presentation of the evolution of EU primary law, the changes since the ECSC Treaty and the Treaties of Rome are presented as comprehensively as possible from a political, historical, and, last but not least, legal point of view. It is only through this synoptic and interdisciplinary presentation that it becomes clear that EU primary law was designed from the outset as a process that will presumably not come to an end with the Treaty of Lisbon.[206]

The individual covering Treaties are summarised in a separate annex following the synoptic overall presentation.

II.0. Preamble

Like most international treaties, both the TEU and the TEC as well as the TFEU are each introduced by a preamble. Both the TEU preamble and the TEC/TFEU preamble are of general political and legal significance. The

205 In addition to the specific changes, however, the ToL provides for a large number of horizontal changes, such as the replacement of the word Community by Union, since the former has ceased to exist under international law and has been replaced by the Union as the successor organisation. In the synoptic presentation, no explicit reference is made to these horizontal changes - and to the renumbering - but only to mandate-related editorial adaptations.

206 The comments on the development of the individual provisions are mainly based on: Fischer: Commentary on (i) the Treaty of Nice, (ii) the Convention, (iii) the Constitutional Treaty and (iv) the Treaty of Lisbon, and have been updated to reflect the latest research and literature.

general political significance derives from the fact that both preambles reflect the political intention of the founding Member States and subsequently of new Member States. While the preamble of the TEU aims at the European integration process in general, emphasises the commitment to certain values in particular, and refers emphatically to the development of the continent, the preamble of the TEC/TFEU strikes a balance between the need for democratic constitution and integration based on the Internal Market. The political intention of the preamble to the TEC was, on the one hand, to bring the peoples of Europe closer together and, on the other, to invite the candidate countries to join.

From a legal point of view, the TEU preamble in the version of the Treaty of Nice had rather less to offer, whereas the TEC preamble contained perfectly concrete approaches. The aforementioned intention to invite states that want to join the EU and the associated integration process - i.e. to submit an application for accession - has not only a political but also a legal dimension, since a legal claim could be derived from it. Not least because of the expiry of the ECSC Treaty, its preamble has more or less disappeared into oblivion. This preamble, which one could almost call the mother of all EU/EC preambles - also alluding to the now almost old-fashioned wording - probably expressed the founding idea most strongly. The founding states were concerned with the noble goal of world peace, with an organised and lively Europe, with overcoming the atrocities of war, and most probably also the resentments that had led to them. Compared to these noble goals, which correspond to the original idea of the Schuman Plan, the demanded effort to contribute to the raising of the standard of living and the progress of the works of peace by expanding their [European] basic productions sounds downright realpolitik. The preamble of the EAEC Treaty is also sometimes regarded as historically significant, although its main concern, the peaceful use of nuclear energy and - beyond that - the intention to create the conditions for the development of an efficient nuclear industry, is more topical than ever.

The ToL made little change to the basic structure and basic orientation of the two preambles and thus relied more on continuity than innovation.

II.0.1. Preamble to the TEU

Reference: Preamble to the TEU

Subject: Fundamental statements on the rationale and task of the Union

The preamble to the TEU was fundamentally amended for the first time by the ToA. Particularly, a confirmation of the importance of fundamental social rights and a firm commitment to sustainable development were added. The original recitals 9 and 10 were retained, but their content was adapted to the changed circumstances. The original recital 9 had made it clear that the Common Defence Policy is part of the Common Foreign and Security Policy, stating that this policy area is intended to strengthen Europe's identity and independence in order to promote peace, security, and progress in Europe and throughout the world. In the original recital 10, the - rather vague - reference to provisions on Justice and Home Affairs was replaced by a clear commitment to promote the establishment of an area of freedom, security, and justice.

The ToN left the preamble to the TEU unchanged.

The ToL takes up the preamble, leaves it essentially unchanged, but adds a new second recital, along the lines of the TEU, dealing with human rights, democracy, and the rule of law, stating that these values are deeply rooted in Europe's cultural, religious, and humanist heritage. This compromise formula made it possible to avoid the same controversial debate as in the Convention and the IGC 2004 on the introduction of a concept of God or the inclusion of a reference to the Christian-Jewish heritage..

Interestingly, during the Convention Turkey (sic!) of all countries was reluctant to accept such a reference, as it would allegedly negate the achievements of Islam for European history and thus discriminate against it.

Turkey did not find much support but in the end one of the Big Four – Germany – sided with Turkey. Added to this was France's objection of secularism, which in turn led to the inclusion of humanism in the text. The other amendments ended in both deleting the term Community and replacing it with the term Union, and the extension of the applicability of the TEU preamble to both Treaties, i.e. also to the TFEU.

However, even the ToL has not changed the basically merely declaratory character of the preamble.

II.0.2. Preamble to the TFEU

Reference: Preamble to the TFEU

Subject: Fundamental statements on the rationale and task of the Union

The TEC preamble, which of course evolved from the preamble to the EEC Treaty, has been almost entirely spared changes over the years. Neither the Merger Treaty, nor SEA, or the ToM intervened in the text. Only the ToA brought the first - and only - adaptation.

The ToA introduced as final recital the determination to work towards the highest possible level of knowledge of the European population through comprehensive access to education and through continuous training. This recital reflects the Community's additional focus on building an educational society.

Apart from editorial adjustments (Community to Union), the ToL introduced no changes.

II.1. Principles and Objectives

II.1.1. Principles and Objectives of the European Union

Reference: Title I Articles 1 to 8 TEU

Subject: Outlining the principles and objectives of the European Union

The original principles and objectives of the Union have been maintained but regularly adapted over the years reflecting political changes. The first treaty to amend the EU Treaty, the Treaty of Amsterdam, added to the second sentence of Article 1 TEU the requirement for transparency in decision-making at European level. Another addition was the obligation of the Council and the Commission not only to ensure the coherence of external action but also to cooperate to this end. An important justification for this addition was by no means a refusal to cooperate by the Council and the Commission, but that this cooperation must be guaranteed across the pillar structure of the Treaty. This addition was also intended to prevent the risk of fragmentation of the Union and the Community as only the first pillar was based on the community method whereas the second and third pillar remained intergovernmental by nature. The boldness to take a permanent decision and, for example, to give the Union legal personality, failed at the IGC 1996, not least because of the United Kingdom's veto. The IGC 1996 retroactively included the Court of Auditors in the list of institutions in Article 5 TEU, which was a reaction to the Court's upgrading by the ToM and the ToA.

The ToL, however, fundamentally reshaped the complex of principles and objectives by adding a Title II to the previous provisions (which were taken over with some changes as Title I), that explicitly deals with the provisions on democratic principles.

The IGC 2007 repealed former Articles 3, 4, and 5, as well as Articles 8 (provisions amending the Treaty establishing the European Economic Community with a view to establishing the European Community), 9 (provisions amending the Treaty establishing the European Coal and Steel Community), and 10 (provisions amending the Treaty establishing the European Atomic Energy Community). Article 3 TEU (AA/ToN) was essentially replaced by Article 7 TFEU and Articles 13(1) and 21(3) second subparagraph TEU (AA/ToL); Article 4 TEU (AA/ToN) was replaced by Article 15 TEU (AA/ToL); Article 5 TEU (AA/ToN) was replaced by Article 13(2) TEU (AA/ToL). Former Article 8 TEU was consequently repealed, as the TEC expired with the entry into force of the TFEU. The repeal of Article 9 TEU (AA/ToN) is also consistent, as the ECSC Treaty expired on 23 July 2002. The last of the listed repeals concerns the former Article 10 TEU, whose amendments were incorporated into the EAEC Treaty.

New provisions have been inserted in place of the repealed articles.

Title I - Common Provisions

The original Article 1 TEU was preserved in its main features throughout all IGCs and merely adapted editorially by the IGC 2007.

In contrast, the ToL introduced a completely new Article 2, which now underpins the EU with its own catalogue of values. This catalogue of values is reminiscent of the previous Article 6 and its references but is far more elaborate and expands the catalogue to include pluralism, non-discrimination, tolerance, justice, solidarity, and equality between men and women. The fathers of the ToL succeeded in creating a legal toolkit in conjunction with the catalogue of values in Article 2 TEU. Such catalogues of values or principles are not binding in general and have at best a declaratory character. However, in connection with the question of the accession of new Member States, as now regulated in Article 49 TEU, this catalogue of values is at least indirectly binding, since new Member States must respect and promote these values in order to be admitted. In addition to this upgrading in connection with the eligibility of new Member States for accession, the catalogue of values has a further indirect binding effect, since the values and their observance play a constitutive role for the initiation of sanction procedures under Article 7 TEU.

The original catalogue of objectives - now contained in Article 3 TEU (AA/ToL) - in the wording of the ToM was not profoundly changed by the ToA; the intended promotion of economic and social progress was supplemented by the objective of a high level of employment, whereby the respective achievement of objectives is to be fulfilled under the premise of sustainable and balanced development.[207] The assertion of identity at international level was extended to include the instrument of gradually defining a common defence policy. A radical change was made to the penultimate indent of Article 2 (AA/ToM). In the ToM, this article referred to the development of close cooperation in the areas of Justice and Home Affairs as an objective and thus corresponded to the intergovernmental pillar introduced by the ToM. However, the ToA became most explicit here: the amended objective was now to maintain and develop the Union as an Area of Freedom, Security and Justice, in which the free movement of persons is ensured in conjunction with appropriate measures with respect to external border controls, asylum, immigration, and the prevention and combating of crime.

The IGC 1996 thus reacted to the civil rights movement in the Union, which in the early 1990s - not least due to the Eurosceptic fear of a European superstate - was gaining increasing momentum. The Heads of State and Government intended with this rewording of the relevant indent in Article 2 TEU on the one hand to underline the will to cooperate more closely at European level in the area of justice and home affairs, and on the other hand, to send a signal that this would not restrict the individual rights of European citizens, but rather that the cooperation would serve to strengthen the safeguarding of citizens' rights. The IGC 2007 intervened massively in this article, which has been completely revised and consequently was embedded as Article 4 TEU. Following the catalogue of

207 Article 2 TEU.

values in the new Article 2, the IGC 2007 decided to draft a comprehensive catalogue of objectives as Article 3 TEU. This Article 3 catalogue of objectives consists of the former Article 2 TEU and the former Articles 2 and 3 TEC, supplemented by the new elements (i) area of freedom, security and justice, (ii) promotion of social justice and social protection, and (iii) preservation of the richness of cultural diversity. With the new Article 3 TEU, the IGC 2007 consistently implemented the principle of the single legal personality and the single legal system of the Union and, at the same time, of overcoming the previous separation of Union and Community.[208] The wording of paragraph 6 is not restrictive, but it does have a cautionary effect, referring to the principle of enumerative individual authorisation and the delimitation and interpretation of competences. Some Member States demanded this double reassurance so as to ensure that the Union could not gain new or novel competences through the back door.

The new Article 4 TEU is at any rate quite definitely a result of the Convention, the IGC 2004, and the subsequent debates on the competences of the Union, or rather on their limitation. The first paragraph is the programmatic part of this article and thus the leitmotif of the debate on competences. The enumerative individual authorisation had never been formulated so clearly in the Treaties, whereby the addition in paragraph 2 that national security would continue to be the sole responsibility of the individual Member States clearly underlines this strict rule. It is not surprising that the United Kingdom in particular - supported by France - regarded the question of national security as a kind of conditio sine qua non, not least against the background of her anti-terrorism legislation following 9/11. The wording of paragraph 1 thus excludes a competence of necessity in favour of the Union, therefore the principle of adhesion in favour of the Union - especially in connection with Article 352 TFEU - is to be interpreted in an absolutely narrow manner; questions of internal security are under no circumstances covered by it.

Article 5 TEU (AA/ToL) has been newly inserted and effectively replaces the former Article 5 TEC, which itself has been repealed in the course of this transfer. The Protocol on the Application of the Principles of Subsidiarity and Proportionality is to be interpreted in the context of Article 5 TEU

208 It is however surprising that despite the comprehensive catalogue of objectives, free competition and protection against distortions are no longer mentioned. France had prevailed with this demand, as a result of which this element of the Internal Market is no longer included in the corpus of the Treaties, but only in the Protocol on the Internal Market and Competition.

(AA/ToL), as it contains, as it were, the implementing provisions for this article, in particular paragraphs 3 and 4.

Article 6 TEU was extended by the various IGCs but fundamentally changed only by the ToL. While the original paragraph 1 referred exclusively to the Union's respect for the national identity of the Member States, since the ToA this paragraph has stated programmatically that the Union is founded on the principles of liberty, democracy, respect for human rights and fundamental freedoms, and the rule of law. At the same time, however, reference was made to the origin of the Union by emphasising that these principles are common to all Member States, i.e. they are conferred on the Union by the Member States themselves. Paragraph 3, which became paragraph 4 as a result of the amendments described above, remained part of Article 6 TEU. Spain was very careful not to change that wording, as she had insisted on its original inclusion in the TEU.[209] The first sentence of the original paragraph 1 of Article 6 TEU was left as a separate - new - paragraph 3 in Article 6. The principle of respect for the nationalities of the Member States by the Union, as postulated there, was thus given greater significance.[210] The IGC 1996 thereby reacted to the spectre of the Union as a European superstate suppressing the respective national identities, characteristics and histories, as conjured up by Eurosceptics.[211] With regard to Article 6, it should also be noted that, until Lisbon, it did not contain any reference to the EU Charter of Fundamental Rights, which was solemnly proclaimed on the eve of the conclusion of the Nice European Council in December 2000. This absolute negation of the Charter can be justified, among other things, by the fact that during the IGC 2000 the vast majority of the Member States - contrary to the explicit and persistently presented demand of the European Parliament - opposed the inclusion of this Charter in the Treaty. Even a reference to this Charter or its incorporation into primary law via a protocol solution was refused then.[212] In contrast, the ToL was negotiated in a radically changed political environment. The Charter and its reference were not even up for debate but were common accord from the outset. Another takeover from the failed IGC 2004 is

209 Spain was less successful in calling for the inclusion of a clause to ensure sufficient transfers to poorer Member States.

210 This is a reference to the origin of the Union and the identity of the Member States to be maintained, both in paragraph 1 and paragraph 3.

211 In particular from the United Kingdom and Denmark.

212 In this case, too, the United Kingdom and Denmark were most vehemently opposed to any inclusion in primary law.

the programmatic commitment that the Union would join the ECHR, a commitment that still seems to be a long way off. The entire debate on fundamental rights and the accompanying discussions both on the EU Charter of Fundamental Rights and the ECHR proceeded along expected fault lines in both the IGC 2004 and the IGC 2007, which, however, were not so fundamental as to lead to an open blockade.

The ToA incorporated a radical innovation at the end of Title I by introducing the legal basis for sanction proceedings against a Member State in Article 7 TEU (AA/ToA). The IGC 1996 had to come to terms with a phenomenon that had developed insidiously over the years and - perhaps against one's better judgement - had been virtually concealed. The Heads of State and Government had become aware of the steadily increasing danger of racist attacks in the Member States and the simultaneous strengthening of the extreme right. In addition, the Union had to face up to its own claim of aspiring to be a political community, which should accordingly be able to protect human rights and democracy. This realisation was promoted not only by a ruling of the German Federal Court in 1993,[213] but also by

213 The discussion in Germany regarding the relationship between the fundamental rights of the FRG and the corresponding development in the Union is essentially based on four decisions of the Federal Constitutional Court (= BGH). In the Solange-I-decision of 1974 (= As long as-I-Decision), the BGH - in reaction to the dictum of the ECJ that Community law takes precedence over national constitutional law (cf. ECJ Case 11/70, [1979] ECR 1125 ff.) - ruled that the protection of fundamental rights is also possible domestically against Community law and that a procedure for the review of EC regulations is permissible. This competence to review is given "as long as" there is no sufficient protection of fundamental rights in the Community. As early as 1979, the BGH questioned this conclusion when it hinted at a possible change in its case law in the "Vielleicht-Decision" (= Maybe-Decision), stating that it had to remain open whether such a review of European norms was still possible in view of the progressing political unification. In the 1984 Solange-II-Decision, the BGH revised its position, stating: "As long as the EC, in particular the case-law of the Court of Justice of the Communities (i.e. the ECJ), guarantees effective protection of fundamental rights against the sovereign power of the Communities in general, which is to be respected as essentially equal to the protection of fundamental rights offered by fundamental law as indispensable, especially since it generally guarantees the essential content of fundamental rights, the Federal Constitutional Court will no longer exercise its jurisdiction over the applicability of Community law, which is claimed as the basis for conduct of German courts or authorities in the sovereign territory of the Federal Republic of Germany." However, of crucial importance in this ongoing series of decisions was the 1993 Maastricht ruling of the BGH, the so-called Solange-III-Decision. In this decision the BGH had to deal with a constitutional complaint on the grounds of alleged infringement of national electoral law, and in this context reviewed the Act

considerations of the stability of possible future Member States. The basic intention behind Article 7 TEU (AA/ToA) was to transpose Article 39 of the UN Charter into the TEU so as to be able to respond to allegations of serious and persistent violations of the principles of liberty, democracy, respect for human rights and fundamental freedoms, and the rule of law by a Member State at Union level. The suspension of the Member State in question from the decision-making procedure was to serve as an adequate reaction. But already in the first - supposed - case, Article 7 TEU (AA/ToA) came to nothing. After the Portuguese Presidency had agreed with the other Heads of State and Government of the Member States in February 2000 to impose sanctions against Austria, which were motivated by the participation of the Freedom Party of Austria (FPÖ) in the Austrian Federal Government, Article 7 TEU could actually have been activated. However, the Presidency had been aware that it would not be able to achieve unanimity in the Council with regard to the allegation of serious and persistent violations of the above-mentioned principles.[214] The sanctions subsequently decided by the Heads of State and Government accordingly only concerned bilateral relations with Austria, whose EU membership, including all rights and obligations, was to remain unaffected.[215] At the time of the Biarritz European Council on 13 and 14 October 2000 - i.e. in the decisive phase of the IGC 2000 - the Heads of State and Government had already agreed to revise Article 7 TEU. The IGC 2000 revision of Article 7 TEU introduces an early warning procedure. Within the framework of the IGC 2000, Austria campaigned as vehemently as successfully for the inclusion of this early warning procedure in the Treaty, which since the IGC 2000 complies with the general principles of the rule of law.[216] Until then, the Council, in its

---

on Approving the Union Treaty and the Treaties as a whole. The BGH rejected the constitutional complaint and declared the Act on Approving the Union Treaty - and thus the Treaties - to be lawful, as long as the national elected legislature still had sufficient control over the Act on Approving the Union Treaty; moreover, the BGH now presented its relationship with the ECJ as a relationship of cooperation.

214 The wording of Article 7 TEU allows the well-founded but nevertheless controversial conclusion that the Member State concerned can vote on this decision.

215 Accordingly, the decision of the Heads of State and Government was taken neither in their formation as European Council nor as Council of Ministers, but outside the framework of the European Union/European Community. The Heads of State and Government who decided on the sanctions were called the Group of Fourteen.

216 Since the Treaty had not provided for an early warning system so far, the sanctions against Austria had been triggered by the Group of Fourteen outside the Treaty and - at least officially - had been of a strictly bilateral nature. Combating these sanctions

composition of Heads of State and Government, could only unanimously determine the existence of a serious and persistent breach of the said principles by a Member State. This provision of Article 7(1) TEU was preceded by a new paragraph 1 introduced by the ToN. This particular paragraph 1 allows the procedure to be initiated at an earlier stage, as the Council can now determine that there is a clear risk of a serious breach of the principles in question by a Member State. Under the new procedure, the Council can now determine on the basis of a risk analysis, which means that the procedure provided for in the Treaty will not only be applied in cases where there is already a serious and persistent breach of the principles but may be launched even before. This early warning procedure is triggered by a reasoned proposal from one third of the Member States, the European Parliament, or the Commission. The determining criterion is that the respective proposal must be accompanied by a statement of reasons. Under the previous procedure, such a statement of reasons was not required. The Council must take the decision by a special majority of four fifths of its members. The Member State concerned has the right to participate in the vote, but cannot block it, as unanimity is not required. Different positions were taken into account at the Nice European Council: unanimity of the Council (including the Member State concerned), unanimity of the Council (without the Member State concerned), majority (with different thresholds) of the Council (including the Member State concerned). The IGC finally agreed on the third option and the above-mentioned threshold. The aim of the early warning system is to avoid a possible escalation by making recommendations to the Member State concerned. However, the procedure cannot continue ad infinitum, as the Council is obliged to regularly check whether the situation that originally triggered the procedure still persists. Article 46 TEU (AA/ToN) must be read in close connection with Article 7(1) TEU. A new letter (e) has been added to Article 46 TEU, which provides that if the Member State concerned wishes a review of the procedural provisions of Article 7 TEU, the Court of Justice shall, at the request of the Member State concerned, give a ruling within one month of the Council's finding under Article 7 TEU. In other words, the procedural review by the Court of Justice applies not only to the newly

within the framework of the Treaty would therefore not have been very promising. Moreover, the state concerned had not been heard. Since these sanctions lacked at least a legal basis within the EU framework, Austria could only have taken action against them according to the general provisions of international law.

introduced early warning procedure, but to the whole of Article 7 TEU. The essential elements of the revision of Article 7 thus include (i) the right of the Member State concerned to be heard, (ii) the obligation to state reasons for the proposal to initiate the procedure, (iii) the consent of the European Parliament to the Council decision, (iv) the legal procedural review by the Court of Justice and (v) the obligation of regular review by the Council. The ToL only changed the sanctions procedure insofar as the mandate of independent persons to submit a report on the situation in the Member State concerned was deleted. Even though it was only optional to request a report until the IGC 2007, it was obviously the will of the Member States to dispense with such reports, otherwise this provision would have been left in the Treaty. The experience from the Austrian case had apparently led to the conclusion that the perceived humiliation of a sovereign state through the expert opinion of a so-called Panel of Eminent Persons is rather detrimental to the overall procedure.

The IGC 2007 inserted a new Article 8 TEU, which provides the legal basis for the Neighbourhood Policy. Already in 2003, the Commission had published a "Communication on Wider Europe - Neighbourhood: A New Framework for Relations with our Eastern and Southern Neighbours",[217] which was followed by a "European Neighbourhood Policy Strategy Paper" in 2004.[218] The political imperative was undeniable, even in the absence of a concrete legal basis. To fill this gap, the IGC 2004 had already intended to anchor the neighbourhood policy in Article I-57 TCEU, and the IGC 2007 adopted this proposal.

Title II – Provisions on Democratic Principles

The ToL added a separate title on democratic principles to the introductory part of the TEU. The provisions are not entirely new, but the prominent placement is an indication of the political symbolic value of this new provision.. The IGC 2007 also wanted to set an example and defend itself against the claim of a democratic deficit.

217 European Commission, COM(2003)104 of 11 March 2003, https://eur-lex.europa.eu/legal-content/EN/TXT/PDF/?uri=CELEX:52003DC0104&qid=1674656999259&from=EN.

218 European Commission, COM(2004)373 of 12 May 2004, https://eur-lex.europa.eu/legal-content/EN/TXT/PDF/?uri=CELEX:52004DC0373&qid=1674657161382&from=EN.

The new Title II TEU replaces the former Title II, which dealt with amendments to the EEC Treaty in view of the establishment of the EC, with the mandatory provisions being incorporated into the TFEU. Title II and Article 8 TEU not only received a new heading but were replaced by Articles 9 to 12 TEU (AA/ToL).

Article 9 TEU is composed of Article I-45 TCEU (first sentence) and Article 17(1) second and third sentence TEC. Systematically, the two provisions clearly fit into one article, as the first sentence deals with the principle of equal treatment of all citizens of the Union, defined as such below. However, this definition creates a legal basis exclusively for Union citizens, which - at least at first glance - does not include citizens of third countries.

Article 10 TEU took over the proposal of the IGC 2004 on Article I-46 TCEU unchanged and thus essentially replaces Article 191 (1) TEC. Ultimately, however, this new primary law provision has a predominantly political function, since it does not make any substantive changes to the previous system. However, this provision is the answer to the question of whether the Union and its institutions are democratically legitimised. Above all, the second subparagraph of paragraph 2 clarifies that the European Council and the Council are also democratically legitimised, albeit it is an indirect clarification.

Article 11 TEU regulates the European Citizens' Initiative. Although this new element of EU law introduces participatory democracy into primary law, it is not a radical innovation since the approach of the institutions called for in paragraphs 1 to 3 has already been practised. In any case, what is new is the concept of a citizens' initiative, which, if not abolishing the Commission's previous monopoly on legal proposals, at least places restrictions on it. The text is relatively general (e.g. a considerable number of Member States) and entrusts Article 24(1) TFEU with the detailed procedural provisions and conditions. The entire provision is very vaguely worded and allows the institutions a great deal of flexibility in the implementation of paragraphs 1 to 3, whereas paragraph 4 is specified in the TFEU and has been implemented by Regulation (EU) No 211/2011 of the European Parliament and of the Council of 16 February 2011 on the Citizens' Initiative (OJ L 65 of 11 March 2011, p. 1). This provision is also to be seen as a political response to the criticism of the Union's lack of democratic legitimacy. It is worth noting that the Union is going further than some Member States.

Article 12 TEU is an addition that can be attributed exclusively to the IGC 2007 and did not find any corresponding provision in primary law de lege lata. Already during the Austrian EU Presidency in the first half of 2006, on the occasion of the subsidiarity conference in St. Pölten, an early involvement of the national parliaments was urged and agreed upon as an informal procedure. However, this new provision goes far beyond this agreement and introduces the following new elements into primary law:

- Catalogue of rights in favour of national parliaments (general information by the institutions, submission of draft EU legislative acts, involvement in certain activities within the framework of the area of freedom, security and justice, information on applications for EU membership)
- Catalogue of duties for national parliaments (ensuring that the principle of subsidiarity is applied in accordance with the procedure, participation in the procedures for amending the Treaties, participation in interparliamentary cooperation)
- Protocol on the role of national parliaments supplementing the provisions of this article

In the course of the IGC 2007, however, to the surprise of all conferees, this innovation was not met with only positive reception. The House of Commons put up massive resistance to this article, as it saw its parliamentary freedom restricted. The House of Commons was particularly offended by the fact that the word "shall" was used in the English language version and not the term "may". The IGC 2007 met these concerns - compulsorily - almost in full and found a wording that allows the justified conclusion that the duties of national parliaments have an optional character (keyword: shall/may) and are by no means justiciable. Rather, they are to be understood as an invitation to the national parliaments to actively participate. Whether national parliaments can successfully bring an action against an institution before the ECJ must also be questioned in the light of these considerations.

II.1.2. Principles, Categories and Areas of Union Competence[219]

Reference: Part 1 Article 1, Part 1 Title I Articles 2 to 6 and Part 1 Title II Articles 7 to 17 TFEU

Subject: Presentation of the principles, objectives, categories, and areas of competence of the European Union

The IGC 2007 made massive modifications to this introductory part of the former TEC, which was transformed and reshaped by the ToL into the Treaty on the Functioning of the Union (TFEU). Accordingly, the following chapter is divided into the development up to the Treaty of Nice and the transformation by the Treaty of Lisbon.

I. Development up to the Treaty of Nice

The principles and objectives section was divided into (a) tasks and activities, (b) limits of competence, and (c) methods.

a) Tasks and Activities

The original Article 1 TEC, which addressed the establishment of the European Economic Community, was adapted by the ToM in that this community was now referred to as the European Community. Article 1 TEC thus remained unchanged as the raison d'être of the Treaty. It therefore also remained unchanged throughout the subsequent IGCs. The catalogue of tasks of the Community was only marginally adapted by the ToM, mainly linguistically, but it was given a new orientation by the ToA, in that (i) the development of economic life also had to be sustainable, (ii) equality between men and women was demanded, (iii) growth lost the attribute environmentally compatible, whereas at the same time (iv) a high level of environmental protection and improvement of the quality of the environment was explicitly demanded.

Although the list in Article 2 TEC is not worded that way, it can hardly be described as taxative, especially since it refers to Articles 3 and 4 TEC, which first list the activities of the Community. The catalogue of tasks has thus not only been extended prima facie but is also more specific than

219 For systematic reasons, enhanced cooperation is dealt with under Chapter II.4.

in the original 1957 version. The ToN has not touched this catalogue of tasks. In its case law, the European Court of Justice has increasingly referred to the catalogue of tasks in Article 2 TEC when interpreting the limits of Community competence, the finality of which it seems to find in Article 2 TEC rather than in the - technical - list of Articles 3 or 4 TEC.

The list of Community activities contained in Article 3(1) TEC had already been significantly modified by the ToM. The introduction of a Common Customs Tariff was deleted from the original letter a - thus reacting to meanwhile developments. The original letter c was not only given a new wording, but was divided into two letters: Whereas Article 3 letter c as amended by the EEC Treaty still spoke of the removal of obstacles to the free movement of persons, services, and capital between the Member States, Article 3 (1) letter c as amended by the ToM deals with an Internal Market characterised by the removal of obstacles to the free movement of goods, persons, services, and capital between the Member States and is supplemented by letter d, which speaks of measures concerning the entry and movement of persons in the Internal Market in accordance with Article 100c TEC. The ToM has extended the activities of the Community in the agricultural sector by including a Common Fisheries Policy. The letters i to q, as well as letters s and t as amended by the ToM represent an extension of the Community's field of activity to the areas of social policy, cohesion, environmental policy, research and technological development, trans-European networks, education and culture, development cooperation, consumer protection, energy, disaster protection, and tourism. This extension of the list was the inevitable consequence of the IGC's deliberations, which, in the course of the establishment of the European Union, had also intended to enlarge the Community's fields of activity. The IGC 1996 added the promotion of the coordination of the employment policies of the Member States to the list of activities with the intention to strengthen their effectiveness through the development of a coordinated employment strategy and thus - in terms of primary law - already anticipated the Lisbon process, which was initiated in 2000, and so prepared its foundation. The ToA also added a second paragraph to Article 3 TEC, which stipulates that the Community shall aim to eliminate inequalities and promote equality between men and women in all the activities referred to in Article 3. This addition is still interpreted as ambiguous insofar as it can be seen on the one hand as a cross-sectional activity, but on the other hand also as an extension of the Community's competences. With this addition, the IGC 1996 at any rate joined the general mainstream, which in the 1990s intensified the political debate on gender equality.

Maastricht brought a significant addition to the Community's field of activity by inserting Article 4 TEC,[220] which dealt with economic and monetary policy. The IGC had two options to choose from: (a) further addition to the list of activities under Article 3(1) TEC or (b) creation of a stand-alone article. The IGC chose option (b) for several reasons: a further addition to the list of activities under Article 3(1) TEC would have led to an overlong list and, moreover, it was intended to give the Monetary Union the place it deserved because of its special position and importance.

b) Limits of Competence

The debate on the limits of Community competence, which took place not least during the Convention and the IGC 2004, had also been the subject of the debates in the Maastricht IGC that led to the Union Treaty. The consequence was the introduction of Article 5 TEC,[221] which deals with enumerative conferral,[222] subsidiarity[223] and proportionality.[224] This article is probably the most politically charged that the ToM has incorporated into the structure of the TEC. The United Kingdom and Denmark relied precisely on this article, referred to in general terms as the subsidiarity article, when it came to ratifying the Union Treaty. Both used it as an argument that national interests could not be overridden by the Community and that the Member States should therefore still be regarded as the Masters of the Treaty, even though the Community as such was undeniably supranational. Subsidiarity is certainly not an invention of the Union or the European Community, but has its roots in Catholic Christian thinking, as expressed

220 i.e. Article 3a TEC AA/ToM.
221 i.e. Article 3b TEC AA/ToM.
222 Subparagraph 1.
223 Subparagraph 2.
224 Subparagraph 3.

in particular in the encyclical Quadrigesimo Anno of 1931,[225] whereby some Protestant Christian roots are also existent.[226]

In the context of European integration, the debate on subsidiarity has been increasingly intensified since the 1980s, when Euroscepticism became more widespread in the Member States. This Euroscepticism - which towards the end of the 1990s gradually began to raise the question of the territorial finality of the European Union - was directed above all against the subliminal fear in some Member States that the Union would become increasingly centralised and ultimately lead to a European superstate.[227] In order to overcome such scepticism, both the Union Treaty and the Community Treaty were designed to be subsidiarity-oriented. At the Maastricht intergovernmental conference, the Heads of State and Government found themselves in the precarious position of seeking, on the one hand, to establish a Union and to extend the competences of the Community, and, on the other hand, to have to allay fears in the Member States and also in the European Parliament. With regard to the enumerative conferral - and the concerns of the Parliament - an adequate solution could be found

---

225 The principle of subsidiarity was explicitly stated in the encyclical Quadrigesimo Anno - On Reconstruction of the Social Order of H.H. Pope Pius XI from 1931 (https://www.vatican.va/content/pius-xi/en/encyclicals/documents/hf_p-xi_enc_19310515_quadragesimo-anno.html). Accordingly, the core sentence of this socio-philosophical principle is that all social activity is subsidiary in its nature and concept, i.e. the lower level is by no means to be deprived of what it can achieve and fulfil for the benefit of the higher level. This can be deduced from the text of the encyclical: "[...] all social activity [...] should support the members of the social body, but must never break them up or absorb them". Moreover, it can be concluded from the encyclical that subsidiarity in the (Catholic) Christian perspective is based on the bottom-up principle, but not on the top-down principle. The former is to be interpreted to the effect that the higher level should only take action when the lower level is either fundamentally no longer able to provide the service or the overall interests can be better safeguarded by the higher level. The second, however, is based on the assumption that all competences are assigned to the highest level and that the subordinate levels only assume responsibility when they are able to perform the tasks better.

226 Based on Part III paragraph 8 of the conclusions of the Emden Synod of 1571 (cf. https://www.emder-synode-1571.de/Teil_3_der_Beschluesse_der_Emder_Synode_von_1571_Synodalordnung-26614-528-0-75.html), Johannes Althusius developed a rudimentary approach to subsidiarity in 1603 in his major work Politica Methodice Digesta.

227 Such scepticism was not only expressed by the "usual suspects", the United Kingdom and Denmark, but also by - in principle - Union-friendly Member States, there however mainly at the level of the regions (= Land), i.e. in federally organised Member States such as Germany and Austria.

relatively easily when the first paragraph of the subsidiarity article took up a draft wording of the European Parliament.[228] This phrasing was neither new in terms of wording nor in terms of content; the IGC simply took up a principle that underlies Western democratic constitutions anyway.

With regard to the actual subsidiarity, the authors of the intergovernmental conference[229] found a solution which - superficially - should put most critics at rest. Subsidiarity is already restricted in the first sentence, which stipulates that this principle should only be applied where the community does not have exclusive competence. This wording, which prima facie seems unambiguous, however leaves open an obviously intended very broad scope, since the Community competences are not necessarily clearly defined in every case, and accordingly can also be interpreted more broadly if necessary. Even on closer examination, the Heads of State and Government did not place too narrow limits on the Community's action when they did not lay down clear rules for subsidiarity in primary law but referred to an - unspecified - principle. The United Kingdom[230] used this range of interpretation to establish that subsidiarity was not a general constitutional principle as interpreted by the federal Member States Austria, Germany and Belgium.[231] The wording that the Community would only act if the measures in question could not be sufficiently achieved by the Member States was inserted by the IGC in order to take account of Germany's concerns in particular. This last-minute insertion did not primarily serve to explain the principle as such but was intended to express explicitly that legislative initiatives at Member State level should also be permissible in principle in the future.

The debates during the IGC 1996 and the IGC 2000 took up these ambiguities, but the Heads of State and Government were unable to agree on a new wording - despite massive interventions, especially by the Belgian government, some initiatives by the Austrian government, and several at-

228 i.c. Text proposed by the European Parliament in 1984 for a Treaty on a European Union, Article 4.

229 To this day, it is claimed - without any genuine proof - that the specific wording originates from Douglas Hurd.

230 Especially under the Tory government of PM Major.

231 The Tory government saw the introduction of the principle of subsidiarity as an opportunity to re-transfer competences into the - exclusive - realm of the United Kingdom.

tempts by some German Länder.[232] Nevertheless, in order to respond to the concerns raised, the Heads of State and Government took up the issue of subsidiarity in the Declaration on the Future of the Union.[233] One of the issues to be resolved in the post-Nice process was how to establish and subsequently maintain a more precise delimitation of competences between the Union and its Member States. The proportionality of Community measures, as demanded in Article 5 paragraph 3 TEC, originates in German law and is to be classified as a liberal constitutional principle. However, like the other two principles of Article 5 TEC, it is not sufficiently concrete to be unambiguously applicable. In retrospect, subsidiarity has served various purposes: it was intended to help the second Danish referendum on the Maastricht Treaty to succeed; at the Birmingham European Council in 1992 it was equated with closeness to the citizens in order to counter the argument of an unapproachable Eurocracy; the insertion of the Subsidiarity Protocol by the ToA, in turn, primarily served the domestic political debate in the federal Member States of Austria, Belgium, and Germany; in later developments, subsidiarity was also used to find a basis for more comprehensible legal acts.

In response to the growing influence of the global environmental movement in the 1990s and the Community's initiatives, especially in the field of sustainability, the ToA inserted the principle of sustainability into the TEC as Article 6. Although the IGC 1996 saw itself confronted with this requirement and had to react accordingly, the more industry-friendly Member States were able to partially assert themselves and thus prevent a more radical language. In the end, the conference agreed that the requirements of environmental protection shall be integrated, particularly in order to promote sustainable development. Although environmental protection was thus elevated to a cross-sectional issue, the restrictions on the application of this consideration requirement have nevertheless remained evident.

232 By their very nature, these initiatives could only be articulated through the German federal government, as IGCs are held at Member State level and not at regional level.

233 Declaration Nr. 23 to the ToN.

c) Methods

The third part of the section on principles and objectives describes the methods by which the tasks and activities of the Community are implemented. Article 7 TEC lists the institutions which carry out the tasks assigned to the Community. Article 11 of the 1970 Treaty amending certain Financial Provisions[234] introduced the exercise of audit by the Court of Auditors, which was elevated to institutional level by the ToM.[235] The ToM had established the Committee of the Regions (= CoR), and accordingly this committee was included as a second advisory committee in Article 4(2) TEC. Neither the ToA nor the ToN amended the list of institutions and advisory committees, although the CoR had vehemently - but in vain from the outset - demanded institutional status.[236] The Union Treaty required the introduction of Articles 8 (European System of Central Banks) and 9 TEC (European Investment Bank). Both the System of Central Banks and the Investment Bank had been established to implement the European Monetary Union. The ToA and the ToN did not alter these provisions. Article 10 TEC, which contains the Member States' duty of loyalty to the Community, has remained unchanged since the TEEC. However, over the years, various opt-outs granted to individual Member States had called into question the general validity of Article 10 TEC.[237] The prohibition of discrimination (Article 12 TEC) was already contained in the original TEEC as Article 7. The first change to this provision was Article 6(2) SEA, which stipulated that the Council could no longer adopt anti-discriminatory measures after simply consulting Parliament, but only in cooperation with Parliament and after consulting the European Economic and Social Committee (= EESC). The ToM had no effect on the prohibition of discrimination. The ToA upgraded the role of the Parliament, as the Council now had to decide on such measures in codecision with the Parliament. No further amendment was made by the ToN, and the CoR's efforts to be granted a right of consultation in this case were not followed.

---

234 https://eur-lex.europa.eu/legal-content/EN/TXT/?uri=OJ:L:1971:002:TOC.

235 As a result, paragraph 3 could be deleted.

236 Nevertheless, the CoR also demanded that status in the course of the Convention and the IGC 2004, but again had to come to terms with the reality that no Member State or the European Parliament supported this demand. Over the years, the CoR's constant and fruitless advances became a kind of never-ending story without any realistic chance of a happy ending.

237 Not least the opt-outs for Denmark, Sweden, and the United Kingdom concerning the introduction of the euro as a common currency.

The general prohibition of discrimination was extended concerning questions of nationality by the ToA, which inserted Article 13 TEC dealing with anti-discriminatory measures against "other forms" of discrimination. Such measures were adopted as amended by the ToA by unanimous decision of the Council after consultation of the Parliament. The ToN extended the scope of application of this specific anti-discrimination article by inserting a new paragraph 2. However, the scope of application of this paragraph 2 is limited to incentive measures by the Community and may under no circumstances lead to harmonisation of legal or administrative provisions. This change was made in pursuit of the IGC 2000 objective of switching from unanimity voting to voting with qualified majority. Moreover, in the case of paragraph 2, the codecision procedure applies, which again met the demands of the European Parliament.

The last three articles of the first part of the TEC, Articles 14 to 16, deal with the Common Market. In the original version of the TEEC, this section comprised only one single article (Article 8 TEEC), which contained those regulations that were to be applied during the transitional period until the implementation of the Common Market. The SEA inserted Articles 8a to 8c of the TEEC,[238] which for the first time introduced the classic definition of the Internal Market into primary law. The ToM left these articles essentially untouched; due to the implementation of the Internal Market in the meantime, the original Article 8 TEEC, subsequently Article 7 TEC as amended by the ToM, was deleted without replacement. The three remaining Articles 8a to 8c TEEC AA/SEA, subsequently Articles 7a to 7c AA/ToM, were amended by the ToA to the extent that a third paragraph was added to what was then Article 14 TEC, stipulating that the Council, acting by qualified majority on a proposal from the Commission, shall determine the guidelines and conditions necessary to ensure balanced progress in all the sectors concerned. The IGC 1996 thus attempted to counter the critics of the Single Market, who feared that the Single Market could - stealthily - lead to an exclusively economic orientation of the Community. Article 8b TEEC as amended by the SEA, subsequently Article 7b TEC as amended by the ToM, was deleted by the ToA, as the deadlines and conditions contained therein had already been met. Article 8c TEEC as amended by the SEA, subsequently Article 7c TEC as amended by the ToM, respectively Article 15 TEC as amended by the ToA, remained in its

238 Article 8a TEEC was inserted pursuant to Article 13 SEA, Article 8b pursuant to Article 14 SEA, Article 8c pursuant to Article 15 SEA.

original version and was also endorsed unchanged by the ToN. However, the IGC 1996 added a new Article 16 TEC, which followed in particular the French idea that some economic activities were not fully compatible with the concept of a single market. The IGC 1996 Reflection Group took up this French proposal while the conference followed the Reflection Group's suggestion but ultimately adopted a rather imprecise and restrictive text. Accordingly, Article 16 TEC only refers to services of general economic interest, but not to public services, although the European Court of Justice had interpreted such services of general economic interest as including telecommunications, postal services, transport, and energy supply. While this is expressed in Declaration No. 13 to the ToA, it was not specifically reflected in Article 16 TEC. The ToN did not take up this issue, although some Member States and above all the Commission wanted clarification. It was not until the Convention that this demand was taken up again, but it faced criticism from the German and Austrian Länder in particular, with the Austrian Federal Government joining in the rejectionist stance of the Austrian Länder - in contrast to the German Federal Government, which did not follow the respective Länder demands.

II. Transformation by the Treaty of Lisbon

As already outlined above, the European Community ceased to exist as a result of the Treaty of Lisbon and the European Union became uno actu the legal successor. Accordingly, the TEC had to be redesigned to take account of this fundamental change. The Treaty on the European Community (TEC) was renamed the Treaty on the Functioning of the European Union (TFEU) and was given a completely new structure. Some of the previous provisions were repealed, replaced, or simply rearranged.

The previous provisions of the first part of the TEC, which dealt with citizenship, were taken out and moved to the second part of the TFEU on citizenship of the Union; the same applies to the provisions concerning the Internal Market, which were moved to the third part of the TFEU. The IGC 2007 consistently pursued its goal of organising the provisions on related issues as compactly as possible in one place in primary law. The same thrust was behind the repeal of those provisions of the TEC that dealt with the tasks, principles, and activities of the - defunct - Community. These provisions were repealed and replaced by adapted provisions of the TEU as amended by the ToL. This becomes particularly evident in the list of institutions (Article 7 TEC), which have become Union institutions through the ToL and are therefore consistently regulated in the new TEU.

In summary, the new first part of the TFEU, which was given the programmatic heading "Principles", presents itself as follows:

Structure

The first part is made up of:

- Title I: Categories and Areas of Union Competence
  The insertion of this title has an almost exclusively political-programmatic intention. This title covers the vertical distribution of competences between the Member States and the Union founded by them and largely replaces the repealed Article 2 TEC. From the point of view of content, it is a summary (a) of the competences previously - explicitly or implicitly - contained in various parts of the TEU and the TEC, as well as (b) of the competences arising from the standing case law of the Court of Justice. This order of competences is taxative, whereby the sources of competence have not only been summarised and codified in primary law, but have also been substantially amended in some areas, be it materially or formally.
- Title II : Provisions having General Application

Amendments to the previous TEC articles

The following Articles have been repealed, replaced, or moved:

- *Repeals*
  - Article 1 ex-TEC
  - Article 2 ex-TEC, which is essentially replaced by Article 3 TEU (tasks and activities)
  - Article 3 paragraph 1 ex-TEC, which is essentially replaced by Articles 3 to 6 TFEU
  - Article 7 ex-TEC, which is essentially replaced by Article 13 TEU
  - Article 8 ex-TEC, which is essentially replaced by Article 13 TEU and Article 282(1) TFEU
  - Article 9 ex-TEC
  - Article 10 ex-TEC, which is essentially replaced by Article 4(3) TEU

- *Replacements*
  - Article 5 ex-TEC, which is replaced by Article 5 TEU
  - Article 11 and 11a ex-TEC, which are replaced by Articles 326 to 334 TFEU and by Article 20 TEU
- *Regroupings*
  - Article 12 ex-TEC becomes Article 18 TFEU (Citizenship of the Union)
  - Article 13 ex-TEC becomes Article 19 TFEU (Citizenship of the Union)
  - Article 14 ex-TEC becomes Article 26 TFEU (Internal Market)
  - Article 15 ex-TEC becomes Article 27 TFEU (Internal Market)

Article 1 TFEU is designed as an introductory article describing the subject matter of the Treaty in question. The IGC 2007 had to be creative in this respect, as it could not fall back on the work of the IGC 2004, which had envisaged a single treaty. The IGC 2007, however, managed this task very elegantly by resorting to the classic instrument of the covering treaty and replacing the repealed TEC with the TFEU by way of the ToL, whereby, however, only those provisions were changed or adapted where necessary. The former Article 1 TEC, which described the tasks of the Community, fell under the category of adaptation.

Article 2 TFEU contains the categories of competences, whereby the previous setting (exclusive Union competences; shared competences; supporting, coordinating and complementary competences) was maintained. However, the IGC 2007 - taking over the work of the IGC 2004 - added a new last sentence in paragraph 2, which regulates the devolution of shared competences to the Member States. In this particular case of devolution, however, a simple non-exercise by the Union is not sufficient; rather, the Union must explicitly decide to no longer exercise the competence in question.

Articles 3 to 6 TFEU regulate the exact division of competences according to policy areas, without changing the structure de lege lata.

Title II of Part I TFEU is introduced by Article 7, which incorporates the text of Article III-115 TCEU. This provision is not new as such but is based on the former Article 3 TEU as amended by the ToN. The principle of enumerative conferral is also explicitly emphasised here.

Article 8 TFEU incorporates the text of Article 3 (2) TEC, whereby Declaration 19 on Article 8 TFEU constitutes a politically significant step, as it states that the Union, in its general efforts to eliminate inequalities between women and men, will work in the various policy areas to combat all forms of domestic violence. In this declaration, some Member States go further - especially in the politico-declaratory area - than they are ready to go domestically.

Article 9 TFEU takes up the requirement of Article III-117 TCEU and thus declares (a) the promotion of a high level of employment, (b) social protection, (c) the fight against social exclusion, (d) a high level of education and training, as well as (e) health protection as cross-sectional issues. However, this only has a declaratory political character, which becomes evident not least by the vague wording.

Article 10 TFEU reproduces Article III-118 TCEU. Both IGCs in 2004 and in 2007 had committed themselves to the goal of combating all forms of discrimination and now also postulate such a goal for the Union in all its activities. Although this is more of a political declaration, it is significant in that such statements underline the Union's claim to be a political organisation.

Article 11 TFEU incorporates Article 6 TEC and thus the fact that environmental protection is a cross-sectional issue for all Union actions. The same applies - mutatis mutandis - to Article 12 TFEU (consumer protection) and Article 13 TFEU (animal protection), which incorporate Article 153 (2) TEC and the previous Protocol on Protection and Welfare of Animals respectively, whereby in the second case the previous protocol text is upgraded by incorporation into the corpus of the Treaty. Although the Convention had considered the inclusion of a separate title on animal welfare in primary law, this was not further pursued by the IGC 2004. During the IGC 2007, there was no longer any effort in this direction either.

Article 14 TFEU deals with services of general economic interest, which were previously dealt with in Article 16 TEC. The IGC 2007, adopting the text of Article III-122 TCEU, specifies the term "conditions". This article had a chequered history, as the Convention had already dealt with it. However, the Convention had only stipulated that the principles and conditions should be laid down by Union legal acts. The IGC 2004 had to deal with this article in numerous debates, as Germany and Austria in particular were of the opinion that limits had to be set to the Union's competences in this area, which is referred to as services of general interest. Both Member States prevailed in the revision of the Convention's proposal at the IGC 2004 to the extent that such EU standards can only be enacted without prejudice to the competence of the Member States. The Member States are by definition obliged to act in accordance with primary law when exercising services of general interest, but their basic competence is no longer called into question by primary law - as actually envisaged by the Convention.

Germany and Austria were able to score another success at the IGC 2007, as a separate Protocol on Services of General Interest was included, which, on the one hand, cites special common values with regard to services of general economic interest in the sense of Article 14 TFEU, and, on the other hand, clarifies that the provisions of the Treaties in no way affect the competence of the Member States to (i) provide, (ii) commission, and (iii) organise non-economic services of general interest.

Article 255 TEC (ex-Article 191a), now Article 15 TFEU, introduced by the ToA, set out the rules for access to Community documents by Union citizens and any natural or legal person residing or having its registered office in a Member State. The IGC 1996 included this new article in response to the post-Maastricht criticism that the Union was not transparent and citizen-friendly enough. However, the solution found by the IGC 1996 got stuck halfway through the reform. Member States could ensure by means of Declaration No. 35 to the ToA that they could prohibit access to documents originating from their sphere to third parties. Although this safeguard clause of the Member States was often criticised in the post-Amsterdam era, the Member States were not willing to deviate from this clause even during the IGC 2000. They were also not inclined to introduce a justification requirement for the use of the clause, arguing that such a requirement would contradict the telos of the clause. Article 15 TFEU reproduces Article 255 of the EC Treaty but develops it further by amending the first sentence of the newly worded third subparagraph of paragraph 3 to ensure the transparency of the activities of the institutions, bodies, offices, and agencies. The IGC 2007 thus went a decisive step further than the ToN, which only provided for an obligation to the effect that the institutions must lay down special provisions in the rules of procedure with regard to access to documents. This new provision not only extends the material scope of application, but also - through the horizontal amendment whereby certain references to institutions are also extended to bodies or agencies - widens the scope of addressees of this provision. The last subparagraph of Article 15(3) TFEU, taking over the text of Article III-399(2) TCEU, additionally stipulates that documents of the legislative procedure must be made publicly accessible.

Article 16 TFEU introduces the protection of personal data into primary law, which is in any case in line with the objective of the IGC 2004 and 2007 to strengthen citizens' rights within the Union.

The concluding Article 17 TFEU incorporates Article I-52 TCEU and deals with the status of churches and non-confessional organisations for the first time in the corpus of primary law. Previously, this matter had only been regulated in Declaration No. 11 of the IGC 1997 on the Protection of Churches and Non-Confessional Organisations. However, its incorporation into primary law does not change the fact that this matter remains within the exclusive regulatory competence of the Member States and thus only serves to clarify that the Union may not affect the status of churches and religious associations or communities as they enjoy it in the individual Member States according to their legal provisions. The open, transparent, and regular dialogue of the Union with churches, religious associations or communities established in accordance with paragraph 3, although of a purely declaratory nature, gives a new and enhanced status to churches and other associations and communities concerned by this provision.

II.2. Non-Discrimination and Citizenship of the Union

Reference:	Part 2 Article 18 to 25 TFEU
Subject:	Prohibition of any discrimination on grounds of nationality Establishment of the citizenship of the Union
Objectives:	Strengthening the protection of the rights and interests of the nationals of the Member States Taking appropriate action to combat discrimination of any kind Making the process of European integration visible Promoting the idea of European identity
Principles:	Citizens of the Union are exclusively those who have the nationality of a Member State Citizenship of the Union is not a substitute for national citizenship of the Member States or an equivalent parallel citizenship, but a complement to national citizenship of the Member States
Instruments:	Labelling of travel documents issued by the Member States[239]

239 e.g. labelling the passports of the Member States as "European Union" and adopting the same colour scheme for these passports throughout the Union.

Although citizenship of the Union was only introduced into the TEC by the ToM, its conceptual origins date back to the 1960s. The TEC already contained a number of individual rights, such as the right of free movement or the prohibition of discrimination on the basis of nationality. Moreover, these rights already gave the possibility to appeal to the ECJ. Accordingly, the ECJ has ruled on such cases since 1963. The Heads of State and Government have been dealing with these issues since the early 1970s, not least at the insistence of Germany. With the so-called Adonnino Report of 1985 at the latest, the policy was extended to a - still very vaguely worded - "Europe of the Citizens", without having a concrete concept in mind at the time. From today's perspective, however, it may seem surprising that questions of the Commission's legitimacy or cushioning the effects of the economic rationalisation efforts of the early 1990s were not included in these considerations. The first concrete steps that ultimately led to the drafting of these articles were taken by Spain, which in the autumn of 1990 - i.e. in the decisive phase prior to the convocation of the IGC 1991 - had, as it were, addressed a reasoned statement to the other Member States aimed at explicitly dealing with the rights, freedoms, and duties of citizens in the future Community. Moreover, Spain was of the opinion that this was an implicit part of the Internal Market anyway. The Spanish proposal, however, aimed at establishing a separate pillar for this purpose, as at that time, Spain had not considered integrating it into the TEC. With the support of the Commission, Spain succeeded in having this proposal accepted by the other Heads of State and Government in December 1990, so that it could be taken up by the IGC 1991. The commitment of the then French President Mitterrand, who was not only open to the Spanish proposal but also believed that it reflected the ideals of the French constitution, was probably instrumental in this success.

Nevertheless, European citizenship still had to overcome three major hurdles before it could find its way into the Treaty. Firstly, the Heads of State and Government concluded that it could not be legally incorporated into the Union Treaty since the Union did not have a legal personality and could therefore not be enforced. Moreover, its scope of application developed in the course of the IGC 1991 in such a way that it did not have any protective effect vis-à-vis the two intergovernmental pillars. The decision was made accordingly, and Union citizenship was embedded in the TEC - contrary to the system, at least, in terms of terminology.[240] Secondly, the rights that were to be derived from citizenship of the Union were not new rights, but those that already existed explicitly or implicitly under existing Community law. The third hurdle was the consideration of the political weight to be attached to this citizenship. The IGC 1991 did not necessarily intend to create a state-like union by means of the ToM, but a political union with strong intergovernmental features.

Embedding citizenship of the Union in the EU Treaty could have been interpreted as a false signal from the point of view of the Heads of State and Government, particularly as a hint that the Union Treaty could be the nucleus for quasi-United States of Europe, since citizenship is regarded in international law as essential for both state-building and constitution-making. In the course of the IGC 1991, various Member States repeatedly opposed the introduction of a citizenship of the Union. Denmark, in particular, read the text in such a way that national citizenship was to be made obsolete and Union citizenship would, if necessary, have a subsidiary effect. However, these Danish reservations were overcome at the Edinburgh European Council in 1992. Taking into account the general objective of the Union within the scope of Article 2 TEU as amended by the ToM, the provisions ultimately adopted on Union citizenship clearly served to strengthen the rights and interests of the nationals of the Member States. Nevertheless, a - not unintentional - placebo effect can also be attributed to them as they offer European citizens something that makes them favourably inclined towards the European idea, without actually granting them new rights. With this formula, even the last critics in the IGC 1991 could be convinced. Despite all attempts to dispel fears of an extension of the scope of European citizenship, Danish concerns were raised again in the course of the IGC 1996, and the Reflection Group under Mr. Westendorp dealt with them in detail. Consistently implemented, these concerns were incorporated into the newly drafted Article 17(1) TEC, which, as amended by the ToA, thus contains expressis verbis that Union citizenship complements national citizenship but does not replace it. At the same time, the Treaty states

240 These concerns were rendered obsolete by the transition from the Community to the Union in the course of the IGC 2007, yet the IGC decided to continue to regulate European citizenship in the successor to the TEC, the TFEU, and not to embed it in the TEU. This decision is inconsistent since the original intention was to deal with all constitutive elements in the TEU. It can only be explained by the fact that Union citizenship is a hybrid one and does not replace national citizenship.

and underlines that the Member States have the sovereign and exclusive competence to decide on citizenship matters of their respective nationals. On the other hand, citizens who only reside in one of the Member States but do not have citizenship of the Member States are excluded from Union citizenship. The restrictive wording was intended not least to make it clear that Union citizenship cannot be granted separately from Member State citizenship. The ToN did not change this wording, as none of the parties of the IGC 2000 wanted this delicate package to be reopened.[241]

In the course of the IGC 2007, the former Articles 17 to 22 TEC were renumbered and are now to be found in primary law as Articles 20 to 25 TFEU. This shift was necessary because the IGC 2007 had drawn the consistent conclusion of combining all provisions relating to non-discrimination and EU citizenship in one part, renaming the relevant part and accordingly prefixing the two articles dealing with non-discrimination, Articles 12 and 13 TEC, as Articles 18 and 19 TFEU. The new Articles 18 and 19 TFEU were embedded with minimal changes, which were necessary in formal terms to comply with the new legislative procedures.

However, the former Article 17 TEC, now Article 20 TFEU, underwent a dramatic extension in the course of the IGC 2007, in which for the first time a demonstrative, non-exhaustive catalogue of Union citizenship rights was listed. The IGC 2007 thus overcame the hesitancy of the IGC 2004, which had listed these rights taxatively in the comparable Article I-10(2) TCEU. Similar to the general enumerative individual conferral, this catalogue of rights also expressly emphasises that these rights are exercised exclusively under the conditions and within the limits laid down in the Treaties and the measures adopted pursuant to them. Here, too, the attitude of some Member States, who wanted to rule out the danger of a creeping expansion of the Union's competences from the outset, becomes evident. This is the same line taken by PM Cameron's call for a reform of social security, which goes hand in hand with the preservation of respect for the

241 In fact, European citizenship is not granted at all; it is an additional element of national citizenship and therefore ceases to exist if national citizenship (of an EU Member State) is lost. The crucial point is that Union citizenship depends on national citizenship and not vice versa. Accordingly, UK nationals who did not have - additional - citizenship of an EU Member State lost EU citizenship upon the UK's withdrawal, as the ECJ has since consistently held (cf. Annex III.5).

reinforcement of national sovereignty, concealing behind it the demand to stop migration into the social systems.[242]

Article 18 TEC (ex-Article 8a), now Article 21 TFEU, was adapted for the first time by the ToA by enshrining the codecision procedure in paragraph 2, whereby the Council still had to decide unanimously. However, the IGC 2000 and the ToN substantially revised Article 18 TEC. Paragraph 2, as amended by the ToA, was once again revised so that the Council now takes decisions by QMV. This change was made in pursuit of the IGC 2000 objective of moving voting from unanimity to qualified majority voting. The scope of application of paragraph 2 was, however, at the same time considerably restricted by the newly added paragraph 3 and relativised in its scope of application. The issuing of documents[243] is excluded, as are the provisions on social security and social protection. The exceptions for the latter area had to be included in paragraph 3 due to massive interventions by Denmark. With this change and at the same time clarification - at least from the Danish perspective - the IGC 2000 was satisfied with regard to Union citizenship. The IGC 2007 revised this article insofar as the ordinary legislative procedure is now applicable. More far-reaching, however, is the amendment of paragraph 3, as the reference to the exception of passports, identity cards, residence permits or equivalent documents has become obsolete, as they are now covered by the application of the article according to the ToL. Denmark was no longer able to maintain her opposition against the application of the article to social measures, but intervened - with substantial British support - in such a way that the relevant decisions would be possible henceforth but would be subject to unanimity. In this case, too, the fear of a dam bursting at the expense of sovereignty in the social sector is apparent once again.

Article 19 TEC (ex-Article 8b), now Article 22 TFEU, was the subject of lengthy and controversial debates both during the IGC 1991 and the IGC 1996, as it represents an extremely integrationist step, since paragraph 1 grants the right to vote and to stand as a candidate in local elections to all those Union citizens who have established their permanent residence in a country other than their home country. Although this provision corresponded to the consistent implementation of the attempt to integrate at least Union citizens in all Member States as far as possible, it would still have

242 https://www.gov.uk/government/speeches/pm-statement-in-madrid-on-aid-for-syria-and-eu-reform.

243 i.e. passports, identity cards, residence permits, or documents equivalent thereto.

to overcome many hurdles in its implementation. The ToA amended this paragraph insofar as it deleted the deadline for the implementation of this provision, since the Council had already adopted the required secondary legislation.[244] Paragraph 2 introduces - just as consistently - the right to vote and to stand as a candidate for the same group of persons with regard to elections to the European Parliament. Even before this granting of the subjective right to every citizen of the Union, three Member States had already granted the right to vote, and in some cases the right to stand as a candidate had also been granted.[245] In the case of paragraph 2, however, the right to vote is already conferred by primary law, and accordingly no implementation acts of the Member States are required. The IGC 1991 thus not only made full use of the legal framework, but at the same time wanted to demonstrate the different quality of the elections in question. During the IGC 2007, this provision remained untouched, as there had been no change of positions. However, the Parliament was given the right to be heard and was thus able to achieve at least a cosmetic success.

Article 20 TEC (ex-Article 8c), now Article 23 TFEU, was uncontroversial until the IGC 2007, since in its original wording it hardly interfered with the sovereignty of the Member States, as its implementation was intergovernmental. However, the IGC 1991 came to the logical conclusion that Union citizenship should not only be made visible internally, i.e. to its own citizens, but also to third countries, in order to send a signal of the internal integrationalist developments to the outside world. The Union/ Community wanted to establish a symbol of its status as a community of solidarity. In the ToL, however, the Member States went one step further by giving the Council the power to act. Critical voices saw in this a tendency towards a standardisation of the right to protection and possibly a first step towards upgrading the EU representations to real embassies and thus possibly replacing small and sometimes extremely cost-intensive embassies of the Member States outside the EU. This could - in the eyes of some Member States - create such a pull that in the long run, not least due to budgetary considerations, a merger of all embassies of the Member States

244 i.e. Council Directive 94/80/EC of 19 December 1994 laying down detailed arrangements for the exercise of the right to vote and to stand as a candidate in municipal elections by citizens of the Union residing in a Member State of which they are not nationals, https://eur-lex.europa.eu/legal-content/EN/TXT/?uri=OJ:L:1994:368:TOC.

245 Belgium, the Netherlands, and the United Kingdom. The latter had granted these rights exclusively to citizens with Irish nationality.

under the umbrella of EU embassies in third countries could not be ruled out.[246]

Article 21 TEC (ex-Article 8d), now Article 24 TFEU, was very short in its original version - contrary to its substantive meaning. It gave EU citizens the right of petition, which can probably be described as one of the fundamental rights in a democracy, and provided uno actu with an adequate field of activity for the Ombudsman, who was also newly introduced by the ToM. However, the ToM did not regulate the question of language, neither with regard to the petitions nor the answers to be given. Only the ToA reacted to this virulent issue in an appropriate way by granting every citizen the right to lodge a petition in one of the official languages and to receive a reply in the same language.[247] The IGC 2000 addressed this provision again because of growing complaints from citizens that responses were not being provided within an acceptable timeframe. Although the complaints were noted, the Heads of State and Government reacted rather evasively. They decided against revising Article 21 TEC to require replies within a reasonable or even definite period of time but contented themselves with a declaration to the ToN. Belgium, which had already insisted on the amendment by the ToA, could not prevail during the IGC 2000. The conference did not amend this provision, but at least requested the institutions to provide a response within a reasonable period of time. This request to the institutions is in itself an embarrassing reprimand, as it can be assumed that the answers will be given within a reasonable period of time. The IGC 2007 only made editorial changes to the article.

Article 22 TEC (ex-Article 8e), now Article 25 TFEU, was ultimately intended to satisfy both sides, the sceptics on the one hand and the integrationists on the other, and in any case to leave open a possibility for evolution. Neither in Amsterdam nor in Nice was there any change, although in the course of the IGC 1996 it was actually proposed that the provisions on

---

246 Austria in particular advocated this perspective in the IGC 2007 and subsequently during the establishment of the European External Action Service (EEAS). In reality, however, this has led to another development that is followed with scepticism by some Member States: Since the establishment of the so-called EU embassies, some third countries no longer turn to the bilateral embassy representing the country holding the Presidency of the Council but to the EU embassy in matters concerning the Union; moreover, the EU ambassador increasingly chairs informal meetings of ambassadors from EU Member States. These tendencies may still depend heavily on the respective personalities, but institutionalisation can hardly be prevented - at least in the long term.

247 European citizens are free to choose which official language they wish to use.

Union citizenship be supplemented by a catalogue of fundamental rights. However, these attempts failed, as did the attempt to incorporate the EU Charter of Fundamental Rights, which had been solemnly proclaimed in Nice in December 2000. In the course of the ToL, the consultation procedure was replaced by the consent procedure.

II.3. External Action and Common Foreign and Security Policy

The IGC 2007, in continuation of the approach of the IGC 2004, had decided to combine the provisions on external action and a common foreign and security policy, some of which were widely scattered in primary law, and accordingly to embed them in a more compact way in the primary law de lege ferenda. However, since the IGC 2007 negotiated a traditional covering treaty, it had to consider, in contrast to the IGC 2004, whose aim had been a single treaty, how it could bring about a logical demarcation between fundamental and implementing provisions without having to return to the old pattern of widely scattered provisions. The decision was made in favour of embedding all basic (= general) provisions in the TEU and all implementing provisions in the newly created TFEU, which replaced the former TEC. This decision also applies to the complex of foreign and security policy. For the first time, therefore, all relevant regulations in primary law have essentially been combined into two large blocks and have accordingly become easier to handle.

II.3.1. The Union's External Action and the Common Foreign and Security Policy

Reference:	Title V Chapter 1 and 2 Articles 21 bis 46 TEU
Subject:	General provisions on external action and common foreign and security policy
Objectives:	Safeguarding common values, fundamental interests, independence, and integrity of the Union Strengthening the security of the Union in all its forms Preservation of peace and strengthening of international security Promotion of international cooperation Development and strengthening of democracy, the rule of law, respect for human rights, and fundamental freedoms
Principles:	Support for the Common Foreign and Security Policy by all Member States Refrain from acts detrimental to the interests of the Union Responsibility of the Council for the coherence and observance of the principles
Instruments:	All legal acts provided for in the Treaties

Introduction

The issue of foreign and security policy has been an extremely delicate political topic since the beginning of European integrational efforts. After initially rather hesitant steps, the ToM incorporated the intergovernmental foreign and security policy pillar into primary law under the umbrella of the Union. It was not until the IGC 2007 that full integration and at least a formal supranational orientation took place.

Since the transition to the Lisbon era is a clear fault line, the analysis of this topic is divided into the pre- and post-Lisbon era.

Development up to the Treaty of Nice

The CFSP can be regarded as the direct successor to the European Political Cooperation established by Article 30 SEA. However, it was not only a simple successor to the EPC, but rather a further development since it extends to all areas of foreign and security policy. Nevertheless, neither the idea nor the concept were new; rather, the CFSP is the overcoming of the failure of the EDC - and thus uno actu of the EPC - in the 1950s, when France, fearing a loss of national sovereignty in foreign and military issues, had paralysed this aspect of European integration with her veto.[248] The Fouchet plans that were subsequently circulated were also unable to find viable approval. France's temporary withdrawal from the Community institutions in 1965 and her withdrawal from the military structure of NATO the following year finally brought these integration efforts to a grinding halt.[249] It was not until the SEA of 1986 that the path of foreign and security policy integration was taken again by providing the EPC with a basis in primary law. The IGC 1991 marked a decisive breakthrough. The Community had drawn the conclusion from both the Yugoslav crisis and the Gulf War that the claim to be a global player and the reality of ineffective and incoherent practice were all too far apart. The IGC 1996 concluded - on the basis of the experience gained in the meantime - that Title V TEU should undergo a thorough adaptation. The IGC 2000 followed this intention but did not go much further than the Amsterdam approach.

Ex-Article J TEU representing only the cornerstone for the establishment of a CFSP, was consequently repealed by the IGC 1996. The original version of Article 11 TEU (ex-Article J.1)[250] laid down the objectives and forms of action of the CFSP (ex-Article J.1(2)), which were adopted by the IGC 1996 as Article 11(1). A new feature, however, was the inclusion of a requirement of coherence with the Charter of the United Nations. The forms of action originally envisaged for the CFSP (ex-Article J.1(3) TEU) were transferred, concretised, and extended under the new Article 12 TEU. The IGC 1996 decided to include a new form of action in the catalogue, so-called Common Strategies, and thus set a counterpoint to the Union's previous occasion-related and thus only reactive actions.

Article 13 TEU (ex-Articles J.3 and J.8(1) and (2)) gave the European Council a virtually unrestricted monopoly in defining the principles of the CFSP, which now also covered defence issues, as can be deduced from the overall context of Title V. The IGC thus overcame resistance from those Member States that covertly regarded defence policy as the almost ultimate

248 cf. above Chapter I.2.

249 cf. above Chapter I.3.

250 References in this chapter to ex-Articles of Title V refer to the ToM version.

prerogative of a sovereign state as well as reservations on the part of neutral Member States.

Article 14 TEU (ex-Article J.3) provides a considerably more precise definition of Joint Action in the ToA version than in its original wording. The most significant adaptation concerns the role of the Commission, which can now submit proposals related to the CFSP upon invitation of the European Council. The IGC 1996 thus reacted to the fact that the Commission was affected in its work by Joint Actions without being able to react to them by way of proposals. That way, the ToA circumvented the fact that the Commission did not have a monopoly on initiative in the intergovernmental pillar as it does in the supranational pillar, thus enabling the Commission to submit proposals on request, as it were.

Article 15 TEU (ex-Article J.2(2)) was more precisely worded at the IGC 1996 than in its original version. The IGC 1996 recognised that common positions, while less concrete in their implications, are nevertheless of eminent political importance. By stating that common positions form the basis for the Union's action on issues of a geographical or thematic nature, the IGC 1996 gave them a higher status than de lege lata.

Article 16 TEU (ex-Article J.2(1)) was reproduced unchanged.

Article 17 TEU (ex-Article J.4) as amended by the ToA goes far beyond the scope of its predecessor. In Maastricht, the Member States had not yet been ready to commit themselves to the future perspective of a common defence policy; rather, they referred to a possible realisation in the longer term. In Amsterdam, the Member States took a further decisive step by also integrating the armament policy aspect.[251] In Nice, the IGC deleted the reference to the WEU and thus placed the Union on its own feet in defence policy and henceforth acted without dependence on and coordination with the WEU, whose life expectancy was already limited anyways.

Article 18 TEU (ex-Article J.5) in its new version responded to the acknowledged need to support the Presidency by establishing the function of a High Representative for the CFSP. This innovation was - at least in part - a response to the criticism that had been voiced for decades that there was no direct and permanent contact person for such issues in the Community

251 This led at some point to the establishment of a European Defence Agency.

and later the Union. Neither in Amsterdam nor in Nice were the Member States willing to take a more radical step.[252]

Article 19 TEU (ex-Article J.2(3) and J.5(4)) and Article 20 TEU (ex-Article J.6) were reproduced unchanged, as were Articles 21 (ex-Article J.7) and 22 (ex-Article J.8(3) and (4)).

Article 23 TEU (ex-Articles J.8(2) and J.3(2)) now consolidated the voting procedure and organised them more coherently than in the ToM. The ToN only introduced a procedural change in that the Special Representative for specific policy issues, to be appointed by the Council under Article 18(5), could now be appointed by QMV.

Article 24 TEU had no substantive counterpart in the ToM and, with its introduction by the ToA, extended the scope of the CFSP to the conclusion of bilateral or multilateral agreements. The amendments by the ToN included, on the one hand, a clarification of the voting modalities with regard to unanimity or qualified majority, and, on the other hand, a substantial adaptation by introducing a new paragraph 6 which postulated that agreements concluded under Article 24 TEU, and thus concerning Titles V and VI TEU, would bind the institutions of the Union (European Parliament, Council, Commission, Court of Justice and Court of Auditors). The IGC 2000 thus took a further step towards integrating the intergovernmental pillar into the supranational sphere of the Union.

Article 25 TEU (ex-Article J.8(5)) established a new committee, called Political Committee, which since the amendments by the ToN has been renamed Political and Security Committee (PSC). Although the rights and responsibilities of the Permanent Representatives Committee under Article 207 TEC were not to be curtailed by this Committee, it was nevertheless given a prominent position when it was entrusted by the Council - due to the ToN - with the task of a political control and strategic management body for operations in the field of crisis management. This upgrade or extension of tasks by the IGC 2000 was a logical consequence of the further development of this title. The Member States nevertheless drew the boundaries of the PSC's competences very tightly in that they were (i) linked to the purpose of the crisis management operation in terms of content, (ii) limited in time to the duration of the operation, and (iii) referred to Article 47 TEU in terms of primary law.

252 Only the embarrassing experience of the Second Gulf War convinced the Member States that they should establish the office of a European Minister for Foreign Affairs.

Article 26 TEU had no equivalent in the ToM and was inserted by the IGC 1996. Neither Article 26 TEU nor Article 27 TEU (ex-Article J.9) were not revised by the IGC 2000.

Articles 27a to 27e TEU are an original product of the IGC 2000. This insertion of new provisions in the CFSP title was based on the debate on a general reorganisation of enhanced cooperation and its extension in the course of the IGC 2000. The newly added Articles 27a to 27e also introduced enhanced cooperation in the area of CFSP. In one respect, however, the IGC 2000 fell short of the expectations of some Member States when it excluded issues with military or defence implications from enhanced cooperation. This exception was justified by the conference on the grounds that at the time of Nice there was still a general exclusion of military or defence policy issues and that the aim was to prevent such references from being established through the back door, as it were, by means of enhanced cooperation. So as to comply with the requirement of transparency and to counter any expected criticism from the outset, the Secretary General of the Council and High Representative for the CFSP was entrusted with informing the European Parliament and all members of the Council, i.e. also those not participating in such enhanced cooperation, in full about the implementation.

Article 28 TEU (ex-Article J.11) was amended by the IGC 1996 to reflect the new provisions of the ToA and was reproduced unchanged by the IGC 2000.

Transformation by the Treaty of Lisbon

As already pointed out in the introduction to this chapter, the IGC 2007 radically intervened in the previous system of foreign and security policy and changed not only the form, but also - and above all - the content. The TEU as amended by the ToL deals with all general regulations regarding this area, the TFEU with the implementation of the overall policy. The IGC 2007 distinguishes for the first time between a general foreign policy and a specific foreign policy, the latter comprising inter alia the Common Foreign and Security Policy, including the Common Security and Defence Policy.

The amendments described below were, by their very nature, agreed before Brexit. Accordingly, the United Kingdom was included as a Member State. This concerns in particular provisions in the relationship with the United Nations and the representation of the EU in the UN Security Council. Therefore, reference is made in this section to France and the United Kingdom as Permanent Security Council Members. As of the date of the United Kingdom's withdrawal, these statements only apply to France.

Not only the heading of the title has been extended, but the entire content was completely restructured. The title, previously not subdivided, has been transformed into a title with two chapters (Chapter 1 - General provisions on the Union's external action, Chapter 2 - Specific provisions on the common foreign and security policy), with the second chapter being subdivided into two sections (Section 1 - Common provisions, Section 2 - Provisions on the common security and defence policy). Enhanced cooperation, which was still dealt with under this title in the TEU de lege lata, was removed by the IGC 2007 and now regulated in Article 20 TEU de lege ferenda (cf. Chapter II.4.1.) on the one hand and in Articles 326 to 334 TFEU (cf. Chapter II.4.2.) on the other. The remaining articles de lege lata have either been renumbered (Articles 17, 22 and 23 TEU de lege lata have been renumbered as Articles 42, 30 and 31 TEU de lege ferenda) or repealed (Articles 26 and 27 TEU de lege lata). The provisions concerning enhanced cooperation de lege lata (Articles 27a to 27d TEU) have been removed and - as explained above - combined in a new single Article 20 TEU.

Article 21 TEU-new serves as the opening article for the entire revised title. The IGC 2007 took over - with editorial adaptations only - Article III-292 TCEU, which itself corresponds to Article III-193 TEC. The Union's new self-image in the field of foreign policy becomes abundantly clear in this article: The Union claims to have more influence on the international stage. The UN is naturally at the centre of this ambition. The Union is acting self-confidently here by claiming to be the guardian of humanist principles. Considering the period of time in which these wordings originated, one could ask whether the Union, in view of its marginalisation on the international level, did not simply want to give itself courage on the occasion of the Gulf crisis in 2002/2003. In the meantime, a balance between aspiration and reality has been established, even if not at the lofty level that many a European politician had hoped for. The requirement of loyalty and coherence had already been contained in Article 11(2) TEU de lege lata, but it was directed exclusively at the Member States. The ToL raises this double requirement to a higher level and now entrusts the Union itself to ensure compliance. This provision contains eminent, if only potential, dynamite. This coherence would naturally have to apply to all international bodies and organisations, especially in the UN World Security Council. Besides the USA, China, and Russia, the United Kingdom and France are represented there as Permanent Members. Realistically, it can hardly be assumed that these two countries, which claim to be world powers, were willing to relinquish their influence or to submit to instructions from, for example, the European Council. With Brexit, France as the only remaining Permanent Member representing the EU, enjoys her powerful position particularly vis-à-vis the EU and its Member States. Equally unrealistic was any expectation that these two states would renounce their membership in favour of a single seat for the Union in the event of a possible reform of the UN Security Council, a situation that has not changed in the course of Brexit. Equally, however, the ambitions of another EU Member State, i.c. Germany, eager to become a Permanent Member of the UN Security Council herself, stand in the way of a coherent common foreign policy. These questions were not addressed during the IGC 2007, as they had already been blocked at the IGC 2004 by the states concerned with the argument of Treaty compliance.

Article 22 TEU new, which takes over Article III-293 TCEU, constitutes a massive extension of the previous Article 13 (2) TEU. The latter still referred very generally to the common - foreign policy - interests of the Member States. The IGC 2007 opted for a clearer wording, which in particular clarifies that the relevant decisions of the European Council apply to the Common Foreign and Security Policy and other areas of the Union's external action. This clearly states that the interests of the Union are to be prioritised and that the interests of the Member States are to take a back seat.

These two new articles conclude the first chapter. The message of the IGC 2007 is explicit. From now on, the common interests of the Union shall determine the actions; particularism on the part of the Member States is to be a matter of the past.

Chapter 2 opens with an original IGC 2007 article. Article 23 TEU constitutes some form of reinsurance against a creeping transfer of competences or the generation of competences in this area to the benefit of the Union and is thus further proof of the latent fear of some Member States. The positive effect of this provision is that it also subjects the Common Foreign and Security Policy to the principles already mentioned. Two declarations were added to the Treaty to further underpin these concerns. Declaration No. 13 emphasises that neither (i) the competences of the Member States existing at the time of the coming into force of the Treaty for the formulation and implementation of their foreign policy nor (ii) their national representation in third countries and international organisations will be affected. Declaration No. 14 emphasises that the provisions on the Common Foreign and Security Policy, including on the High Representative of the Union for Foreign Affairs and Security Policy, and on the External Action Service, are without prejudice to the existing legal bases, competences and powers of the individual Member States with regard to the formulation and conduct of their foreign policies, their national diplomatic services, their relations with third countries, and their participation in international organisations, including the membership of a Member State in the United Nations Security Council. The question of what then remains for the Union may be raised, whereby reality partly answers this question in a sobering manner at the expense of the Union.

The following Article 24 TEU is also an original product of the IGC 2007 with regard to paragraphs 1 and 2, while paragraph 3 is an adapted version of the former Article 11(3) TEU. This very article exemplifies the dilemma of the IGC 2007. On the one hand, there was a strong desire to dissolve the previous pillar structure and fully integrate the CFSP (communitarising it, as it were); on the other hand, this exercise also required finding a justifiable position on defence policy. The IGC 2007 could not bring itself to include a clear statement in favour of a Common Defence Policy, but only to include it in the Treaty as an option. The automatism between the definition of a policy and the establishment of common defence, which some had hoped for, failed to materialise, not only due to Austria's special status under international law, but also due to the concerns of other Member States, which are either not NATO members or were concerned about the very existence of NATO. The interests of the USA were also expressed at least indirectly, since the latter would also have to fear for the continued existence of NATO in its current structure if the Union became independent in terms of defence policy. In practice, this mixture of interests made it impossible to take a clear and unambiguous direction. The continued intergovernmental character of the CFSP is further reflected in the wording of this provision, which establishes a special procedure for this policy area in which the European Council and the Council must decide unanimously, the Court of Justice has no jurisdiction and, moreover, no legislative acts may be adopted. The future effectiveness of the CFSP, including defence policy, in the face of all these restrictions, was quickly demonstrated by the crises in the Maghreb and the Mashreq in the course of the so-called Arab Spring and the Ukraine crisis. In all these cases, the Union could not play a decisive role, neither politically nor even less militarily.

Article 25 TEU incorporates Article III-294(3) TCEU, but is not a novelty in terms of content, as it reproduces the instruments of ex-Article 12 TEU.

Article 26 TEU is a mixture of ex-Article 13(1) and (3) TEU as well as Article III-295 and Article I-40(4) TCEU. The main innovations are the strengthening of the European Council and its President. The latter is responsible for the decision to convene an extraordinary European Council if s/he considers an international development to be critical in this respect. In reality, this decision does not really lie with the President, but will be taken in consultation with the Member States. In other words, the President will convene a meeting when there is a prospect of political agreement or at least a unified statement by the European Council. Moreover, it is a question of step-by-step escalation. The inflationary convening of Special European Councils could lead to a weakening of this institution and thus run counter to the intentions of the Treaty. The European Council itself is upgraded to the extent that it no longer determines the principles of the CFSP but its strategic interests. This may be a semantic finesse and hardly changes anything in reality, since in the absence of a legal definition of this term, the competence of the European Council de lege ferenda effectively remains unchanged. However, the fact that the European Council de lege ferenda defines not only the general guidelines, but also the objectives, can certainly be seen as an increase in competences.

Article 27 TEU incorporates Article III-296 TCEU and describes the field of activity of the High Representative. The IGC 2007 thus turned away from the failed, lofty plans of the IGC 2004, which still intended to introduce a European Foreign Minister. However, with a new nameplate, this function was ultimately incorporated into primary law. This article introduces the following innovations to primary law: (a) Introduction of the office of High Representative of the Union for Foreign Affairs and Security Policy, who is responsible for the following tasks: (i) submitting proposals defining the CFSP, (ii) ensuring the implementation of CFSP decisions, (iii) representing the Union externally in the field of the CFSP, (iv) conducting the political dialogue, (v) representing the Union's position in international organisations and at international conferences, (b) the High Representative taking over the function of High Representative for the CFSP, which is abolished at the same time, and (c) establishing a European External Action Service. This article, as short as it may be, shows on the one hand an unbelievable self-confidence of the Union, but on the other hand also the indecisiveness to create truly straight conditions in this policy field. The wording does not allow any definite conclusion as to how the competing situation between the High Representative on the one hand and the two European Permanent Members of the World Security Council, France and England, is to be resolved. Brexit has in no way alleviated the dilemma. In any case, the provision of Article 34 paragraph 2 last sentence TEU is not necessarily useful. Likewise, the relationship between the European External Action Service and the corresponding services of the Member States remains unresolved.

Article 28 TEU reproduces - only slightly adapted - ex-Article 14 TEU and thus remains on safe ground; the same applies to Articles 29 to 31 TEU, which reproduce ex-Articles 15, 22 and 23 TEU, with the only innovation being the addition of the High Representative.

Article 32 TEU amends the former Article 16 TEU fundamentally by merging Article I-40(5) and Article III-301(1) and (2) TCEU. This new provision is almost an appeal to the necessary coherence at political and technical level. Precisely because of its wording, this article has a clearly political and declaratory orientation, because none of the provisions contained is justiciable, but it does indeed exert political pressure on the Member States. The IGC 2007 saw itself very clearly as a political conference and expressed this explicitly in this article.

Article 33 TEU takes over only paragraph 5 of ex-Article 18 TEU, granting the High Representative wide-ranging powers. Without his proposal, there are no Special Representatives, so it is up to the High Representative to decide whether to delegate his agenda or to exercise it himself. The High Representative, who is otherwise heavily dependent on the Member States, is given exclusive competence in this case. At the same time, however, his/her hands are politically tied, as any holder of the post can only be successful with the full support of the member states.

Article 34 TEU essentially reproduces ex-Article 19 TEU and adapts this provision to the effect that the organisation of coordination is entrusted to the High Representative. This change is not necessarily significant, but the new concluding subparagraph of paragraph 2 restricts the manoeuvring power of the Member States, which are now obliged to request that the High Representative presents the Union's position in the UN Security Council. The restriction on France and the United Kingdom may still be resolved internally within the EU, although the provision does not preclude EU Permanent Members of the UN Security Council from exercising their right to take the floor, nonetheless. A completely different question is whether the Security Council agrees. In the event of a refusal to exercise this right to speak, the question arises as to whether France or the United Kingdom could be entrusted with this task on a subsidiary basis, as it were. Prima facie, the Treaty does not provide for such a devolution. The IGC 2007 may have been driven by a perhaps somewhat exaggerated self-confidence, or for political reasons could not lag behind the IGC 2004. The provision as such is the result of an occasionally hypereuphoric IGC, whose wording did not always think everything through to the last consequence.

Article 35 TEU, on the other hand, is relatively conservative and only adapts the ex-Article 20 TEU to the necessary extent.

Article 36 TEU consequently transfers the role of information vis-à-vis Parliament from the Presidency to the High Representative, without making any further substantial changes.

Article 37 TEU represents an almost revolutionary shortening of ex-Article 24 TEU. The previous procedure for concluding agreements with third countries or international organisations had been extremely complex and had included numerous exceptions and emergency brakes. The IGC 2007 again applied its principle of regulating general matters in the TEU and specific matters in the TFEU to this succinct text. The precise procedural provisions were not abolished by the revision of Article 24 TEU, but now appear in Articles 139, 207, 216 and 217 TFEU. However, this shift corresponds to the telos of the Convention and streamlines the TEU accordingly.

Article 38 TEU - editorially adapted - reproduces ex-Article 25 TEU.

Article 39 TEU is an original addition of the IGC 2007 and simultaneously repeals the former Article 26 TEU, outlining the support tasks of the Secretary General of the Council and the former High Representative, as well as the former Article 27 TEU, which regulated the participation of the Commission in the area of CFSP, as both provisions have been rendered obsolete by the ToL. This new article introduces the legal basis for a Council Decision on personal data protection in the context of the CFSP. The IGC found an innovative solution for the implementation of the supervision of these provisions by entrusting them to independent authorities, thus outsourcing them from the institutional framework of the Union. Probably for political rather than legal reasons, the IGC 2007 introduced an independent data protection basis for the CFSP, whereby the intergovernmental element in this case is that a Council Decision is provided for as an instrument, so that the Parliament is still excluded from the decision making.

Article 40 TEU reproduces the former Article 47 TEU and adapts it editorially. The subject matter of the provision continues to be the relationship between the CFSP and the other policies of the Union in terms of collision, which remains unchanged in terms of content.

Article 41 TEU, on the one hand, maintains the existing Article 28(2) and (3) TEU, but adds to these two provisions new specific provisions concerning the financing of CFSP initiatives.

Article 42 TEU opens the second section of the second foreign and security policy chapter.[253] This provision is composed of parts of the former Article 17 TEU, parts of Article I-41 TCEU, and original considerations of the IGC 2007. Thus, this newly worded article reflects the entire development of the Common Foreign and Security Policy since the Maastricht negotiations. With the new text, the IGC 2007 already emphasises in the first paragraph that CSDP is now an integral part of CFSP and must not be regarded as a separate policy. This emphasis may only be important from a declaratory political point of view, but it was necessary as a signal to point to the primacy of foreign policy. Another new aspect is that primary law assigns the CSDP the task of providing the Union with the necessary operational capability in both the civilian and military sector. Primary law also goes far beyond what is required de lege lata in the area of making the capabilities of the Member States available. From now on, this is to be comprehensively interpreted and no longer limited to cooperation in the field of armament policy. Paragraph 3 leaves no doubt about the obligatory character of all these provisions, whereby the Member States have the obligation to (i) make civilian and military capabilities available as a contribution to the realisation of the objectives set by the Council, as well as to (ii) progressively improve military capabilities. The TCEU had still contained the call for the establishment of a European Defence Agency, which, however, had become superfluous since this agency had already been established by the time of the IGC 2007. Article I-41(3) TCEU has been reworded accordingly and continues to contain the profile of requirements for this agency. However, Article 42 TEU contains even more far-reaching provisions that were taboo at the time of the Nice negotiations. One of these previously taboo subjects is the so-called Permanent Structured Cooperation. Those Member States that wish to go further in the field of CSDP can establish

253 The wording of this section, in particular who is entrusted with the respective decision-making competence, testifies to the still existing intergovernmental character of this policy field. The Council continues to play the dominant role in the entire section, a role it shares with the Member States, who in any case remain the masters of proceedings by virtue of the principle of unanimity.

such cooperation as described in Article 46 TEU. The IGC 2004 built on the results of the Convention in this field, the IGC 2007 adopted them almost without any further debate. Historically, this possibility of cooperation, which was intended to enable greater flexibility in the field of defence, can be understood as a response to the unilateral actions of some Member States on the one hand and the inability of the Union to act in a coordinated manner on the other. It is questionable whether the European Council's power to mandate a group of Member States to carry out missions in order to uphold the values of the Union and to act in its interests (paragraph 5) is really breaking uncharted territory. Ultimately, it is a more compact wording of the former paragraph 2, as it can probably be assumed that these missions will encompass the areas of joint disarmament measures, humanitarian and rescue tasks, tasks of military advice and assistance, tasks of conflict prevention and peacekeeping, as well as combat missions in the context of crisis management, including peace-making measures and operations to stabilise the situation after conflicts. The two paragraphs (Article 17(2) TEU and Article 42(5) TEU) have a common telos, the new wording is more precise and unambiguous, the previous wide scope for interpretation is narrowed to a minimum. The most controversial innovation is certainly the mutual assistance clause in paragraph 7. The Member States had already come to the conclusion during the Convention that the Union's military presence was not only suboptimal, but simply non-existent, or at least so poorly developed that in case of emergency only recourse to NATO resources would bring relief. It was precisely the growing disparity with the USA that emerged during the Convention that made it appear necessary to develop an independent European stand-by solution. Within the framework of the obligation to provide assistance in the event of an armed attack on a Member State's territory, the Member States must provide all aid and support in their power in accordance with Article 51 of the Charter of the United Nations. As unambiguous as this wording appears to be, it is fraught with several provisions. The reference to the UN Charter served the Member States as a basic safeguard or rather as a direct reference to a legal definition already recognised under international law. The open wording as to what is actually meant by assistance and support (... everything in their power ...), however, leads to the conclusion that there is no unconditional obligation to provide military assistance or support. This becomes all the clearer when the second sentence of paragraph 7 is read into it, which states quite clearly that this assistance clause is without prejudice to the special character of the security and defence policy of certain Member States. That group of "certain" Member States included the neutral states Sweden, Finland, Ireland, Malta, Cyprus and Austria, whereby Austria has the strongest commitment to neutrality under international law.[254] Finally, in this context, reference should be made to the double safeguard vis-à-vis the special character of the security and defence policy of certain Member States, which is already - programmatically - contained in paragraph 2 and does not leave it at this point with the general wording, but explicitly refers to the stipulated NATO obligations of some Member States. The IGC 2007 had certainly endeavoured to carry along the spirit and momentum of the Convention and the IGC 2004, but in the end it could not contribute to a clearer solution, as certain Member States were not willing to take any further step towards a European orientation of their defence policy.

Although Article 43 TEU does not have a direct corresponding article in primary law de lege lata and accordingly reproduces Article III-309 TCEU, on closer examination it very much takes up the descriptive elements of ex-Article 17(2) TEU, which - and this is the genuine new feature - it extends by including the so-called Petersberg missions.[255]

Article 44 TEU takes over Article III-310 TCEU with editorial adaptations and introduces a new element into primary law, respectively it describes the procedure for the missions already mentioned in Article 42(5) TEU. There is one restriction that makes the intergovernmental character recede somewhat, as the Member States carrying out the mission are bound to inform the Council immediately in the event of a drastic change in the situation. In this way, the Council remains the master of the procedure; those Member States participating in the mission may not take an independent decision in this specific case. This restriction was already considered necessary by the IGC 2004 in order to dispel any doubts about the Council's leadership competence and to make it impossible for the Member States carrying out the mission to act on their own. It is not ensured by the provision itself how such a procedure can produce a timely reaction.

---

254 Following the Russian attack on Ukraine, Finland and Sweden applied for NATO membership, which Finland joined in mid-2023 and Sweden - only after Hungary and Turkey lifted their veto - in March 2024.

255 The Petersberg missions, also known as Petersberg tasks, can be divided into the following categories: (i) humanitarian operations, (ii) rescue operations, (iii) peacekeeping operations, and (iv) combat operations in the course of crisis management, including peace-making.

Article 45 TEU is without precedent in primary law and comprises the catalogue of tasks of the European Defence Agency, which was established by the Council Joint Action of 12 July 2004.[256] This catalogue of tasks is a simple copy of Article III-311 TCEU. The IGC 2007 was not in a position to restrict the content of this catalogue, since the Defence Agency had already been established in accordance with the provisions of the TCEU. Although the IGC 2007 would have had the opportunity to broaden the agency's remit, it left the TCEU catalogue unchanged.

Article 46 TEU is the last provision of the foreign and security policy title and regulates the implementation of the Permanent Structured Cooperation. By its very nature, there is no corresponding provision in primary law; rather, the IGC 2007 adopted the text of Article III-312 TCEU, which had already been agreed in the IGC 2004. The most important elements of this form of cooperation concern the question of transparency. Both the Convention and the IGC 2004 and 2007 agreed that this particular form of cooperation should not be a "closed shop" but shall be open to all Member States that fulfil the criteria for participation and are willing to do so. The wording was drafted accordingly. In order to comply with the transparency requirement, it was swiftly decided that a list of the participating states would be published in order to prevent any secrecy. The rejection of the closed shop approach is also made clear by the fact that not only can no Member State be excluded from participation at the time of the founding, but it is also possible for any Member State to join at any time after the cooperation has been established. It is interesting, however, that a Member State can also withdraw again - in the form of a unilateral declaration - without requiring the approval of the other participating Member States, non-participating Member States or the Council. Even more interesting, though, is the procedure if a participating state no longer fulfils the conditions for participation or can no longer meet its obligations. In this case, it is not necessary to wait for the declaration of withdrawal, but the Council can act on its own initiative and suspend the participation of the state in question. With this solution, primary law only suspends membership and at the same time denies the Council the possibility of excluding a state. The final termination of this cooperation thus lies in the decision-making power of each individual Member State, which can decide on this sovereignly and

256 Council Joint Action 2004/551/CFSP of 12 July 2004 on the establishment of the European Defence Agency, OJ L 245 of 17 July 2004 (https://eur-lex.europa.eu/legal-content/EN/TXT/HTML/?uri=CELEX:32004E0551&from=EN).

unilaterally. The IGC 2004 even took a decisive step back from the outcome of the Convention, which had stipulated in Article III-213 TCEU that a non-participating state should even be excluded from the deliberations and would only be informed by the EU Foreign Minister (now: High Representative). This rather odd regulation could neither be justified by the preservation of military secrets, nor would it have complied with the coherence requirement. Speculation in the aftermath of the conference that this provision was originally intended to exert pressure on Member States not willing to participate to bring their capacities up to the appropriate level and to request participation cannot be substantiated and is ultimately futile. The IGC 2004 decided relatively soon that the same automatism as for a common currency should by no means be envisaged for Permanent Structured Cooperation. Moreover, such an undermining of the voluntary nature and the special obligation of some Member States would have been diametrically opposed to the spirit and telos of the Treaty.

The evolution of these provisions shows by way of example that the IGC 2004 did not adopt the results of the Convention unconditionally and that the IGC 2007 made some substantial changes to the results of the deliberations of the IGC 2004.

II.3.2. General Provisions on the Union's External Action

Reference: Part 5 Title I Article 205 TFEU
Subject: Introduction to the topic

The ToL inserted this introductory article into the TFEU, which once again reminds us that the policies of Part 5 TFEU must be conducted in accordance with the fundamental requirements of the TEU. Legally, this provision is not necessary, since the TEU applies to the TFEU in all its parts anyway; it was a political demand of the IGC 2007 with a declaratory character, emphasising this necessity.

II.3.3. Common Commercial Policy

Reference:	Part 5 Title II Articles 206 and 207 TFEU
Subject:	Development and application of a Common Commercial Policy
Objectives:	Harmonious development of world trade through the abolition of customs and other trade barriers in international trade Taking into account the increased competitiveness of European companies
Principles:	Abolition of trade barriers Liberalisation of world trade
Instruments:	Adoption of safeguard measures Association Agreements Measures in the field of import policy Conclusion of multilateral trade agreements Taking an active role in particular in the World Trade Organisation (= WTO)

The position of the Common Commercial Policy in primary law as amended by the ToN seemed somewhat peculiar. Embedded, as it were, in a sandwich position between classic domestic policies, this particular type of foreign policy was an alien element in any case. This was due to the many changes in Part 3 TEC, especially the numerous additions of titles, which had taken the Common Commercial Policy further and further away from its original position. Nevertheless, these changes had also had a positive effect on this policy, as it was given a new quality by the ToM when it was elevated from a chapter of the economic policy title to a title in its own right. The ToL finally assigned the Common Commercial Policy the place it systematically deserves, namely in the newly created fifth part on the Union's external action. This transfer had become possible as the IGC 2007 had decided to examine the entire Treaty for systematics and conformity and, if necessary, to make radical shifts. In the course of this reorganisation, Articles 132 and 134 TEC were repealed, which contributes significantly to the streamlining of this topic. As a result, this section only contains two articles, namely Article 131 TEC, which is now Article 206 TFEU, and Article 133 TEC, which has been incorporated as Article 207 TFEU.

The trade policy chapter of the TEEC comprised seven articles dealing with objectives (Article 110 TEEC), transitional provisions (Article 111 TEEC), the standardisation of export subsidies (Article 112 TEEC), the Common Commercial Policy (Article 113 TEEC), agreements on behalf of the Community (Article 114 TEEC), measures to remedy difficulties (Article 115 TEEC), and Common Action in International Organisations (Article 116 TEEC). These articles were incorporated - with the same numbering - into the TEC, whereby articles that had become obsolete in the meantime as a result of the ToN were repealed by the ToM, but nominally continued to appear in the Treaty.[257] Articles 111 and 114 TEEC/TEC were repealed when the deadline laid down therein was reached, and Article 116 TEEC/TEC became obsolete through the inclusion of Article 19(1) TEU (ex-Article J.2(3)), the latter placing the necessary coordination among the Member States under the umbrella of the Common Foreign and Security Policy. The Commission had made numerous attempts to bring about substantive changes in trade policy, which it tried again during the IGC 1996, but failed because the Member States could not decide between liberalising international trade and national protectionism. The remaining amendments concerning the trade policy title were - as in the cases already mentioned - merely adaptations in the course of the IGC 1991, which had become possible due to the expiry of deadlines.[258]

The IGC 1996 also failed to bring about a reorientation of trade policy and merely (i) adapted Article 132 (1) subparagraph 2 TEC (ex-Article 112), since the second stage mentioned there had been reached by then, (ii) deleted the articles already declared obsolete in Maastricht, and (iii) added a new paragraph 5 to Article 133 TEC (ex-Article 113), which opened up the possibility of including international negotiations and agreements on services and intellectual property.

After the ToA, the four remaining trade policy articles only underwent a profound change at the IGC 2000. The antagonism between free traders and protectionists was still palpable during this conference, whereby these

257 i.c. Article 111 by Title II, paragraph 27 ToM, Article 114 by Title II, paragraph 29 ToM, Article 116 by Title II, paragraph 31 ToM.

258 i.c. Article 113(1) first sentence TEEC/TEC, Article 113(3) last sentence (new) TEEC/TEC, Article 115 second subparagraph first sentence TEEC/TEC, Article 115 third subparagraph TEEC/TEC.

two positions were prominently represented by the United Kingdom on the one hand and France on the other.[259]

The changes made to the trade policy title by the ToN only affect Article 133 TEC, although quite profoundly. The history of the revision of Article 133 TEC in the course of the IGC 2000 can arguably be described as one of the most eventful in this conference. In any case, it was marked by the rejection of a majority of Member States to create the possibility of transferring Member State competences to the Community through an amendment by unanimous Council decision. Some delegations saw this as nothing more than a simplified form of treaty revision. Over a long period, the conference had a double proposal on the table, which dealt with a revision of Article 133 TEC on the one hand and a new protocol on the details of the participation of the European Union in the WTO's proceedings on the other. Finland had commented extensively on these issues in the conference and contributed to the revision of Article 133 TEC substantially. In a key document, Finland stated that the following points should be included in the considerations: (i) decisions on external relations should be taken unanimously in those matters where unanimity is also required for internal rules, (ii) those areas where harmonisation of laws and regulations of the Member States is excluded should not fall within the scope of the article, (iii) consistency of external actions with internal actions should be ensured, (iv) Member States retain the right to conclude agreements with third countries as long as these agreements do not impede the Common commercial policy, (v) with regard to intellectual property, only the commercial aspects of intellectual property should be covered, and (vi) investment should only concern direct investment, whereas investment in the areas of social services and culture should not be covered.

In the final version of the revised Article 133 TEC, the conference essentially came closer to the issues raised in the Finnish document. At first glance, Article 133 TEC, as amended by the ToN, would not appear to be suitable for solving the hitherto existing problems in the area of the

259 However, these different approaches were not only introduced to the Community by the United Kingdom's accession. Considering the wording of the TEEC, these conflicting positions were already present in the Founding Member States, as the wording of Article 110 of the TEEC clearly shows. On the one hand, the Member States aim to contribute to the harmonious development of world trade; on the other hand, the Common Commercial Policy is intended to reflect the common interests of the Member States. In short: common trade policy through liberalisation of the world market where it benefits the Member States.

Common Commercial Policy. The content of the previous paragraphs 1, 2, and 4, were kept unchanged with the same numbering. In paragraph 3, a requirement of coherence was included, according to which the Council and the Commission must ensure that negotiated agreements are compatible with the internal policies and regulations of the Community.

New - and controversial - was the first subparagraph of paragraph 5. Previously, the Council, acting unanimously on a proposal from the Commission and after consulting the Parliament, could extend the application of Article 133 TEC to international negotiations and agreements on services and intellectual property rights, insofar as these were not already covered by Article 133 TEC. The new paragraph 5, first subparagraph, extends the scope of application of paragraphs 1 to 4 in general to the negotiation and conclusion of agreements concerning trade in services and trade aspects of intellectual property, insofar as they are not already covered by the said paragraphs. Thus, qualified majority voting is also applicable to these areas. However, this general clause was subsequently massively restricted. Accordingly, qualified majority voting does not apply under the following conditions: (i) where agreements referred to in the first subparagraph of paragraph 5 contain provisions for which unanimity is required for the adoption of internal rules, (ii) where such an agreement concerns an area in which the Community has not yet exercised its competence under this Treaty when adopting internal rules, and (iii) where the agreement is of a horizontal nature, in so far as it concerns agreements relating to (a) trade in services, (b) trade aspects of intellectual property, (c) trade in cultural and audiovisual services, (d) services in the field of education, (e) the social and health fields, which fall within the shared competence of the Community and its Member States. Agreements (c) to (e) require a Community decision under Article 300 TEC and the consensual agreement of the Member States. France vehemently demanded and successfully claimed these massive exceptions in Article 133 TEC.[260]

As if that were not enough, the negotiation and conclusion of international agreements in the transport sector were generally excluded from the scope of Article 133 TEC. In addition, two safeguard clauses were added to Article 133 TEC, which were intended, on the one hand, not to restrict the sovereignty of the Member States too much (clause 1), whereby the

260 France was particularly concerned about her film industry, which she saw threatened by US productions.

antagonism between the Member States more inclined towards free trade and the Member States more inclined towards protectionism was once again documented here, and, on the other hand, it was to be prevented (clause 2) that a creeping expansion of Community competences could occur.[261]

The IGC 2007 radically modified the content of the Common Commercial Policy title. These changes are of a political nature on the one hand and of a technical one on the other. With regard to the politically motivated changes, the European Parliament was able to almost assert its demands completely: for one thing, the former codecision procedure, now the ordinary legislative procedure, was extended to trade policy and new control rights of the European Parliament during the drafting of mandates and the negotiation of international trade agreements were included. The Parliament had even more far-reaching ideas, such as an equal say throughout the negotiation process, but this demand was denied by the Member States. Nevertheless, the new opportunities for the Parliament turned out to be more far-reaching than the Member States had assessed, as the negotiations on CETA and TTIP impressively demonstrated.

In terms of content, the IGC 2007 opted to extend the scope of application, which now also includes trade agreements with aspects relating to intellectual property and foreign direct investment. It was precisely the gradual removal of restrictions on foreign direct investment that exposed traditional fault lines: protectionism was pitted against liberalisation. The liberalisers, however, were able to prevail with the argument of the necessary conformity with Article XXIV (5) a GATT. Whether conformity is achieved by the new wording in the TFEU remains to be seen, but the more protectionist Member States were not willing to go further. In addition to this issue, other problem areas also come to the fore: (i) How should the diverse and numerous bilateral trade agreements of the individual Member States with third countries be dealt with, are they in their entirety subject to exclusive Union competence as a result of this wording?, (ii) Do these agreements therefore have to be renegotiated or even revoked?

261 During the debate on the second clause, the IGC's opposition to such general clauses extending Community competences had become apparent. This position, which already dominated the domestic EU debate in Germany at that time, was advocated above all by the conservative-dominated federal states, as they feared being creepily robbed of their competences. The issue of the division of competences between the Union and the Member States was also to occupy a prominent position during the Convention and the IGC 2004.

One cannot assume that the Fathers of the ToL had rewritten the text in ignorance of these questions; on the contrary, it may be presumed that the indirect aim was to consolidate foreign trade relations.

II.3.4. Cooperation with Third Countries and Humanitarian Aid

II.3.4.1. Development Cooperation

Reference:	Part 5 Title III Chapter 1 Article 208 to 211 TFEU
Subject:	Developing a common policy in the field of development cooperation that complements the policies of the Member States concerned
Objectives:	Promoting the sustainable economic and social advancement of developing countries, in particular the most disadvantaged ones Harmonious, gradual integration of developing countries into the world economy Fight against poverty in developing countries
Principles:	Supporting the general objective of developing and consolidating democracy and the rule of law, while respecting human rights and fundamental freedoms Taking into account the objectives of development cooperation in the implementation of other Union policies insofar as they affect development cooperation Contribution of the Member States to the implementation of Union aid programmes
Instruments:	Coordination of Union and Member State development cooperation policies Coordination of the respective aid programmes Coordination of the approach to international organisations

The focus of the TEC towards international policies, in particular with regard to developing countries, was brought about by the ToM, which introduced this title into the Treaty. Even before the incorporation of development cooperation, the Community had been active in this field, based on Part 4, Association of Overseas Countries and Territories, but limited in territorial scope to these specific regions. The only way out of this territorial limitation was to invoke Articles 308 and 310 TEC. The Netherlands had unsuccessfully called for a separate title on development cooperation during the SEA negotiations. During the IGC 1991, the Dutch were finally able to get their way, this time being supported by Italy, Denmark, and the Commission. Nevertheless, the conference had been considering for some time integrating development cooperation not into the TEC but into the TEU, with the CFSP being identified as the appropriate anchor. However, the conference decided against this intention as this would have led to development cooperation being seen purely as a foreign policy instrument. The conference had assumed that the foreign policy effect would have been rather negative; furthermore, the Community had already understood and operated development cooperation as a development aid policy within the framework of international development law for some time. Luxembourg was able to provide the conference with a compromise document in the early stages of the negotiations. The principle of taking account of the objectives of development cooperation in the course of implementation of other Community policies, insofar as they affect development cooperation, emphasised the character of this title as a cross-sectional issue. The political-ideological determination of the Community's development cooperation policy - which in any case was to be understood as a radical departure from the colonial policy pursued in the past by various Member States - goes clearly and exclusively in the direction of recognising the states concerned as equal members of the international community, which are not to be regarded as dependent on the donor countries, so to avoid any comparison with colonial policy.

The IGC 1996, which led to the ToA, changed decision-making from unanimity to majority voting. The ToN did not affect the title of development cooperation.

Contrary to that, the ToL intervened massively in this subject area. The fundamental decision of the IGC 2007 was to remove this field from its original position and to embed it in the newly created Part 5 on the Union's external action. In doing so, this topic lost its independence as a title and is now integrated as chapter 1 of the title on Cooperation with Third Countries and Humanitarian Aid. With this decision, the IGC 2007 consistently stuck to its line of merging all provisions on external competences. The previous introductory Article 177 TEC was replaced by Article 208 TFEU with drastic changes. Whereas development cooperation under the Nice regime was still aimed at promoting the sustainable economic and social development of the countries concerned and the harmonious and gradual integration of these countries into the world economy, its new objective is the fight against and eradication of poverty in these countries. The IGC 2007 thus followed the IGC 2004, but in no way resolved those issues that had already arisen with the TCEU. On the one hand, the Union wanted to get away from the quasi-colonialist approach that was - allegedly - reflected in the rather paternalistic wording of the original objectives. On the other hand, however, the Union is deprived of any competence when it comes to questions of support for integration into the world economy. Prima facie, this competence has reverted to the exclusively bilateral sector, unless the term "main objective" is interpreted in extremis. In individual cases, such semantic sensitivities can lead to negative consequences that are not necessarily justified by the facts. The rest of the text of the TEC - apart from editorial changes - remained untouched. Fortunately, the cross-sectional nature was preserved.

II.3.4.2. Economic, Financial and Technical Cooperation with Third Countries

Reference: Part 5 Title III Chapter 2 Articles 212 and 213 TFEU

Subject: Legal basis for the conclusion of agreements with third countries

Objectives: Conclusion of agreements with third countries on economic, financial, and technical cooperation

Principles: Complementing the activities in the field of development cooperation
Compliance with the principle of equivalence with the Union's general development policy

Instruments: Agreements with third countries

This policy was only incorporated into primary law by the ToN. The rationale for the integration of this topic was based on the demand to the IGC 2000 that agreements on economic, financial, and technical cooperation with third countries should be concluded by QMV. Until the ToN, such agreements had been launched via the general clause of Article 308 TEC. Owing, among other things, to the fact that hardly any Member State was prepared to take decisions under Article 308 TEC by majority vote, the conferees sought a clean legal solution, as it were.

In addition, the Community could emphasise its increased commitment as a global player. However, the conference drafted this policy in such a way that, on the one hand, no duplication with the title of development cooperation could arise and, on the other hand, no limitation of the competence of the Member States at international level could be interpreted in this regard.

The IGC 2007 intervened in this area insofar as it removed it from the previous context - similar to development cooperation - and incorporated it into the foreign affairs part of the TFEU. The content of the former Article 181a TEC remained unchanged, apart from the fact that the distinction to development cooperation was formulated more clearly. The IGC 2007, though, went a decisive step further by creating a legal basis for emergency financial assistance. Article 213 TFEU, which has no corresponding article in the TEC, gives the Union a clear authorisation to act. This explicit financial authorisation to act is at the same time the transition to the also newly created Part 5 Title III Chapter 3 TFEU (humanitarian aid) which by its very nature requires financial resources. The entire field of cooperation with third countries is a product of the Member States' awareness that the Union will only be able to remain a global key player if it acts quickly and, above all, if it acts in unison.

II.3.4.3. Humanitarian Aid

Reference:	Part 5 Title III Chapter 3 Article 214 TFEU
Subject:	Humanitarian aid for third countries
Objectives:	Provision of ad hoc assistance, relief, and protection for people in third countries who are victims of natural or man-made disasters
Principles:	Mutual complementarity and reinforcement of the actions of the Union and the Member States
Instruments:	International cooperation European Voluntary Humanitarian Aid Corps

This chapter is a new element in primary law introduced by the ToL. The provision is the result of the political commitment to a robust engagement of the Union in this field. The Union had already provided humanitarian aid before the TFEU, so Article 214 TFEU has, as it were, a catch-up significance, which, however, must not be undervalued politically.

II.3.4.4. Restrictive Measures

Reference:	Part 5 Title IV Article 215 TFEU
Subject:	Imposing restrictive measures on third countries
Objectives:	Clarification of procedural issues

The provision embedded in Article 301 TEC, which became necessary in the course of the ToM due to the establishment of the foreign and security policy pillar, was embedded in the field of the Union's external action in the course of the IGC 2007, whereby no substantive change was made.

II.3.4.5. International Agreements

Reference:	Part 5 Title V Articles 216 to 219 TFEU
Subject:	Competences to conclude international treaties Impact of the treaties
Objectives:	Clarification of procedural issues

In the course of the IGC 2007, this subject area was separated from its previous and quite diverse contexts and merged into a single title. According to the previous case law of the European Court of Justice, the Union has the competence to conclude international agreements with third countries or international organisations if this is explicitly provided for in the Treaty or if the conclusion of an agreement within the framework of the Union's policy is either necessary to achieve one of the objectives laid down in the Treaty or provided for in a binding legal act of the Union. The new Title V is strictly in line with this case law and thus serves to strengthen legal certainty.

Article 216 TFEU reproduces the telos of Article 300(7) TEC and closely follows Article III-323 TCEU. The provision thus adapted anchors the binding effect of such agreements in primary law. Moreover, the provision clarifies that these agreements are binding legal acts of the Union and thus also take precedence over Member State law, even if they do not appear in the list of Article 288 TFEU. With regard to the embedding of such agreements in the tiered structure of EU law, they are therefore to be classified between primary and secondary law in the sense of the so-called mezzanine theory, as is already the case de lege lata.

Article 217 TFEU reproduces Article 310 TEC almost unchanged and merely replaces the term "state" with "third countries" and thus restricts the scope of application exclusively to non-EU countries.

Article 218 TFEU, like Article 300 TEC, describes the procedure for concluding international agreements, the suspension of such agreements, and the possibility of advisory opinions by the European Court of Justice. The previous paragraphs 1 to 7 and 9 to 11 were merely editorially and linguistically adapted by the IGC 2007, but paragraph 8 underwent two substantial innovations:

- Inclusion of a taxative list of those cases in which - by way of derogation from the first subparagraph - the unanimity requirement for Council decisions is established, whereby this list includes, inter alia, accession to the European Court of Human Rights (= ECHR);
- In addition to the listing of the ECHR Accession Agreement, it is further stipulated that this decision will only enter into force after the Member States have given their consent. As a result, this decision, like the decision to amend the Treaties in accordance with the simplified procedure pursuant to Article 48 (6) or (7) TEU, will be subject to the consent procedure under international law with no transfer of competences to the Union in this case either.

The section on ECHR once again shows the ambiguity of the IGC 2007. On the one hand, accession to the ECHR is presented as a given ("...accedes ..."), on the other hand, a double approval procedure by the Member States is required. Although a binding effect on the Member State parliaments cannot be derived from the objective, it is nevertheless in contradiction to the free mandate. Despite these antagonisms, the IGC 2007 opted for the political variant in the general programmatic introductory section and only regulates the procedure later, the exact study of which makes the impossibility of rapid accession apparent.

Article 219 TFEU takes up the provisions of Article 111 (1) to (3) and (5) TEC and deals with questions concerning monetary agreements. The ToL made no change to the content.

II.3.4.6. The Union's Relations with International Organisations and Third Countries and Union Delegations

Reference: Part 5 Title VI Article 220 and 221 TFEU

Subject: Regulating cooperation with international organisations

Objectives: Clarification of procedural issues, i.a. the position of Union delegations

Originally, the Community's relations with international organisations were addressed at the very end of the TEC in the so-called General Provisions laid down in Articles 302 to 304 TEC, with Article 302 TEC regulating relations with the United Nations and all other international organisations, Article 303 TEC dealing with cooperation with the Council of Europe, and Article 304 TEC stipulating that the Community shall establish close cooperation with the OECD.

In the ToL - following the approach of the IGC 2004 in Articles III-327 and III-328 TCEU - these three articles have been merged into a single new Article 220 TFEU, with all three former articles now forming a single paragraph. The new paragraph 2 states that the implementation of this article is the sole responsibility of the High Representative of the Union for Foreign Affairs and Security Policy and the Commission. The changes made clearly show the handwriting of the integrationists. It is no longer the Commission that maintains relations with the United Nations and other international organisations, but the Union itself. In the case of the other two organisations, the term Community is simply replaced by Union. The Union is thus declared the unambiguous authority for all relations with other international organisations. The Commission thereby loses its previous general competence for these activities. The Commission remains responsible for external economic affairs, while the High Representative is responsible for relations in the field of the Common Foreign and Security Policy.

The newly added Article 221 TFEU has no corresponding provision in primary law de lege lata, but is an original addition by the ToL, editorially adapting and updating Article III-328 TCEU. The background to this provision, which in itself does not appear to be spectacular, was already one of the most controversial areas of the negotiations during the IGC 2004; the sometimes very emotional debates continued seamlessly in the IGC 2007. The main question was to whom these delegations - which are now vaguely labelled as EU embassies in legal terms - should ultimately be answerable.

The Commission insisted on continuing to exercise this sovereignty, not least with the historically justified argument that these were the former Commission delegations. The solution may sound Solomonic, but it is only so to a limited extent. The High Representative, as the supreme authority of the European External Action Service, is the source of directives, exercising his/her right to issue such directives vis-à-vis the Head of Delegation. The Commission, however, continues to have direct technical access to the Commission staff seconded to the delegations not active in the area of the Common Foreign and Security Policy; these staff members exclusively report to the Head of Delegation in matters of protocol. This also weakened the position of the Head of Delegation - at least indirectly - as he/she cannot exert any influence on the work of these seconded Commission officials. This reveals a new phenomenon: supranational does not equal supranational. The Commission pays strict attention to its (sphere of) influence and defends it vigorously, with the support of those Member States that want to avoid subordinating further EU policies to foreign policy.

The second sentence of paragraph 2, which states that the delegations will work in close cooperation with the diplomatic and consular missions, is also ambiguous. In principle, delegations are not called upon to carry out consular tasks, such as passport management or the issuing of visas. At both IGCs, some Member States were clearly opposed to such assignments, whereas other Member States did not want to rule out this development for the future. At present, it is not possible to give a clear answer as to the direction to be taken, but it should be borne in mind that, as a rule, options will be taken at some point; the nucleus for joint diplomatic missions and, where appropriate, the merging of Member States' embassies into these delegations is certainly in place.

II.3.4.7. Solidarity Clause

Reference:	Part 5 Title VII Article 222 TFEU
Subject:	Support during terrorist attacks and disasters Assistance clause
Objectives:	Mobilisation of all the instruments at the Union's disposal, including the military resources made available by the Member States Assisting a Member State in its territory at the request of its political authorities in the event of a natural or man-made disaster
Principles:	Joint action of the Union and its Member States in a spirit of solidarity
Instruments:	Regular assessment of the threats facing the Union Unspecified instruments at the disposal of the Union, including the military resources made available by the Member States

The IGC 2004 endorsed the proposals of the Convention to introduce such a clause into primary law (Article I-43 and Article III-329 TCEU). The literature describes this clause, which was updated and only editorially adapted by the IGC 2007, as an original provision that is completely new in primary law. While this radical statement is formally correct, Article 2 TEC already specified the promotion of solidarity between Member States as an objective of the Community. Accordingly, solidarity was not provided for as a task of the Community, but it did exist as a basic principle. Just as the Union Minister for Foreign Affairs (now: High Representative) is a child of event-driven legislation, the solidarity clause is also a reaction to the attacks of 11 September 2001 in New York and Washington, DC, on the one hand, and the attack in Madrid of 11 March 2004 on the other.

The Convention still had a holistic approach in that it wanted to anchor a comprehensive solidarity and assistance clause, which, however, seemed to some Member States to be one-sidedly military. Accordingly, it was divided into (i) a (military) assistance clause under Article 42(7) TEU in the event of an armed attack on a Member State and (ii) a solidarity clause in the event of a terrorist attack, natural disaster, or man-made catastrophe. However, this distinction is not entirely clear-cut since military means are also part of the support instruments in the solidarity case. However, support is only granted at the request of the affected Member State. Especially neutral states like Austria received additional reassurance in the form of Declaration No. 37, which underlines the right of a Member State to choose the most appropriate means to fulfil its obligations. The Union can therefore under no circumstances force Member States to provide certain assistance by means of a Council decision. However, this particular freedom of choice of means does not conflict with the obligation of solidarity and is not likely to undermine this obligation.

II.4. Enhanced Cooperation

Enhanced cooperation was introduced into primary law by the Member States in order to enable cooperation at Community level in areas where there was no exclusive Community competence.

With this political mechanism, a kind of graduated integration was achieved which, on the one hand, is only authorised at the level of secondary law and, accordingly, is not capable of transferring competences to the Union in a covert manner.

The introduction of the title of enhanced cooperation was one of the major adaptations of the TEU by the IGC 1996. Due to the complete reorganisation of this thematic complex in the course of the IGC 2007, this chapter is divided into two sections, one dealing with the provisions laid down in the TEU, the other addressing the provisions laid down in the TFEU.

II.4.1. Enhanced Cooperation as laid down in the TEU

Reference:	Title IV Article 20 TEU
Subject:	Measures of enhanced integration of some Member States under the Treaty
Objectives:	Promoting the objectives of the Union Strengthening the integration process
Principles:	Compliance with the principles of primary law Ultima ratio Non-impairment of the acquis communautaire Non-impairment of trade between Member States
Instruments:	Unspecified actions

Development up to the Treaty of Nice

Enhanced cooperation represented a further development of what had become known as flexibility but was considered inopportune in that it could have been equated with the negatively connoted term "differentiated integration"aka multi-speed Europe. The IGC 1996 provided an institutional framework for these concepts and was intended to enable more integration-minded Member States to take such steps within the framework of primary law. Although the debates were already rather heated in Amsterdam before this title could be agreed upon, no use was made of enhanced cooperation following the entry into force of the ToA.

Nevertheless, enhanced cooperation was at the centre of the IGC 2000 deliberations from the very beginning. Despite the fact that this title could almost be described as dead letter as the Member States never made use of it, it was nevertheless considered a necessary instrument for further development. The IGC 2000 was confronted with two schools of thought. One school of thought did not want to re-discuss the title and wanted it to remain unchanged, but a minority of Member States - at least at the beginning of the conference - were in favour of a revision aimed at removing obstacles to its applicability. Those who were sceptical about enhanced cooperation in any respect even at the IGC 2000 were countered by the latter group that - from a purely technical point of view - Article 306 TEC (ex-Article 233) had already allowed for such models. The Portuguese

Presidency, however, felt compelled to declare enhanced cooperation as a conference item. Portugal may even have felt obliged to take the bull by the horns, since some Member States had indirectly expressed their wish to be able to take integrationalist steps outside primary law, if necessary, in cases where the Treaties did not provide for this. Already in the first rounds of negotiations, the Commission proposed to remove the quasi-veto of an opposing Member State and some Member States wanted to lower the threshold for establishing enhanced cooperation. The United Kingdom, Finland, and Greece, however, remained sceptical and justified this, among other things, with the fact that not a single field of application had yet been identified and it would therefore be kind of shot in the dark. Although support from the Benelux countries and Italy was rather cautious, Portugal stuck to its line and kept enhanced cooperation on the agenda, supported in particular by French President Chirac and German Foreign Minister Fischer. France, as successor to the Portuguese Presidency, took a more offensive approach to the issue, proposing that enhanced cooperation should be uniform across the three pillars, thus creating a general approach to improved integration. France mainly relied on the initial opinion of the Commission, in which it had had argued that "the character of the forthcoming enlargement justifies making these new provisions [on enhanced cooperation] as practicable as possible. The greater diversity within a larger Union must not be allowed to stand in the way of the wishes of some members to make use of the Union's institutional framework to cooperate more closely together".[262] France subsequently received massive support from Germany and Belgium in particular, both of whom reiterated that in a Europe of up to twenty-eight Member States, it would be essential to enable those Member States that wished to be the first to proceed along the path of integration to do so, while respecting the single institutional framework and the rules in force. When the United Kingdom, Spain and Austria also joined the supporters of a radical reform, the French Presidency was in a position to present a completely new approach to enhanced cooperation to the intergovernmental conference in Nice and finally to obtain its approval.

262 European Commission: Adapting the Institutions to Make a Success of Enlargement - Commission Opinion in accordance with Article 48 of the Treaty on European Union on the calling of a Conference of Representatives of the Governments of the Member State to amend the Treaties, COM(2000) 34 final, Brussels, 26.1.2000, p 32. The very document was republished as document of the IGC 2000 on 1 February 2000 as CONFER 4701/00.

The most important elements of enhanced cooperation in the TEU as amended by the ToN are based on the fact that it must be (i) the ultima ratio (Article 43a TEU), (ii) open to all Member States when it is established (Article 43b TEU), and (iii) carried out within the institutional framework of the Union. Moreover, it shall have the objective of enabling the Union to develop more rapidly into an area of freedom, security and justice, while respecting the competences of the European Union and the objectives of Titles V and VI TEU (Article 40 TEU). Eight Member States must meet in order to pass the threshold, whereby the authorisation is granted by the Council with a qualified majority and without an opposing Member State being able to veto (Article 40a (1) TEU). The participating Member States must intend to strengthen the integration process within the meaning of Article 43 (a) TEU. The Commission and the Member States involved in enhanced cooperation are called upon to ensure that as many Member States as possible are encouraged to participate (Article 43b TEU). However, the TEU explicitly stipulates that legal acts and decisions pursuant to Article 44 TEU are not part of the acquis communautaire. The financing of enhanced cooperation from resources other than those of the participating Member States can - as before - be decided unanimously by all Council members. What is new, however, is the requirement of prior consultation of the European Parliament (Article 44a TEU).

Transformation by the Treaty of Lisbon

The IGC 2004 was already aware that the preconditions for the implementation of enhanced cooperation were too narrow and too inflexible to breathe life into this instrument. In particular, the IGC 2004 did not want to adhere to the previous restriction according to which such cooperation would not applicable in the area of security and defence policy. The IGC 2007 essentially followed the approach of the Convention and the IGC 2004 and eventually removed this restriction. In one essential point, however, the IGC 2007 deviated from the IGC 2004. The latter had still provided for the flexible system of one third of the Member States. Yet the IGC 2007 assumed that this could be too high a threshold for future enlargements and agreed on nine Member States as threshold. In doing so, the IGC 2007 aimed to ensure that this instrument would not become dead letter again from the outset; in particular, it had anticipated the discussions that would have been triggered if the number of Member States had not been divisible by three.

In consistent implementation of the objective of regulating the general provisions in the TEU and the related provisions in the TFEU, the IGC 2007 divided the regulations on enhanced cooperation into a general part (Article 20 TEU new) and the implementing provisions (Articles 326 to 334 TFEU).

II.4.2. Enhanced Cooperation as laid down in the TFEU

Reference:	Part 6 Title III Article 326 to 334 TFEU
Subject:	Measures of enhanced integration of some Member States under the Treaty
Objectives:	Strengthening the integration of part of the Member States
Principles:	Limitation to a faster achievement of the Union's objectives No overstepping of the powers conferred by the Treaty No interference with intra-Union trade and no distortion of competition No interference with Union policies, actions and programmes No link with citizenship of the Union No discrimination between nationals of Member States Permissible only if authorised by the Council
Instruments:	Unspecified actions

Development up to the Treaty of Nice

The ToA introduced a completely new element into the TEC by means of enhanced cooperation. The IGC 1996 had been aware that with the rigid limits of the Treaty a dynamic further development of integration would hardly be possible, so that the Community could only progress at the speed that the slowest - which would actually be the most non-integration-friendly - Member State would allow. Article 11 TEC as amended by the ToA was the subject of tough and controversial negotiations and ultimately had to accommodate all, even the most hesitant Member States. Accordingly, its wording was complicated and complex. In Amsterdam, a safeguard clause was added to the enhanced cooperation, which made it possible for a Member State that wanted to oppose such cooperation to prevent it de facto by means of a simple communication. Under the ToA, an opposing Member State only had to remonstrate in order for the European Council to deal with the matter; since this body only takes decisions unanimously, notification by the opposing Member State was sufficient.

The experiences between Amsterdam and Nice on the one hand, and the forthcoming enlargement on the other, led to a revision of Article 11 TEC by the IGC 2000. During the IGC 2000, a wide variety of models were discussed, some of which were more far-reaching, but some of which were even more restrictive. In the end, the conference agreed on a wording which, on the one hand, radically shortened the original Article 11 and made it more readable and, on the other hand, added a new Article 11a. The wording of Article 11(1) TEC as amended by the ToN is strongly based on the relevant provisions of the TEU. The original version of the Council of Ministers in its formation of Heads of State and Government was replaced by the referral to the European Council and thus the Commission was also - formally - involved in the development of enhanced cooperation, since the President of the Commission is a member of the European Council. The safeguard clause of the ToA has been dropped by the ToN, which has caused lasting concern, especially among Eurosceptics in the United Kingdom. However, Article 11 (3) TEC as amended by the ToN - as it were to calm the sceptics - stipulated that closer cooperation can only take place within the limits of the TEC. The new Article 11a TEC introduced by the ToN takes up the former Article 11 (3) TEC as amended by the ToA. The new version of Article 11 TEC was also the subject of the campaign for the Irish referendum on the ToN. However, the Heads of State and Government agreed to not renegotiate this provision, as a new package solution that would have satisfied all sides was not on the horizon.

Transformation by the Treaty of Lisbon

The IGC 2007 assigned a specific title to this subject area thus formally emphasising the importance of enhanced cooperation. In conjunction with the above-mentioned Article 20 TEU, the provisions of Articles 326 to 334 TFEU replace Articles 27a to 27e, 40 to 40b and 43 to 45 TEU, as amended by the ToN, as well as Articles 11 and 11a TEC. The IGC 2007 introduced a number of substantive innovations, above all it brought together the provisions that had been scattered in the most diverse places of primary law.

Article 326 TFEU essentially reproduces ex-Article 43(1) TEU and presents it in a more compact form, whereby the preconditions and limits for enhanced cooperation remain unchanged. The reference to full respect for primary law continues to serve as a general barrier; in terms of content, the following four barriers apply: (i) Common Market and cohesion barrier, (ii) trade barrier, (iii) discrimination barrier, (iv) competition barrier. The inclusion of cohesion, which is the only new provision, was based on the corresponding adaptation of the cohesion provisions by the IGC 2007.

Article 327 TFEU is a further compact update of ex-Article 43 TEU.

Article 328 TFEU reproduces parts of Article 43 and Article 45 TEU but introduces two new elements. In order to break up the implicit closed-shop system, the participating Member States and the Commission are now obliged to ensure and promote that as many Member States as possible participate. On the one hand, this provision has a positive underpinning (keyword: promotion), but on the other hand it expresses the fear that a multi-speed Union could emerge (keyword: closed shop). The second innovation relates to the question of who must inform whom; here the Council becomes the informed party, which can be seen as a downgrade, whereas its former task being taken over by the High Representative, thus upgrading this position.

Article 329 TFEU builds on Article 10 TEU and supplements it by introducing detailed provisions for the authorisation to establish enhanced cooperation. Above all, the three different procedures (First Pillar - Article 11 TEC, Second Pillar - Article 27c TEU, Third Pillar - Article 40a TEU) are merged into a single uniform procedure. However, the IGC 2007 had to take into account the concerns of some Member State and include a derogation from this uniform system for the area of the Common Foreign and Security Policy, including the Common Security and Defence Policy, in paragraph 2.

Article 330 TFEU is a classic implementing provision that describes the actual rules to be applied.

Article 331 TFEU essentially reproduces the procedure of Article 11a TEC. Here too, the restriction of Article 329 TFEU applies, so the uniform procedure applies to all areas except the Common Foreign and Security Policy, including the Common Security and Defence Policy.

Article 332 TFEU reproduces (editorially adapted) Article 44a TEU.

Article 333 TFEU introduces a passerelle clause in favour of the transition from unanimity to the ordinary legislative procedure. This clause is clearly to be regarded as a flexibility instrument and had already been provided for by the IGC 2004.

Article 334 TFEU reproduces the editorially adapted ex-Article 45 TEU.

II.5. Internal Market and Free Movement of Goods

Reference:	Part 3 Title I Article 26 and 27, Title II Article 28 to 37 TFEU
Subject:	Ensuring the free movement of goods
Objectives:	Removal of all relevant barriers, be they non-tariff, physical, or technical in nature
Principles:	Mutual recognition Recognition of minimum standards
Instruments:	Harmonisation of standards, whereby minimum standards are defined in principle Establishing basic safety regulations for products

Prior to the ToA's radical restructuring of this title, which was at the heart of the TEC, the free movement of goods was governed by no less than thirty articles. This fundamental restructuring suggests that it is necessary to recall the Maastricht structure[263] and, building on this structure, to describe the changes of the Amsterdam era, with the numbering in brackets in the following column referring to the TFEU as amended by the ToL.[264]

For structural reasons, Article 135 TEC was brought forward in the course of the IGC 2007 and Article 33 TFEU was inserted into this title as Chapter 2. Furthermore, Articles 14 and 15 TEC were placed before the entire Title I as Articles 26 and 27 TFEU in order to combine all articles relevant to the Internal Market in a single title.

ex-Article^X	Content	ToA	Article^Y
7a	Common Market		14 (26)
7c	Exemptions		15 (27)
9	Customs Union	modified	23 (28)

263 Marked with X in the following overview.

264 Marked with Y in the following overview.

ex-Article[X]	Content	ToA	Article[Y]
10	Free movement of goods coming from third countries	modified	24 (29)
11	Member States' measures	repealed	
12	No new tariffs or increases	modified	25 (39)
13	Gradual abolition of import duties	repealed	
14	Starting point for tariff, timing and level of reduction	repealed	
15	Further reduction	repealed	
16	Abolition of export duties	repealed	
17	Financial tariffs	repealed	
18	Agreement on the reduction of customs duties	repealed	
19	Common Customs Tariff from the simple expedient	repealed	
20	Tariff rates for products in list G	repealed	
21	Directives to remedy technical difficulties and adjustment measures	repealed	
21	Directives to remedy technical difficulties and adjustment measures	repealed	
22	Inclusion of financial tariffs	repealed	
23	Modification of tariff rates vis-à-vis third countries	repealed	
24	Accelerate alignment with the Common Customs Tariff	repealed	
25	Granting of tariff quotas at lower rates of duty	repealed	
26	Postponement of adjustment	repealed	
27	Approximation of laws, regulations and administrative provisions	repealed	
28	Autonomous amendments to suspensions of Common Customs Tariff rates	modified[265]	26 (31)
29	Tasks of the Commission	modified	27 (32)
116	Customs cooperation		135 (33)
30	Prohibition of quantitative restrictions between Member States	modified	28 (34)
31	No new quantitative restrictions; liberalisation	repealed	

265 This article has already been subjected to a first change by the SEA.

ex-Article[X]	Content	ToA	Article[Y]
32	No further restriction of quotas, but abolition	repealed	
33	Creation and increase of global quotas	repealed	
34	Prohibition of quantitative restrictions on exports	modified	29 (35)
35	Faster removal of import and export restrictions	repealed	
36	Exemptions	modified	30 (36)
37	Treatment of state trading monopolies	modified	31 (37)

The Internal Market provisions, which concern not only a core of the entire primary law, but the nucleus of the former EEC, have been subject to multiple and sometimes radical changes since the ToM. However, the most recent amendments by the ToL - in addition to the changes in content - finally led to the entire Internal Market complex being governed by a single title and thus to the creation of a compact section. Above all, it was placed at the beginning of Part 3. Following this programmatic orientation, the IGC 2007 moved two articles of the former Part 1 TEC, namely Articles 14 and 15, to the Internal Market title in order to include the provisions establishing the Internal Market in the title in question. Article 26 TFEU (ex-Article 14 TEC), which introduces the new Title I Part 3, was merely given a reworded paragraph 1, since the Internal Market was already established at that time. Article 27 TFEU (ex-Article 15 TEC) was also reproduced unchanged, except for editorial adaptations. Otherwise, the ToL did not interfere further with the Internal Market provisions, except in Article 33 TFEU (ex-Article 135 TEC) where Council and Parliament are now declared joint legislators.

However, the most significant changes of a substantive nature were made by the ToA. Even the programmatic headings of the repealed articles allow a conclusion on the reason for their declaration of obsolescence: they simply had become outdated in the course of time. In other words, the IGC 1996 did not necessarily have to be innovative in terms of content, but merely had to check which articles were already to be regarded as fulfilled on the grounds of the deadlines on which they were based. It is nevertheless of the utmost interest to know what world of ideas the Founding Fathers had in mind when they drafted the preconditions for the Internal Market with regard to the free movement of goods. The very structure of Title I Part 3, shows that the primary instrument for ensuring the free movement of goods is the establishment of a customs union in which properly imported goods may circulate freely.

The first two articles of the original provisions were - inevitably - taken over unchanged by the ToA, while the third article could be repealed, since the deadline for the establishment of the Customs Union had been met and the Member States accordingly no longer had to make such arrangements. In the following chapter, which describes the Customs Union in greater detail, the pre-Amsterdam text had contained regulations that served to eliminate customs duties among the Member States and to establish a Common Customs Tariff. The ToA took over only ex-Articles 12 (= Article 25), 28 (= Article 26), and 29 (= Article 27) of this set of provisions. The content of these articles had to be revised accordingly. Whereas ex-Article 25 still required Member States to refrain from introducing new import or export duties and charges having equivalent effect or from increasing those applied in their mutual trade relations, Article 25 as amended by the ToA succinctly stipulates that import and export duties or charges having equivalent effect are prohibited between Member States, as are financial duties. Before the IGC 1996, as already pointed out, the meticulously defined steps to achieve the customs union had become obsolete and the IGC was therefore able to repeal these articles. Ex-Article 28, which was also kept in force, had already been amended by the SEA and underwent a further revision by the ToA. However, this essentially represents a simplification of the text - probably also due to the repeal of the preceding articles - and henceforth stipulates that the Council, acting by a qualified majority on a proposal from the Commission, shall determine the rates of the Common Customs Tariff.[266] It is remarkable that neither at the IGC 1996 nor at the IGC 2000 the European Parliament was involved in such decisions, not even by simple consultation. The amendment of ex-Article 29 is limited to the wording but does not affect any substantive issues.

The second chapter of Title I, which deals with the prohibition of quantitative restrictions between Member States, has not been changed as radically as the first one, but merely shortened from seven to four articles. The current Article 28 (ex-Article 30), which was referred to by the European Court of Justice in its judgement in the case Commission v. France as an indispensable instrument for the Internal Market on the basis of its provi-

266 Initially, such Council decisions referred to all autonomous amendments or suspensions of the Common Customs Tariff.

sion that all quantitative restrictions on imports and all measures having equivalent effect are prohibited between Member States, has only been simplified compared to its original wording, the tenor remaining unchanged.[267] The repeal of the following pre-Amsterdam articles follows the logic and justification that had led to the repeal of the articles in Chapter 1 already mentioned. Article 30 in its current version is the unchanged continuation of ex-Article 36. The final Article 31 of the Title Free Movement of Goods was also repeated almost unchanged; due to the repeal of the Articles of Chapter 1, the part concerning the - previously necessary - removal of customs duties and quantitative restrictions between the Member States was reworded to the extent that it now refers to a prohibition.

In conclusion, it can be said that the pre-Amsterdam era was more concerned with the establishment of the Customs Union as a necessary precondition for the Single Market than the post-Amsterdam era. The title Free Movement of Goods was from then on more dedicated to the prohibition of possible barriers, not so much to the removal of such barriers. The IGC 2000 had not seen any reason to take up this title during the entire deliberations. Apart from editorial adaptations and the consolidation of all relevant provisions, the ToL did not change the content of this thematic complex.

267 Cf. https://curia.europa.eu/juris/document/document.jsf?docid=43536&doclang=EN, esp. recital 28.

II.6. Agriculture and Fisheries

Reference:	Part 3 Title III Article 38 to 44 TFEU
Subject:	Establishment and safeguarding of a Common Agricultural Policy (CAP)
Objectives:	In principle, the CAP aims to achieve the following five objectives: • Increasing agricultural production through modernisation • Ensuring fair living conditions for farmers • Stabilising markets • Ensuring the availability of agricultural products • Ensuring comprehensible consumer prices
Principles:	Market unity (through freedom of movement for agricultural products in a common market). Community preference (by giving preference - in principle - to products produced in the Community) Financial solidarity (through a common agricultural budget) Shared responsibility (through burden sharing by all farmers in the Community)
Instruments:	Common Market Organisations (which support freedom of movement, price structures, financial solidarity, through (i) common competition rules, coordination of the different national market organisations, a single European Market Organisation, (ii) price regulations, support for production, marketing, storage and transport, and (iii) a common mechanism to stabilise imports and exports) Price support mechanisms Agrimonetary instruments Financial instruments[268]

The provisions concerning agriculture were originally regulated in Part 2 Title II TEEC, containing the foundations of the Community. This allocation can very well be considered programmatic and gave agricultural policy a distinctive position in the structure of the Treaty. If the name of the Treaty were more likely to suggest that it was an economic community, the

268 i.e. European Agricultural Guidance and Guarantee Fund (EAGGF).

founding states wanted to give agricultural policy its own importance by placing it so prominently.

Left as unaffected by the ToM as it was by the SEA, the agricultural title underwent its first radical change with the ToA.[269]

The most important changes were the deletion of ex-Articles 44 [minimum price systems], 45 [agreement on the removal of all discrimination], and 47 [group on agriculture of the EESC] TEC. The deletion of these articles was based on the fact that they dealt with matters that had become obsolete with the creation of the Customs Union, the CAP, and the organisation of the EESC. However, in order to clearly safeguard and reflect the previous decisions of the Court of Justice on ex-Article 44 TEC, the IGC 1996 adopted Declaration No. 14 on the repeal of Article 44 as amended by the TEEC, which served as an assurance that the case law that developed from this article would not be called into question. The deletion of ex-Article 47 TEC was justified by the conference on the grounds that the EESC should be granted greater flexibility with regard to its organisation.[270]

The remaining amendments served primarily to simplify the legal text without derogating from its original content. The deletion of the second sentence in ex-Article 38 TEC, which dealt with the decision on the extension of the list of agricultural products covered by the agricultural title, had been superseded by the decisions taken in the meantime and its deletion was intended to allow more flexibility for future decisions.[271] The adaptation of ex-Article 40 TEC (common organisation of agricultural markets) caused the deletion of paragraph 1, that had called on the Member States to develop the CAP progressively, which had already been accomplished by the time of the ToA. The adaptation of ex-Article 43 TEC concerned the fact that the original Treaty provided that during the first two stages of the development of the CAP the Council should adopt the necessary legal acts unanimously on a proposal from the Commission. Since this had become obsolete, this provision could be deleted without replacement.

---

269 Ex-Articles 38 to 47 TEC became Articles 32 to 38 TEC, with ex-Articles 44, 45 and 47 deleted without replacement.

270 The conference thus followed the legitimate intervention of the EESC, having been able to credibly demonstrate that this restriction on its self-organisation was not substantiated in factual and technical terms. The lifting of this restriction had thus ended an anomaly in the Treaty that was difficult to argue from the outset.

271 The conference came to the correct conclusion that the Commission's right to propose such decisions was to be interpreted as an obligation anyway and accordingly did not have to be explicitly laid down in primary law but was an inherent part of the system.

The provisions on agriculture did not change substantially over the years, as the various IGCs had concluded that they did not want to open this notorious Pandora's box. The Heads of State and Government, however, were fully aware of the ever louder criticism of the CAP and chose an indirect way to improve the situation. The alleged negative environmental impacts of the CAP were at the centre of criticism. It was precisely this criticism that led to the drafting of the SEA, in particular the introduction of environmental policy, and the strengthening of environmental concerns in the course of the IGC 1996. But criticism against the CAP also came from animal welfare NGOs and culminated in Declaration No. 24 to the TEU. Despite this success, it must be noted that this declaration is not only of a purely declaratory nature from a legal point of view but has also hardly led to any tangible consequences in the decisions of the institutions. The IGC 1996 - under massive pressure from animal protection and environmental NGOs - took up this issue again and adopted Protocol No. 24 to the TEC on the protection and welfare of animals.[272]

The IGC 2000 came to the conclusion that the previous regulations, protocols, and declarations were sufficient and thus left the entire agriculture complex untouched. The same applies mutatis mutandis to the IGC 2007. The ToL moved the agriculture title one place backwards, added the term fisheries to the title, but changed the content of the title only to the extent that was necessary due to the general application of the ordinary legislative procedure to this part as well. The change in the numbering of the articles was purely editorial. However, animal welfare was included as a cross-sectional issue in Article 13 TFEU.

272 Although this protocol is similar to Declaration No. 24, it turns the former request into an obligation to take animal welfare into account. In addition, however, this protocol contains a restrictive reference to taking into account the laws, regulations, and practices of the Member States, in particular with regard to religious rites, cultural traditions, and religious heritage. So far, this protocol has not contributed much to the improvement of animal welfare either. However, the reference to the consideration of Member State circumstances could become even more important in view of possible future enlargements of the Union.

II.7. Free Movement of Persons, Services and Capital

II.7.1. Workers

Reference:	Part 3 Title IV Chapter 1 Article 45 to 48 TFEU
Subject:	Ensuring the free movement of persons
Objectives:	Unrestricted freedom of movement within the Union Unrestricted exercise of profession within the Union
Principles:	Member States may refuse entry and/or establishment only for extraordinary reasons
Instruments:	Regulations that guarantee the harmonious development of the labour market and prevent distortions of competition Rules laying down the conditions of admission of nationals of other Member States, which may include, where appropriate, rules on the harmonisation or coordination of social security legislation

With Part 3 Title III Chapter 1 TEC - now Part 3 Title IV Chapter 1 TFEU - the Treaty, after having dealt with agriculture in the previous title, returns to the market economy aspect and regulates the remaining three freedoms, which are a constitutive element of the Common Market.

The first chapter deals with the issue of workers. The basic principles of the free movement of workers enshrined in Article 39 (ex-Article 48) TEC, now Article 45 TFEU, were adapted for the first time by the ToA. The original wording that the free movement of workers within the Community shall be established at the latest by the end of the transitional period until the establishment of the Internal Market, was replaced by the statement that this particular free movement is guaranteed. The IGC 1996 thus implemented in text - and in law - what had been brought about by the passage of time and legislation. The introductory article remained unchanged in the course of IGC 2007.

The following Article 40 TEC (ex-Article 49, now Article 46 TFEU), addressing measures to establish freedom of movement, was amended for the first time by Article 6(3) SEA. Following the systematic of the SEA, the legislative procedure was adapted and from now on the Council had to decide by qualified majority on a proposal from the Commission in cooperation with the European Parliament and after consulting the EESC. The same passage was amended again by the ToM, in that the codecision procedure was applied instead of the cooperation procedure. The amendment by the ToA has essentially a linguistic background without affecting the content, the same applies to the IGC 2007. Article 41 TEC (ex-Article 50, now Article 47 TFEU), which deals with the exchange of young workers, has remained exempt from any amendment so far.

The concluding article of Chapter 1 - Article 42 TEC (ex-Article 51), now Article 48 TFEU - which deals with the system of guaranteeing rights and benefits, was thoroughly revised for the first time by the IGC 1996 with regard to the decision-making procedure by switching to codecision. The ToL includes the self-employed in the group of persons concerned but maintains the previous position of the Member States that third-country nationals and non-active persons should not be covered by this provision in the future either.[273] With this restraint, the IGC 2007 had already anticipated the debates of 2015, when hundreds of thousands of people attempted to migrate to the Union through the unexpected influx of refugees. The amendment that is certainly more far-reaching is the addition of paragraph 2. After the ordinary legislative procedure is also applied in this area, the IGC 2007 takes up the text of the failed Constitutional Treaty and introduces a reflection mechanism into the TFEU to ensure that substantial concerns of a Member State must be observed. This observation is far-reaching, as it leads to the ordinary legislative procedure being suspended. This derogation was further secured by Declaration No. 22, as it had been made a conditio sine qua non by some Member States at both the IGC 2004 and the IGC 2007 in order to preserve the highest degree of national sovereignty in this area and to prevent or at least discourage the feared migration to more developed social systems.[274]

---

273 The so-called Residency Directives of the early 1990s, granting residence rights to certain groups of people by stipulating that one must not be a worker or economically active, but economically self-sufficient, remain unaffected (e.g. Directives 90/365 (pensioners/retired workers), 93/96 (students), 90/364 (all others), the first known as "Pensioners Directive", the latter known as "Playboy Directive").

274 Even this arrangement did not seem sufficient to PM David Cameron, who claimed additional exceptions for the UK in the run-up to the EU referendum scheduled for June 2016. Among other things, Mr Cameron demanded that the British pound be permanently protected from being scrapped in favour of the euro and that the ever-closer-union clause should not apply, at least to the UK; the list of exceptions also included a safeguard clause in favour of the City of London.

II.7.2. Right of Establishment

Reference:	Part 3 Title IV Chapter 2 Article 49 to 55 TFEU
Subject:	Ensuring the freedom of establishment
Objectives:	Unrestricted freedom of establishment of Union citizens within Union territory Unrestricted freedom of establishment within the Union for companies established in accordance with the law of a Member State if they have either (i) their registered office, (ii) their central administration, or (iii) their principal place of business within the Union
Principles:	Right to self-employment General prohibition of discrimination General prohibition of restrictions
Instruments:	Guidelines for establishment Promotion of the development of production and trade Coordination of the protection of companies (e.g. harmonisation of European company law and adoption of company law directives)

In its original wording, the TEEC provided for a total of seven articles dealing with the Freedom of Establishment (= ex-Articles 52 to 58). On the one hand, the Freedom of Establishment covers the area of establishment of companies, on the other hand, it complements the right to Freedom of Movement for natural persons by also enabling self-employed persons to access the market in Member States other than their own. The ECJ interprets this right of establishment as the effective pursuit of an economic activity through an establishment for an indefinite period.

Ex-Article 52 TEC (= Article 43, now Article 49 TFEU) was adapted for the first time by the ToA and henceforth states succinctly that subject-matter restrictions are prohibited insofar as the Treaty so provides. The original wording had become obsolete because the transitional period for the creation of the Single Market had already expired.

Due to the expiry of this transitional period, the entire former Article 53 TEC had also become obsolete, as it had stipulated that no new restrictions on establishment could be introduced; it subsequently was deleted without replacement by the ToA.[275] The entire subject of Freedom of Establishment remained unaffected by the ToN.

Ex-Article 54 TEC (= Article 44), now Article 50 TFEU, underwent its first amendment through Article 6(4) SEA. Until then, the Council had adopted guidelines for the implementation of the general programme for the lifting of restrictions on a proposal from the Commission and after consultation of the EESC and the Assembly. The SEA changed the decision-making procedure according to ex-Article 54(2) to the effect that the Council now had to take decisions in cooperation with the European Parliament. The ToA deleted ex-Article 54(1), which dealt with the procedure in the first stage of the transitional period. Accordingly, Article 44 TEC henceforth only comprised two paragraphs, whereby the amendment of paragraph 1 (ex-paragraph 2) does not affect any substantive issue, but only incorporates the expiry of the transitional period and stipulates that it concerns directives for the implementation of the Freedom of Establishment.

Ex-Article 55 TEC (= Article 45), now Article 51 TFEU, remained in its original version, whereas ex-Article 56 (= Article 46), now Article 52 TFEU, was amended by both the SEA and the ToA. The amendment of ex-Article 56(2), second sentence, in accordance with Article 6(5) SEA, mainly related to the upgrading of the position of the European Parliament, which became involved in the legislative process through the cooperation procedure. The ToA radically shortened paragraph 2 by deleting all passages related to the transitional period, on the other hand it gave the European Parliament more influence by conferring on it the right to the codecision procedure.

Ex-Article 57 TEC (= Article 47), now Article 53 TFEU, has undergone several modifications since the SEA. The first revision was introduced by Article 6(6) SEA, which stipulated that the Council would no longer issue directives on the recognition of diplomas, certificates and other evidence of formal qualifications (ex-Article 57(1)) after simply consulting the Parliament, but from then on in cooperation with it. The same change was made for decisions under ex-Article 57 as defined in Article 6(7) SEA. The ToM further strengthened the position of the Parliament insofar as the Council henceforth had to decide in codecision with the Parliament. The ToA reinforced the position of the Parliament further by requiring decisions under paragraph 2 to be taken by codecision - in the pre-Amsterdam era

275 However, the prohibition of introducing new restrictions has by no means been lifted by this deletion, but is in any case still covered by Article 43 TEC.

only consultation of the Parliament was provided for.[276] The requirement of unanimity in the Council remained, as no IGC could bring itself to impose such measures against the will of an affected Member State.

Ex-Article 58 (= Article 48), now Article 54 TFEU, which deals with the equal treatment of companies and natural persons, has only been adapted once in its history, whereby this was limited exclusively to a linguistic change in the German version, which had no effect on the content.

In the course of the IGC 2007, only renumbering and editorial adjustments were made; the content of these provisions remained unaffected. In order to summarise all relevant provisions, Article 294 TEC was transferred to this chapter as the final Article 55 TFEU.

276 This paragraph shall apply to directives whose implementation in at least one Member State involves the amendment of existing legal principles governing the profession with regard to training and conditions of access of natural persons to the profession.

II.7.3. Services

Reference:	Part 3 Title IV Chapter 3 Article 56 to 62 TFEU
Subject:	Freedom to provide services, generally against remuneration, in so far as they are not subject to the rules on the Free Movement of Goods and Capital and the Free Movement of Persons, within the territory of the Union
Objectives:	Freedom to provide services within the Union Abolition of all restrictions, even if they apply indiscriminately to domestic service providers as well as to service providers of other Member States, if they are likely to prevent, hinder or render less attractive the activity of the service provider established in another Member State and lawfully providing similar services there[277]
Principles:	Permissibility of active and passive services [278] Recognition of existing permits and licences
Instruments:	Liberalisation of the services sector through sectoral or profession-specific directives Establishment of a Single Market for Financial Services Abolition of existing monopolies

The first modification was introduced by the SEA. Until then, the Council had had to decide unanimously (ex-Article 59(2)) whether this chapter also applied to service providers who were nationals of a third country and established within the Community. The SEA, i.c. Article 15(3), facilitated this procedure by introducing qualified majority voting in the Council in this field.

Unaffected by the ToM, the provisions on the Free Movement of Services were significantly amended by the IGC 1996. The ToA shortened this chapter from originally eight to seven articles (ex-Articles 59 to 61 and ex-Articles 63 to 66 became Articles 49 to 55). On the one hand,

277 Cf. inter alia ECJ Case 76/90, https://curia.europa.eu/juris/showPdf.jsf;jsessionid=4B25300439B646006D3386327F82DC87?text=&docid=97112&pageIndex=0&doclang=EN&mode=lst&dir=&occ=first&part=1&cid=3032170,
and ECJ Case 222/95, https://curia.europa.eu/juris/showPdf.jsf?docid=43688&pageIndex=0&doclang=EN&mode=lst&dir=&occ=first&part=1&cid=3032670.

278 Active: provision of services in every Member State; passive: search for services in every Member State.

an entire article was deleted (ex-Article 62, which postulated a ban on new restrictions on trade in services for the Member States during the transitional period, had become obsolete due to the expiry of the deadline), and on the other hand, further provisions were simplified (Article 49) and adapted to the expired transitional period (Article 52). The ban on new regulations, which had actually been deleted, was legally secured in the new version too, insofar as Article 49(1) states that restrictions on the subject matter are prohibited. A special feature in the area of Freedom to Provide Services is the Protocol to the ToM and to the TEC. It succinctly states that the Contracting Parties have agreed that the Treaty on European Union, the Treaties establishing the European Communities and the Treaties and Acts amending or supplementing them are without prejudice to the application of Article 40.3.3 of the Irish Constitution. The protocol addresses the primacy of the Irish Constitution as far as abortion is concerned, which was strictly prohibited in Ireland at that time. The Irish government had insisted on this protocol during the ToM negotiations so as to be able to maintain this prohibition in any case without running the risk of it being undermined by the requirement of Freedom to Provide Services. Apart from this prohibition and its exception with regard to the Freedom to Provide Services, Irish nationals remained free to have an abortion outside the territory of Ireland.[279]

The ToL left the entire chapter apart from editorial changes and the editorially necessary renumbering untouched.

279 The Irish government also insisted - successfully - on the taking over of this protocol at subsequent IGCs. The abortion ban was lifted only in 2018, when on 26 May 2018 a referendum resulted in a landslide win for the repeal side.

II.7.4. Capital and Payments

Reference:	Part 3 Title IV Chapter 4 Article 63 to 66 and Part 3 Title V Chapter 1 Article 75 TFEU
Subject:	Unrestricted freedom of capital movements and payments between Member States on the one hand, and between Member States and third countries on the other hand
Objectives:	Abolition and prohibition of all restrictions conflicting with this freedom. Liberalisation of capital and payment transactions, including the abolition of foreign exchange restrictions, as well as of restrictive investment regulations and tax regulations.' Establishment of a European Financial Area
Principles:	Harmonisation of the relevant provisions in the Member States Possibility of adopting protective and emergency measures vis-à-vis third countries Possibility of imposing economic sanctions on third countries that restrict capital movements and payments, if these are necessary in the context of the implementation of the Common Foreign and Security Policy
Instruments:	Directives and regulations that remove or prevent such restrictions Directives and regulations designed to prevent the illegal exploitation of this freedom (e.g. Money Laundering Directive)

The provisions on the Free Movement of Capital and Payments have undergone the most fundamental revision over the years, at least in relation to the other chapters of this part. The IGC on the ToM did not change the original articles of this chapter (ex-Articles 67 to 73 TEC) but felt compelled to add eight additional articles (ex-Articles 73a to 73h TEC). According to ex-Article 73a TEC, the additions by the ToM provided that ex-Articles 67 to 73 TEC (the original articles of this chapter) would be repealed with effect from 1 January 1994 - i.e. the beginning of the second stage of the Economic and Monetary Union (EMU) - and replaced by ex-Articles 73b to 73g TEC. This somewhat peculiar construction led to the chapter becoming almost twice as long and could only have been reduced by a republication of the Treaty in a consolidated version. The original provisions regulated the definition of the Free Movement of Capital (ex-Article 67 TEC), foreign exchange authorisations and the capital market (ex-Article 68 TEC), the adoption of necessary directives (ex-Article 69 TEC), the coordination of foreign exchange policy (ex-Article 70 TEC),[280] the further liberalisation of capital movements (ex-Article 71 TEC), the information and opinion of the Commission (ex-Article 72 TEC), as well as safeguard measures (ex-Article 73 TEC). The provisions applicable from 1 January 1994 took over the telos of ex-Articles 67 to 73 TEC, but repealed all those provisions which had become obsolete through reaching the second stage of the EMU. These articles dealt with the prohibition of restrictions (ex-Article 73b TEC), capital movements with third countries (ex-Article 73c TEC), derogations (ex-Article 73d TEC), a deadline for maintaining the rules for Member States which would still have a derogation under existing Community law on 31 December 1993 (ex-Article 73e TEC),[281] Council safeguard measures (ex-Article 73f TEC), economic sanctions against third parties (ex-Article 73g TEC), as well as the liberalisation requirement and transitional measures (ex-Article 73h TEC). In the course of the IGC 1996, ex-Articles 73a, 73e, and 73h TEC were repealed in conformity with the system due to the expiry of the deadline and were not incorporated. In the ToA version, this chapter therefore only comprises five articles.[282] The changes made by the IGC in the revision of this chapter were limited to the repeal of the obsolete provisions and the adaptation of the remaining provisions to the new numbering. The IGC did not make any changes to the content.

The ToN left the chapter on Free Movement of Capital and Payments untouched.

The ToL was equally neutral in terms of content, merely moving the former Article 60 TEC to Title V (Area of Freedom, Security and Justice) as Article 75 TFEU.

---

280 This provision had already been amended by Article 16(4) SEA, which introduced the principle of QMV for directives on the subject.

281 This period lasted until 31 December 1995 at the latest.

282 i.e.: Article 56 = ex-Article 73b, Article 57 = ex-Article 73c, Article 58 = ex-Article 73d, Article 59 = ex-Article 73f, Article 60 = ex-Article 73g.

II.8. Area of Freedom, Security and Justice

Reference:	Part 3 Title V Article 67 to 89 TFEU[283]
Subject:	Contributing to establishing an Area of Freedom, Security and Justice
Objectives:	Gradual establishment of the Area of Freedom, Security and Justice Communitarisation of the Schengen system (pre-ToL era) Cooperation in the fields of justice and home affairs
Principles:	Application of the Community method (pre-ToL era) Possibility of transferring measures in the area of the Third Pillar of the TEU to the TEC via passerelle (pre-ToL era) Extension of the jurisdiction of the ECJ
Instruments:	Measures in the field of asylum, immigration, and protection of the rights of third-country nationals Measures in the field of judicial cooperation in civil matters Measures to promote and strengthen administrative cooperation

I. The development up to the Treaty of Nice

I.1. Police and judicial cooperation in criminal matters

Like the preceding Title V TEU, Title VI, now Title V, was also subjected to a radical reorganisation by the ToA. The new title is already a clear indication of this, as the provisions on cooperation in the fields of justice and home affairs became provisions on cooperation in police and judicial criminal matters. When this Title was originally drafted, it was essentially a systematic approach, designed to remedy the unsystematic and incoherent approach of the pre-Maastricht era. In addition to this technical aspect, political pressure was also exerted, in particular by German Chancellor Kohl, who, supported by other Member States, called for provisions on asylum, immigration, and a European Police Authority to be established, with these provisions to be incorporated into primary law. Title VI in

283 Until its complete realignment by the ToL, this policy area was regulated in Title VI Article 29 to 42 TEU and Part 3 Title IV Article 61 to 69 TEC.

its final ToM version even went beyond these demands. The scope of application extended from asylum issues to the fight against drug-related crime and fraud. Even the establishment of Europol was envisaged. The IGC 1991 actually allowed for the possibility of transferring Title VI matters to the supranational pillar by means of a passerelle clause, which was never used, however. The IGC 1996 continued the work of the IGC 1991 and transferred parts of Title VI to the TEC, allowing the United Kingdom and the Republic of Ireland to opt out in order to obtain their consent. The IGC 2000 left Title VI essentially unchanged, although it extended the possibilities for enhanced cooperation, and was therefore heavily criticised by the European Parliament, which felt that the Member States had been too hesitant. In particular, the Parliament complained that (i) communitarisation had not gone far enough, and (ii) no European Public Prosecutor had been established to prosecute fraud offences against the Union. In contrast, some Member States, notably the United Kingdom, saw the changes introduced by the ToN as a creeping threat to Member State competences in home affairs and autonomy in police matters.

Article 29 TEU (ex-Article K.1)[284] introduces as a new and more concrete objective a high level of security for citizens and thus links directly to the Area of Freedom, Security and Justice to be established. In line with the political mainstream, the new provision is also intended to prevent and combat racism and xenophobia. Articles 30 and 31 TEU now define more precisely which areas are covered by police and judicial cooperation respectively, whereas Article 32 TEU regulates the conditions under which the Council determines the exact limits of the application of these two articles by authorities in the territory of another Member State. Article 33 TEU (ex-Article K.2(2)) was reproduced unchanged, Article 34 TEU (ex-Articles K.3 and K.4(3)) was also maintained apart from technical adaptations. Article 35 TEU can be considered an innovation in that the IGC 1996 grants the Court of Justice the competence to give preliminary rulings. This amendment was to be understood as a reaction of the Member States to increasing criticism regarding a democratic deficit of this title. Article 36 TEU (ex-Article K.4(1) and (2)) and Article 37 TEU (ex-Article K.5) were maintained with the necessary editorial adaptations. Article 38 TEU was incorporated by the IGC 1996 into the provisions of Title VI in alignment with those of Title V, in order to enable the conclusion of such agreements here as well. Article 39 TEU (ex-Article K.6) is a continuation of the ori-

284 References in this section to ex-Articles of Title VI relate to the ToM version.

ginal provisions, but gives the Parliament more concrete options, whereby the Member States have endeavoured to accommodate the criticism of the Parliament, but only go as far as is absolutely necessary. Although Articles 40 (ex-Article K.7), 40a, and 40b TEU have been the clear expression of the Member States to allow enhanced cooperation also under this title, the wording shows that some Member States are extremely sceptical about such initiatives. Due to strong UK reservations about such innovations, the IGC 2000 included the clause that a Member State opposed to such cooperation could appeal to the European Council. Article 41 TEU (ex-Article K.8) and Article 42 TEU (ex-Article K.9) were taken over apart from necessary editorial and technical adaptations.

I.2. Visa, Asylum, Immigration and other policies related to the Free Movement of Persons

The former Title IV TEC on visa, asylum, immigration, and other policies related to the free movement of persons is a result of the IGC 1996 and was introduced into the TEC by the ToA.

Until the ToL, this title consisted partly of (i) provisions of the TEU as amended by the ToM, (ii) ex-Article 100c TEC, and (iii) genuine innovations. The complexity of the origins combined with numerous Member State reservations made Title IV a unique construct compared to the other parts of the TEC. It reflected the Community's efforts to complete the free movement of persons, but it also showed the national reservations with which the Community would have to live in the future, as was again evident in the course of the negotiations on the ToL. Moreover, it should be noted that Title IV cannot be considered independently of the Schengen Agreement, its acquis, and the - partial - incorporation into the TEU by the IGC 1996.

In total, Title IV comprises nine articles and is supplemented and legally interpreted by a number of protocols and declarations. The aim of Title IV is to create the legal basis for the establishment of an Area of Freedom, Security and Justice, as stated in Article 61 TEC. Although this title is in line with Article 2 TEU and Preamble Recital 11 TEU, and certainly also with Article 14(2) TEC, the IGC 1996 did not provide for a specific equivalent in the catalogue of activities of the Community under Article 3 TEC, but only incorporated the - quite cryptic - description of activities of measures relating to the entry and movement of persons under Title IV.[285]

The IGC 1996 thus refrained - deliberately or unknowingly - from defining this new area. Accordingly, this area has been the subject of the most diverse and diametrically opposed interpretations. However, if one considers the countless hurdles that the IGC had to overcome before the incorporation of this title was accepted by all Member States, this decision becomes comprehensible.

The genesis of this title originated in ex-Article 8a TEC (= Article 14), the Commission's White Paper on the Implementation of the Internal Market, the Schengen Agreement, and the third pillar of the TEU (= Cooperation in the Fields of Justice and Home Affairs (CJHA)). Ex-Article 8a TEC, inserted by Article 13 SEA, has clarified that an area without internal borders should be established, in which not only goods, capital and services should enjoy freedom of movement, but also persons. In conformity with the system, this means free, unrestricted, and - in particular - uncontrolled movement of persons. However, resistance and reservations in the Member States prevented the implementation of this goal. Over the years, the Member States became more and more aware of the fact that crime and terror did not stop at the borders and that transnational cooperation was just as desirable as it was necessary, but they were unable to bring themselves to establish such cooperation at Community level. Moreover, a complete freedom of movement of persons stood in the way of these security interests. The logical consequence - the creation of the free movement of persons with the simultaneous creation of the necessary flanking measures to prevent illegal exploitation of this freedom - was indeed accepted by some Member States, but a stable majority to implement this realisation could not be established. In its White Paper on the completion of the Single Market in the 1990s, the Commission did not necessarily act in the most helpful way by considering the abolition of internal border controls on persons without any substitution. As flanking replacement measures, the Commission proposed to provide for security measures at the intergovernmental level. In the eyes of some Member States, the Commission had clearly exceeded its competences with this initiative, although it had merely followed the "avant-garde politique", which at that time was shaped and moved by the discussion on a citizens' Europe. The Commission's initiative was not crowned with

285 cf. Article 3 (1) d TEC.

success, at least in the medium term. In particular, the intergovernmental element of the accompanying substitute measures was - at least in the pre-Maastricht era - almost inconceivable, or at least incompatible with the Community idea of that time.[286] Any cooperation did take place at Council level but could not rise above the level of ad hoc groups.[287]

Belgium, Luxembourg, the Netherlands,[288] France, and Germany decided to implement this Internal Market objective outside the Community framework, not least because of the hesitant behaviour of the other Member States, and joined forces in 1985 in the Schengen Agreement.[289] The Schengen Agreement consisted essentially of initial facilitation of border controls on the one hand[290] and longer-term objectives on the other.[291] The five Schengen founding members decided in mid-1990 to abolish controls at the shared borders altogether and to take flanking substitute measures to prevent crime.[292]

286 Only the enhanced cooperation took up this idea again and raised it to Union and Community level respectively, thus remedying the reservation of system conformity.

287 e.g. the so-called TREVI group, which comprised several ad hoc groups and, from 1975 onwards, dealt in particular with the fight against international terrorism. The origin of this acronym is lost in the darkness of the Council annals, TREVI could therefore be derived as an abbreviation of the fields dealt with (Terrorisme, Radicalisme, Extrémisme, Violance Internationale) or - as is probably more prosaic - after the first meeting place (in the vicinity of the Fontana di Trevi in Rome). Wherever the name may be derived from, it is certainly interesting to note that the Member States had already been dealing with such issues at Council level - irrespective of the legal quality - some thirty years before the terrorist attacks of 2001. How, against this historical background, the urgent and sudden need for action, but especially the call for new institutions and procedures, can be justified remains unanswered.

288 It should be noted here that the Benelux countries already formed a passport union.

289 This can probably be interpreted as the first real anticipation of the enhanced cooperation that was introduced at a later stage.

290 e.g. restriction to simple visual inspections and randomly performed detailed examinations.

291 i.e. gradual abolition of controls at the common borders.

292 With the exception of the United Kingdom and Ireland, all Member States joined the Schengen Agreement. Not all states that joined the Union on 1 May 2004 are Schengen members to this day, but they all had accepted the obligations of the first stage. Full accession can only be accomplished once all criteria have been met. Bulgaria's and Romania's entry to the Schengen realm was blocked by Austria in late 2022 on the eve of the respective Council meeting to the surprise of all Members States, Parliament, and the Commission. Early in 2024, Austria agreed to the opening of Schengen Air and Schengen Sea for Bulgaria and Romania, entering into force on 31 March 2024, but continued to veto the full Schengen accession of these two countries.

The IGC 1991 took up the already existing ideas, combined them for the first time in the Third Pillar, the Cooperation in the Fields of Justice and Home Affairs, and raised them to the Union level. Not least because the reservations in some Member States about communitarising this matter were still extremely high, this pillar remained outside the supranational structure and in the realm of intergovernmentalism. However, the IGC 1991 and its legacy, the ToM, had laid the foundation for communitarisation of - almost - the entire complex.

The IGC 1996 had set itself the goal of taking up the experiences with the TEU and the revised TEC and, if necessary, taking measures to improve both. In the opinion of the Reflection Group which preceded the IGC 1996, cooperation in legal and domestic policy gave sufficient cause for this, as it considered the results of this cooperation to be simply rather poor, whereby above all the complicated construction of soft law and an instrument mix of elements of international law and Community law did the rest. The conclusion of the Reflection Group, which the IGC gladly followed - at least in this general aspect - was the transfer of essential elements of the Third Pillar of the TEU to the TEC, i.e. the communitarisation of this subject matter. However, the Reflection Group did not limit itself to the Third Pillar of the TEU but looked beyond Union and Community law and devoted detailed consideration and assessment to the Schengen Agreement, which resulted in the transfer of this acquis to the Community level as well. The IGC 1996 finally agreed on the insertion of Title IV into the TEC with a total of nine articles.

Article 61 TEC, which contains the basic considerations on the movement of persons and the fight against crime, stipulates which measures are to be adopted by the Council so that the Area of Freedom, Security, and Justice - which, as already pointed out, is not defined in detail - can be gradually built up. The IGC felt compelled to include the term "gradual" at the very beginning of Title IV in order to accommodate the particularly hesitant Member States. For the same reason, the deadline in Article 61(a) TEC for ensuring the free movement of persons in accordance with Article 14 TEC was set at a longer period than originally planned. The IGC had proposed that these measures should be in place by 1 January 2001. In the end, only a five-year transitional period, i.e. 1 May 2004, was acceptable as a compromise.

Article 62 TEC, which essentially deals with visa measures, adopts the five-year period for the implementation measures in question. It is noteworthy that the IGC chose - as it has done several times in this title - the means of a declaration to limit the applicability of Article 62 TEC. Declaration No. 16 refers to Article 62(2)(b) TEC, concerning measures relating to the crossing of the external borders of the Member States, in concreto rules on visas for intended stays. In the declaration, the conferees agreed that foreign policy considerations of the Union and the Member States would be taken into account in the application of the provision concerned. While this declaration does not necessarily give primacy to the Common Foreign and Security Policy in this case, it does at least recognise the need to establish coherence between these two policies.

Article 63 TEC, covering measures in the field of asylum and immigration, again shows the difficult situation of the IGC 1996. On the one hand, reference is made of course to the 1951 Geneva Convention on Refugees and the 1967 Protocol thereto; on the other hand, the Member States retain the freedom not only to maintain other measures in conformity with the Treaty and the Convention, but also to continue to introduce them. Declaration No. 17, which provides for consultations with the UN High Commissioner for Refugees and other relevant international organisations in matters of asylum policy, is fitting in this regard. The freedom of Member States is further underlined by Declaration No. 18, which allows them to negotiate and conclude agreements with third countries, provided they are in conformity with Community law. The mechanism of the original Third Pillar of the TEU, which was considered too cumbersome and complicated, was adopted cum grano salis and presents itself as a mix of international law and Community law, as well as of the Community method and the sovereignty of the Member States.

Article 64 TEC, dealing specifically with public order and emergencies, is - at least indirectly - a restriction on the applicability of Article 63 TEC, as it allows the Council to take decisions with QMV to assist Member States in emergency situations due to a sudden influx of third-country nationals.[293] Even more noteworthy is the clause in paragraph 1 according to which the exercise of the responsibilities incumbent upon Member States with regard to the maintenance of law and order and the safeguarding of internal security shall not be affected by Title IV, it being noted that this derogation is not limited to asylum matters but covers the whole of Title IV. Protocol No. 20 on asylum for nationals of Member States of the European Union and Declaration No. 48 to this protocol are remarkable in this context. Spain had pushed for this protocol and the corresponding

293 Article 64 TEC derives from ex-Article 100c(2) and (5) TEC.

declaration in order to prevent terrorists - proven or suspected - from seeking asylum in other Member States. Specifically, Spain was referring to Basque separatists, in particular members of ETA, and to Belgium as a host country to such particular asylum seekers. This Protocol aims to ensure that Member States are classified as safe third countries in asylum matters and that asylum-seeking EU citizens are granted a correspondingly mitigated asylum position. Belgium, which was not comfortable with the Spanish move but wanted its sovereignty clarified, stated in Declaration No. 5 to Protocol No. 20 on asylum for nationals of Member States of the European Union, which was taken note of by the conference, that in accordance with its obligations under the 1951 Geneva Convention and the 1967 New York Protocol, it would examine separately any application for asylum made by a national of another Member State, in accordance with letter d of the sole Article of that Protocol. In plain language, Belgium let Spain know that she intended to settle the question of granting asylum - and thus also the question of whether the person seeking asylum was a terrorist - sovereignly. This almost open conflict between two Member States showed, on the one hand, how carefully this title had to be handled, and on the other hand, the achievement of the conference in reaching a compromise.

Article 61 letter c TEC gives the Council the task of adopting measures in the field of judicial cooperation in civil matters in accordance with Article 65 TEC, and - in letter d - the task of adopting appropriate measures to promote and strengthen administrative cooperation in accordance with Article 66 TEC. With this mandate, the TEC took a very bold and far-reaching step - at least in the eyes of some conferees - which seemed likely to restrict the sovereignty of the Member States in the field of civil jurisdiction. The United Kingdom, in particular, felt obliged to clarify that certain limits to communitarisation would be drawn. This can also be understood in the - interpretative - Declaration No. 20 to the ToA on Article 65 TEC, which states that any measures adopted under Article 65 TEC are not suitable to prevent Member States from applying their constitutional rules on freedom of the press and freedom of expression in other media.[294] Nevertheless, the wording of Articles 65 and 66 TEC clearly point to an increased intensity of cooperation between the Member States and the - arguably still -

294 In this context, it should again be pointed out that Article 64(1) TEC in any case emphasises the primacy of the Member States to regulate their respective internal security and order (cf. above).

embryonic communitarised immigration and asylum policy. The Action Plan adopted at the Vienna European Council in December 1998 under the Austrian EU Presidency should also be understood in this context, and it was given an unexpected dynamic by the Finnish EU Presidency.[295] At the latest through the Vienna Action Plan, which culminated in the Tampere Process, the intention of the Member States to implement the Area of Freedom, Security, and Justice at Community level[296] and to formulate and implement - peu-à-peu - common objectives in the field of immigration policy, social integration of asylum seekers and immigrants had clearly emerged.[297]

In this context, it is also necessary to look back at the ToM, which already contained the nucleus of a communitarised policy in this area. The subject areas listed in Title IV TEC were originally envisaged in the Union Treaty as those areas that were to be implemented under the Third Pillar in the form of intergovernmental cooperation; only a very few exceptional areas were transferred to the TEC. Even in the ToM, however, this division was not intended as a petrification of the allocation of competences, but as a temporary determination. The remaining facts could have been transferred to the TEC via he already above mentioned passerelle clause. In Declaration No. 31 to the ToM on asylum, the Member States had envisaged considering transferring the relevant acts from the TEU to the TEC towards the end of 1993. However, the Member States did not make use of this clause; no such attempt even came close to being made. Although the ToA - with the explicit exception of customs cooperation in criminal matters and combating fraud - brought about the communitarisation of a large part of the Third Pillar, this attempt at communitarisation also remained partially stalled.

The IGC 1996 had not managed to implement communitarisation consistently and in one go; on the other hand, the window of opportunity was not supposed to be closed. Accordingly - albeit complicated in its wording - Article 67 was included in the TEC, containing the regulations according

295 This process was launched at the Tampere European Council in December 1999 under the Finnish Presidency and included a package of approximately 200 legal proposals.

296 Due to the measures that were enacted subsequently, critics of this system came up with the term Fortress Europe.

297 The burden that was to fall on the individual Member States in this area was not balanced enough in the eyes of some Member States - e.g. Germany - but eventually all Member States agreed.

to which the legal implementation measures for Title IV TEC would have to take place. In conformity with the system, the Commission does not have the usual exclusive monopoly of initiative in this case but shares it with the Member States, which can very well be seen as a relic of the intergovernmental approach. However, this shared competence was only intended for a transitional period, which was to last from 1999 to 2004. Only after the end of this period would the systemic state of affairs be established, and the exclusive monopoly of initiative be transferred to the Commission. But even this monopoly on initiative is indirectly curtailed as the Commission is obliged to examine every application from a Member State. The position of the European Parliament can be regarded as rather weak. Contrary to its demands on adopting the codecision procedure for Title IV, the consultation procedure applies; this again is a reference to the original intergovernmental source of the subject matter. The only concession to Parliament was made with regard to the adoption of acts under Article 62(2)(b)(ii) and (iv), regarding rules on visas for intended stays of no more than three months, including (subparagraph (ii)) the list of third countries whose nationals must be in possession of visas when crossing the external borders and those whose nationals are exempt from that requirement, and (subparagraph (iv)) the rules on a uniform visa. Only in these two exceptional cases should the codecision procedure be introduced after the five-year period. However, the IGC kept open the possibility of development by including a passerelle clause, according to which other areas could also be transferred to codecision if the Council unanimously so decides. This passerelle also remained dead letter. The conference had not been able to decide under the ToA to adopt a more rigorous communitarisation approach directly in the TEC. Declaration No. 21 to the ToA on Article 67 TEC, however, clearly shows that the more integrationalist Member States did not want to be completely slowed down. Without specifying a precise target date, the Member States agreed to examine the possibility of a passerelle before the end of the transitional period, if necessary, in order to ensure at least in this way that the transition could take place immediately after the expiry of the deadline.

By and large, the Parliament considered itself the clear loser of the IGC and criticised the fact that Title IV was not subject to parliamentary control. The Parliament had thus not been able to assert itself with its demands in the course of IGC 1996 and therefore hoped - as a quasi-compensation - for a strengthening of its position through the IGC 2000. However, in the eyes of the Parliament, the conference once again fell short of its potential, although a new paragraph 5 was added to Article 67 TEC by the ToN, which provides that measures according to Article 63(1) TEC (measures relating to asylum) and the measures according to Article 63(2)(a) TEC (minimum standards for temporary protection) are transferred to QMV. The Parliament's renewed annoyance was caused by the restriction that this transfer would only be possible once the Council had unanimously created a so-called acquis in principle. At the same time, however, paragraph 5 decreed that measures under Article 65 TEC (i.e. judicial cooperation in civil matters) would be transferred to QMV without delay, although family law aspects were to remain excluded also in the future. The ToN's protocol on Article 67 TEC, according to which, as of 1 May 2004, the Council must act by qualified majority on a proposal from the Commission and after having consulted the European Parliament when adopting measures under Article 66 TEC (i.e. cooperation between the relevant departments of the authorities), did not satisfy the Parliament at all. However, in the course of IGC 2000, the Member States were also confronted with the dichotomy between maximum maintenance of national sovereignty on the one hand and increasing communitarisation of this matter on the other. In any case, the IGC did not see itself in a position to fulfil the Parliament's demand for an automatism between qualified majority and codecision.

Nevertheless, the IGC 2000 has been a major step towards communitarisation of Title IV TEC, as an agreement was reached in Declaration No. 5 on Article 67 TEC, which allows for the transition to qualified majority voting. In this declaration, the parties to the IGC 2000 agreed that as of 1 January 2004, the Council may decide unanimously to move to qualified majority voting in the following cases: Freedom of movement of third-country nationals (Article 62 number 3 TEC), measures in the field of illegal immigration (Article 63 number 3 letter b TEC), as well as procedures for the control of persons at the external borders (Article 62 number 2 letter a TEC). In the first two cases, no specific condition was included in the declaration, but in the third case, an agreement on the scope of the measures was postulated as a precondition. The conference was unable to agree on a more far-reaching extension, but in the same Declaration No. 5 it stated that the Council would endeavour to transfer the other provisions of Title IV TEC, or at least parts of them, to QMV and the codecision procedure from the same date or as soon as possible thereafter. At the last minute, a reference to the target date of 1 May 2004 was deleted from the text, as some Member States had considered this to be too concrete a commitment on the part of the Council. Despite all this,

Parliament criticised the fact that IGC 2000 had only made this single change in Title IV, i.e. the addition of paragraph 5 to Article 67 TEC.

Article 68 TEC takes a new direction. Although much of Title IV TEC falls under the jurisdiction of the ECJ, the Court does not have jurisdiction over any measures or decisions taken by Member States to maintain internal security and order under Article 62(1) TEC. The same applies with regard to the admissibility of national measures under Article 64 TEC.[298] However, the jurisdiction of the ECJ is not finally defined, as the evolution clause in Article 67(2) TEC allows the Council to amend the jurisdiction of the Court by unanimity. Article 68 TEC also expresses the disagreement and indecision of the Member States as far as the question of communitarisation is concerned. Not only the United Kingdom, Ireland, and Denmark insisted at the IGC 1996 on national prerogatives in the field of visas and asylum, but other Member States also saw national sovereignty at risk, especially if jurisdiction were to be transferred to the European level, as it were. The opt-outs of the three Member States mentioned are particularly unique, as they imply that the jurisdiction of the ECJ is not only to be regarded as extremely limited in general terms but is also almost taken ad absurdum by the special position of certain Member States. Several conferees pointed out this asymmetry,[299] but ultimately had to acknowledge that without this compromise the inclusion of the entire title would have been jeopardised.

Probably the most striking anomaly contained in Title IV is Article 69 TEC. Contrary to the general clause of Article 311 TEC, according to which all protocols annexed to the Treaty are an integral part of the same Treaty, Article 69 TEC explicitly refers to three protocols.[300] At first sight, the three protocols mentioned imply a complete opt-out of the Member States concerned from Title IV TEC, at least as far as its provisions, the measures to be taken and the jurisdiction of the ECJ are concerned. Furthermore, they imply an exemption from any financial consequences arising from the application of Title IV TEC. For Denmark, the whole package of Article 69 TEC is a pragmatic approach resulting from the desire to be part of it on

298 The resemblance to the provisions in Article 33 TEU is certainly not accidental.

299 The situation was classified as asymmetrical in that some Member States can continue to take measures ex contractu, unaffected by EU competences, without being subject to EU jurisdiction.

300 i.e. Protocol on the Application of certain Aspects of Article 14 TEC to the United Kingdom and Ireland (1997), Protocol on the Position of the United Kingdom and Ireland (1992) Protocol on the Position of Denmark (1997).

the one hand and the consideration of public concerns in Denmark on the other; moreover, it is - at least from the Danish point of view - the corollary of the decision of the Edinburgh European Council 1992 regarding the restrictions on the applicability of the Third Pillar TEU to Denmark. For the United Kingdom, it is the consistent implementation of the British approach to Third Pillar issues. Ireland's position - in contrast to the UK's - is characterised by being torn between the need to maintain certain legal conditions with the UK, especially with regard to the Common Travel Area, at the same time as seeking more integration.

Critics of the Danish, British, and Irish "Sonderweg" (aka special way) describe these protocols - together with other exemption provisions for these three Member States - as classic opt-outs. In contrast, however, the three states concerned - especially Denmark and Ireland - regard this setting as opt-ins. This becomes particularly evident in the case of Denmark when one considers the clause, according to Denmark has agreed to adopt those measures dealing with visa requirements and visa formats and may - within six months of an extension of the Schengen acquis - decide to adopt any such decision. In the case of Denmark, one can speak of a so-called pipeline acquis.[301] The situation is even more complicated for the United Kingdom and Ireland, whose autonomous follow-up does not even take place under the EU regime but uses the international law track.[302] To further complicate the situation, Ireland and Denmark can, by simple unilateral declaration, abrogate their respective protocols and participate fully in Title IV, whereas the UK's participation would require a Treaty amendment.

In general, the United Kingdom and Ireland have achieved a unique exceptional position vis-à-vis Title IV, which is mainly reflected in the Protocol on the Application of certain Aspects of Article 14 TEC. This protocol allows both countries to maintain their Common Travel Area, established since the 1920s,[303] while at the same time carrying out checks on persons at their external borders with the other EU Member States, notwithstanding Article 62(1) TEC. The principle of reciprocity on the part of the other Member States is allowed to apply, thus enabling Spain to continue to carry

301 i.e. the state concerned cannot actively participate in the process of bringing about the legal act, but implements its content in a quasi-autonomous manner.

302 i.c. both states can participate via notification to the Presidency.

303 The Common Travel Area is not based on a written agreement, but on a permanent administrative practice and has never been written into law. The first written recognition of the Common Travel Area originated from the ToA of all places.

out border controls at Gibraltar. The Irish delegation to the IGC 1996 was under heavy pressure on this point in particular; if it had detached itself from the United Kingdom, border traffic with Northern Ireland would no longer have been possible within the framework of the Common Travel Area regime, which would not have made the Republic of Ireland's relationship with the United Kingdom - and in particular with the British province of Ulster - any easier and would probably not have met with any support from the Irish populace. In the end, Ireland had to bow to the normative power of the factual and find a way forward that seemed acceptable in realpolitik terms. The balancing act between the official position of wanting the freedom to participate in Title IV at any time and, on the other hand, maintaining the Common Travel Area with the United Kingdom, is the reason for the complicated and sometimes difficult to understand solution in Article 69 TEC. At the same time, it should be noted that the other conferees also had to reach beyond their shadows in order to accommodate the special wishes of the two island states in such a way that it was still possible to claim an intact Title IV regime.

The genesis of Title IV shows the conflicting relationship between some Member States and the communitarisation of certain policies, especially in connection with the possible (if partial) relinquishment of national sovereignty. This also reflects the respective self-image of these countries, which do not necessarily see themselves as Member States in this very context, but nevertheless do not want to stand in the way of an overall agreement, as such a policy of obstruction would be counterproductive. Despite all this, it should be noted that critics of the Title IV solution are not wrong to complain that it represents a radical departure from the absolute basic principles of Community law: (i) the uniform nature of Community law, (ii) the uniform interpretation and application of Community rules, and (iii) the Community-wide maintenance of the acquis communautaire. However, this criticism must be countered by the fact that the conference was faced with the task of finding a feasible way of placing the Schengen acquis on a sounder, more Community-oriented basis, despite the massive opposition of at least three Member States - although some other Member States also had a latent mental reservation regarding Title IV. Only the acceptance of the three protocols mentioned above cleared the way for a fourth protocol, which was proposed by the Netherlands and aimed at integrating the Schengen acquis into the framework of the European Union. The 1997 Protocol No. 2 to the TEU on integrating the Schengen acquis into the framework of the European Union opened up the possibility of partial communitarisation of - at that time - some 3 000 pages of secondary legislation. This protocol applies to all Member States with the exception of Ireland and the United Kingdom, whereby France, through Declaration (No. 7) on the Situation of the Overseas Departments, which was taken note of by the IGC 1996, granted itself a special position with regard to the Schengen acquis protocol in that the Schengen acquis protocol does not apply to the overseas departments. France justified the necessity of this particular regulation with the special geographical situation of these departments and the difficulty of implementing the Schengen acquis, especially vis-à-vis the other states surrounding them. For Ireland and the United Kingdom, an opt-in variant applies in this case. However, such an opt-in cannot be made by unilateral notification, but requires unanimous acceptance by the other Member States. This tightening of the opt-in requirement goes back to a Spanish reservation, which only agreed to support this protocol if unanimity is set instead of QMV acceptance. The background to this tightening is to be found in the Gibraltar conflict between Spain and the United Kingdom, in which Spain - primarily for domestic political reasons - could not afford to weaken its position. Border traffic between Spain and Gibraltar without identity checks would have contributed considerably to a blatant weakening from the Spanish point of view.

On 20 May 1999, the Council adopted the necessary decisions to implement the acquis. This decision was thus taken much later than originally intended, though this was not necessarily due to the opposition of the Member States, but ultimately to the fact that there was no clear decision as to which parts were to be taken over and not all the relevant legal acts had been published.

Moreover, Title IV TEC and its application contains another specificity. Not only did two EU Member States achieve an à la carte position, but two non-EU Member States entered into an association with Schengen. Norway and Iceland felt the need to associate with Schengen in order to maintain the Nordic Passport Union between Denmark (excluding the Faroe Islands and Greenland), Sweden, Finland, Norway, and Iceland.

II. The Realignment by the Treaty of Lisbon

As noted in the introduction to this chapter, the IGC 2007 completely revised this title by bringing all the relevant provisions into a single legal framework. The old title, which had a very technocratic feel, was replaced by a new, highly programmatic one. The new title was headlined by the ToL with "Area of Freedom, Security and Justice". The IGC 2007 thus followed the IGCs 2004's demand to dissolve the pillar structure of the Union Treaty and to communitarise not only foreign and security policy, but also the entire complex of cooperation in the areas of justice and home affairs as well as the Schengen area. In this way, the intergovernmental approach of these policies was to be abandoned in favour of a supranational one. As already described in detail above, these sectors had been regulated in various sections of the Treaties. The origins of these policies were found on the one hand in Article 2 indent 4 TEU as amended by the ToN, which defined the area of freedom, security and justice as an objective of the Union. This area included, according to Article 61 letter e TEC, the adoption of measures in the field of police and judicial cooperation in criminal matters aiming at a high level of security by preventing and combating crime in the Union. The relevant Title IV TEC provided for the gradual establishment of this area, whereby the Council had been given a deadline of 1 May 2004 to adopt all measures to ensure the free movement of persons in accordance with Article 14 TEC. However, this provision, which sounds lapidary in itself, went far deeper into the matter than its wording would suggest, as it also included related flanking measures concerning external border control, asylum, and immigration. The details of all these provisions were derived from Articles 29 to 42 TEU as amended by the ToN, and, with regard to the special aspect of combating fraud against the Community, from Article 280 TEC. The IGCs 2004 and 2007 were thus faced with the task of combining these provisions on the one hand, and on the other of avoiding too many new opt-outs (or rather euphemistically: opt-ins) being demanded by individual Member States. The merger was successful, but both IGCs failed in their attempt to avoid new opt-outs. Nevertheless, this reorganisation must be considered a success since the window for dissolving the pillar structure and above all for communitarising the Schengen acquis would probably never again have been as wide open as it was at the beginning and in the middle of the first decade of this millennium. The enormous wave of refugees in late summer and autumn 2015 showed this quite clearly. If Schengen had still been regulated in an intergovernmental manner, the effects in this regard would have been incalculable. The sub-optimal solution capacity in this most recent period also showed that the pooling of competences alone is not sufficient to manage such crises.

II.1. Innovations and Principles, Structure, Rearrangements

Innovations and Principles

The fundamental innovations and principles of this now quite compact policy field can be summarised as follows:

- The European Council provides the Strategic Guidelines;
- The regular procedure is the ordinary legislative procedure;
- The Council is responsible for issuing regulations on administrative cooperation;
- The national parliaments are called upon to monitor compliance with subsidiarity regarding judicial cooperation in criminal matters and police cooperation;
- Inclusion of an explicit requirement to take account of fundamental rights and the legal traditions and systems of the Member States, thereby establishing the highest possible common denominator for the implementation of this policy;
- The agreements already concluded, such as the Schengen Agreement and the Europol Agreement, are an integral part of the implementation of this policy;
- Upholding the principle that the maintenance of law and order and the safeguarding of internal security are the exclusive responsibility of the Member States;
- The Commission's monopoly of initiative, although inherent in the Union system, is breached insofar as the Member States may also take initiatives on the basis of which legal acts may be adopted. According to Article 67(2) first indent TEC, the Commission's monopoly of initiative was also restricted for the period after 1 May 2004, since - in addition to its own right of initiative - it had to examine every request from a Member State and then submit a proposal to the Council. However, the provisions of the TFEU give the Member States an independent right of initiative alongside the Commission;
- Introduction of the possibility of establishing a form of European criminal law;
- Introduction of the possibility of setting up a European Public Prosecutor's Office to combat serious crime with a cross-border dimension, as well as offences detrimental to the interests of the Union;
- Provision for so-called emergency brakes in selected areas (i.e. enactment of minimum provisions in criminal law, operational police cooper-

ation, establishment of a European Public Prosecutor's Office), which trigger a conciliation procedure by way of the European Council, whereby this must be seen in the light of the former intergovernmental character of this policy area;
- Introduction of special transitional rules vis-à-vis the newly added competences of the Commission and the ECJ in the area of police and criminal law cooperation;
- Extension of the opt-outs of the United Kingdom, Denmark, and Ireland to police and criminal law cooperation.

Structure
The new Title V contains the following chapters:

- Chapter 1: General provisions
- Chapter 2: Policies on border checks, asylum and immigration
- Chapter 3: Judicial cooperation in civil matters
- Chapter 4: Judicial cooperation in criminal matters
- Chapter 5: Police cooperation

Repeals, Replacements, and Rearrangements
The following repeals, replacements, and rearrangements were made by the ToL:

Repeals

- Article 67 to 69 ex-TEC

Rearrangements

- Article 60 ex-TEC to be Article 75 TFEU

Replacements

- Article 61 ex-TEC is replaced by the new Chapter 1 and Articles 67 to 76 TFEU, with Article 67 TFEU also replacing Article 29 TEU de lege lata
- Article 63(1) and (2) ex TEC is replaced by Article 78(1) and (2) TFEU;
- Article 64(1) ex-TEC is replaced by Article 72 TFEU, which also replaces Article 33 TEU de lege lata
- Article 64(2) ex-TEC is replaced by Article 78(3) TFEU
- Article 66 ex-TEC is replaced by Article 74 TFEU

II.2. The Provisions of the Area of Freedom, Security and Justice in Detail

Chapter 1: General provisions (Article 67 to 76 TFEU)

Article 67 TFEU replaces Article 29 TEU de lege lata and Article 61 TEC on the one hand, and repeats Article III-257 TCEU on the other. This article is intended as a programmatic introductory provision and serves as a parenthesis between the existing legal framework and the new one. The other articles of this first chapter describe the general procedure, but also the fundamental exception concerning the exclusive competence of the Member States for questions of maintaining public security and order.

The IGC 2007 deviated decisively from the IGC 2004 in one aspect and extended the first chapter by clarifying in Article 73 TFEU that - although the entire policy area has now become supranational due to the dissolution of the pillar structure - the Member States still have intergovernmental possibilities in this particular area and can conclude bilateral agreements. This provision has been a concern of many Member States, which wanted to preserve their freedom of action - at least to a limited extent - whereby the restriction of the general principle that the Member States may not set any activities that conflict with or hinder the implementation of the Treaties also makes this scope very narrow. However, the fiction of national sovereignty has been maintained.

Chapter 2: Policies on border checks, asylum and immigration (Article 77 to 80 TFEU)

Article 77 TFEU raises the Schengen criteria to the level of primary law and describes which areas may be regulated by Union measures. The IGC 2007 went a decisive step further than the previous intergovernmental conferences by declaring Union measures concerning passports, identity cards, residence permits or documents equivalent to these as authorised.

Article 78 TFEU, dealing with asylum policy, describes (i) in general the criteria of the Common Asylum System and (ii) in particular the situation of Member States in an emergency due to a sudden influx of third-country nationals. This emergency situation regulation came into play more quickly than the IGC had imagined in 2007, when hundreds of thousands of refugees attempted to reach EU territory via the Balkans in the late summer and autumn of 2015 as a result of the civil war in Syria and the aggressive spread of the so-called Islamic State across Syria and Iraq.

Article 79 TFEU postulates the development of a Common Immigration Policy, as was already provided for in Article 63(3) and (4) TEC. The history of this provision also testifies to the will of the Member States, but at the same time to its failure in reality, because in 2015 there was no functioning immigration policy either at the level of the Union or at the level of the Member States.

Article 80 TFEU recalls the principle of solidarity and fair sharing of responsibility - including financial responsibility - among the Member States. Here, too, the statement on Article 79 applies in full.

Chapter 3: Judicial cooperation in civil matters (Article 81 TFEU)

The sole article of this chapter replaces Article 65 TEC, further developing and adapting it to the realities and competences provided by the newly set primary law. The previously intergovernmental character is - once again - called to mind by the veto clause for national parliaments introduced by the IGC 2007.

Chapter 4: Judicial cooperation in criminal matters (Article 82 to 86 TFEU)

Articles 82, 83, and 85 TFEU essentially take up the provisions of Article 31 TEU de lege lata and develop these further. Article 84 TFEU, dealing with crime prevention, was already proposed by the IGC 2004 and taken over by the IGC 2007. However, the IGC 2007 went one - decisive - step further by introducing the mechanism for a facilitated enhanced cooperation for the regulatory domains of Articles 82 and 83 TFEU.

The provisions of Article 86 TFEU, which deals with the European Public Prosecutor's Office, are entirely new. The idea for these regulations came from the Convention and was taken over by the two IGCs in 2004 and 2007. Also in this case, the IGC 2007 introduced the mechanism for facilitated enhanced cooperation.

Chapter 5: Police cooperation (Article 87 to 89 TFEU)

Articles 87 and 88 TFEU refer to and develop the provisions of Article 30 TEU, whilst Article 89 TFEU also adopts this approach, the reference

Article in this case being Article 32 TEU de lege lata. The IGC 2007 also introduces the mechanism for facilitated enhanced cooperation for Article 87 TFEU.

II.9. Transport

Reference:	Part 3 Title VI Article 90 to 100 TFEU
Subject:	Establishment and ensuring of a Common Transport Policy
Objectives:	Eliminating anomalies and gaps in the European transport network that prevent the completion of the Internal Market Ensuring an effective, efficient, safe, and accessible transport system that supports the free movement of goods, people, and services Increasing competition in the transport industry, reducing state aid, reducing obstacles for European transport companies to do business in other Member States
Principles:	Balancing the need for an effective EU transport system on the one hand and environmental protection on the other, in order to achieve sustainable mobility Ensuring the needs and interests of individual citizens as (i) consumers, (ii) transport users, (iii) residents of transport-related or direct transport zones
Instruments:	Financial support (regional and structural policy, low-interest loans from the European Investment Bank, loan guarantees from the European Investment Fund, financing of feasibility studies) Research and technological development International agreements

Addressing the issue of transport has been a Community task since the Treaties of Rome. The Treaties specified a common policy in the field of transport as one of the activities in the Community's task list from the outset of European integration. Transport policy is one of the policies that has undergone only minor changes in terms of content, with a focus on procedural and terminological aspects in the individual steps of the development of the treaties, with one exception only.

Transport policy should by no means be seen as an isolated issue or even as a stand-alone policy. It has always served and continues to serve to support and safeguard the Internal Market as a flanking policy. A functioning Internal Market requires, as one of its basic prerequisites, an efficient and effective transport system at all three dimensions: land, air, and water. This transport system must be designed to support the economic, environmental, and social objectives of the Union at the same time. If one includes the four Internal Market freedoms in this comprehensive approach, it becomes evident that the - physical - freedom of goods, persons, and services would be meaningless without an adequate EU transport system. Beyond the intra-Community area, transport policy should also contribute to enabling and strengthening transport links with third countries in order to make a contribution to trade policy.

Originally, transport policy at Community level had been considered almost dead letter. According to the original wording of the Treaty, the rules on the Common Transport Policy would have had to be adopted by 31 December 1969. Whether the Community of Six did not have transport problems is a moot point. The fact that railway, at that time the most important mode of land transport, was state-owned in all Member States and that the state also owned the infrastructure, i.e. the rail network and its maintenance, as well as the influence of various interest groups resulted in the Council remaining inactive.

In 1983, the Parliament brought an action against the Council before the ECJ under Article 232 TEC for this failure to act.[304] The Court delivered a judgement that was as Solomon-like as it was spectacular,[305] holding that while the Council was not at fault in that it could not be accused of failure to act with regard to the establishment of a Common Transport Policy since the Treaty did not sufficiently define the content of such a policy, the Council had been culpably inactive with regard to the adoption of Community rules implementing Article 71(1)(a) and (b) TEC. The ECJ held that the Council had failed to ensure the freedom to provide services in the field of international transport and to lay down the conditions under which carriers may operate transport services within a Member State in which they are established. Until this ruling, the Council had justified its

304 The Commission joined this case as a litigant on the side of the Parliament. One of the reasons for the Commission's role as a litigant was that it had identified a rich field of activity in the transport sector and saw itself as being negatively affected by the Council's inaction in implementing the Internal Market.

305 Cf. ECJ 13/83, Parliament vs. Council, 1985, 1603.

reluctance in this area mainly on the grounds that transport policy was not covered by the general rules of the Treaty, in particular regarding the applicability of competition rules, the freedom of establishment, and the freedom to provide services. The ECJ undermined this position of the Council through further rulings, which ultimately led to a change of attitude on the part of the Member States. In the meantime, the prevailing doctrine is that the purpose of a separate Treaty title on transport is to give the Council the possibility of responding to the special needs of this policy vis-à-vis the other Community policies, underlining the flanking policy character.

Another ECJ ruling that had a significant influence on the development of transport policy was delivered in 1986. In the so-called Nouvelle Frontière Case, the Court held that the Council not only had an obligation to act on land transport and sea transport, but that this obligation also applied to air transport and implicitly to sea transport.[306] The Council had abstained from any implementation of policy in air and sea transport, using as its primary legal argument Article 80(1) TEC, which made transport policy applicable in general to transport by rail, road, and inland waterway. The possibility to adopt such regulations also for sea and air transport is a purely optional provision according to Article 80(2) TEC. The Member States had applied the very narrow interpretation of Article 80 TEC, among other reasons, because these two modes of transport were considered to be closely related to national security and thus national prerogatives. In the Nouvelle Frontière ruling, the ECJ deprived this view of any basis. Since 1986, decision-making in the Council has been facilitated insofar as the SEA brought about an amendment to Article 80(2) TEC and since then the Council has also voted by qualified majority on regulations for maritime shipping and aviation.

The first substantive change since the original version was made by the ToM. Originally, the scope of application according to Article 71(1) TEC included explicit legislative competences of the Council with regard to (letter a) international traffic from or to the territory of a Member State or for transit traffic through the territory of one or more Member States, as well as (letter b) the admission of carriers to traffic within a Member State in which they are established. As a general clause, the original letter c provided for the Council to adopt any other appropriate provisions. In the course

306 Cf. ECJ 209-213/84, Nouvelle Frontière, 1986, 1425.

of the intergovernmental conference, competence for measures to improve road safety was added as a new letter c.[307] This extension of competence proved to be extremely far-sighted, and the Council has frequently made use of this competence in recent years.

The ToL amended the transport title in three aspects. Firstly, paragraph 2 of the former Article 71 TEC, now Article 91 TFEU, was adapted rather in the wording than content. The Convention had intended to delete the voting requirement completely, but the IGC 2004 had already returned to it - with the wording taken over by the ToL. The second amendment relates to the now Article 98 TFEU. A second sentence was added, which contains a repeal clause of this article. Already in the course of the IGC 2004, some Member States intended to delete this special provision in favour of Germany, as it was generally regarded as dead letter. Germany opposed this deletion; whereby no objective necessity had been cited for its retention. The IGC 2004 reacted to this German position by issuing a declaration to ensure that Germany could not take advantage of it in an improper manner. This indecisive conduct, which would have led to legal distortions and politically incomprehensible consequences, could be remedied by the IGC 2007 by introducing the repeal clause after Germany had given up its opposition. The third amendment relates to Article 100 TFEU, formerly Article 80 TEC. Here, the very vague possibility of introducing appropriate regulations for maritime shipping and aviation was simply converted into a direct authorisation to act; the resulting increase in the Union's competence was made in the sense of closing a gap, which ultimately addresses the developments since the SEA.

II.10. Common Rules on Competition, Taxation and Approximation of Laws

Since the coming into force of the ToA, Title VII, formerly Title VI, contains - under a new and more precise heading - those regulations that were originally contained in Title I of Part 3. Unless otherwise specified, the regulations contained here refer to all relevant community activities in the TEC or rather, since the ToL, in the TFEU. The division into three chapters, however, does not represent a tiered structure as such or even a kind of ranking; the IGC 1996 merely intended to make this title more concise and more manageable. Those provisions dealing with questions of the free

307 This general clause is now contained in letter d.

movement of persons in connection with visa policy that were transferred from the TEU to the TEC were included in Title IV TEC by the IGC 1996. The ToL did not make any major changes to either the system or the content but contented itself - apart from renumbering - with editorial changes.

II.10.1. Rules on Competition

Reference:	Part 3 Title VII Chapter 1 Article 101 to 109 TFEU
Subject:	Ensuring fair intra-Union competition
Objectives:	Ensuring a system that protects competition within the Internal Market from distortions Ensuring an open market economy with free competition
Principles:	Prohibition of abuse of a dominant market position Prohibition of certain state aid
Instruments:	Prohibition of cartels Prohibition of monopolies Merger control Block exemptions State aid control Control of public procurement Control of public enterprises

The first six articles dealing with the rules for companies were taken over almost unchanged in their original 1957 version. The IGCs saw no reason to change the substance of the existing system and retained the provisions on the prohibition of anti-competitive agreements or decisions (Article 81 TEC (ex-Article 85)), abuse of a dominant position (Article 82 TEC (ex-Article 86)), decisions on the admissibility of agreements (Article 84 TEC (ex-Article 88)), infringement proceedings (Article 85 TEC (ex-Article 89)) as well as public enterprises and monopoly enterprises (Article 86 TEC (ex-Article 90)) as they have stood for decades. The IGC 1996 only adapted paragraph 1 of Article 83 TEC (ex-Article 87), now Article 103 TFEU, regarding the issuance of regulations and directives, whereby no substantive change was made here either, but merely a reaction to the fact that the deadline requirement for the application of this article had already been met.[308] The same applies to Article 85 TEC (ex-Article 89), now Article 105 TFEU, which has been merely simplified.

However, this acceptance by the various IGCs should not necessarily be interpreted as meaning that this is petrified law.[309] Rather, the ECJ, by developing the de minimis principle in 1969, has been instrumental in making dynamic interpretation possible. Otherwise, the conferences might have been forced to adopt the system established by the Court of Justice in primary law, which would, however, have led to the complicated question of how to determine the respective threshold for the application of this principle, which otherwise prohibits agreements or decisions that are contrary to the Treaty only if they have significant market effects.

Although the primary law provisions remained unchanged, Germany succeeded during the IGC 1996 in her bid to ensure that a Declaration of the Intergovernmental Conference (No. 37) was included, which takes note of the Commission's view that the existing competition rules allow full account to be taken of services of general economic interest[310] provided by the public-law credit institutions existing in Germany, as well as facilities granted to them to compensate for the obligations associated with these services.[311] Germany tried up to the last minute of the IGC 2000 to have the same declaration adopted, but failed - much to the displeasure of the German Länder - due to the resistance of the other Member States, which considered it an inconsistent exception.

Only ex-Article 91 TEC, which dealt with dumping, was deleted. This deletion was made possible by the expiry of the deadline. The original Section 2 of Chapter 1, which had consisted of this sole article, was also deleted.

Today's Section 2 (Section 3 before the deletion of the dumping articles mentioned above) went through several changes. It deals with state aid and basically defines which such aid is considered compatible with the common market (Article 87 TEC (ex-Article 92)). In particular, Article 87(3) TEC

308 i.e. three years after the entry into force of the TEC as amended by the ToM.

309 The term "petrified law" derives from the Austro-German legal theory that legal texts shall be interpreted exclusively on the terms of their issuance. This theory can best be compared to the "originalism theory" of the Anglo-American legal system.

310 This thematic complex is collectively referred to as services of general interest.

311 The public-law credit institutions of the German Länder were affected by this declaration. Austria and Luxembourg made a corresponding unilateral declaration to the IGC 1996 stating that they assume that Declaration No. 37 also applies to credit institutions in Austria and Luxembourg with comparable organisational forms.

(ex-Article 92), now Article 107 TFEU, listing which aid can be considered compatible,[312] underwent a major change in the course of the IGC 1991, when aid in the cultural sector was added to the list. This issue had arisen primarily due to large-scale events in the cultural sector, as such events had increasingly morphed into commercial ones with massive economic effects.[313] Moreover, the IGC 1991 changed the order without any apparent necessity so that the original letter c became the new letter b, the original letter b became the new letter c, cultural issues were inserted as the new letter d and the original letter d became the new letter e. The IGC 1996 took up this very paragraph 3 again and - also without pressing necessity - exchanged letters b and c again, so that they henceforth reappear in their original order in the Treaty. The content of letter b, dealing with aid to promote the development of certain economic activities or of certain economic areas, was modified. The reference to shipbuilding aid, insofar as it existed on 1 January 1957 and merely corresponded to a lack of customs protection, was deleted from this provision. This derogation had become obsolete as a result of the fulfilment of the condition that such aid should be phased out in accordance with the provisions applicable to the abolition of customs duties. A minimal but, from the European Parliament's point of view, important amendment was made to Article 89 TEC (ex-Article 94), now Article 109 TFEU, already in the course of the IGC 1991, when the Council could still only adopt implementing regulations on a proposal from the Commission with a qualified majority, but since the ToM only after consulting Parliament.

312 Unlike those under paragraph 2, which are compatible by definition.

313 These effects occurred - and still occur - not so much through the events per se, but through their marketing in the course of and after the respective event (broadcasting rights, sound and video carriers). During the accession negotiations, Austria claimed such an exemption, especially for its renowned festivals in Salzburg and Bregenz.

II.10.2. Tax Provisions

Reference:	Part 3 Title VII Chapter 2 Article 110 to 113 TFEU
Subject:	Complementary policy for the establishment of the Internal Market
Objectives:	Exercising the tax sovereignty of the Member States in compliance with Union law
Principles:	Prohibition of tax discrimination Harmonisation of indirect taxes No applicability of the harmonisation mandate to direct taxes
Instruments:	Directives Cooperation between tax administrations (Bilateral) Double taxation agreements

Tax regulations had already been part of the original TEEC. Over the years, the SEA, the ToM, and the ToA made small, not too far-reaching changes to them. The last major opportunity to amend these provisions could not be seized in the course of IGC 2000, as this failed due to the opposition of some Member States.

The inclusion of this complex of issues in Title VII of the Treaty already indicates the intended objective. The aim of this title is to ensure fair competition within the Union by eliminating as far as possible any discrimination against goods imported from other Member States, especially in view of the fact that such discrimination is based on different indirect taxation systems in the Member States, such as VAT, excise duties, registration fees, vehicle taxes and the like. In this context, the provisions of Title VII are to be seen as complementary to the free movement of goods, in particular Article 25 TEC, now Article 30 TFEU. This applies specifically to Article 90 TEC, now Article 110 TFEU, which is intended to prevent Member States from abusing the right to levy national taxes to the extent that such taxes serve to discriminate against imports from other Member States. In other words, no national tax - direct or indirect - may be levied on such imported products that does not apply to comparable domestic products. Thus, since Article 90 TEC stipulates which type of taxation is excluded, Article 91 TEC, now Article 111 TFEU, specifies that the tax rebate in the case of export to another Member State may not be higher than the direct or indirect taxes originally levied. This provision clearly serves to prevent indirect export support, which would also amount to discrimination. This very provision actually goes beyond the original scope of application of the Treaty, especially in connection with Article 90 TEC, now Article 110 TFEU. In various decisions, the ECJ has additionally extended the scope of application of Article 90 EC and applied it to exports as well, arguing that higher indirect taxation of exported goods affects free trade and is therefore not permissible. Based on this case law, the application of incentive-reducing taxes levied with the intention of preventing the export of scarce goods is prohibited as being inconsistent with the provisions of the Treaty.

The original provision of ex-Article 97 TEC that Member States levying VAT under the cumulative multiple tax system may set average rates for goods or groups of goods for domestic duties levied on imported goods and for refunds granted on exported goods, while respecting the principles set out in ex-Articles 95 and 96 TEC, was deleted by the ToA. Article 92 TEC, now Article 112 TFEU, stipulates that for charges other than Value Added Tax (= VAT), excise duties and other indirect taxes, relief and drawback on exports to other Member States, and countervailing charges on imports from Member States may be granted only if the Council, acting by qualified majority on a proposal from the Commission, has previously authorised such charges for a limited period.

However, the provisions of Article 93 TEC, now Article 113 TFEU, are of outstanding importance at any rate. This article explicitly deals with the harmonisation of indirect taxes. Article 93 TEC gives the Council the competence, on a proposal from the Commission and after consulting the European Parliament and the Economic and Social Committee, to adopt provisions for the harmonisation of indirect taxation legislation. The Council can only adopt these provisions unanimously and is restricted both economically and by the Treaty. In economic terms, the Council has to demonstrate a need for such provisions in relation to the establishment and functioning of the Internal Market. In Treaty terms - and arguably also in political terms - it has to be demonstrated that these provisions are necessary in order to meet the deadline set in Article 14 TEC, now Article 26 TFEU. In other words, the harmonisation of indirect taxes does not follow an automatism. Moreover, the pressure on the Council is increased by the fact that the deadline of Article 14 TEC - 31 December 1992 - has long since passed. The reference to this deadline could or even should have been removed by the ToA at the latest. However, the IGC decided to keep it in order to support the argument that the harmonisation of indirect taxes is an integral part of the establishment and functioning of the Internal

Market - in particular the free movement of goods and services - and is long overdue.

During the IGC 2000, Article 93 TEC and its possible amendment had been the subject of intense controversy. On the one hand, several Member States wanted to abandon the requirement of unanimity in the Council and introduce qualified majority voting for these measures; on the other hand, the European Parliament demanded the co-decision procedure in consistent pursuit of its aim of creating an automatism between qualified majority voting in the Council and the co-decision procedure. Even those Member States who were in favour of a qualified majority wanted to limit the scope of application to a minimum. In the end, however, Luxembourg, Ireland, and the United Kingdom prevailed with their blockade against an amendment of Article 93 TEC, so this article remained unchanged.

In Nice, it was not only an attempt to simplify the procedure for the harmonisation of indirect taxes that failed. After the IGC had reached the point that industrial policy measures under Article 157 TEC, now Article 173 TFEU, would be decided by co-decision (paragraph 3), the three Member States cited succeeded in having the following passage inserted into the second subparagraph of Article 157(3) TEC: "This Title shall not provide a basis for the introduction by the Community of any measure which is likely to result in distortions of value or which contains tax provisions [...]". These states have thus also prevented tax harmonisation measures from being adopted through the back door of the Industry Title, so to speak. The Member States did make attempts to initiate a kind of harmonisation in the tax area, with a group of eleven Member States trying to establish enhanced cooperation for a stock exchange sales tax, but the attempt stalled for a long time and has not been properly realised to date.

II.10.3. Approximation of Laws

Reference:	Part 3 Title VII Chapter 3 Article 114 to 118 TFEU
Subject:	Contribution to the establishment of the Single Market
Objectives:	Facilitating the effective exercise of the freedom of establishment Abolishing obstacles to legal transactions with companies and legal persons incorporated under foreign law
Principles:	Structuring the Freedom of Movement granted to companies in accordance with the Union's economic and social objectives Ensuring that differences in the structure of national company law in the Member States do not lead to distortions of competition across the Union
Instruments:	Approximation of company law in the Member States Introduction of European company law standards Community agreements in the field of company law Introduction of minimum standards in stock exchange law

The ToN reduced Chapter 3 to four articles, which have evolved and changed radically over the years since the TEEC (three articles), the SEA (five articles), and the ToM (seven articles); in its current - ToL – version it contains five articles.

Article 94 TEC (ex-Article 100), now Article 115 TFEU, has remained unchanged in content and regulates the issue of establishing directives for the approximation of legislation. However, the ToM adapted the procedure itself insofar as the Council is no longer the sole deciding body, acting unanimously on a proposal from the Commission, but can only issue such directives after consulting Parliament and the Economic and Social Committee. During the IGC 1991, the Parliament did not yet have the self-confidence to push for a higher level of integration, or at least the cooperation procedure; at the subsequent IGCs, such attempts were nipped in the bud, as the Member States argued - successfully - that such adjustments by definition affected existing national regulations and that it was therefore unacceptable for the national parliaments to be overruled by the European Parliament.

The first - rather dramatic - change of Chapter 3 was introduced by Article 18 SEA through the insertion of Article 95 TEC (ex-Article 100a), now Article 114 TFEU. The ToL has placed this article at the beginning of the chapter as an introductory article. The inclusion of ex-Article 100a TEC is justifiably regarded as probably the most important provision of the SEA. Article 95 TEC is the basis for so-called harmonisation directives in the Internal Market context and thus became the solution to the smouldering problem of adaptations which, by their very nature, could only take the form of special directives before the SEA.[314] The Member States had realised that such individual directives and the cumbersome unanimity procedure could no longer keep pace with the requirements of the Internal Market and, by making the QMV admissible, opened the way to a faster solution. Moreover, the Parliament was granted the cooperation procedure and the Economic and Social Committee the right to be consulted. Already during the IGC 1991, the next revision of ex-Article 100a was carried out, in particular through the introduction of the codecision procedure. The ToA affected this article again and even more profoundly. In the pre-Amsterdam era, paragraph 3 required the Commission to take a high level of protection as a basis for its proposals in the fields of health, safety, environmental, and consumer protection, while Council and Parliament were not bound by this requirement. However, the ToA required the Council and the Parliament to strive for these objectives as well. The IGC 1996 could not bring itself to include a stricter link to these principles in the Treaty, although it was not necessarily the industrially strong Member States that sought to prevent this. However, the political commitment was - as was subsequently shown - sufficient to give these principles a stronger position. At the same time, the Treaty stipulated that the Commission should base its proposals in particular on the scientific results of the latest developments. The IGC 1996 thus raised the principles of state-of-the-art and best-available-technique to the level of primary law.

The UK successfully intervened in favour of animal welfare and secured Protocol 24 on the Protection and Welfare of Animals in the ToA, which requires both the Community and Member States to take full account of the relevant requirements when defining and implementing Community policy

314 The first harmonisation directive adopted on the legal basis of ex-Article 100a TEC was Council Directive 88/378/EEC of 3 May 1988 on the approximation of the laws of the Member States concerning the safety of toys, the so-called Toys Directive.

on agriculture, transport, the Internal Market and research.[315] A special feature of this protocol is that it must take particular account of religious rites, cultural traditions, and regional heritage.[316] In this context, the IGC 1996 also adopted Declaration No. 22 on persons with disabilities, according to which the institutions of the Community shall take into account the needs of this societal group when developing measures under Article 95 TEC.

These changes and extensions to paragraph 3 are to be seen as a reflection of the discussions in the early 1990s, which had placed a major emphasis on the environment.

The remaining parts of Article 95 TEC (now Article 114 TFEU) underwent an equally profound change through the IGC 1996. Paragraph 4 in its ToA version facilitates the maintenance of more stringent Member State standards, where justified by the protection of the working environment or the natural environment, simply through the notification by the Member State concerned to the Commission. The remaining subparagraphs of paragraph 4 have been deleted and replaced by new paragraphs 5 to 9, which place the procedure following such notification on a more precise legal footing. These provisions address the delicate balance between the right of Member States to maintain stricter levels of protection on the one hand and the need not to tolerate discrimination or disguised barriers to trade on the other. Whether the list of permissible cases of intervention deliberately omitted the justifying facts of consumer protection or whether this was simply a drafting error cannot be ascertained in retrospect; the sources do not provide any clear information on this. The new regulations solved the dilemma of the previous text, which was short, but correspondingly cryptic and thus the cause of numerous interpretation issues. The IGC 1996 took up in particular the fact of derogation on the basis of - alleged - specific health problems, which had been used as a gateway to far-reaching Member State derogation provisions. Should a Member State request an exemption on the basis of this reasoning, the Commission must immediately examine whether it should propose appropriate (harmonisation) measures to the

315 In the following years, the United Kingdom continued to spearhead the protection of animals at Community level, which was to become apparent not least through the introduction of the Council Directive 1999/22/EC of 29 March 1999 relating to the keeping of wild animals in zoos (so-called Zoo Directive), under the UK EU Presidency.

316 This reference in particular was to prove important in subsequent years, as it was precisely on this basis that the demands for ritual slaughter of animals carried out according to Jewish or Islamic tradition could be justified.

Council on that basis. Thus, unilateral measures by Member States on the basis of these grounds would be more or less ruled out. Paragraphs 9 and 10 of Article 95 TEC are a reiteration of the original sub-paragraph 3 of paragraph 3 as well as the original paragraph 5, as no substantive changes have been made.

Ex-Article 100b TEC, which was inserted by Article 19 SEA and dealt with the equivalence of national regulations, had only a short retention period in the TEC and was deleted already during the IGC 1996, as the time limit contained in this article had expired.

Ex-Article 100c TEC (visa obligation and the uniform format for visas) and ex-Article 100d TEC (coordination committee in accordance with ex-Article K.4 TEU), which were inserted by the ToM, were - in line with the system - moved to Title IV TEC during the IGC 1996.

The remaining two articles of this chapter as amended by the ToN - Article 96 TEC (ex-Article 101), now Article 116 TFEU, and Article 97 TEC (ex-Article 102), now Article 117 TFEU - have, with one exception, remained unchanged since the TEEC. In its original version, the reference in the second subparagraph of Article 96 stated that the Council had to decide unanimously in the first stage and only then with QMV. This clause was deleted due to the fulfilment of the deadline in 1992.

During the IGC 2007, a new Article 118 TFEU was added, the origin of which lies in the IGC 2004. This provision had no corresponding provisions in primary law de lege lata. It aims to introduce a legal basis for ensuring improved and uniform protection of intellectual property rights in the Union into Treaty law. The IGC 2007 thus expanded the competences of the Union on the one hand, but quite specifically created a legal basis for the functioning of the Internal Market, not so much for its realisation.

II.11. Economic and Monetary Policy

Reference:	Part 3 Title VIII Article 119 to 144 TFEU
Subject:	Establishment of a Common Economic and Monetary Union
Objectives:	Coordination of economic policy Promotion of the efficient use of resources Establishment of a Monetary Union
Principles:	Actions of the EMU shall be in accordance with the principle of an open market economy No liability of the Union for the debts of the Member States Avoidance of excessive deficits Compliance with budgetary discipline
Instruments:	Coordination of Member State economic policies Common currency

Arguably one of the most profound and lasting innovations brought about by the ToM was the inclusion of Title VII (now Title VIII), Economic and Monetary Union (EMU), in the TEC. EMU was seen by the IGC 1991 as the ultimate step towards the completion of the Single Market and its further development. As in other cases, this policy was only incorporated into primary law by the ToM, but its roots go back far into the history of the Community. In a particularly broad interpretation, the fifth recital of the Preamble to the original TEEC could be regarded as the basis for the later EMU, since the Founding States had stated there that they had concluded this Treaty in an effort to unify their economies. Even if there is no explicit reference to a monetary union, the long-term goal of an economic union is nonetheless mentioned. The next, more concrete reference in primary law is to be found in the eighth recital of the Preamble to the SEA.[317]

317 In any case, the Member States were aware of one decisive economic point from the very beginning: The participating states of a single market must commit themselves to essentially similar economic goals and accordingly coordinate their respective national economic policies at least to such an extent that functioning competition can indeed take place in the single market to be established. Accordingly, the leeway of the Member States of a single market is limited only to the scope and intensity of coordination; further restrictions - even at the level of primary law - would run counter to the achievement of the objective. Despite agreement on the problem (too low a degree of convergence of the Internal Market economies has an impact on

However, at their meeting in The Hague on 1 and 2 February 1969, the Heads of State and Government had already decided to press ahead with the development necessary to strengthen the Community and develop it into an economic union; in concrete terms, they agreed to have a step-by-step plan drawn up in the course of 1970 for the establishment of an economic and monetary union and entrusted this work to the then PM and Finance Minister of Luxembourg, Pierre Werner, whose working group subsequently presented the so-called Werner Plan. The Council and the Representatives of the Governments of the Member States, meeting within the Council, defined the objective of an EMU in a quasi-genuine Council Resolution[318] in such a way that, at the end of the process of its achievement, the Community would (i) constitute an area in which the free movement of persons, goods, services, and capital would be ensured, without distortions of competition and without structural or regional imbalances, and under conditions which would allow economic agents to (ii) constitute an autonomous monetary area within the international system, characterised by the full and irreversible convertibility of currencies, the removal of exchange rate fluctuation margins, and the irrevocable fixing of parity ratios, which are indispensable conditions for the creation of a single currency, and in which a Community central banking system operates. Although the political circumstances of the 1970s did not yet allow this resolution to be implemented, the European Monetary Cooperation Fund and the European Monetary System (EMS) were nevertheless introduced.

After the thrust of integration had been relaunched by the SEA in 1986, the Hanover European Council set up another group of experts on this subject at its meeting on 27 and 28 June 1988, this time under the chairmanship of the then President of the Commission, Jacques Delors, to develop a concrete step-by-step plan. This phased approach was presented on 17 April 1989 and called Delors Plan. Mr Delors proposed to remove all trade barriers in the Single Market and to strengthen the coordination of economic and structural policy in the first phase; furthermore, all Community

---

the Internal Market through exchange rate problems, which impedes the emergence of a common capital market as well as the free exchange of goods and services), there were two almost irreconcilable schools of thought in the Member States, the monetarist approach on the one hand and the Keynesian approach on the other. This directional dispute should continue to smoulder - albeit diminished - even after the achievement of stage three of EMU.

318 cf. OJ C 28/1971 p.1. In this case, one refers to a legal act of the European Council sui generis, as there was no explicit basis for the Committee in the TEEC for this issue.

currencies were to be integrated into the EMS, whereby the - then - ECU was also to be used without restriction in private transactions. In a second phase, the Treaties were to be amended with regard to the establishment of the European System of Central Banks (ESCB) and the European Central Bank (ECB). In a third and final phase, large proportions of power of the Member States in the economic policy and monetary field were to be transferred to Community institutions, the exchange rates of the currencies were to be irreversibly fixed, and a single monetary policy was to be worked out by the ESCB. At the end of this process, the national currencies were to be replaced by a single Community currency. The Community implemented the first phase of the Delors Plan without changing the structure of primary law until 1 July 1970. The second and third phases of the Delors Plan, however, required primary law provisions and a fundamental adaptation of primary law, respectively, and became one of the central issues of the ToM.

The ToM completely revised ex-Articles 102a to 109 TEEC, indicating clearly that the IGC 1991 intended to make a clean break with the pre-Maastricht era. This is also expressed by the structure of the new provisions, since the final stage of EMU was regulated in the first part (Articles 98 to 115 TEC (ex-Articles 102a to 109)),[319] and the transitional provisions (Articles 116 to 124 TEC (ex-Articles 109e to 109m)) only afterwards. The provisions on EMU as laid down in the ToM were not changed by the IGC 1996 at all and by the IGC 2000 only in a few aspects. Article 100 TEC (ex-Article 103a), which regulates financial assistance, was changed to QMV in general by the ToN, whereby Declaration No. 6 of the IGC on Article 100 TEC was incorporated into the ToN at the instigation of the United Kingdom. This declaration is intended to ensure that such decisions are consistent with the financial perspective and the inter-institutional agreements on budgetary discipline. The second amendment made by the ToN concerns Article 111(4) TEC (ex-Article 109), which deals with agreements with third parties and monetary agreements. Subject to paragraph 1 of this article, QMV is also introduced here in general. The third ToN amendment - Article 123(4) TEC (ex-Article 109), which deals with the beginning of the

319 From a historical point of view, it should be noted that the chapter on Cooperation in Economic and Monetary Policy (Economic and Monetary Union) had been inserted into the EEC Treaty as Chapter 1 under Article 20 SEA, and the subsequent Chapters 2 (Conjunctural Policy), 3 (Balance of Payments), and 4 (Commercial Policy) - which was later moved by the ToM - had been renumbered in accordance with Article 20(2) SEA.

third stage, the reporting obligation and voting rights - also concerned the switch from unanimity to QMV.

The ToL fundamentally reformed this title for the first time since its inclusion into primary law. On the one hand, the title was renumbered, and on the other hand, it underwent changes that had become necessary for reading purposes. In addition to these purely formal-technical changes, the IGC 2007 also made substantive changes to this title.

The IGC 2007 decided to place a programmatic introductory article at the beginning of the monetary and economic policy title and moved the former Article 4 TEC to the top as Article 119 TFEU. The content of the article itself was not changed, but the decision to place it here was made with a view to bringing related parts of the Treaty together as far as possible and thus giving them a spatial connection.

In Chapter I, Economic Policy, the current Article 121 TFEU (formerly Article 98 TEC) is strengthened in that from now on the Commission can directly warn a Member State that is not complying with the system. This was the IGC's response in 2007 to increasingly frequent deviations against which the Commission could not react directly; moreover, the Member State concerned is deprived of the right to vote on its own case.[320] The amendment of the current Article 122 TFEU, formerly Article 99 TEC, introduces the principle of solidarity at the level of energy supply into primary law, whereby the IGC reacted here in 2007 to various energy policy developments in the neighbouring countries to the east, which subsequently proved to be prescient. The first corresponding energy crisis took place under the Austrian EU Presidency in 2006. However, it was averted with relatively little complaint. Further dramatic developments in Ukraine eight respectively sixteen years later vindicated the IGC's decision to introduce such a solidarity clause relatively quickly in 2007.

Chapter 2, Monetary Policy, and Chapter 3, Institutional Provisions, remained essentially unaffected by the ToL.

The IGC 2007 decided to introduce a completely new Chapter 4 in this title dealing with provisions for the Member States whose currency is the euro. In doing so, the IGC 2007 intended on the one hand to emphasise the special position of the euro states, and on the other hand to follow the normative power of the factual. At the time of the IGC 2007, the Euro Group had already gained such importance that it had set the tone for the

320 This principle applies to the entire title. The aim was to prevent the state concerned from being the deciding factor in narrow decisions.

ECOFIN in its formation as Council of Finance Ministers. Although the IGC 2007 did not go so far as to elevate the informal ministerial meetings of the Eurogroup to the corpus of the TFEU, it did adopt a protocol to this effect, whereby these provisions are at least present in primary law. It was clear to all Member States involved that the inclusion of this chapter could be the nucleus for future Treaty changes if the Eurogroup were to become further independent. Here, too, the IGC 2007 anticipated developments that were to manifest themselves in the course of the Greek debt crisis in 2014 and 2015.

The previous Chapter 4, Transitional Provisions, consequently, became Chapter 5 and was - radically - adapted to reality by the ToL. The following overview summarises the repeals and changes made by the ToL:
Repeals

- Article 116 ex-TEC;
- Article 117 paragraphs 1, 2 second indent, and paragraphs 3 bis 9 ex-TEC;
- Article 118 TEC;
- Article 121 paragraphs 2 to 4 TEC;
- Article 122 paragraphs 1, 2 first sentence, and paragraphs 3 to 6 TEC;
- Article 123 paragraphs 1, 2 and 4 TEC;
- Article 124 paragraph 2 TEC.

Renumberings

- Article 117 paragraph 2 indents 1 to 5 TEC become Article 141 paragraph 2 TFEU;
- Article 121 paragraph 1 TEC becomes Article 140 paragraph 1 TFEU;
- Article 122 paragraph 2 Satz 2 TEC becomes Article 140 paragraph 2 subparagraph 1 TFEU;
- Article 123 paragraph 3 TEC becomes Article 141 paragraph 1 TFEU;
- Article 123 paragraph 5 TEC becomes Article 140 paragraph 3 TFEU;
- Article 124 paragraph 1 TEC becomes Article 141 TFEU.

Article 139 TFEU takes over Article III-197 TCEU - editorially adapted, but unchanged in content - regulating issues concerning those Member States with a derogation in respect of the euro.

Article 140 TFEU takes over the wording of Article 121(1) TEC in general but introduces a highly substantive change. The beginning of the first sub-paragraph of the previous provision stipulated that the Commission and the European Monetary Institute (EMI) were obliged to report. This provision is now amended so that at least once every two years, or at the request of a Member State with a derogation, the Commission and the European Central Bank must report. This amendment specifies the reporting obligation in terms of timing and the party entitled to make the request.

The first paragraph of Article 141 TFEU adopts the text of Article 123(3) TEC, whereas the second paragraph adopts indents 1 to 5 of Article 117(2) TEC. The introductory phrase of paragraph 2, in turn, is taken from Article III-199 paragraph 2 TCEU, which, however, does not represent a substantive innovation, but merely an adaptation to the reality of the Eurozone or rather the non-members.

Article 142 TFEU reproduces, with editorial adaptations, the provisions of Article 124(1) TEC.

Article 143 TFEU adopts the provisions of Article 119 TEC, whereby the obsolete reference to the gradual realisation of the Common Commercial Policy has been deleted, as has the entire paragraph 4, since the third stage was already reached.

Article 144 TFEU repeats Article 120 TEC, but deletes the entire paragraph 4, as the third stage was already reached, and grants the Commission the right of recommendation in paragraph 2 instead of the previous right of opinion.

II.12. Employment

Source:	Part 3 Title IX Article 145 to 150 TFEU
Topic:	Coordinated strategy for employment
Objectives:	Promoting employment as a matter of common concern with a view to reach a higher level of employment rate in the Union
Principles:	No harmonization of legal and administrative provisions of the Member States Exclusively promoting a skilled, trained and adaptable workforce and labour markets responsive to economic change
Instruments:	Obligatory coordination of the Member States' actions in this respect within the Council; Support of Member States' actions by the Union

The chapter on employment is one of the most recent supplements to EU primary law. After severe debates and fundamental discussions between the United Kingdom and the other Member States, employment became part of EU law in the course of the IGC 1996. The incorporation of that particular policy mirrors the substantial changes of the European political landscape of the 1990s more than any other change to the Treaties by the ToA.

Legend goes that employment was a totally new addition to the Treaties when it was incorporated as Title VIII to the TEC. The creation of this myth was intended to emphasise the achievement of a balance with social policy, which had long been enshrined in the Treaties. Already in the pre-Amsterdam era several indications to employment policy could be found in the Treaties. Even the original Article 104 TEEC contained a reference of ensuring high levels of employment.[321] The Treaty on the European Community comprised clear indications to employment policies, e.g. the new reference to a high level of employment in Article 2 (as amended by the Treaty of Maastricht).[322]

Despite all this criticism, with the incorporation of Title VIII employment policy got a prominent position within the Treaty framework. The

321 The content of Article 104 TEEC was deleted by the ToM.

322 That particular addition might be seen as a compensatory measure - at least from the employment policy perspective - to the deletion of article 104 TEEC as mentioned above.

Member States had been confronted with growing unemployment[323] on the one hand and tightening public spending in the course of implementing (and reaching) the Maastricht criteria. They came under severe pressure by the public and the organized civil society, namely the trade unions. As direct reaction, the Member States intended to put down a marker to let the stakeholders know they care about these calamities. Next to the civil society, the European Commission strongly advocated the introduction of employment measures. All these efforts lead to the so called "Essen Strategy", adopted by the European Council in December 1994, and – two years later – to the "Dublin Declaration on Employment".[324]

The last years of the pre-Amsterdam era had been coined by fierce resistance of the United Kingdom under the premiership of Margaret Thatcher and her successor John Major. Both fought an all-out battle against any further competences of Brussels in the field of social and employment policy. When Tony Blair became Prime Minister after a crushing victory of "New Labour", the United Kingdom did not change her position, but the new UK leader was at least open for negotiations.[325] At the end of the IGC 1996, the Member States persuaded the United Kingdom to give up her resistance against that new title.[326]

Sweden, backed up by the European Trade Union Confederation (= ETUC), fulfilled all prejudices when trying to establish the general target

323 Unemployment in Europe had reached the previously unknown quota of 10 % on average.

324 That process had become irreversible. The Essen Strategy had been followed by the Dublin Declaration and the establishment of the Spring Meeting of the European Council that is since dedicated to economic and employment topics. The 1999 Lisbon Strategy was thought to be the final cornerstone. According to the Lisbon Strategy, the Union was meant to be striving to become the most competitive economic area in 2010. Unfortunately, the financial crisis started in 2008.

325 As a result of Tony Blair's extraordinary position within the European Heads of State and Government and his impact on the IGC 1996, one is tempted to call it a *Blairite Treaty* that led the way from neoliberalism to a kind of regulated capitalism. Conservative critics feared the worse, namely the renaissance of Keynesianism. They argued that the 1996 revision of the Treaties not only incorporated employment policy but adapted social and environment policy in that direction. Today's assessment shows that their worries had been exaggerated.

326 Employment policy became one of the strongest arguments of the Brexeteers (in connection with intra-EU migration). For them it was the perfect example of the excessive meddling of Brussels.

of "full employment" rather than "high level of employment".[327] The United Kingdom had not to ask long for support amongst the Member States to torpedo that push. The then conservative German government shared the sceptical position of the United Kingdom. Chancellor Helmut Kohl had won the 1998 elections with the promise of "blossoming landscapes" in former Eastern Germany,[328] but the reality showed quite a different picture: rising unemployment rates, unexpected rows of insolvency and business failure, and rural-urban migration to the western part caused huge transfer payments. Furthermore, the employment situation deteriorated even in the so called "Old Provinces" in the West, resulting in a considerable budget gap. Mr Kohl's situation became even more tricky as he needed the support of the social-democrat opposition in the German Bundestag (1st Chamber) as well as in the Bundesrat (2nd Chamber) to secure the ratification of the Treaty of Amsterdam. At the end, Germany signed the ToA and went along with the new employment title.

The IGC 2000 did not take up Title VIII any further. In particular, the question of whether the goal of full employment should be discussed no longer arose, since unemployment rates in the Member States had risen to such an extent in the meantime that it was no longer necessary to speak of a goal, but at best of wishful thinking. Moreover, it was already foreseeable in Nice that the negotiations with at least ten candidate countries would be concluded in the near future, and that their labour market situation would be even more drastic than that of the EU-15 Member States.

The fact that Title VIII remained unchanged in Nice clearly shows that a proverbial window of opportunity had opened up in the course of the IGC 1996, which the Heads of State and Government had taken advantage of. Neither before nor after the Amsterdam conference would the political framework have permitted such a radical adaptation of primary law in the area of employment. This statement can also be directly applied to the IGC 2007, which left the employment title untouched, only renumbering and editorially adapting the respective provisions.

---

327 Sweden's initiative was certainly triggered in memory of the glorious days of Olof Palme, when the so called "welfare state" became axiomatic. Given the situation twenty years later, even radical social romantics would rule out that objective. During the IGC 2000 no Member State took up the idea of full employment and no stakeholder asked for it. The Union had become realistic on its own limits – and on the considerable damage to its image such unattainable promises might cause.

328 Cf. https://www.chronik-der-mauer.de/material/180425/rundfunk-und-fernsehansprache-von-bundeskanzler-helmut-kohl-2-oktober-1990.

II.13. Customs Cooperation

Reference:	Part 3 Title II Chapter 2 Article 33 TFEU
Subject:	Further development and strengthening of customs cooperation
Objectives:	Mutual assistance of the customs authorities of the Member States Combating fraud through customs measures
Principles:	Restriction to customs cooperation Exclusion of criminal law aspects, which remain within the exclusive competence of the Member States
Instruments:	Exchange of information Measures that seem likely to increase cooperation and limit opportunities for fraud

The Treaty of Maastricht added customs to the original Title VI Article K.1(8) TEU, Provisions on Cooperation in the Fields of Justice and Home Affairs, Cooperation in Judicial and Home Affairs Policy. However, Article K.1 TEU clearly stated that the policies covered by it were to be considered by the Member States only as matters of common interest, without prejudice to the competences of the Community. Moreover, the area of customs was not covered by the evolutionary clause of Article K.9 TEU, containing a passerelle clause for a transition of certain policies into the Community method. Customs were thus exclusively part of the intergovernmental pillar of Cooperation in the Fields of Justice and Home Affairs. The results of an EP Committee of Inquiry into the Community Transit Procedure, which had been set up to investigate cases of fraud in this procedure, as well as initial approaches to transferring the Third Pillar to the Community method, prompted the IGC 1996 to include a separate title for customs cooperation in the TEC through the Treaty of Amsterdam. Although this area has been part of the TEC since the Treaty of Amsterdam, essential elements of the intergovernmental pillar remained, in particular the restriction of competence to a pure cooperation mechanism. The Treaty of Nice did not touch the title of customs cooperation, neither in text nor in content.

The Treaty of Lisbon brought together all the relevant Internal Market and customs provisions in a coherent whole, thus embedding Article 135 TEC as Article 33 TFEU.

II.14. Social Policy and the European Social Fund

Reference:	Part 3 Title X Article 151 to 161 and Part 3 Title XI Article 162 to 164 TFEU
Subject:	Ensuring economic and social progress in the Member States
Objectives:	Constant improvement of living and working conditions Establishment and operation of a European Social Fund (ESF) Ensuring social justice Strengthening social cohesion Ensuring high employment rates and a high level of social protection
Principles:	Maintaining the balance between the Internal Market and the development of a social equilibrium Joint action of economic and social forces
Instruments:	The main instrument for implementing social policy is the ESF

In its original version, the TEC wording showed a clear intention to constantly improve working and living conditions, harmonizing them as far as possible as they developed. The Commission was called upon to bring about the closest possible cooperation between the Member States in social policy areas, particularly in matters relating to (i) employment, (ii) social security, (iii) labour law and conditions, (iv) vocational training, (v) job security, and (vi) employee representation. The original text already included the requirement that pay should be gender neutral. The ESF, which was created under primary law, was assigned the tasks of (i) improving employment opportunities and (ii) supporting the development of increased labour mobility.

Although the SEA expanded these social provisions, it did not increase their enforceability. The Commission was empowered to facilitate a social dialogue at Community level, but the SEA did not specify in any way how the Commission should proceed, let alone what the objectives of such a dialogue should be. Nevertheless, the SEA should not be seen as a failure for the further development of the social chapter. After all, for the first time a provision was introduced that allowed the adoption of legal acts dealing with issues of the working environment, including health and safety of workers. This harmonization was to take the form of minimum standards.

The Treaty of Maastricht did not introduce any innovations in the field of social policy, but only a simple renumbering. However, the so-called Social Protocol was introduced. It was not until the Treaty of Nice that there was a significant push toward stronger social policy at Union level.

Denmark had long been reluctant to allow for an adaptation of Article 137 TEC in particular and was opposed to the transfer of social provisions to QMV. Nevertheless, Article 137 TEC was eventually redrafted. Measures to combat social exclusion and measures to modernize social protection systems were added as new objectives. Denmark's agreement was ultimately achieved through two clauses: (i) for the transition from unanimity to QMV in certain cases, the Council must decide unanimously on this transition and (ii) a new safeguard clause was added to the former Article 137(5) TEC (now Article 137(4)), which stipulates that the competence of the Member States to determine their social security system must not be affected by provisions adopted on the basis of this article and that the financial equilibrium of these systems must not be significantly affected by them.[329] Article 144 TEC was completely redrafted, dealing with the delegation to the Commission of tasks relating to the implementation of common measures, in particular in the field of social security for migrant workers referred to in Articles 39 to 42 TEC. The Portuguese Presidency of the IGC 2000 had initially proposed the deletion of this article, whereas the French Presidency proposed that this article should now form the legal basis for the establishment of a Social Protection Committee. The conference agreed on the French proposal and so the new Article 144 TEC provided the legal basis for the establishment of a Social Protection Committee. This Committee is advisory in nature with the task of promoting cooperation between the Member States and the Commission in the field of social protection. The Committee may draw up reports and opinions for the area of competence assigned to it or act in unspecified ways.[330]

The provisions on the ESF, which now form Title XI TFEU, originally comprised six articles.[331]

---

329 Despite much criticism, especially from the Commission, the IGC could not bring itself to define the term more precisely.

330 On the question of more precise texting cf. footnote above.

331 i.e. ex-Article 123 to 128 TEC in the pre-Maastricht version.

The Treaty of Maastricht already led to a drastic shortening of this chapter. In the TEC as amended by Maastricht, only the first two articles remained unchanged and continued to deal with the establishment and purpose of the European Social Fund as well as its administration. The IGC 1991 agreed to open up the narrow primary law corset of the former Articles 125 to 128 TEC and to regulate the question of implementation in a single and compact article. The authority for implementation was transferred to the Council, which had to collaborate with the Parliament in a cooperation procedure and had to consult the Economic and Social Committee before taking a decision. The IGC 1996 saw no reason to make any significant changes to this setting. However, the conference met the Parliament's demands by introducing the codecision procedure for implementing decisions, and it also fulfilled the Committee of the Regions' wish to be consulted. The Committee had successfully argued that both the European Regional Development Fund and the European Social Fund were jointly involved in regional and structural policy activities and the situation de lege lata had thus to be considered inconsistent. [332] Since neither the Parliament nor the Committee of the Regions had made new requests to the IGC 2000 and the Maastricht regime – according to the unanimous view of the participants in the conference – had proved its worth, Chapter 2 of Social Policy remained untouched by the Treaty of Nice.

The ToL intervened more structurally in this title by separating the European Social Fund from the Social Title and anchoring it in the Treaty as an independent title. The IGC 2007 did not have a legal or substantive justification for this, but rather followed the ostensible goal of more clearly separating the actual policy from the fund, which, however, was not further pursued in the case of regional and structural policy and the associated funds. In Title X, now devoted exclusively to social policy, the IGC 2007 introduced a new Article 152 TFEU, which is inserted between the general description of social policy (introductory Article 151 TFEU (Article 136 ex-TEC) and the description of tasks in Article 153 TFEU (Article 137 ex-TEC). The IGC 2007 thus followed the IGC 2004, which had already adopted this text as Article I-48 TEU and had given it the programmatic title "The Social Partners and the Autonomous Social Dialogue". Although the IGCs 2004 and 2007 did not intend to confer directly applicable or even subjective rights, they nevertheless sent a clear political signal by

332 This was to be one of the few successful attempts by the Committee of the Regions to improve its position.

recognising social partnership at European level. No other fundamental changes were made in the course of the IGC 2007. However, the IGC 2007, not least as a result of Austrian pressure, granted greater emphasis on the social component, which ultimately manifested itself in this new article.

II.15. Education, Vocational Training, Youth and Sport

Reference:	Part 3 Title XII Article 165 and 166 TFEU
Subject:	Promoting high quality education
Objectives:	Developing a European dimension in education Promoting the mobility of learners and teachers Promotion of academic recognition of diplomas and of study periods Promotion of cooperation between educational institutions Strengthening exchange of information and experience on common problems within the education systems of the Member States Encouraging the development of youth exchanges and exchanges of socio-educational instructors Promoting the development of distance learning Promoting cooperation with third countries and international organisations competent in the field of education, in particular the Council of Europe
Principles:	No harmonisation of laws and regulations of the Member States Promotion of cooperation without any harmonisation
Instruments:	Funding programmes Council recommendations

The Founding Treaties did not comprise any Community competence in either the field of education or youth policy; only individual competences in the field of vocational training and - since the SEA - in the field of promoting training and the mobility of researchers could be interpreted as approaches in this direction. However, the Heads of State and Government paved the way towards an at least partial Community competence as early as 1961[333] and 1983,[334] when they expressed in several declarations their conviction that education, culture, and research were very much matters of common interest. It was not until the ToM, however, that education and youth became Union policies by being included as a separate chapter in the TEC. The following intergovernmental conferences did not bring any substantial change to these provisions.

The IGC 2007 expanded the scope of application while at the same time extending the Union's competences to the field of education, thus turning a former sub-chapter into a separate title; all other adaptations were of editorial nature. The entire change (including the inclusion of sport) was rather due to the spirit of the times and must accordingly be understood as pure political symbolism.

333 Final Communiqué of the Heads of State and Government of 18 July 1961.
334 Solemn Declaration of the European Council of 19 June 1983.

II.16. Culture

Reference: Part 3 Title XIII Article 167 TFEU

Subject: Contribution to the development of the cultures of the Member States, while preserving their national and regional diversity as well as simultaneously highlighting the common cultural heritage

Objectives: Encouraging cooperation between Member States and, if necessary, supporting and supplementing their action in the following areas:

- Improvement of knowledge and dissemination of culture and history of the European peoples
- Conservation and safeguarding of cultural heritage of European significance
- Non-commercial cultural exchanges
- Artistic and literary creation, including in the audiovisual sector.

Principles: No harmonization of legal and administrative provisions of the Member States
Exclusively promoting cooperation

Instruments: Funding programs and recommendations of the Council

Together with the chapter on education, culture was incorporated into the EU primary law only with the ToM. First approaches to a common cultural policy go back to the 1970s.[335] Furthermore, the ministers responsible for culture held informal meetings since 1982, ten years before culture became part of EU primary law. The origins of European cultural policy are essentially rooted in the application of fundamental rights in the context of primary law, insofar as they relate to culture or have been the subject of cases before the European Court of Justice.

In the run-up to the IGC 1991, a bizarre discussion arose. Purists criticised that a principally economic treaty – as the TEC – had been kind of

335 Resolution of the European Parliament on the motion for a resolution submitted on behalf of the Liberal and Allies Group on measures to protect the European cultural heritage, 15 May 1974, OJC 62/1974, p 5; Communication of the Commission to the Council: Community Action in the Cultural Sector, COM (1977/560)fin, 2 December 1977.

abused by being applied to cultural questions. Some critics even went so far as to complain about a possible transgression of competences, by claiming that culture was not within the scope of the Treaties.

The Fathers of the IGC 1991 had thus been confronted with the question of either closing their eyes, not changing the Treaty, and so allowing the practice to continue, or creating a new competence. Besides the above mentioned economic purists' critique, culture purists on the opposite side of the Great Divide worried that an incorporation into the Treaties might end in a communitarisation and harmonization of culture, which would kill Europe's diversity. The result was an exemplary European compromise. The IGC 1991 decided to declare culture as Community policy without granting the Community any tools or competences that would allow it to pursue any substantial policy in that field. The only actions permitted have since been EU funding programs and recommendations of the Council.

In its initial wording, the cultural aspects, in particular cultural diversity, should only have been taken into account in the Community's actions. The ToA extended the range of application substantially, stipulating that the Union shall act in particular in order to respect and to promote the diversity of its cultures.

Neither the ToN nor the ToL revised that title.

II.17. Public Health

Reference:	Part 3 Title XIV Article 168 TFEU
Subject:	Ensuring a high level of health protection in the Union
Objectives:	Improving the health of the population Preventing human disease and eliminating causes of danger to human health Combating widespread major diseases Research into the causes, transmission, and prevention of such diseases Promotion of health information and education
Principles:	Complementing the policies of the Member States Promoting cooperation between Member States
Instruments:	Measures to establish high (minimum) quality and safety standards for organs and substances of human origin as well as for blood and blood derivatives Measures in the veterinary and phytosanitary fields with the aim to protect public health Support measures aimed at protecting and improving human health, excluding any harmonisation of the laws and regulations of the Member States

The ToM incorporated health care into primary law, although initially formulated rather vaguely, without assigning real competences to the Community. Contrary to that, the ToA set new standards in that field. During the IGC 1996, particularly Belgium pushed for a strengthening of this policy competence at Union level, especially due to the disastrous effects of the BSE crisis and multiple cases of Creutzfeldt-Jakob syndrome. Under the impression of general consumer uncertainty, the intergovernmental conference decided to tighten up the first paragraph of Article 152 TEC and to text it in such a way that a high level of health protection must be ensured in the definition and implementation of all Community policies and measures, whereas the ToM had still demanded that a contribution be made to ensuring a high level of health protection.[336]

336 It was precisely this insertion that was likely to cause tensions with other EU policies, especially in the area of the Common Agricultural Policy, which supports the cultivation of tobacco plants, among other things. However, the development of

However, the Heads of State and Government were not content with this amendment but decided on a complete redrafting of the article in question. In particular, a catalogue of measures under paragraph 4 was added, which now disclosed concrete areas of application.

Nevertheless, a kind of safeguard clause had to be included in paragraph 5 to ensure that Community action in the field of public health fully respects the responsibilities of the Member States for the organisation and delivery of health services and medical care.[337] Furthermore, it was specified that in particular measures setting high standards of quality and safety for organs and substances of human origin, blood and blood derivatives are without prejudice to national regulations on the donation or medical use of organs and blood.

In the course of the IGC 2000, the title on health care was left untouched.

The IGC 2007 adapted the article on health care, now Article 168 TFEU. The IGC 2007 did not go back to the failed TCEU, but adapted the provision de lege lata, especially in the light of the developments of the past years. It even went further than the IGC 2004 and significantly extended the scope of the Union's competences. Overall, this article is an example of successful consolidation, as the delimitation of competences between the Union and the Member States is drawn more clearly. For example, the IGC 2007 also took over insights from medicine by no longer speaking of health in general, but in the sense of a holistic approach to physical and mental health.

This clarification is also in line with the trend to recognise mental illness as such and not to make it an unspoken taboo subject. Another new aspect is the recognition of the challenge posed by cross-border health threats, which are not to be tackled by isolated Member State measures, but by joint action. Along the same lines is a new provision, according to which the cooperation of the Member States in the field of improving the complementarity of health systems in border areas is to be promoted. The previous instruments, i.c. Interreg, do not seem to have been suitable for removing obstacles under social security law or for preventing the simultaneous establishment and operation of specialised hospitals by several Member

the last few years has shown that this cultivation, and thus also its support by the EU budget, is to be regarded as an obsolete model in the medium to long term.

337 Along with other Member States, Denmark in particular pushed for the insertion of this clause.

States in border areas. However, this treaty initiative will certainly not be able to solve a fundamental problem of medical care, namely the language issue. It is rather questionable whether the language training of doctors and medical staff is also covered by this treaty provision. Ultimately, this provision will remain dead letter if it is not possible to bring about permeability of the social security systems through other treaty provisions.

During the COVID pandemic, this title proved to be completely inadequate. There were calls for a communitarised health policy with far-reaching executive powers at EU level. However, due to the sub-optimal performance of the European Commission in vaccine procurement, it was rejected by a significant number of Member States, especially those with highly developed and solidly funded social and health insurance systems.

II.18. Consumer Protection

Reference:	Part 3 Title XV Article 169 in conjunction with Part 1 Title II Article 12 TFEU
Subject:	Ensuring a high level of consumer protection
Objectives:	Contribution to the protection of the health, safety, and economic interests of consumers Contribution to the promotion of the right of consumers to information, education, and the formation of associations to defend their interests
Principles:	Consumer protection requirements shall be considered in defining and implementing other Community policies and activities
Instruments:	Measures adopted in the framework of the realisation of the Internal Market Measures to support, supplement, and monitor the policies of the Member States shall not prevent any Member State from maintaining or introducing more stringent protective measures, while ensuring that such measures are compatible with the Treaty Measures to support, supplement, and monitor the policies of the Member States

Consumer protection has been a Community policy since the ToM, but originally it was to be regarded as absolute soft law, since the Community was only supposed to contribute to achieving a high level of consumer protection.[338] The basic principles of a specific Community consumer protection policy can already be found in the declaration of the Heads of State and Government at their meeting in Paris in 1972, when they demanded that measures shall be taken at Community level to strengthen and coordinate consumer protection measures. The ToA extended the competence in particular to the promotion of consumer interests and clearly defined the scope of Community intervention.

The IGC 2000 did not touch the title Consumer Protection and thus it remained unchanged.

338 The introduction of this title as an EU policy in its own right shall be seen above all in connection with the simultaneous introduction of the title Public Health.

The IGC 2007 remained consistent with this title and removed the part of the text that falls under the category of objectives of the Treaty. Accordingly, Article 153(2) TEC was removed and inserted as Article 12 TFEU.

II.19. Trans-European Networks

Reference:	Part 3 Title XVI Article 170 to 172 TFEU
Subject:	Contributing to the Common Transport Policy through coherent planning of a European transport network
Objectives:	Ensuring a coherent transport policy through efficient and interconnected transport routes
Priciples:	Community action shall be aimed at promoting the interconnection and interoperability of, and access to, national networks within the framework of a system of open and competitive markets, and shall take particular account of the need to link island, landlocked and peripheral regions with the central regions of the Community
Instruments:	Development and implementation of priority project lists

As a result of the ToM, the Trans-European Networks were incorporated into the TEC and adapted by the ToA in terms of text, but not in terms of content. The IGC 1991 justified the inclusion of the Trans-European Networks in the Treaty with a necessary contribution to the completion of the Internal Market.

The Trans-European Networks remained unaffected by both the ToN and the ToL and were therefore incorporated into the TFEU in their original version.

II.20. Industry

Reference:	Part 3 Title XVII Article 173 TFEU
Subject:	Shared commitment between the Union and the Member States to ensure that the conditions necessary for the competitiveness of the Union industry are met
Objectives:	Facilitation of the adaptation of industry to structural changes Promoting a favourable environment for the establishment and development of businesses throughout the Community, in particular small and medium-sized enterprises Promotion of an environment favourable to cooperation between enterprises Promotion of better use of the industrial potential of innovation, research and technological development policies
Principles:	Consultation and coordination between Member States, with the Commission being involved The right of initiative of the Commission for measures promoting such coordination Exclusion of measures under this Title which could lead to distortions of competition, or which contain tax provisions or provisions relating to the rights and interests of workers
Instruments:	Science and research policy Supporting economic activities in economically underdeveloped regions, through measures under the European Regional Development Fund (= ERDF) regime in particular Use of sectoral policies, especially in steel, shipbuilding and textiles

Introduced by the ToM, industrial policy remained unaffected by the ToA. The origins of industrial policy go far back into the 1970s, when the Community had already begun to pursue industrial policy on a massive scale, but without having a concrete legal basis at its disposal. During the IGC 1991, the industry title - along with the provisions on Economic and Monetary Union - was one of the most hotly contested. France, above all President Mitterrand, had made the inclusion of an industry title a conditio sine qua non. Germany - under pressure from her domestic associations - was opposed to this French proposal and justified her rejection with the argument that such a title would be contrary to the German approach of a liberal industry policy. This argument was strongly supported by the United Kingdom. During the IGC, German and French text proposals alternated in rapid succession, with the French being regularly rejected as too dirigiste and the German as too imprecise by the respective opposing side. In particular, those French text passages concerning external relations and the voting procedure were unacceptable to economically liberal Member States such as Germany, the United Kingdom, Denmark, and the Netherlands. However, the Dutch Presidency - supported by the Commission - presented a compromise text, which could finally be accepted by the conference except for two last-minute amendments.

The ToN adapted the content of this title insofar as one of the objectives of the IGC 2000, namely, to shift voting from unanimity to QMV as far as possible, was implemented here, while at the same time applying the co-decision procedure.

However, the agreement of some Member States could only be achieved when the last sentence of the compromise text was added to the second subparagraph of paragraph 3, which clearly states that this title shall not provide any basis for the introduction by the Union of any measure which could lead to a distortion of competition or contains tax provisions or provisions relating to the rights and interests of employed persons. Those Member States that had opposed tax harmonisation - notably the United Kingdom and Luxembourg - or harmonisation in social affairs - notably Denmark - followed the overwhelming majority of Member States only after any form f harmonisation had been ruled out expressis verbis by this provision.

The IGC 2007 only adopted editorial changes and specified the content of the measures to be taken by the Commission.

II.21. Economic, Social and Territorial Cohesion

Reference:	Part 3 Title XVIII Article 174 to 178 TFEU
Subject:	Establishing economic and social cohesion in the Union
Objectives:	Supporting the most disadvantaged regions Supporting regions affected by structural difficulties Supporting disadvantaged groups in society Supporting the achievement of gender equality Promoting the adaptation and modernisation of education, training and employment policies
Principles:	Concentration of funds on priority objectives Programming Partnership of those involved in the actions Additionality (Community funds complement but do not replace Member State funds) Control
Instruments:	Structural Funds Cohesion Fund Community Initiatives Specific actions

Title XVII of the EC Treaty, now Title XVIII TFEU, which deals with the policy that, together with agricultural policy, accounts for the lion's share of the Union budget, [339] has been renumbered several times in the course of its history. The policy of economic and social cohesion (in short: cohesion policy) was added by the SEA as Title V of Part 3. The new objective expands the title's heading and content by including the issue of territorial cohesion but essentially amends only Article 158 EC Treaty, now Article

339 Until the 2013 budget, the split was about 1/3 (structural policy) to 2/3 (agricultural policy). In the medium-term financial framework 2014-2020, € 351.8 billion were earmarked for cohesion policy, while € 373.2 billion were allocated to agriculture (= sustainable growth), for a total commitment of € 959.9 billion. This meant a massive cut in agricultural funding with a comparatively minimal increase in cohesion funding. The ratio of the budget share for the period mentioned was thus 36.7 % (structural policy) to 38.9 % (agricultural policy). The following medium-term financial framework 2021-2027 continued in this direction: € 377.8 billion are earmarked for cohesion, resilience, and values and € 356.4 billion for sustainable growth (= natural resources and environment), for a total commitment of € 1074.3 billion.

174 TFEU; all other provisions remain unchanged (apart from editorial adjustments).

The objective for cohesion policy seems strange, since the former Article 130 TEC stated that the Community shall develop and pursue its policies leading to the strengthening of its economic and social cohesion. Only the second subparagraph betrayed the intention to include this title in primary law. The Founding States had seen no reason to include cohesion policy in the EEC Treaty, since the economic theory of the time assumed that the general economic upswing, which was undoubtedly expected and to which the establishment of the Economic Community was to contribute, would ensure a balanced development of the regions.[340] However, the thesis that the establishment of the Common Market alone would suffice proved to be mistaken over the years.

Regional policy was already included in the Founding Treaties, in particular through the reference to the need to take regional differences into account within the framework of agricultural policy. Further references to such consideration can also be found in the provisions on the realisation of freedom of movement, the shaping of the common transport policy, and the admissibility of subsidies. The Commission seems to have been aware of this gap early on and began to develop an independent Community regional policy in the 1970s. This step was partly a reaction to the regional policy measures of the individual Member States, which did not necessarily contribute to a balanced development of the Community.[341] The oil crisis, the steel crisis, and the growing gap between the well-developing regions and those lagging behind, eventually undermined the fabric of cohesion[342]

---

340 The only possible basis for such a policy was therefore Article 235 TEEC.

341 It is in the nature of things that financially better-off Member States and regions were able to absorb crises more easily with interventions than less well-off Member States and regions. This imbalance was exacerbated by the interventions carried out and, in the medium term, increased by migration to the better-off regions.

342 In addition to the crisis-like developments mentioned above, there was also a negative development in shipbuilding, which had a massive impact on the affected regions because the labour market was almost monoculturally oriented. The concept of monoculture, which originates from the agricultural sector, is transferable insofar as the exclusive orientation of the labour market towards one product - in the broadest sense - leads to the mass of the labour market in the region concerned being dependent on the weal and woe of the main industry and, accordingly, no other economic sectors emerge or establish themselves. The decline of the main sector almost inevitably leads to the decline of the peripheral sectors. Examples of this were not only shipbuilding in the coastal regions, but - in the early 1990s - the

and threatened to distort competition in the Community. In developing cohesion policy, the Commission sought to apply Community-specific measures, while most Member States were interested in a mere inflow of funds from the Community budget to be distributed according to their specific situation.[343] Despite the obvious need to counteract this tendency, in the 1970s the Member States could not bring themselves to create a legal basis for a Community cohesion policy in the Treaties. On 20 October 1971, a first resolution of the Member States on the coordination of regional aid schemes was adopted, in which the Member States committed themselves to respecting certain principles, such as limiting the intensity of aid in the most industrialised regions. However, it did not go beyond a Commission Communication on general regional aid schemes.[344]

The Commission's Community approach failed despite the creation of the first regional fund at Community level,[345] as this fund was intended as a complementary element to the regional policy activities of the Member States, but in no way to replace them. Moreover, it did not provide a basis for Community-wide regional policy activities. It was not until the revision of the Fund Regulation in 1979[346] that the Community aspect was accentuated as a supporting element and finally anchored in the revision of 1984[347] in the form of coordination of Community regional policy. The programmes adopted in implementation of the Fund Regulation increasingly exceeded the objectives - and the resources - of the regional fund. This conclusion led the intergovernmental conference, which had been convened to draw up the SEA, to decide to create a primary law basis for a comprehensive Community policy and to include it in the TEC.

---

final decline of the steel industry in the Belgian Hainaut region around the city of Charleroi, from which this region never fully recovered.

343 To speak of financial equalisation at community level in this context is perhaps too one-sided, but cannot be dismissed out of hand. On the one hand, the Member States contribute to the common budget and - of course - want to benefit from it; on the other hand, such a financial equalisation increases the position of some Member States as net contributors. In addition, there is the (Community) political element of redistribution, which aims at a community of solidarity among the Member States. Finally, there is also the (domestic) political argument, according to which it is seen as a domestic and community policy success to negotiate as much cohesion funding as possible for one's own Member State.

344 cf. OJ. C 111/1971, 7.

345 cf. Regulation 724/75, OJ. L 73/1975, 1.

346 cf. OJ. L 35/1979, 1.

347 cf. Regulation 1787/84, OJ. L 169/1984, 1.

The debate on the future of cohesion policy has been extended to include the facet of territorial cohesion. The Hanoverian Academy for Spatial Research and Planning defines this term as follows: "Territorial cohesion is a fundamentally pragmatic concept. It is the highest expression of solidarity within Europe and thus an expression of equality between citizens. It is the way forward for making the most of territorial diversity across Europe and thus represents a significant competitive advantage in the age of global change, which is crucial for Europe's economic future. As a spatial principle, it must permeate a range of European policies and strengthen their effectiveness".[348] Originally, the term cohesion originates from the French language and only becomes understandable in this context. It describes the spatial dimension holistically and thus acquires almost philosophical dimensions. However, this was not enough for a reorientation of the content of this title, but a buzzword has found its way into the Treaties without better clarifying what had not been clearly explained before.

Article 158(2) TEC (ex-Article 130a), now Article 174 TFEU, originally set the objective of reducing disparities between the levels of development of the various regions and the backwardness of the least favoured regions. The IGC 1991 felt compelled to clarify this very general wording and modified the objective to the effect that the differences in the level of development of the various regions should be reduced. This change may still be called only an editorial adjustment, but the change in the second half of paragraph 2 went beyond that. While the SEA still referred to disadvantaged areas - without defining them in more detail - the passage introduced by the ToM targeted the most disadvantaged areas, including rural areas. The explicit extension to agricultural areas was a reaction to the one-sided promotion of industrial areas, which ran counter to the economic structure of some Member States, but especially of many regions.[349] The IGC 1996 was confronted with the next wave of demands from Member States that had a significant insular share of their territory. Regional support for such zones had already been possible on the basis of the wording de lege lata, but the Member States concerned pushed for an explicit inclusion of island regions, as this opened up better conditions in the negotiations on the Structural Funds Regulation. At the IGC 2000, there were several proposals to expand

348 http://www.arl-net.de/lexica/de/territoriale-koh%C3%A4sion?lang=en.

349 Member States with a strong agricultural sector, such as France, were particularly interested in such an adaptation, as it would significantly expand the group of applicants.

this catalogue of objectives, but in the end only the text in the ToA version was acceptable, as otherwise the entire catalogue would have had to be included, which - at least in Nice - was seen as a dilution of regional policy. The IGC 2007 added a new paragraph 3 to the former Article 158 TEC, which makes the dilemma of IGCs in general abundantly clear. Each Member State saw the opportunity to write its specific problem regions into primary law as eligible, after considerations arose in the course of the IGC 2004 to draw a clear demarcation between eligible and non-eligible regions. The result was the greatest possible compromise, which - if Declaration No. 33 on Article 174 TFEU is taken into account - effectively declares all regions of the Union to be particularly eligible regions. After this text had been included in the TEU, the IGC 2007 could not bring itself to delete this "compromise" and so it was also included in the ToL. However, this rather comprehensive definition has not led to any significant change for the better.

Article 159 TEC (ex-Article 130b), now Article 175 TFEU, which describes the tasks of the Member States and the Community, originally contained only one paragraph stating that Member States shall formulate and direct their economic policies in such a way as to attain the objectives of cohesion policy, the Community assisting them with the means assigned to it. The IGC 1991 added two new subparagraphs to this article and invited the Commission to make proposals for improving cohesion policy in its triennial cohesion report, if deemed necessary.[350] Closely related to this addition is the insertion of paragraph 3, which provides that the Council, acting unanimously on a proposal from the Commission and after consulting the European Parliament, the EESC and the CoR, may adopt the necessary measures if they require specific action outside the funds, without prejudice to measures adopted under other policies. The very fact that such decisions were to be taken only (i) unanimously and (ii) through the consultation procedure again clearly shows that the Member States had not yet fully committed themselves to a communitarised cohesion policy. The IGC 1996 denied Parliament the right of co-decision and adhered to unanimity and the consultation procedure. It was not until the IGC 2000 - and not least under the pressure of the forthcoming enlargement - that a revision of paragraph 3 was undertaken.

Article 160 TEC (ex-Article 130c), now Article 176 TFEU, which lists the objectives for the ERDF, remained unchanged.

350 ex-Article 130b (2) TEC as amended by the ToM.

In contrast, Article 161 TEC (ex-Article 130d), now Article 177 TFEU, was amended several times fundamentally. Article 161 TEC, as amended by the SEA, provided that immediately after the entry into force of the SEA, the Commission had to present an overall proposal to achieve the objectives of cohesion policy and the Council had to decide unanimously on this proposal within one year after consulting the Parliament and the EESC. This provision was already a dead letter at the time of the IGC 1991 and could therefore be rephrased. Article 161 (1) TEC (ex-Article 130d as amended by the ToM) stipulates how the tasks, objectives and organisational structure of the Structural Funds are to be defined. According to the ToM, the Council had to take these decisions unanimously after obtaining the consent of Parliament and consulting the Economic and Social Committee and the Committee of the Regions. This procedure was not changed at the IGC 1996, as particularly Spain successfully resisted the introduction of QMV in this field.[351] Article 161(2) TEC (ex-Article 130d as amended by the ToM), which provided the basis for the establishment of the Cohesion Fund, was adapted by the IGC 1996 only insofar as it responded to the expiry of the original deadline; it subsequently remained unaffected by the ToN. However, the IGC 2000 was again confronted with the question of how decisions on the structural funds should be taken after enlargement. It was foreseeable that enlargement would only bring in new Member States that would be net beneficiaries in the medium to long term. It was also clear that these Member States would follow the same hard line as Spain - and other old net beneficiary countries - in the distribution of funds. From the beginning of the IGC 2000, the intention and necessity was expressed to transfer the structural funds and the cohesion fund to QMV - on the one hand, to follow the goal of a general reduction of unanimity, on the other hand, to prevent individual Member States from blocking such decisions as long as the funds earmarked for them were too low from their point of

351 Spain feared - probably not without good reason - that with QMV the distribution of funds could turn out differently than before, in particular that the lever of the veto would be lost for Spain, which had always used this instrument successfully in previous years when she felt she was not receiving enough funds. To Spain's credit, however, it must be noted that some net beneficiary states simply hid behind Spain's back, as they were pursuing the same objectives, but had no reason to doubt Spain's tough stance on this issue. Thus, neither Portugal, nor Greece, nor Italy were forced to take an openly blocking position against such a change.

view.[352] The majority of Member States followed this line from the start of the IGC 2000. Spain remained the only exception, steadfastly refusing, even until the last minute in Nice, to agree to the transition to QMV directly with the entry into force of the ToN.[353] The argument that future Member States could use the means of unanimity against the current Member States was not striking enough to convince Spain, especially considering their long-term macroeconomic situation. The IGC 2000 nevertheless found a compromise that persuaded Spain to give in: Article 161 TEC was to remain in the realm of unanimity for the time being. As of 1 January 2007, the Council would decide by qualified majority if the following conditions were met: At the time of the vote in question, the Council must have adopted (i) the multiannual financial perspective applicable from 1 January 2007 and (ii) the Interinstitutional Agreement relating to it. Spain thus achieved that the next Structural Funds and Cohesion Fund period was still subject to unanimity, but probably fatally miscalculated her assessment of the dynamics of the enlargement process. But Spain was not satisfied with the compromise reached either. In Declaration No. 2 of Greece, Spain and Portugal, which was taken note of by the IGC 2000, these three states express their interpretation of Article 161 (3) TEC very clearly. Their agreement to move to qualified majority voting was given only on the basis that the term "multiannual" means that the Financial Perspective and the corresponding Interinstitutional Agreement, which would apply from 1 January 2007, would have a duration equivalent to the referring Financial Perspective, i.e. seven years. Denmark, Germany, the Netherlands, and Austria replied in their (counter-)Declaration No. 3,[354] which was taken note of by the IGC 2000, that this Greek-Spanish-Portuguese declaration would not have any adverse effects on the European Commission, in particular on its right of initiative.[355]

---

352 This is all the more the case for the Cohesion Fund, as the subsidies granted there are particularly high.

353 Spain apparently calculated to have the cohesion period 2007 to 2013 decided unanimously in order to secure - possibly for the last time - a corresponding share of the funds. In Nice, Spain apparently still assumed that enlargement would only take place after this decision, which in retrospect turned out to be a misjudgement.

354 Critics of the Spanish position saw this adherence to unanimity as already threatening the end of cohesion policy. It should be noted that the Spanish position also had to be reconsidered in the light of an enlarged Union and that new coalitions have formed accordingly.

355 Such declarations have been a tradition since the ToM. Declaration No. 9 to the ToM states that the Community should take account of nature conservation

The last Article of Title XVII, Article 162 TEC (ex-Article 130 d), now Article 178 TFEU, deals with the implementing decisions of the Council.[356] The changes made by the IGC 1991 are justified by the fulfilment of the original conditions. However, the ToA had already changed the procedure from cooperation to co-decision. Neither the ToN nor the ToL revised this provision.

requirements in the context of cohesion policy, Declaration No. 26 to the ToM also directs the attention of cohesion policy to the French overseas departments, the Azores, Madeira, and the Canary Islands, a declaration reinforced by Declaration No. 30 to the ToA concerning the special situation of island territories. The Protocol on Economic and Social Cohesion (1996) is a clearly political protocol, which is simply intended to ensure that the relevant political decisions are implemented via secondary legislation.

356 Article 162 TEC (ex-Article 130d).

II.22. Research and Technological Development and Space

Reference:	Part 3 Title XIX Article 179 to 190 TFEU
Subject:	Guaranteeing and promoting research and technological development that supports the Union's international industrial position
Objectives:	Strengthening the scientific and technological bases of the Union's industry Promoting the development of the international competitiveness of the Union's industry Supporting all research activities necessary for this purpose
Principles:	Support for enterprises in the Union, in particular small and medium-sized enterprises. Promotion of and support for research centres and universities Promotion of intra-Union cooperation efforts Coordination of Member State and Union activities in the field of research and technological development
Instruments:	Conducting research, technological development and demonstration programmes Promoting cooperation with third countries and international organisations Disseminating and evaluating the results obtained in the field of research Promoting the training and mobility of Union researchers Establishing a framework programme for science and research

The Founding Treaties did not provide for an independent policy on research and technological development. However, the Community decided to act in this field long before the ToM. Accordingly, the SEA extended the Community's field of intervention to research and technological development in order not only to promote but above all to focus Community efforts, the latter to be achieved through cooperation. By introducing this new policy, the IGC was responding to the threat that the Community might fall behind the USA in the field of science.

The title Research and Technological Development underwent a number of changes under both the ToM and the ToA but remained unaffected by the ToN. The ToM considerably strengthened the position of the European Parliament, which until now only had to be consulted; the Union Treaty gave the Parliament the right of codecision for the Framework Programme. At the same time, the EESC was given the right to be consulted. However, decisions in the Council continued to be taken by unanimity. The original Article 130i TEC was also completely revised, listing explicitly the specific tasks and objectives of the Framework Programme. The ToA also renumbered the title Research and Development. However, the fact that the IGC 1996 was able to stipulate that the Council from now on adopts these programmes with QMV in a codecision procedure was important for facilitating decision-making regarding the implementation programmes for the Framework Programme. The CoR was left empty-handed in both the IGC 1996 and the IGC 2000 and was not granted the right to be consulted.

The IGC 2007 reacted to the developments of the previous years and extended the scope of this title by including space, although this was not an original initiative of this IGC, as the failed TCEU had already addressed this issue. However, the ToL substantially supplements this title in that it introduces the creation of a European Area of Research as an overarching objective in paragraph 1 of the introductory article. The IGC 2007 concretised this area very comprehensively in paragraph 1. Paragraph 2 also sends a clear signal against national protectionism in research when it demands that researchers be able to cooperate freely across borders. Article 189 TFEU is a new addition, which has had no corresponding provision in the Treaty. After the IGC 2004 had already agreed to include space policy as a Union competence in primary law, the IGC 2007 followed this proposal and thus created a legal basis for relevant activities of the Union.

II.23. Environment

Reference:	Part 3 Title XX Article 191 to 193 TFEU
Subject:	Ensuring a sustainable environmental policy of the Union
Objectives:	Protection, preservation, and improvement of the quality of the environment Protection of human health Sustainable use of natural resources Supporting measures at the international level that address regional or global environmental problems
Principles:	Polluter pays principle Avoidance principle Integration principle Prevention principle Principle of applying the highest possible level of protection
Instruments:	Legislative measures Economic measures (promotion of environmentally friendly techniques, productions and products) Financial instruments (e.g. LIFE, Structural Funds, Cohesion Fund, EIB support) Horizontal instruments (e.g. improvement of environmental data and databases, support for environmental research, integration of environmental factors into planning processes)

It was not until the SEA that environmental policy was directly incorporated into primary law. Already in the 1970s, environmentally relevant Community legislation had been adopted, based on the former Articles 100 and 235 TEEC.[357] The SEA placed this auxiliary construction on a transparent and secure primary legal basis by introducing Title XIX TEC (ex-Title XVI) in accordance with Article 25 SEA. Alongside this legally required insertion there is also a very well-founded political motivation. The Community was reacting to the environmental movements emerging in an increasing number of Member States, which also relatively soon voiced their criticism

357 E.g. legal acts to combat and control environmental pollution as well as to protect endangered species. The so-called Birds Directive, 79/409, was to develop its full economic implications only in later years, especially through its integration into the Natura 2000 Network.

on the Community's lack of commitment to environmental issues. In its further genesis, the environmental title was to be specified more precisely, anchored even more firmly by the ToM and extended in its applicability by the ToA. It was only on the occasion of its last revision to date by the ToN that more restrictive changes were to be made for the first time.

Article 174 TEC (ex-Article 130r), now Article 191 TFEU, which defines the objectives of the Community's environmental policy, as well as cooperation with third countries and international organisations, has been extended by the ToM in so far as the promotion of measures at international level to deal with regional or global environmental issues has been explicitly included in the list of objectives under paragraph 1.[358] Since its first version, Article 174(2) TEC has provided the fundamental principles on which the Community's environmental commitment is based, namely the principle of prevention, the principle of origin and the polluter-pays principle. The ToM introduced the regional dimension, or rather the regional policy dimension, in that the Community should take account of the conditions in the individual regions in its environmental policy activities. In contrast to this rather soft request, the second amendment in subparagraph 1 cannot be classified as soft law. The SEA wording was that environmental protection requirements were an integral part of other Community policies. Since the IGC 1991, environmental protection requirements must be integrated into the formulation and implementation of other Community policies. What had been a rather general requirement to take account of environmental protection requirements had become a strict - and, if necessary, legally enforceable - mandatory provision. This compliance requirement was removed from the environmental title by the IGC 1996 and reintroduced in a more prominent place, namely in Article 6 TEC (ex-Article 3c). In the pre-Maastricht era, Article 174 TEC had consisted of only one paragraph; the ToM added a subparagraph to it to ensure that, in the case of harmonisation measures meeting environmental protection requirements,[359] safeguard clauses are built in to allow Member States to take provisional measures subject to a Community control procedure, permissible only for environmental policy motives.

---

358 The Union's involvement in the Rio Process in 1992 thus took on a completely different dimension since the preparatory work for this process had not yet included this explicit reference to goals.

359 And thus, due to the general wording, not only includes measures adopted exclusively under the environment title, but also equivalent measures from other titles, such as agriculture, energy, or transport.

The rather cryptic wording allows only reinforcing safeguard clauses, although these would already be permissible under Article 176 TEC. The original paragraph 4, which stipulated that the Community should only take action in the environmental field if the objectives could not be sufficiently achieved at Member State level, was deleted in the course of IGC 1991.[360]

The ToL added only one new element by including the fight against climate change as a target in the introductory Article 191 TFEU. This addition is an original innovation of the ToL, as the IGC 2004 had not yet identified climate change as a topic for the Constitutional Treaty. The IGC 2007, however, was under massive political pressure to redraft the environmental title in a suitable way, otherwise facing massive criticism from environmental associations and respective NGOs. Yet the environmental provisions turned out to be so well-balanced de lege lata that any change to the status quo would meet with resistance from the various Member State interests. Expanding the catalogue of objectives seemed to be the only solution to this dilemma - and was also in keeping with the Zeitgeist.

Article 175 TEC (ex-Article 130s), now Article 192 TFEU, is also a typical example of the position of environmental issues in the overall structure of Community policies, especially with regard to their value and importance. Article 130s TEC as amended by the SEA stated succinctly in the first subparagraph that the Council, on a proposal from the Commission and after consulting the Parliament and the EESC, votes unanimously on environmental legal acts; according to the second subparagraph, it had the possibility of deciding unanimously, in accordance with the same procedure, which legal acts could be adopted with QMV. The SEA thus made the unanimity principle in conjunction with the consultation procedure the standard procedure and voting with QMV the exception. Exactly this stipulation was reversed by the ToM, which now made the codecision procedure the standard procedure and listed the exceptions that had to be adopted unanimously in the consultation procedure. This was in response to parliamentary demands for the introduction of the codecision procedure as well as to the pressure of the increasingly strong environmental associations and environmental NGOs, which had complained about the cumbersome

360 These changes in the environmental title alone show that the Community had become more environmentally friendly oriented, a process that was reinforced by the accession of Sweden, Finland, and Austria, three countries that had already prioritised environmental issues during the accession negotiations.

nature of the procedure and the focus on Member State interests - ensured by the veto option under the unanimity procedure. The IGC 1996 was not supposed to make any substantive changes to this new setting; it merely complied with the CoR's insistence that it be given the right to be consulted.[361]

During the IGC 2000, a crisis arose - albeit only temporarily - with regard to Article 175 TEC. The question of unanimity in Article 175(2) TEC was hotly disputed until the end of the IGC. This article had been submitted to the conference from the outset with the aim of abolishing the requirement of unanimity. However, an alliance of convenience was quickly formed between the United Kingdom and Austria, albeit for completely different motives. From the outset, Austria had strongly opposed such a change for substantive and political reasons.[362] The French Presidency had for the first time proposed a revision of the text that would have removed the provisions of a predominantly fiscal nature from the scope of Article 175(2), thus bringing into play the United Kingdom, which feared justifiably that tax harmonisation measures in the codecision procedure would be made possible, as it were, through the back door. Austria's problem lay less in the tax issue than in the management of water resources.[363] In the first synthesis document in preparation for the Nice European Council, the French Presidency had reintroduced the provisions of a predominantly fiscal nature into the scope of Article 175(2) TEC, as the pressure from the United Kingdom had become overwhelming. The Austrian reservations had been met insofar as the complex of water management had been clarified along the Austrian line. In the final text of the Treaty, both the United Kingdom and Austria were able to prevail. The conference was thus unable to achieve an extension of qualified majority voting in the area of

361 The Committee of the Regions had successfully argued that the requirement to take regional circumstances into account fully justified its consultation.

362 Halfway through the conference, other Member States, such as Spain, also agreed with the Austrian position; nevertheless, at the Nice European Council, Austria had ended up in a more or less isolated position.

363 Under massive pressure from the domestic yellow press and some far-right politicians, Austria raised reservations about a co-decision clause for water management. The unsubstantiated criticism claimed that this clause would allow the Community to access Austrian groundwater resources. These far-fetched fears were fuelled by corresponding demands from the Spanish side - in particular due to the increasing drought disasters on the Iberian Peninsula.

Article 175 TEC. No further amendments were envisaged during the IGC 2000.[364]

Article 176 TEC (ex-Article 130t), now Article 193 TFEU, has seen only one change in its history. In its SEA version, it had contained the general clause that safeguard measures taken did not prevent individual Member States from maintaining or adopting enhanced safeguard measures as long as they were compatible with the Treaty. The ToM limited the Member States' space of manoeuvre by imposing on them a notification obligation vis-à-vis the Commission in case they made use of this option.[365] The IGC 1991 was criticised for its decision to retain this article, as were subsequent IGCs. The criticism was based on the argument that such enhanced protection measures were actually contrary to the Internal Market and its principles, especially since the question of the admissibility of such measures was difficult to contest. The more environmentally oriented Member States, however, vehemently defended this article, as they saw it - especially in terms of domestic policy - as an important lever to raise the level of environmental protection of the entire Community in the long run.

364 And would not have been appropriate due to the probable failure in view of the blockade regarding paragraph 2.

365 However, this notification is merely declaratory or informative in nature and therefore only has an optical effect per se.

II.24. Energy

Reference:	Part 3 Title XXI Article 194 TFEU
Subject:	Energy policy of the Union and the Member States
Objectives:	Guaranteeing the functioning of the energy market Guaranteeing the security of energy supply in the Union Promoting energy efficiency and energy savings as well as the development of new and renewable energy sources Promoting the interconnection of energy networks
Principles:	Solidarity-based cooperation of the Member States Maintaining national sovereignty with regard to the right of a Member State to determine the conditions for the use of its energy resources, its choice between different sources of energy and the general structure of its energy supply
Instruments:	All legal acts that may be adopted under the ordinary legislative procedure

The energy title is an innovation in primary law. Even before the ToL, the Community had energy competences, although the legislative bodies had to make use of a wide variety of articles, i.c. Article 175 TEC (environmental protection), Article 95 TEC (Internal Market), Article 155 f TEC (TEN), and Article 100 TEC (supply difficulties). These auxiliary constructions meant legal and political twists and turns each time, in addition to which different voting and majority modalities were applied. The IGC 2007 combined all energy issues in one article, which as Article 194 TFEU is also the sole article of Title XXI. The question of competence is already clarified in Article 4(2) TFEU to the effect that this is a competence shared between the Union and the Member States. Nevertheless, it should be noted that this new article will not have any relevant legal impact, which was not necessarily intended by the IGC 2007. The background for this new title is merely a political signal and the intended consolidation in a single compact provision.

II.25. Tourism

Reference:	Part 3 Title XXII Article 195 TFEU
Subject:	Tourism sector of the European economy
Objectives:	Improving the business environment of this industry Cooperation amongst the Member States
Principles:	Supporting the Member States
Instruments:	Supportive measures excluding any harmonisation

The tourism title is an innovation in primary law and has no equivalent provision in the previous Treaties. The debates at the Convention and the IGC 2004 took place along the fault line as to whether this title should be created at all and, if so, whether it should be dedicated exclusively to the economic aspect. Belgium and Italy had argued strongly both in the Convention and in the IGC 2004 that historical and natural heritage should also be promoted, while Germany had in general been opposed to the inclusion of the tourism title until the end of the IGC 2004. All three failed with their particular demands, Germany was even isolated in the end, as Italy and Belgium renounced their demands in order to save the tourism title as such. The IGC 2007 did not return to fundamental debates and adopted the text of the TCEU. Legally nothing changes, but the Union saved itself the trouble of having to construct auxiliary structures whenever it intends to provide support.

II.26. Civil Protection

Reference:	Teil 3 Title XXIII Artikel 196 TFEU
Subject:	Designing effective systems to prevent natural or man-made disasters
Objectives:	Enhanced cooperation between Member States in this field
Principles:	Support measures by the Union Promotion of fast and efficient cooperation Improvement of coherence
Instruments:	Supportive measures excluding any harmonisation

The title on civil protection is an innovation in primary law, which is not matched by any corresponding provision in the previous Treaties. The decision to include civil protection in primary law is a classic piece of knee-jerk legislation. The experience of the flood disaster of 2002, which affected large parts of Austria, the Czech Republic, and Germany, had led to the establishment of a Disaster Relief Fundat Union level. Although this did not require a new legal basis in primary law, the Member States had become painfully aware that no coordinated action would be possible at Union level without resorting to all kinds of auxiliary constructions. The Convention had proposed to call this measure civil protection, but at that time the this was considered too narrow a concept. The IGC 2007 nevertheless adopted the text of the TCEU and incorporated it into primary law.

II.27. Administrative Cooperation

Reference:	Part 3 Title XXIV Article 197 TFEU
Subject:	Administrative cooperation between Member States
Objectives:	Proper functioning of the Union
Principles:	Voluntariness
Instruments:	Supportive measures excluding any kind of harmonisation

The administrative cooperation title is an innovation in primary law that is not matched by any corresponding provision in the previous Treaty versions. This innovation is probably one of the best examples of the negative aspects of the failed Constitutional Treaty, which for incomprehensible reasons has nevertheless found its way into the ToL and thus into EU primary law. The very statement that the effective implementation of Union law by the Member States, which is essential for the proper functioning of the Union, is to be regarded as a matter of common interest raises the question of how such trifles end up in the Treaty and are even given their own title. This article seems to be unobjectionable insofar as the Member States neither have to accept the Union's support nor otherwise run the risk of losing competences. On the other hand, however, the Union is in no way restricted in adopting such support measures, since the possibilities for intervention remain completely unspecified. The non-affection clause in paragraph 3 emphasises even more clearly this already subordinate function of the Union's supportive competence. The archives reveal little when one searches for the origin of this provision, which made its first appearance in the Convention. This provision may have been intended as a general reminder of the need for administrative cooperation between Member States, but it still does not deserve an article, let alone a title, of its own. The IGC 2007 adopted this provision not least because it was not included in the mandate and therefore could not be dealt with in terms of content.

II.28. Association of the Overseas Countries and Territories

Reference:	Part 4 Article 198 to 204 TFEU
Subject:	Association of those non-European countries and territories which have special relations with Denmark, France, the Netherlands, and - until Brexit - the United Kingdom
Objectives:	Equal treatment of the territories concerned with the Member States in trade issues Participation of Member States in investments
Principles:	Equal treatment of the territories concerned with regard to the trade provisions applicable among the Member States on the basis of the TFEU Most-favoured-nation clause vis-à-vis the territories concerned, so that each Member State treats these territories in trade matters in the same way as it treats a European State with which it has special relations
Instruments:	As in the TFEU laid down for the policies concerned

The origins of the policy of Association of the Overseas Countries and Territories lie in France's request that the other Founding Members undertake to support France in her commitment to her former colonies. This commitment was intended to ensure French ratification of the TEEC in return. In essence, the provisions in question were aimed at the French Overseas Territories, as can be seen from the original Annex IV.[366] The Greenland Treaty inserted Article 188 TEC (ex-Article 136a), now Article 204 TFEU, after Greenland exited the Community.

366 Subsequently Annex II to the TEC.

The ToM did not affect the provisions concerning the association of the overseas territories. The ToA, on the other hand, brought several changes and adaptations. Firstly, the reference to the non-European countries and territories of Belgium was deleted and Annex IV was renamed Annex II. The evolution clause concerning the abolition of customs duties on goods from these territories into the Community was adapted insofar as it had been worded as a declaration of intent in the original version; due to developments since then, Article 184 (1) TEC as amended by the ToA (now Article 200 TFEU), stated that such customs duties were prohibited. Accordingly, the evolution clauses in Article 184(2) and (3) TEC were also redrafted and transformed into a prohibition clause.

The ToN did not affect the provisions on the Association of the Overseas Countries and Territories, although the Member States had recognised the need for reform in the IGC 1996 in Declaration No. 36 to the ToA and had requested the Council to review the current association system by February 2000. The reform resulted in a secondary legal act,[367] but not in a change of the provisions in primary law.

The ToL did not make any substantive changes.

II.29. The Institutions

Reference:	Title III Article 13 to 19 TEU
Subject:	Common framework for the institutional structure Specific regulations for the individual institutions
Objectives:	Establishing a precise legal framework for the composition and tasks of the institutions Establishing an institutional framework with clear rules for the performance of tasks and for cooperation
Principles:	Establishment of a clearly defined tiered institutional structure

367 i.e. recast of the Association Decision.

Introduction

The penultimate part of the TEC consisted of two titles and was devoted to institutions on the one hand and financial regulations on the other. The title on institutions was based on a very narrow approach, which was ultimately limited to a more detailed explanation of the institutions listed in Article 7 TEC, whereby it extended the otherwise taxative list of this article by adding the European Investment Bank. In contrast, Article 288 TEC (ex-Article 215), which dealt with questions of liability of the Community and its staff, clearly assumed a broader view, as expressed in particular in the 1992 ECJ judgement in SGECM v. EIB,[368] thus almost going beyond the narrowly chosen framework of Article 7 and Part 5 Title I TEC.[369]

In principle, it should be noted that the way in which institutions are treated in primary law is essentially limited to defining the framework of political decision-making but does not establish administrative infrastructures. This is significant insofar as criticism of the institutional structure is always ignited by this administrative framework. Moreover, the embedding of the institutions in the TEC structure allowed conclusions to be drawn about their significance. The institutions were only dealt with in the TEC after the individual policies had been presented. This implied that the institutions do not derive their value eo ipso, but rather from their function of carrying out or implementing what the Member States regard as Community tasks. The reference to the institutions of the European Union in the preamble to the ToN,[370] however, allows the legitimate conclusion that they are assigned an essential role in integration, since they represent the uniform institutional framework of the Union and the Community.[371]

---

368 ECJ, Case C-370/89 of 2 December 1992, Société générale d'entreprises electromecaniques s.a. et Roland Etroy vs. EIB - Public works contracts in an ACP State, EIB co-financing, non-contractual liability towards an unsuccessful tenderer, jurisdiction of the Court of Justice - 1992 I-06211.

369 The European Central Bank is not dealt with in this title. The reason for not including the European Central Bank is its being considered an independent institution with its own statute.

370 i.c. Recital clause 2 [...] DESIRING to complete the process started by the Treaty of Amsterdam of preparing the institutions of the European Union to function in an enlarged Union, [...].

371 This reference in the preamble of the Treaty of Nice is misleading - if not contrary to the legal context - insofar as the Union had no institutions of its own; even the European Council did not have the character of an institution under the Nice setting but was - at best - to be described as an institutionalised meeting without

Since the institutions were already introduced in Article 7 TEC, Part 5 Title I TEC was limited to implementing provisions. These provisions essentially comprised two thematic sections. Firstly, they contained more detailed descriptions of the institutions, their competences, basic regulations and - at least rudimentarily - procedural regulations. Secondly, this title described the institutional framework by dealing very carefully with the definition and the course of the interrelated decision-making processes.

Prima facie, Part 5 TEC was organised in thematic sections, each dealing with a specific institution. However, this approach is misleading in that, firstly, each of these blocks shows the close interconnectedness of the institutions and their balance within the structure; secondly, all institutions, despite their fundamental independence from each other, are subject to common rules and, ultimately, essential questions of their respective competence are not regulated in this title, but are given in those parts, titles, and sections of the Treaty that regulate the specific policies.

It is precisely this interdependence of the institutions on the one hand, and their substantive determination in the policy provisions on the other, that is one of the most important reasons why, within this uniform institutional framework, no clear roles can be assigned to the institutions in the sense of Montesquieu's Principle of the Separation of Powers - executive, legislative, judiciary. On the contrary, the institutions actually fulfil overlapping functions. This design has been and continues to be criticized to the effect that the lack of separation leads to lack of transparency and remoteness from the citizens; moreover, this structure does not meet the requirements of a democratic order. Nevertheless, and precisely for this reason, the Community institutions are the key to understanding European integration in general and the European Union in particular. The institutions are the expression of how much competence the Member States intend to transfer to the Union. On the one hand, the institutions are to be seen as an independent bloc vis-à-vis the Member States; on the other hand, they play a wide variety of roles among themselves. The institutional structure is also determined by the antipolar position of the Council as an intergovernmental body vis-à-vis the supranational bodies and institutions of the Commission and the ECJ.

The Treaty itself did not - and does not - establish a hierarchy between the institutions, although it does of course distinguish between institutions

---

legislative competence. The Union made use of the Community institutions and bodies to fulfil its tasks.

and advisory bodies in the principal classification of the institutions. This means, for example, that putting the Parliament first in no way implies that it is the most important or highest ranking institution. Rather, this embedding or the place of this embedding signifies a reference to the European peoples whose representative at European level is this very Parliament. In any case, the institutions have an eminent significance for the shaping of the Union. They form one of the pillars on which the Union - from the point of view of international law - can be classified as supranational. Only the fact that these institutions can take binding decisions vis-à-vis the Member States is constitutional for the supranational character of the Union.

They also mirror the different legitimacies on which the Union is based:

- the Parliament is the expression of the democratic approach
- the Council represents the Member States
- the Commission embodies the European approach
- the Court of Justice is the expression of a European legal order
- the European Court of Auditors stands for compliance with the proper use of European financial resources

However, these different legitimacies are at the same time an expression of the balance between the two fundamental approaches on which the Union (and the then Community) is based, the supranational and the intergovernmental approach.

The changes that this title has undergone over the years can also be interpreted as a mirror for the evolution of European integration:

- the Assembly became a European Parliament, whose members are elected by universal, equal, and direct suffrage - an expression of the path towards more democracy at Union level
- the more or less informal meeting of Heads of State and Government was formalised over the years and ultimately elevated to the status of an institution – an expression of consideration of the reality of decision-making power
- the Council, which originally had - almost - sole decision-making power, became a co-legislator acting jointly with the Parliament - an expression of an integrative approach
- the High Authority became the European Commission, which was to become increasingly independent – which can be seen as an expression of the system moving in the direction of federalism

- the Economic and Social Committee was joined by a Committee of the Regions - an expression of recognition of the role of the regions and local authorities

This development can rightly be seen as decisive for the past, present, and future of the European Union; it sets the course, especially in the changing relationship between the Member States and the supranational community they founded, formed, and developed over the years.

The Treaty of Lisbon intervened in this structure, which had remained unchanged since Maastricht, both in terms of content and organisation, by removing the fundamental provisions on the institutions and their designation from the defunct TEC and transferring them to the TEU de lege ferenda. With this important decision, the institutions finally receive the place in primary law that they deserve both legally and in terms of content. This step has been taken in consistent implementation of the maxim of anchoring the fundamental regulations in the TEU, the executive provisions, however, in the TFEU. Accordingly, the procedural provisions on the individual institutions and bodies are found in the latter. The position of the TFEU becomes particularly clear in Article 13 TEU as amended by the ToL, when paragraphs 2 and 3 state that the implementing provisions are not regulated in the TEU, but in the TFEU.

In the course of the IGC 2007, the following essential changes were made in the institutional structure: (i) The number of institutions was increased by proclaiming the European Council and the European Central Bank as institutions, although the European Council was not assigned a legislative function, (ii) the distribution of power was reorganised in that the Parliament now stands opposite the Council as an equal and - with a few exceptions - co-legislator with the same rights, (iii) at the same time, three new positions were created, namely the permanent President of the European Council, the High Representative of the Union for Foreign Affairs and Security Policy, and the President of the Eurogroup. However, the ToL was inconsistent insofar as it claimed to locate the general regulations of the institutions in the TEU but did not take the Central Bank and the Court of Auditors into account.

The Institutions – Fundamental Principles

Article 13 TEU as amended by the ToL is constitutive for the structure in that it establishes that the Union has an institutional framework whose purpose is to implement the values, objectives, and interests of the Union. While the EESC and CoR had hoped to become institutions, this upgrade did not happen. Instead, their status as advisory bodies is clearly emphasised [372]

The European Parliament

Article 14 TEU as amended by the ToL contains the constitutive elements with regard to the European Parliament and brings together the existing provisions of Article 189, Article 190 (1) to (3) and Article 197 (1) TEC with completely new elements, such as the election of the President of the Commission by the Parliament. Article 189 TEC, now Article 14 (1) and (2) TEU, was amended for the first time by the ToA by introducing a maximum number of MEPs, namely 700. The reason for this restriction is that the Parliament has grown with each enlargement by granting the new Member States the number of seats that comparable Member States had under the cluster system.[373] The consequence of this would have been that the Parliament would have become ever larger and thus ultimately would have lost any efficiency. This IGC 1996 move was a consequence of Declaration No. 15 to the ToM, which addressed the issue of the number of Members of the Commission and the European Parliament. In this declaration, the IGC 1991 agreed to examine these issues no later than the end of 1992 with a view to reaching an agreement that would allow the legal basis for determining the number of Members of the Parliament to

372 The CoR does not seem at all comfortable with this subordinate role and sees itself as a complementary institution of the Union, which is not covered by primary law and could lead to conclusions that are not necessarily desirable. However, this did not stop the CoR Bureau from informally renaming the CoR as the European Committee of the Regions. This arbitrary renaming, which is not covered by the Treaty, has no legal significance whatsoever; at best, it caused additional administrative costs.

373 According to the cluster system, comparable Member States receive an equal number of seats, whereby the number of inhabitants is used as a benchmark. Contrary to what is thought or claimed, there is no mathematical formula behind the cluster allocations. The number of seats is rather subject to an aleatory system.

be established in time for the 1994 elections. These decisions should be reached taking into account, inter alia, the need to fix the total number of Members of Parliament in an enlarged Community. This maximum number was not only raised to 732 by the IGC 2000 but was further extended by an overriding clause in a possible transitional period from enlargement to the next parliamentary elections. The only substantive demand for a change in Article 189 TEC was raised by Germany during the IGC 1991, when she suggested that the Parliament should not be composed of the representatives of the peoples of the states united in the Community, but of representatives of the citizens of the Union.[374] This demand corresponded to the new citizenship of the Union but was rejected by the other conferees and not pursued further by Germany.

Article 190(1) to (3) TEC (ex-Article 138), now Article 14(1) to (3) TEU, deals with the number of MEPs and the electoral procedure. As mentioned above, the Direct Election Act fundamentally changed the electoral procedure.[375] The original paragraphs 1 and 2, which referred to the composition of the Parliament before the introduction of direct elections, were repealed and replaced by the current version, which corresponds to the rules in Articles 1 to 3 of the Direct Election Act. The number of MEPs also changed as a result of the various enlargements, but the cluster system had been maintained at all times. The IGC 2000 was confronted with the problem that the forthcoming enlargement with at least ten states could make the distribution of seats in Parliament extremely controversial. The small Member States insisted on a minimum number of seats that would make democratically legitimate elections meaningful, while the large Member States insisted on a representation that was more adequate to their population. In the IGC 2000, Luxembourg stated dryly that a European election for one or two seats would in no way be justifiable and almost undemocratic, and ultimately prevailed with her demand for a minimum number of five seats, as did the large Member States, which had demanded an increase in their seats relative to the other Member States; the medium-sized states, which were proportionally most likely to lose influence, are to be seen as

374 Apart from the fact that the ToM has shortened and simplified the original text by referring only to powers, this amendment is a consequence of what had already become necessary through the two treaties on the budgetary and financial provisions, as well as through the substantial changes brought about by the ToM itself.

375 Act concerning the election of the representatives of the Assembly by direct universal suffrage, OJ. L 278, 08/10/1976 P. 0005 - 0011.

obvious losers of this system. Although these changes only came into force on 1 May 2004, they were already taken into account in the parliamentary elections in June 2004. Since the IGC 1996, this issue had been acute and already at that conference it had been Luxembourg that had vehemently demanded her claim for a minimum representation in the Parliament. The consequence of this demand was the new subparagraph 2 in paragraph 2, which, since the ToA, stipulated that an adequate representation of each Member State had to be guaranteed in any future change in the distribution of seats. Paragraph 3 was amended for the first time in the course of the IGC 1991. In the pre-Maastricht era, it had been the Council alone which - unanimously - made the relevant provisions for the elections to the Parliament. The ToM gave the Parliament a respective right of assent, which clearly corresponded to the upgrading of this institution. The ToA added a new paragraph 3, which stipulates that the term of office of MPs is five years. The former paragraph 3 was redrafted into a new paragraph 4, with the substantive change being that the Parliament should prepare its proposals for elections by direct universal suffrage not only according to a uniform procedure in all Member States, but in eventu in accordance with principles common to all Member States. The IGC 1996 justified this change by stating that the possibility should be opened up that there should not be a draft for an identical electoral procedure in all Member States, but a draft with common principles, which would leave the Member States free to choose the modus operandi.[376] Paragraph 5 is also a product of the IGC 1996 and deals with the statute for Members of Parliament for the first time on primary law level. This issue had become virulent as a result of criticism of the way in which some MEPs exercised their mandate. Paragraph 5 enables the Parliament to draw up a proposal for a Statute, which is then adopted by the Council after consultation of the Commission. In the first version under the ToA, the Council had to act unanimously, but the IGC 2000 split this decision on the statute by stating that the Council shall in principle act by QMV, except on rules and conditions concerning fiscal arrangements, which remain subject to unanimity.[377]

---

376 This new passage mainly took into account the majority voting system in the United Kingdom, which had also switched to proportional representation since the 1999 elections, however only for elections to the European Parliament. For national elections, the UK retained the first-past-the-post system.

377 Thus, the United Kingdom had once again prevailed, keeping a watchful eye to ensure that there would be no transition to QMV in any matter concerning any tax issue. However, this statute regularly failed in Council votes.

In the last night of the negotiations, the IGC 2007 was confronted with an almost insoluble problem regarding the number of parliamentarians. The Member States had agreed to keep the maximum number already set by the IGC 2004, according to which the European Parliament should not have more than 750 members. Italy, however, steadfastly refused to accept the envisaged reduction of her members and insisted on retaining an additional seat. This would naturally have required another Member State to give up a seat, which - as expected - no Member State was prepared to do. At the literally last second, a compromise was found that seems Kafkaesque: the future Parliament would have a maximum of 750 members plus its President. The ToL thus creates the fiction of maintaining the nominal upper limit, whereby the President is of course a Member of Parliament, since he or she must be elected from among its members; there is also no doubt that the President is entitled to vote, since no Treaty provision deprives him or her of that right. One can therefore accuse the IGC 2007 of many things, but lack of situational flexibility is certainly not one of them. Furthermore, the ToL introduces a change to the situation de lege lata that will have massive effects not only on Treaty law, but on the entire system of composition of the Parliament, the EESC, and the CoR. The ToL abandons the numerical distribution of seats in all three cases and stipulates that this distribution will be determined by the European Council (in the case of the Parliament) or by the Council (in the case of the EESC and the CoR).[378] This change has several effects. Firstly, there is no longer any such distribution of seats in primary law, but in future the respective decisions are taken by the European Council or the Council. Secondly, it cannot be ruled out that these seat distributions must be renegotiated or decided before each election or each mandate period. Thirdly, a hitherto always controversial chapter in accession negotiations will be avoided. The latter had always been contested, as accession negotiations could not be concluded before an agreement had been reached on the distribution of seats, which, in the case of maximum numbers, naturally leads to Member States having to give up seats. This decision will now be outsourced (or delayed) and will probably be dealt with in a less emotional - though still highly controversial - manner.

378 The subordinate position of the two committees becomes also obvious from this very clear classification.

The European Council

Article 15 TEU introduces a new body to the institutional set-up, namely the European Council. This provision removes an anomaly of the previous system. This anomaly was due to the fact that the Heads of State and Government had not actually been assigned a clear position at European level, and although they already informally met, they were not an institution. The previous wording of Article 4 ex-TEU had only assigned basic target-setting competences to the European Council. The primary law situation was thus adapted to reality. The specification of two - ordinary - meetings per six months and thus the discontinuation of the informal European Councils also serves to bring the Treaty closer to reality. Should the European Council meet, it must be decided whether it is an ordinary or an extraordinary meeting, which only the President of the European Council can convene. However, the Member States and their Heads of State and Government quickly found a way around this self-imposed obstacle and reintroduced the informal European Councils, which had actually been abolished, through the back door. The big losers of the IGC 2007 were clearly the foreign ministers. According to the de lege lata provision, they were not voting members of the European Council, but due to their expertise they were substantially involved in the deliberations. On the occasion of the IGC 2007, the Heads of State and Government were able to finally get rid of their foreign ministers; all attempts to revise this plan, which had already been decided at the IGC 2004, failed. The Heads of State and Government can now call in ministers, but - as practice has shown - they refrain from doing so and remain among themselves. Even during the economic and financial crisis and the negotiations with Greece, neither the foreign ministers nor the finance ministers were consulted or invited to take part at the meetings of the European Council. The last fundamental innovation is the introduction of a - permanent - president, elected by the European Council for two and a half years with the possibility of re-election once. With this decision, which had already been incorporated into the TCEU, the IGC 2007 took a step towards continuity of the Union's external appearance. The Union had often been accused of changing its leader every six months and thus not providing continuity in terms of content or personnel. This has been remedied with the introduction of both the President of the European Council and the High Representative of the Union for Foreign Affairs and Security Policy.

The Council

Article 16 TEU as amended by the ToL addresses the Council and contains little that is revolutionary, at least not in the first three paragraphs.

Article 202 TEC (ex-Article 145), now Article 16(1) TEU, which deals with the rights and duties of the Council, was revised for the first time by Article 10 SEA adding a third indent allowing the Council to delegate the implementation of acts adopted by it to the Commission. This addition laid the foundation for the so-called comitology procedure. Article 202 TEC subsequently remained unchanged.[379]

Article 203 TEC (ex-Article 147), now Article 16(2) and (9) TEU, dealt with the composition of the Council and the question of the presidency. In its original version, it contained only two terse sentences, according to which the Council shall consist of representatives of the Member States, each of which shall appoint one of its members, and that the presidency shall be held in turn in the alphabetical order of the Member States for six months each. Article 7 Merger Treaty repealed ex-Article 147 TEC and replaced it in accordance with Article 2 Merger Treaty. Article 2 Merger Treaty replaced the order of presidencies, which had been based on the alphabet, with an order based on primary law. The Merger Treaty established an order for a total of twelve years. These changes were hardly of any substantive relevance. The ToM, however, was to bring about a radical change particularly in terms of content. The IGC 1991 was confronted with demands from the federal states of Germany and Belgium - and also from Austria, although not yet a Member State but still in the midst of accession negotiations - which pressed for a solution that would enable these Member States to also send Länder or state ministers to the Council. These demands initially met with little approval, especially from centrally oriented Member States, but for Germany and Belgium they were a conditio sine qua non in the institutional sector. The IGC 1991 decided on a wording that allowed both sides to save face: the representation of a Member State must continue to be at ministerial level, but the person seconded must no longer necessarily be a member of the government, but merely hold the rank of minister and be authorised to act in a binding manner for the government of the Member State concerned. The question of representation

379 The IGC 1996, however, annexed Declaration No. 31 on the Council Decision of 13 July 1987 to the ToA, in which it called on the Commission to submit a new proposal for a comitology decision before the end of 1988.

was thus delegated to the respective national law. The ToM adopted the existing wording on the order of presidencies, but the IGC 1996 decided to remove the order of presidencies from primary law and make it subject to a unanimous decision of the Council. This change had been made in the belief that otherwise this question would also be the subject of every accession negotiations and that a consensual solution would be correspondingly difficult to achieve. Moreover, this wording allowed for the option that the order of presidencies could be changed - even without enlargements - if necessary, without having to amend primary law.

However, Article 216(4) in conjunction with (5) TEU new introduces a fundamental change that puts Council voting on a completely new footing, although - to stay with this image - the Council would be dependent on a walker and crutches until 31 March 2017. The IGC 2007 had to admit its inability to make clear decisions on essential issues on yet another point. The requirement to switch from the previous cluster system to the double majority could only be achieved step by step, as Poland refused to give up her disproportionately high weighting of votes. Accordingly, the IGC 2007 had to find a way to settle both the double majority issue and the blocking minority together with the Ioannina Clause[380] in a package that would allow the conference to be concluded without giving too much ground to Poland. With regard to the double majority, it was decided to delay the entry into force following a Kafkaesque sequence: (i) until 31 October 2014, the Nice regime (weighting of votes in the Council) continues to apply, (ii) from 1 November 2014 until 31 March 2017, the double majority system applies, unless a Member State requested a vote under the Nice regime, (iii) from 1 November 2017, only the double majority system applies. The Ioannina Clause from 1994 (OJ C 1 of 1 January 1995), which was introduced in the course of the accession of Austria, Sweden

380 The term goes back to an informal meeting of foreign ministers on 27 March 1994. The Ioannina Clause describes the option of creating a kind of blockade on decision-making even before the actual blocking-minority threshold is reached. Before Finland, Austria and Sweden joined the EU on 1 January 1995, the blocking minority in the Council amounted to 23 votes. Due to their accession, this threshold was raised to 26 votes out of a total of 87. Spain, though, enforced the so-called Ioannina clause, according to which the Council would have to make every effort to find a solution within a reasonable period of time that could be adopted with at least 65 votes, if there were 23 to 25 votes against a decision. The 65-vote threshold is the same as the number of votes needed to overcome a blocking minority before the aforementioned accessions.

and Finland at the intervention of Spain, fearing for her influence, was also adapted with an inbuilt time delay. In this case, however, the adaptation is not linear, but exclusively in favour of Poland. Accordingly, the original Ioannina formula was valid until 31 October 2014. From 1 November 2014 until 31 March 2017, in cases where members of the Council reach at least 75% of the threshold required for the blocking minority with regard to either the population or the state criterion and at the same time declare that they oppose the adoption of the decision by qualified majority, the Council was to continue to discuss the issue concerned, making every effort to reach a satisfactory solution for those Member States having invoked the clause. Declaration No. 7 provides for a reasonable period of time for this purpose, but within the limits stipulated for the legislative procedure. So far, the IGC could still be considered a success in 2007, as this time shift was drafted in parallel with the question of double majority. However, the solution adopted for the period from 1 April 2017 onwards reduces the objective of making it easier to achieve majorities in the Council to absurdity: from 1 April 2017, the threshold required to trigger the clause is lowered from 75% to 55% of the population or number of states required for the blocking minority. Poland had prevailed against the other Member States and thus at the same time nullified the advantages from the introduction of double majority. Apart from this negotiating defeat, the other innovations are completely overshadowed, although the anchoring of the Marlia procedure at the level of primary law and the reorganisation of the presidency rotation are certainly positive achievements. The so-called Marlia procedure, i.e. the competence of the General Affairs Council to ensure the coherence of the work of the Council formations at primary law level, had hitherto been a recognised procedure without a robust legal basis, which, due to the wording of the ToL, the General Affairs Council now also holds vis-à-vis the Foreign Affairs Council.[381] Another bitter defeat of the Foreign Ministers is manifested in the new provision according to which the High Representative of the Union for Foreign Affairs and Security Policy also holds the chair of the Foreign Affairs Council. The Treaty does not provide for details on the rotation of the Presidency in its corpus; the rotation - including the new system of team presidencies - is laid down in Declaration No. 9.

381 The term dates back to an informal ministerial meeting at Villa Marlia, near Lucca, Tuscany, in October 1975, where the procedure was developed and agreed. This provision also testifies to the relative loss of importance of the foreign ministers.

The Commission

The ToL regulates the fundamental issues and questions regarding the European Commission in the new Article 17 TEU. In total, this article consists of eight paragraphs, which essentially replace the previous articles 211, 213, 214, 217 and 251 TEC, while substantially modifying them. In order to make the complexity of this compilation comprehensible, these compilations are presented in the following overview - in which the corresponding articles of the Constitutional Treaty are also included - in the order of the new provisions. Following this, the historical development is presented. As this overview shows, the IGC 2007 decided to deal with all general questions regarding the Commission in a single article, thus deviating from the approach of the IGC 2004, which had still created two provisions, one dealing with the Commission as a collegial body and the second with its president; as in some other cases, this decision also testifies to a stricter approach of the IGC 2007, whose aim was to provide a compact and clear text.

Article 17 TEU new	TEC	TCEU
para 1	Article 211	Article I-26 para 1
para 2	Article 250 para 1	Article I-26 para 2
para 3 subparagraph 1	Article 214 para 1 subparagraph 1	Article I-26 para 3
para 3 subparagraph 2	Article 213 para 2 subparagraph 1	Article I-26 para 4
para 3 subparagraph 3	Article 213 para 2 subparagraph 1 and 2	Article I-26 para 7
para 4	Article 213 para 1 subparagraph 4	Article I-26 para 5
para 5	Article 213 para 1 subparagraph 3	Article I-26 para 6
para 6	Article 217	Article I-27 subparagraph 3
para 7 subparagraph 1	Article 214 para 2 subparagraph 1	Article I-27 para 1
para 7 subparagraph 2	Article 214 para 2 subparagraph 2	Article I-27 para 2 subparagraph 1
para 7 subparagraph 3	Article 214 para 2 subparagraph 3	Article I-27 para 2 subparagraph 2
para 8	Article 201	Article I-26 para 8

Article 17 TEU as amended by the ToL deals with the Commission and introduces a series of new elements in response to earlier shortcomings, the strengthening of the European Parliament and lessons learned since the turn of the millennium (i.e. election of the Commission President by the

Parliament, with the proposal being made by the European Council, taking into account the result of the parliamentary elections; stipulation that the High Representative is Vice-President of the Commission; extension of the organisational rights of the Commission President). The basic tenor of the new Commission regulations, however, is the decision to politicise the Commission more strongly or, in other words, to give it greater political influence.[382]

This redrafting of the basic provisions vis-à-vis the Commission is a clear breach with past Treaty developments in this sector.

In contrast to most of the other articles dealing with the Commission, the basic provisions have been unchanged since the TEEC. The latter was modelled on Article 8 TECSC, which succinctly stated that the Commission's task is to ensure that the purposes laid down in the Treaty are achieved in accordance with the provisions of the Treaty. The TEEC - and subsequently the TEC - no longer seemed to be able to cope with this very general allocation of competences, whereby the experiences of the first years of the Coal and Steel Community had also contributed to this respect. Article 214 TEC regulated the appointment of the Commission on the one hand, and the vote of approval by Parliament on the other. The original TEEC article contained only two subparagraphs, which stated that (subparagraph 1) the Members of the Commission shall be appointed by common accord of the governments of the Member States and (subparagraph 2) their term of office shall be four years, with the possibility of reappointment. The ToM introduced several innovations in this respect. On the one hand, the term of office of the Commission was extended to five years (paragraph 1), on the other hand, a detailed procedure for the appointment of the Commission was introduced (paragraph 2).[383]

This new system had become necessary since the IGC 1991 had complied with the Parliament's demand to be included in the appointment

382 The so-called "politicisation" of the Commission already existed in principle insofar as any Member State appointment reflected the party-political orientation of the respective government. However, the consideration of the results of the parliamentary elections when nominating the Commission President is a real game changer. Until the ToL, the party-political orientation of the Commission President reflected the party-political distribution in the European Council. Now this alignment switches to the European Parliament. This massively limits the range of choices on the part of the European Council and - as happened with Jean-Claude Junker's appointment - the European Council had to follow the pressure of the European Parliament nolens volens.

383 Paragraph 3, inserted by the ToM, was deleted in the course of the IGC 1996.

of the Commission. In Maastricht, however, Parliament was only permitted to participate in the hearing procedure for the appointment of the Commission President, whereas it already had the right to participate in the approval procedure for the appointment of the entire Commission. The appointment as such, however, remained the exclusive competence of the governments of the Member States. The IGC 1996 took this one step further and granted the Parliament the right of assent also with regard to the President of the Commission. The IGC also strengthened the function of the Commission President for the first time by stipulating that the Commissioners shall be appointed by the Member States in agreement with the Commission President-designate. The IGC 1996 felt compelled to compensate for the concession to the Parliament and found this in the strengthening of the Commission President, who was at the same time elevated to the level of the national governments of the Member States as they now had to carry out their appointments in agreement with the President. The next step towards a strong Commission President was taken by the IGC 2000. For the first time, the Heads of State and Government were involved expressis verbis in the procedure by giving the Council, in its composition of Heads of State and Government, the task of nominating by qualified majority the person they intended to appoint, this nomination being subject to the approval of the Parliament. The second major change introduced by the IGC 2000 concerned the nomination procedure for the other Members of the Commission. According to the wording of the ToA, the governments of the Member States - in agreement with the designated President of the Commission - nominated the persons they intended to appoint as Members of the Commission. According to the ToN, the Council - still in agreement with the President-designate of the Commission - adopts a list of the persons to be appointed, which is drawn up on the proposal of the Member States. The change relates to the fact that it is no longer the Member States that decide which persons occupy the respective positions, but the Council. This change is clearly to be seen as a step away from the intergovernmental towards the supranational regime. The final amendment to Article 214(2) TEC shall also be seen against that background. At the end of the whole process, the President and the Commissioners will not only be appointed by qualified majority, but by the Council, no longer by the governments of the Member States. However, one demand of the European Parliament was not met by the IGC 2000. At the latest since the Commission crisis in 1999, the Parliament had demanded that it be able to reject individual Commissioners. The IGC dismissed this demand and insisted on the principle of collective acceptance or rejection.

Article 213(1) TEC (ex-Article 157), dealing with the composition of the Commission, was repealed by Article 19 Merger Treaty and re-inserted by Article 10 Merger Treaty. Prior to the TEU, the TEEC had stipulated that no more than two members of the Commission could be of the same nationality. Under the Merger Treaty, this provision - paragraph 1 subparagraph 4 - was amended to the extent that it was stipulated for the first time that the Commission must have at least one member from each Member State. This principle had never been questioned, but the conference felt compelled to guarantee it in primary law. Even in the early days of the Communities, the size of the Commission had been the subject of a wide variety of opinions; the fact that the College should comprise at least as many members as the Community has Member States was not necessarily to be seen as a dogma, but rather the result of Member State positions. Accordingly, Article 213 TEC was not rewritten during the IGC 1996, but only the maximum number of Commissioners was adapted to the circumstances after the enlargement of the Community to include Austria, Sweden and Finland. The IGC 2000 was confronted with this so-called Amsterdam-left-over and found a protocol solution which was supposed to make it possible to bring about a consensual clarification in due course. In the Protocol on the Enlargement of the European Union, Article 4(1), the IGC agreed that Article 213(1) TEC - and Article 126(1) TEAEC - would be replaced by the following on 1 January 2005:

> *1. On 1 January 2005 and with effect from when the first Commission following that date takes up its duties, Article 213(1) of the Treaty establishing the European Community and Article 126(1) of the Treaty establishing the European Atomic Energy Community shall be replaced by the following:*
> *"1. The Members of the Commission shall be chosen on the grounds of their general competence and their independence shall be beyond doubt.*
> ***The Commission shall include one national of each of the Member States.***
> *The number of Members of the Commission may be altered by the Council, acting unanimously."*

The IGC 2000 thus broke with the principle that the big Member States would provide a second Commissioner.[384] Three options regarding the applicability of the transition to the principle of one Commissioner per Member State were presented to the IGC 2000. The first option, which would have brought the provision into force at the same time as the new Treaty was immediately rejected as it would have led to a change to the Commission in office. The second option would have taken effect with an enlargement and would have meant replacing the second commissioners of the Member States concerned. This option was also rejected for similar reasons. The third option was linked to the assumption of office by the subsequent Commission and ultimately prevailed because it had the advantage of including a specific date and being unrelated to any accession.

However, this meant that the IGC 2000 did not meet all the demands for a reduction in the number of Commissioners. Nevertheless, the pressure in Nice had at least been so strong that the following rendez-vous clause was adopted by Article 4(2) and (3) Protocol on the Enlargement of the European Union:

> *2. When the Union consists of 27 Member States, Article 213(1) of the Treaty establishing the European Community and Article 126(1) of the Treaty establishing the European Atomic Energy Community shall be replaced by the following:*
> *"1. The Members of the Commission shall be chosen on the grounds of their general competence and their independence shall be beyond doubt.*
> *The number of Members of the Commission shall be less than the number of Member States. The Members of the Commission shall be chosen according to a rotation system based on the principle of equality, the implementing arrangements for which shall be adopted by the Council, acting unanimously.*
> *The number of Members of the Commission shall be set by the Council, acting unanimously."*
> *This amendment shall apply as from the date on which the first Commission following the date of accession of the twenty-seventh Member State of the Union takes up its duties.*
> *3. The Council, acting unanimously after signing the treaty of accession of the twenty-seventh Member State of the Union, shall adopt:*
> *- the number of Members of the Commission;*

384 This regulation was brought forward and already applied to the composition of the Commission as of 1 November 2004.

- the implementing arrangements for a rotation system based on the principle of equality containing all the criteria and rules necessary for determining the composition of successive colleges automatically on the basis of the following principles:
(a) Member States shall be treated on a strictly equal footing as regards determination of the sequence of, and the time spent by, their nationals as Members of the Commission; consequently, the difference between the total number of terms of office held by nationals of any given pair of Member States may never be more than one;
(b) subject to point (a), each successive college shall be so composed as to reflect satisfactorily the demographic and geographical range of all the Member States of the Union.
4. Any State which accedes to the Union shall be entitled, at the time of its accession, to have one of its nationals as a Member of the Commission until paragraph 2 applies.

During the IGC 2000, the big Member States had always insisted on capping the number of Commissioners, i.e. introducing a maximum number. The main argument was that a Commission with more than twenty members would not be efficient. The group of small and medium-sized Member States, however, strongly resisted this demand - and eventually succeeded. They argued that efficiency would not depend on size, but rather be a question of internal organisation. The underlying reason for this debate, however, was certainly not a question of efficiency, but of representation in this institution. The small and medium-sized Member States feared that they would no longer be represented in this body and would therefore lose a great deal of influence. They also argued that the national Commissioner virtually embodied the Union in the respective Member States and should therefore not be surrendered to a principle, as he or she made essential contributions to facilitating identification with European integration. Before the summit in Nice, Germany offered that it could also agree to an equal rotation, but at the latest during the actual debate on this rotation, the limits of the respective tolerance were quickly reached. The IGC 2000 discussed a further proposal - put forward by the big Member States - for a hierarchisation of the Commission. According to this idea, the Commission President would have appointed a certain number of Vice-Presidents to whom the other Commissioners would have been assigned, who would be called Junior Commissioners. This variant was rejected by the other group, as they feared that this hierarchisation would be to the detriment of the small and medium-sized Member States. The IGC 2000 had thus managed the balancing act between all the proposals, in particular it had been able to postpone the actual decision on the size and composition of the Commission indefinitely.[385] It should not be forgotten that the particular piquancy lay in the fact that this final decision should have been taken unanimously.

Article 17(1) TEU as amended by the ToL, which is based on Article 211 TEC, introduces the provisions on the Commission with a description of its tasks. Above all, its function as Guardian of the Treaties, which it has held since the founding of the Communities, is highlighted. The ToL does not change this essential position of the Commission in the institutional structure in any way that would not be editorially or systemically necessary through other amendments to the Treaties.

Article 17 (2) TEU reaffirms the Commission's monopoly on proposals for legal acts, which was already laid down in Article 250 (1) TEC. The derogation (...unless otherwise specified...) was already part of primary law de lege lata, and the ToL did not change either principle.

Article 17(3) TEU contains three basic elements: (i) the duration of the Commission's term of office, (ii) the conditions of appointment of Commissioners, and (iii) the Code of Conduct for Commissioners. The duration of the term of office remains unchanged at five years, while the passage in Article 213(1) TEC that reappointment is permitted has not been taken over. The IGC 2007 did not see the need to include this option expressis verbis, thus applying the principle that what is not explicitly prohibited is permitted. Here too, the IGC 2007 was consistent in its intention to keep the text as compact as possible. The previous conditions for the appointment of Commissioners were taken from Article 213(1)1 TEC and expanded by the new condition that the candidates would also be selected on the basis of their commitment to Europe. This passage was taken from the TCEU and reflects the staunch pro-EU approach of the IGC 2004; whether it was intended to exclude EU sceptics from the office of Commissioner is a moot point, as is whether such a wording is politically correct. The Code of Conduct is modelled on the one contained in Article 213(2) 1 and 2 TEC. The explicit reference to the prohibition of secondary employment, wheth-

385 Such decisions taken by the Heads of State and Government have become a tradition since. It is precisely the postponement of the actual decision to a time when those Heads of State and Government who have adopted the decision in principle may no longer be in office that makes the decision so much easier. In particular, the solution by means of a rendez-vous clause, which does not include a specific date, is particularly helpful in such situations.

er paid or unpaid, as contained in Article 213(2) subparagraph 3 TEC, has been transformed into the rather cryptic sentence that Commissioners shall refrain from any action incompatible with their office or the performance of their duties.

Article 17(4) and (5) TEU as amended by the ToL deal with the number of Members of the Commission, with para 4 addressing the number of Members of the first Commission appointed between the entry into force of the ToL and 31 October 2014, and para 5 addressing the number of Members of the subsequent Commission to be appointed. The reception of Articles 213 and 214 TEC can at best be described as rudimentary, and concerns on the one hand the fact that they must be citizens of the Member States and that - in relation to the paragraph 4 Commission - each Member State is represented by one member. The IGC 2007 had originally also agreed to drastically reduce the number of Members of the Commission to a number corresponding to two thirds of the Member States. The ToN, as explained above, had already envisaged such a reduction, but the Member States became increasingly reluctant to do so as the trigger date approached. Officially, they could not back down, but Austria had insisted on introducing a solution satisfactory to all Member States in the course of the IGC 2004. The reduction would come into force, unless the European Council unanimously decided to change this number. The elegance of this arrangement is not so much to be found in its obvious appeal as in the fact that no IGC is necessary for this essential change, but rather a regular meeting of the European Council and a unanimous decision.[386] This is exactly what happened rather quickly. On 22 May 2013, the European Council took the decision that the Commission, including its President and the High

386 The Convention had gone one step further than even the otherwise progressive IGC 2004, which, however, contradicted the Convention on this essential point: in an equally inconsistent and ill-conceived attempt to bring about a compromise between one party, which demanded that the Commission be smaller than the number of Member States, and the second party of like-minded, which wanted an unspecified reduction in numbers, the Convention had proposed the introduction of two levels of Commissioners: European Commissioners with a dossier, seat and vote, and so-called Junior Commissioners who have no dossier of their own and no vote. This nonsensical division led to protests in almost all Member States. Denmark, in particular, stated that it would not send a Junior Commissioner, as it could not be made clear to the Danish people why such a second-class Commissioner had no task and no responsibility, but instead had an official residence, an official car, a fully-fledged staff, and an exorbitantly high salary. The discussions on this subject lasted only a short time and the Junior Commissioners disappeared from the scene and into the abyss of the archives.

Representative of the Union for Foreign Affairs and Security Policy, shall consist of a number of members equal to the number of Member States (OJ L 165/98 of 18 June 2013). The European Council determined to review this decision in view of its impact on the work of the Commission. This review should be carried out in due time either (i) before the appointment of the first Commission following the accession of the thirtieth Member State, or (ii) before the appointment of the Commission due to take office on 1 November 2014, whichever of these events occurs sooner. Officially, the European Council based its decision on Ireland's demands in this regard, but it was obvious that the other Member States would not be opposed. It is not so much the fact of the u-turn as such that is the stumbling block, but the circumstances that accompanied it. Both during the IGC 2004 and the IGC 2007 it was evident that the Member States could not come to terms with the idea of not being represented in the Commission and, accordingly, not being able to have their say and take part in decision-making, especially with regard to infringement proceedings. This also reveals an inherent mistrust among the Member States and the perception that the Commission is by no means a supranational body but is ultimately seen as the extended arm of the Member States, because one expects one's own Commissioner to represent national interests if necessary. Against this background, the decision to include the reduction in the number of Commissioners in the Treaty makes little sense and is more of a face-saving exercise.

The content of Article 17(6) TEU as amended by the ToL is very much based on Article 217(1), (3) and (4) TEC. Until the ToN, these provisions only stated that the Commission could appoint one or two Vice-Presidents from among its members. The IGC 2000 fundamentally changed this article. As part of the so-called Lex Prodi, this article comprised four paragraphs since the ToN, which regulated the position of the President of the Commission, the division of competences, and the resignation of Members of the Commission. Article 217(1) TEC was preceded by the ToN by the former Article 219(1) TEC (which was of course deleted uno actu), according to which the Commission must carry out its activities under the political leadership of its President. Paragraph 1 thus gave the President for the first time expressis verbis the imperium to decide on the internal organisation of the Commission, which he had implicitly held in the pre-Nice era, but which could not be derived directly from primary law. In this decision, the President was only limited in so far as he or she had to exercise it in the light of coherent and efficient action and had to ensure that the principle of collegiality was complied with. The Member States have assured themselves an unspoken indirect right of co-determination or at least the right to be consulted, as the Commissioners are in reality still representatives of the Member States.

The explicit reference to the principle of collegiality results from the sustained debates in the IGC on the size and composition of the Commission and was intended to ensure - in the eyes of the smaller and medium-sized Member States - that all Commissioners are on equal footing. Paragraph 2 also codifies customary law. Even before the IGC 2000, the President had - officially - distributed the dossiers among the individual Commissioners, whereby the influence of the Member States had been no less. A change of competences during the term of office was considered unusual, as the Commissioners concerned would have been formally disavowed. By defining this as a competence of the President, such a change not only becomes possible under primary law, but above all ensures that it is the sovereign decision of the President to take such a step. However, the Member States inherently assumed that the President of the Commission would also consult with them on such occasions in the future. The supervision by the President was already undisputed. However, the anchoring in primary law also meant that the President could commit a breach of his duty of supervision.[387]

During the pre-Nice era, the Vice-Presidents were appointed from among the Commission's Members. The ToN assigned this competence to the President. In any case, the proposal must be approved by the College, by which the IGC 2000 secured the collegiality principle of the Commission - despite the extension of the executive power of the President. Since the ToN, it has been up to the President to determine the number of Vice-Presidents - likewise after approval by the College - and he has thus no longer been bound to a maximum number. With this option, the IGC 2000 acted proactively towards a Commission in an enlarged Union. The right of the President to ask a Member of the Commission to resign is known as Lex Prodi.[388] The entire revision of Article 217 TEC was to be seen under the political motto of strengthening the President in order

387 This treaty change must be considered in particular against the background of the events surrounding the former French Commissioner for education, Edith Cresson, and the unanimous resignation of the Santer Commission in the spring of 1999.

388 The President-designate of the Commission, Romano Prodi, had taken a promise from his future colleagues in the Commission that they would resign if he asked them to do so. This rigorous lex Prodi was not adopted because the IGC 2000 was not yet ready to strengthen the Commission President in this way.

to compensate for the fact that Parliament had to be granted more rights in numerous areas. The strengthening of the Commission was intended to counterbalance Parliament's increased rights. The ToL merged these provisions, gave them a more compact structure, and only made editorial and mandate-related adjustments without adapting the content; except for one crucial issue: the IGC 2007 reinforced the Lex Prodi by granting the President of the Commission a monocratic decision to ask a Member of the Commission to resign, which is tantamount to coercion, since this Member is obliged to comply with the request. Accordingly, the prior consent of the College to a request for resignation has been deleted.

Article 17(7) TEU deals with the election and appointment of the President of the Commission and the Members of the Commission, whereby, although Article 214 TEC has been formally used, the IGC 2007 introduces a number of completely new elements. Basically, this new procedure for appointing the Commission President or the entire Commission is a conglomerate of the Nice era, the Convention draft and the IGC 2004, with the ToL not having affected the content of the draft of the IGC 2004. Anyhow, the Commission is now definitely turning into a political body. Nothing else is meant by the requirement that the European Council, in its choice of personnel for the Commission President, must take into account the majority ratios in the European Parliament; whichever group has the majority in the Parliament or is in a position to form a majority coalition provides - (party) politically - the Commission President. The European Parliament elects the President of the Commission by simple majority on the basis of a proposal of the European Council, but the President of the Commission can still only be referred to as designated, since after the European Council has drawn up the list of Commissioners in agreement with the President of the Commission, the President of the Commission, together with the High Representative and the proposed other Commissioners, must stand a vote of approval by the Parliament. Only on the basis of this vote of approval the European Council appoints the Commission by qualified majority. Although this means that the Commission President is more or less party-politically predetermined, as he or she reflects the party-political majority in the Parliament, the political-factional relationship in the entire Commission is preserved, as the Commission encompasses the entire political spectrum of the Member States. Unfortunately, the ToL retains a vagueness of the TCEU with regard to the majorities with which the Parliament must vote. In the case of the Commission President, the TEU gives a clear answer since it stipulates a simple majority of the Members of Parliament for approval. In the case of the Commission list, this is not specified. That gap has to be closed by means of an analogy. The Parliament thus gained an enormous increase in competence, however, the IGC 2007 denied it the right of appointment for the Commission and the Commission President. This is not just a nuance of protocol, but of considerable importance, because it is ultimately the Member States - through their Heads of State and Government - that appoint the Commission and its President.

The last paragraph of Article 17 TEU, paragraph 8, stipulates the procedure for the motion of censure by the Parliament. As de lege lata, the Parliament can only withdraw its confidence from the entire Commission, but not from individual Commissioners. Here, too, the IGC remained conservative and did not give in to the Parliament's vehement and years-long demands to take action against individual Commissioners, either at the time of their appointment or during their term of office.

The High Representative of the Union for Foreign Affairs and Security Policy

Article 18 TEU introduces the function of the High Representative of the Union for Foreign Affairs and Security Policy into primary law. This function is due to a foreign and security policy disaster of the European Union. On the eve of the European Council of 20 and 21 March 2003, the USA, together with the Members of the Coalition of the Willing, attacked the Iraqi regime under Saddam Hussein. Accordingly, the European Council had to reschedule its agenda and uninvite the Chairman of the Convention, Giscard d'Estaing, for the first day of the meeting and offer him to present the first draft text of the Convention on the afternoon of the second day. Giscard d'Estaing rejected this as humiliating and boycotted the European Council. At best, this would have gone down in the annals as a personal state of mind and the merciful cloak of oblivion would have been placed over it. However, the disastrous performance of the Union and its Member States obstructed this cheap escape from embarrassment. As Europe was more divided than ever, the USA was able to divide the Europeans into an Old Europe (i.e. war opponents) and a New Europe (i.e. Coalition of the Willing). The Greek EU Presidency was faced with a shambles but was able to save the situation with a unique volte-face by converting the signing of the Accession Treaties with the former Warsaw Pact states planned for 16 April 2003 in Athens into a Special Meeting of the European Council and even managed to persuade the UN Secretary General Kofi Annan to attend. At a special morning meeting of the Heads of State and Government, the Convention Chairman was heard and as reaction to the foreign policy disaster, the European Council agreed on anchoring the office of EU Foreign Minister in the TCEU. The TCEU failed but the office of this EU foreign minister remained under a different name. Whether such an office would be created the same way today is debatable; that function is definitely a child of the circumstances at the time of its creation. However, the coherence of foreign and security policy is not ensured by an office alone, but to a large extent by the person holding that office. If one takes into account the simultaneous loss of image of the foreign ministers of the Member States and the parallelisms created by the European External Action Service, any positive effect can at best be ascertained in the long term.

The Court of Justice

Article 19 TEU deals with the European Court of Justice, which is now called the Court of Justice of the European Union, whereby this is used as an umbrella term for the Court of Justice, the General Court and Specialised Courts. The renaming is arbitrary, the ToL hardly intervenes in terms of content.

Article 220 TEC (ex-Article 164), now Article 19(1) TEU, was taken over verbatim from the TECSC when the European Economic Community was established and was only amended for the first time by the ToN. Since the ToN, Article 220 has been divided into two subparagraphs. Article 220 TEC underwent two major changes as a result of the ToN: On the one hand, the Court of First Instance was given a completely new position by being named on an equal footing with the Court of Justice as the Guardian of the Law, both instances within the scope of their respective jurisdiction; on the other hand, judicial panels were introduced - in accordance with the new Article 225a TEC - which are attached to the Court of First Instance.

Article 221(1) TEC (ex-Article 165), now Article 19(2) TEU, which regulates the composition of the Court of Justice, was also adapted by the ToN. The previous changes were only limited to adjusting the number of judges due to the respective enlargements. For the first time, it is stipulated that each Member State can send one judge to the Court. The IGC 2000 had decided to codify the common practice according to which appointments had been made since the establishment of the Court in primary law. This had been triggered by the next wave of enlargement, as some Member States had feared that they would no longer be able to send a judge or that the number of judges would be reduced below that of the Member States. This redefinition of the number of judges of the Court of Justice thus allows for its dynamic adjustment in the course of enlargements without having to amend Article 221 TEC, now Article 19(2) TEU.

II.29.1. Parliament

Reference: Part 6 Title I Chapter 1 Section 1 Article 223 to 234 TFEU

Originally, a so-called Common Assembly had been set up by the Founding States in the TECSC, consisting of seventy-eight deputies sent by the - at that time - six national parliaments. With the Treaties of Rome, this nucleus developed into an Assembly consisting of 142 deputies. Although this Assembly had already been calling itself the European Parliament since 1962, it was not until the SEA that this designation became official and legally binding, as it were.[389] The Common Assembly had already been established as an institution in the TECSC and, with the entry into force of the TEEC and the TEAEC, had become responsible for all three Communities through Articles 1 and 2 of the Agreement on Common Institutions.

The competence originally granted to Parliament was limited exclusively to the right to be consulted by the Council on Commission proposals. This competence was extended for the first time in 1970 by the Treaty amending Certain Budgetary Provisions and subsequently in 1975 by the Treaty amending certain Financial Provisions. These two treaties granted the Parliament far-reaching budgetary powers.[390] In addition to the extension of its powers by the subsequent treaties amending the Founding Treaties,[391] however, the position of Parliament was certainly strengthened by the Direct Election Act, since it was only through these treaties that it developed in the direction of a genuine parliament. The TEEC regulated the parliament in

389 i.c. by Article 3(1) in conjunction with Article 6 (2) SEA.
390 These changes were essentially reflected in Article 272 TEC.
391 i.e. SEA, ToM, ToA, ToN.

eight articles;[392] in the meantime, this set of rules grew to thirteen articles and has been reduced again to twelve articles since the ToL.

In the course of the IGC 2007, the former Article 189 TEC was repealed and essentially replaced by Article 14 (1) and (2) TEU; the provisions on the exact composition of the Parliament were thus transferred to the TEU.

Also as part of the IGC 2007, the former Article 190(1) to (3) TEC was repealed and essentially replaced by Article 14(1) to (3) TEU. The former provisions of Article 190 paragraphs 4 and 5 TEC were embedded in Article 223 TFEU. The IGC 2007 decided - in line with the IGC 2004 - to move the general provisions concerning the Parliament to the TEU and to embed the implementing provisions in the TFEU. Since the ToL, the provisions concerning the Parliament therefore begin with the arrangements for its election. The IGC 2007 stipulates as the only real innovation that the Council shall unanimously adopt the necessary provisions for the election of the Parliament, which shall enter into force after approval by the Member States. This wording should actually allow for a uniform electoral law throughout Europe, which is determined in a Union phase and a Member State phase. However, this fictional approach has been reduced to absurdity by the United Kingdom's Declaration No. 64 on the ToL, according to which the foundations of EP electoral law are not to be changed. The United Kingdom had made no secret of her position and had already articulated it in the Convention and at the IGC 2004. Nevertheless, the IGC 2007 seems to have wanted to maintain the fiction that such a franchise is possible.

The first significant change to the provisions concerning parliament was made by the ToM. The ToM extended the provisions by Articles 191 to 195 TEC (ex-Articles 138a to 138e). This block is in any case an expression of the upgraded position of Parliament in the institutional triangle. Subsequently, the ToL had a lasting effect on the structure of these provisions, too.

Article 191 TEC for the first time introduced political parties at European level. However, it is not only the fact that such European political parties are included in primary law that lends this article such outstanding significance. Rather, it is the expression that the IGC drew the - compelling - consequence from the foundation of the European Union. This Union is to be seen much more as a political Union than the Community had ever been. Article 191 TEC recognises the important contribution of political parties in the integration process. The IGC 1991 thus departed from

392 Article 137 to 144 TEEC.

the previous approach that it is actually the Member States - and almost exclusively them - that carry integration by assigning competences to the Community and thus - indirectly - also defining the limits of integration. Unchanged by the ToA, Article 191 TEC was extended by the ToN by subparagraph 2, which assigns to the Council the competence to determine the regulations concerning European political parties - and in particular their financing - in a codecision procedure. At the same time as recognising the role of political parties in the European structure, criticism was voiced from various camps. Eurosceptics argued that this article could exclude critical parties, while Euroenthusiasts criticised the fact that it was not acceptable that parties critical of the EU could be financed from European funds. In response, the IGC 2000 agreed on Declaration No. 11, which states that all parties represented in Parliament must be treated equally and that, moreover, no competence would be transferred to the Community, but that national regulations concerning parties would remain unaffected. Nevertheless, the Parliament felt that its autonomy was severely restricted, since it was the Council, and not the Parliament itself, that had to lay down such regulations. The ToL removed paragraph 1 from what is now Article 224 TFEU and embedded it in Title II (Provisions on Democratic Principles) Article 10(4) TEU, without making any substantive changes. This intervention was carried out in implementing the aim to merge content.

Article 192 TEC (ex-Article 138b), which deals with the participation of Parliament in law-making, remained unaffected by the IGCs following Maastricht. Critics - also from the parliamentary side - accused the IGC 1991 of restricting the rights of the Parliament by the way the text was formulated. However, the conference decided - arguably justifiably - to include this provision, which for the first time regulated a framework for the Parliament's participation in the legislative procedure. Since the IGC 1991, the Parliament has always argued that it is denied the key right of legislative initiative, not least by Article 192 subparagraph 2 TEC. Each IGC countered this criticism with the following argument: if the Commission's monopoly on initiative is abolished in favour of the Parliament, the Council must also be granted the right of proposal. This would drastically change the delicate interplay between the institutional triangle Council-Parliament-Commission and thus also the whole institutional structure. Above all, it would contradict the dual nature of the Union, which could best be preserved by the - supranational - Commission. The ToL shared this approach and moved the first paragraph to the new Article 14(1) TEU without changing the content. The former paragraph 2 became the only paragraph of Article

225 TFEU. Here, Parliament at least achieved that the Commission has to give reasons if it does not follow a parliamentary proposal.

In any case, Article 193 TEC (ex-Article 138c), now Article 226 TFEU, is to be seen as a reference of the IGC 1991 towards the Parliament and its increased influence, since it grants it the right of enquiry in the case of alleged infringements of Community law or alleged maladministration in the application of Community law, as long as these are not sub judice. But here, too, there is constant criticism from the Parliament, which considers it unacceptable that the committee concerned (a) may not have a permanent character and (b) the rules for the exercise of the right of enquiry must be determined by agreement between Council, Parliament, and Commission. Again, however, all IGCs remained convinced that the dual nature of the Community must be preserved, and that Parliament could not be granted a special position in the institutional triangle without significantly affecting this very structure. The ToL did not change these provisions.

Article 194 TEC (ex-Article 138d), now Article 227 TFEU, on the other hand, represents an innovation by the ToM that has been received above all criticism. This provision establishes a right of petition at the European level, which gives every citizen the right to address complaints to Parliament about maladministration in the activities of the institutions or bodies of the community. However, this right of petition is limited in two respects. Firstly, complaints against the Court of Justice or the Court of First Instance are inadmissible insofar as these complaints are connected with their exercise of the power of jurisdiction; secondly, there must be a subjective justification on the part of the complainants, i.e. a popular complaint is inadmissible. The IGC 1991 introduced the second exclusion on the grounds, among others, that a popular complaint to the Court of Justice is also inadmissible. The IGC 2007 adopted these provisions unchanged.

Article 195 TEC (ex-Article 138e), now Article 228 TFEU, which introduces the function of Ombudsman, who is appointed by Parliament in an independent decision, is also non-controversial. With the inclusion of this article, the IGC 1991 followed the demand for more democracy, proximity to citizens, and transparency in the Community. The only change in the course of the IGC 2007 is the election of the Ombudsman instead of his/her former appointment. This change is due to the approach of introducing as many democratic elements as possible, but in reality there is no change. The remaining six articles dealing with Parliament (Articles 196 to 201 TEC, now Articles 229 to 234 TFEU) have remained essentially unchanged over the years. Only Article 196 TEC has been amended in subparagraph 1 by Article 27(1) Merger Treaty, but this did not lead to any change regarding competence. The ToL introduced an innovation into the former Article 201 TEC by adapting paragraph 2 of the current Article 234 TFEU to the effect that the office of the High Representative was introduced and that the High Representative is affected by the censure procedure as a member of the Commission, but at the same time not in his position as High Representative. In other words, the office-holder remains High Representative, but as a Member of the Commission he or she may have to resign.

II.29.2. European Council

Reference: Part 6 Title I Chapter 1 Section 2 Article 235 to 236 TFEU

With the conferral of institutional status to the European Council, the IGC 2007 had to also incorporate corresponding implementing provisions into primary law. These are modelled on those of the Council and contain a single deviation in that the President of the European Council does not have the right to vote. Prima facie, this may seem strange, but it is consistent insofar as only representatives of the Member States are entitled to vote. Already in the pre-Lisbon era, the President of the Commission had only the right to address the European Council. The ToL did not change this restriction.

II.29.3. Council

Reference: Part 6 Title I Chapter 1 Section 3 Article 237 to 243 TFEU

The Council is often regarded as the Community institution which is ultimately nothing other than the representation of the Member States, although this assessment would suggest an intergovernmental nature rather than a supranational one. However, this is contradicted by the actual orientation of the Treaty text, which already in its original version speaks of the Council exercising its powers in the cases and in the manner provided for in this Treaty, in particular in order to coordinate the activities of the High Authority and the governments responsible for the general economic policy of their countries (Article 26 TECSC). This wording in itself leads to the conclusion that the Council is a body with a clear Community orientation.

The ToL intervened in this section in the same way as in the case of the Parliament and the Commission by removing the fundamental provisions from what is now the TFEU and moving them to the adapted TEU. This concerns i.c. Articles 202, 203 and 205 paragraphs 2 and 4 TEC.

Article 204 TEC (ex-Article 147), now Article 237 TFEU, which deals with the convening of the Council, has remained unchanged over the years.[393]

Article 205 TEC (ex-Article 148), now Article 238 TFEU, deals with the decision-making procedure of the Council. However, its changes before the ToL were not of a substantive nature - i.e. changes to the voting systems - but were the result of accession negotiations in which the newly acceding Member States were granted a certain voting weight within the existing cluster system. The TEEC had taken over this cluster system from the TECSC, whereby it should be noted that it was particularly favourable to the smaller Member States. Since the cluster system had also been retained in the individual waves of enlargement and the weighting had shifted more and more in favour of the medium-sized and small Member States, the question of the weighting of votes became the subject of the most heated disputes in the IGC 2000. In a package deal with the redistribution of seats in the European Parliament and the relinquishment of the second Commissioner by the five big Member States, the weighting of votes in the Council was redistributed for the first time in the ToN and the demands of the big Member States were met.[394]

The enlargement of the European Union to twenty-five Members States on 1 May 2004 had triggered a transitional mechanism for the weighting of votes in the Council in accordance with Article 26 of the 2003 Act of Accession, which applied from 1 May to 31 October 2004. This transitional solution is an arithmetical continuation of the status quo with the addition of the ten new Member States. As of 1 November 2004, the new - and definitive - weighting of votes in the Council, as laid down in the ToN and reproduced in Article 12 of the 2003 Act of Accession, was applied.

393 Although it was repealed by Article 7 of the Merger Treaty, it was reinserted uno actu by Article 3 of the same Treaty with identical wording.

394 The distribution of votes for the future Member States was also decided by protocol in the ToN, whereby Poland in particular received an excessive weight of votes, which it did not intend to give up in the course of the IGC 2004, however ultimately failed with this demand.

According to the ToN, this new system of weighting of votes would also include the clause that a Member State may request that it be verified that the qualified majority represents at least 62% of the total EU population. Should this threshold not be met, the decision in question would not be adopted. The General Affairs Council accordingly adopted a decision to amend its Rules of Procedure on 12 October 2004. The ToL abolished the cluster system and introduced the so-called double majority in the voting system of the Council. This new system, which had already been proposed by the Convention and subsequently been adopted by the IGC 2004, introduces a dynamism into the voting procedure that had previously been almost unimaginable. In the previous system of clusters, the sensitivities of the Member States could be served by allocations of voting weights which were not subject to any mathematical formula. Thus, the smaller Member States received a disproportionately high voting weight, while the large Member States, which saw their position threatened by the enlargements, could also be served. The medium-sized Member States, which were in a sandwich position, had been treated rather neglectfully, but formed the largest bloc (without ever having used this position in their favour). Poland had definitely been disproportionately well integrated in the ToN regime but did not want to give up this negotiating success and went into the 2004 and IGC 2007s with pithy slogans whose vehemence was indirectly proportional to the success of the negotiations; the only thing Poland achieved was a delayed entry into force of the double majority system.

Ex-Article 149 TEC dealt with the procedure in case of a Commission proposal and the procedure of cooperation with the Parliament. This article, which had been amended by Article 7 SEA, originally only stipulated how the Council had to proceed when considering amending a Commission proposal. The SEA introduced the cooperation procedure with the Parliament and thus strengthened its position in the institutional structure to an unimagined extent for the first time. As a consequence of the IGC 1991, this article was repealed by Title II paragraph 45 ToM and transferred to the - then new - ex-Article 189a (now Article 293 TFEU) and 189c TEC, which itself was repealed in the course of the IGC 2007.

Article 206 TEC (ex-Article 150), now Article 239 TFEU, regulates the transfer of voting rights in the Council and remained in its original version over the years.

Article 207 TEC (ex-Article 151), now Article 240 TFEU, deals with the Permanent Representatives and the Rules of Procedure of the Council. The original version of ex-Article 151 TEC provided that the Council (first subparagraph) shall adopt its Rules of Procedure and that these rules (second subparagraph) may provide for the establishment of a Committee of Member States, the composition and powers of which shall be determined by the Council. Article 7 Merger Treaty repealed ex-Article 151 and recast that provision by Articles 5 and 4. Since the Merger Treaty, subparagraph 1 states that the Council shall adopt its rules of procedure. Subparagraph 2 introduces the Permanent Representatives Committee at the level of primary law by stating succinctly that this committee shall have the task of preparing the work of the Council and carrying out the tasks entrusted to it by the Council. The ToM radically changed this article. It reproduced subparagraph 2, which became paragraph 1, but added a new paragraph 2, which raised the existence of the secretariat-general of the Council to the level of primary law. The original subparagraph 1 was added to this article as paragraph 3. The IGC 1996 went one step further by granting the Permanent Representatives Committee the right to take procedural decisions in cases provided for by the Council. The conference thus implemented reality in a legal form, as the work of the Committee had become increasingly important for the preparation of Council meetings and the workload had made it necessary to give this Committee more competences. Paragraph 2 was expanded by the ToA in that the function of Secretary General and High Representative for the CFSP was introduced. This was the conference's response to the need to provide the CFSP with a public face. The original office of Secretary General had only covered the organisational management of the secretariat-general; this task was entrusted by the ToA to the Deputy Secretary General of the Council. The IGC 2000 did not change the substance of this setting but decided to have both functions filled by the Council with a qualified majority - in contrast to the previously applicable unanimity principle. Paragraph 3, which in the pre-Amsterdam era only dealt with the Council's Rules of Procedure in principle, was significantly extended by the ToA. Article 207(3)2 regulated for the first time the procedure by which the Council - in its Rules of Procedure - must regulate public access to its documents. The IGC 1996 faced fierce criticism in this area, both from the Parliament and from Eurosceptic circles who had criticised the lack of transparency of the Council. Nevertheless, the conference fell short of the demands when it ultimately left it up to the Council to decide which documents it intended to release.[395]

Article 208 TEC (ex-Article 152), now Article 241 TFEU, which deals with requests of the Council to the Commission, remained unaffected by the individual primary law amendments, as did Article 209 TEC (ex-Article 153), now Article 242 TFEU, on the rules governing the status of committees.

Article 210 TEC (ex-Article 154), now Article 243 TFEU, addresses salaries and allowances. This article was only amended for the first time by the ToN, in which the Council was declared primarily responsible for determining the salaries, allowances and pensions of the Members and Registrar of the Court of First Instance.

II.29.4. Commission

Reference: Part 6 Title I Chapter 1 Section 4 Article 244 to 250 TFEU

The provisions on the Commission changed over the years, but it was not until the IGC 1996 that the differing views of Member States on the size, composition, and internal organisation of this most supranational of institutions became evident. However, the conference was unable to come up with a workable solution, making the Commission one of the three notorious Amsterdam-left-overs. The IGC 2000 was only able to agree on the future of the Commission in the form of a rendez-vous clause, and even the IGC 2004 found a solution supported by all Member States only at the very last minute. Naturally, the circumstances that had led to the fall - or rather the resignation - of the Santer Commission played a significant role in the decision-making of the Heads of State and Government. The ToL again intervened in this section, whereby - as with Council and Parliament - the fundamental provisions were transferred to the TEU or assigned a new location in the TFEU.

The original introductory article, which is now to be found in the TEU, was replaced by a completely new Article 244 TFEU, dealing with the modalities of the rotation of the Commission to be reduced. In the meantime, this Article - as it were with its entry into force - has become dead letter, since the European Council has taken a decision which in turn grants each

395 During the IGC 1996 itself, it was only the Scandinavian Member States that advocated - albeit very cautiously - for more transparency in the Council.

Member State one Commissioner. Nevertheless, it is of utmost importance that Article 244 TFEU remains in primary law, as it cannot be ruled out that the European Council will at a later date come back to that question and eventually decide to reduce the size of the Commission.

Article 212 TEC (ex-Article 156), now - unchanged in content - Article 249 (2) TFEU, regulates the Commission's obligation to publish an annual general report.

Article 213 (2) and (3) TEC (ex-Article 157), now Article 245 TFEU, were only condensed in the course of the IGC 2007 without being changed in content.

Article 215 TEC (ex-Article 159), now Article 246 TFEU, deals with the provisions concerning termination of tenure and succession. The basic concept of these provisions remained unaffected by the various intergovernmental conferences.

Article 216 TEC (ex-Article 160), now Article 247 TFEU, deals with impeachment and has so far remained unchanged.

Article 217 TEC (ex-Article 161), which was very comprehensive until the ToL, was split, with paragraphs 1, 3 and 4 being incorporated into a new Article 17(6) TEU and paragraph 2 being converted into Article 248 TFEU.

Article 218(1) TEC (ex-Article 162) was embedded in the new Article 295 TFEU. Article 218(2) TEC, now Article 249 TFEU, which regulates questions concerning the Rules of Procedure of the Commission and the cooperation with the Council, remained unchanged in its original version.

Article 219 TEC (ex-Article 163), now Article 250 TFEU, which deals with the decision-making of the Commission, was first amended by the ToA by prefixing the principle of political leadership of the Commission by its president as subparagraph 1. However, this change was reversed by the ToN insofar as subparagraph 1 was transferred to Article 217 TEC, which was revised by the ToN. The ToL did not affect this article.

II.29.5. European Court of Justice

Reference: Part 6 Title I Chapter 1 Section 5 Article 251 to 281 TFEU

The Court of Justice is one of the so-called original institutions of the Community, as it was already part of the institutional setting of the Coal and Steel Community. The most significant adaptations of the Court of Justice were made by the ToN, until then only minor adjustments were undertaken, apart from the establishment of the Court of First Instance.

Until the amendment by the ToN, Article 221 TEC had specified in extenso how the Court of Justice was to sit, and which chambers it could establish - in particular with regard to the number of judges constituting these chambers. The Nice version shifts the decision on how the Court meets to the level of the Statute of the Court of Justice; it is now up to the Statute of the Court of Justice how the chambers are composed and according to which criteria the selection is made.[396] The so-called Grand Chamber was introduced as a new element. The Court of Justice sits as a Grand Chamber if a Member State or Community institution involved in the proceedings so requests. Moreover, if the Court considers that a case before it is of exceptional importance, it may decide, after hearing the Advocate General, to refer the case to the full Court. The transfer of the procedural questions from that article to the aforementioned protocol was made by the IGC 2000 for reasons of simplification and ease of reading. The ToL split this article, with paragraph 1 becoming Article 19(2) TEU and the remaining part becoming Article 251 TFEU, without having to adapt the content of the latter provisions.

Article 222 TEC (ex-Article 166), now Article 252 TFEU, deals with the Advocates General. Apart from the number of advocates general, this article has not been changed in substance.

Article 223 TEC (ex-Article 167), now Article 253 TFEU, regulates the appointment of judges and advocates general and their term of office. As with Article 222 TEC, this article - with two minor exceptions - has not been substantially amended. The IGC 2000 merely added the former Article 224 TEC as subparagraph 5 (appointment of the Registrar by the

396 Article 16 of the Statute of the Court of Justice, as laid down in the Protocol to the ToN, provides that the Court of Justice shall form Chambers of three or five Judges. The Chamber of seven Judges will therefore be abolished. The Grand Chamber will be composed of eleven judges.

Court of Justice) to this article in order to be able to redraft the latter article. The IGC 2000 did the same with the former Article 245 subparagraph 3 TEC (Rules of Procedure of the Court), which was added to Article 223 TEC as subparagraph 6.[397]

Article 224 TEC (ex-Article 168), now Article 254 TFEU, dealt with the Registrar of the Court in the pre-Nice era. This article remained unchanged during the entire pre-Nice era. Due to the general redrafting of Section 4, the IGC 2000 had to find a new place for the rules concerning the Court of First Instance. For systematic considerations, Article 224 TEC was chosen for this purpose, which directly follows the comparable regulations for the Court of Justice. Also for systematic reasons, the rules for the Court of First Instance have been aligned with those of the Court of Justice.

A new Article 255 TFEU was inserted in the course of the IGC 2007 ahead of the previous Article 225 TEC, the subject matter of which is referred to in Article 254 TFEU. This refers to a committee that precedes the appointment of judges and advocates general. The committee has no executive function but gives an opinion on the suitability of the candidates. The aim of the procedure is to objectify the selection process. Regarding the introduction of an objectification process, it should be noted that throughout the history of the Court, there has never been any doubt about the excellence of the candidates - and subsequently - appointed judges. This provision is more due to the political Zeitgeist than to the abolition or prevention of maladministration.

Article 225 TEC (ex-Article 168a), now Article 256 TFEU, essentially contained the provisions of Article 224 TEC in the version of ToN in the pre-Nice era. As amended by the ToN, Article 225 TEC deals with the jurisdiction of the Court of First Instance. In the pre-Nice era, the competences of the Court of First Instance had been established by a Council decision under Article 225(2) TEC, as amended by ToA.[398] The conference came to the political conclusion that the Court of First Instance had to be institutionally strengthened. The proposals of the appointed expert groups, however, did not aim at any stage at an equality with the Court of Justice; among other things, the definition of competences in primary law was

397 In keeping with the aim of the IGC 2000 to transfer as many provisions as possible from unanimity to the QMV, these rules of procedure are now adopted by the QMV.

398 cf. Council Decision of 24 October 1988, OJ EC L 319/1988, p. 1, as amended by the Amending Decision of 1 January 1995, OJ EC L 1/1995, p. 1.

identified as an adequate solution, without thereby diminishing the general claim of the Court of Justice. The ToL did not change this article.

Article 225a TEC, now Article 257 TFEU, was inserted into primary law by the ToN. Although this insertion contradicted the IGC's claim to remove so-called "bis articles" from primary law, neither the IGC nor the aforementioned expert groups had been able to identify an adequate article into which the provisions of the new Article 225a TEC could have been inserted. Article 225a TEC allows for the establishment of judicial panels to relieve the Court of Justice and the Court of First Instance. In Declaration No. 16 to the ToN, the conference invited the Court of Justice and the Commission to prepare as soon as possible a draft decision on the establishment of a judicial panel to hear disputes at first instance between the Community and its staff. While this provision and the declaration suggest that the conference was unable to reach agreement on which such chambers should be established, this conclusion must be considered inadmissible insofar as the conference wanted to include an evolutionary clause in the Treaty so to avoid primary law amendments whenever there was a need for such chambers. The ToL amended this article by changing the consultation procedure into an ordinary legislative procedure.

Article 226 (ex-Article 169), now Article 259 TFEU (action for failure of a Member State to fulfil its obligations), and Article 227 TEC (ex-Article 170), now Article 260 TFEU (referral to the Court of Justice by a Member State and preliminary proceedings), were not amended.

Article 228 TEC (ex-Article 171), now Article 260 TFEU, deals with the declaration of an infringement by a Member State, its obligations to act, and penalty payments. The ToM has considerably extended its field of application by empowering the Commission to draw the attention of a Member State in default of a judgement of the Court of Justice to the fact that it is in default and subsequently to bring the matter before the Court of Justice. The IGC 1991 had thus reacted to the default of individual Member States, in particular to the fact that this default had remained - more or less - without sanctions. In the course of the IGC 2007, this provision was tightened up on the basis of an explicit demand by the Commission. De lege ferenda, the Commission is given the possibility, in the case of non-implementation of an ECJ judgement by a Member State, to refer the matter to the ECJ again after only a one-off request by this Member State for an opinion and to directly indicate the amount of the lump sum or penalty payment in the case of a new conviction. De lege lata, the preliminary procedure following a condemnatory decision of the ECJ was also two-step, comprising a letter of formal notice and a reasoned opinion. The Commission will therefore no longer have to issue a reasoned opinion in such cases. The IGC 2007 was ultimately a reaction to the way some Member States reacted to ECJ rulings.

Article 229 TEC (ex-Article 172), now Article 261 TFEU, was adapted by the ToM only insofar as it responds to the new rights of Parliament as co-legislator. Article 229a TEC has been newly incorporated into primary law by the ToN. The conference had been confronted with a proposal by the Commission to create a separate court for such matters but saw it as inopportune to create a special court. In order to avoid such an institution, but at the same time to take up the Commission's proposal, the competences of the Court of Justice were extended and Article 229a TEC, now Article 262 TFEU, was included. The ToL did not affect these provisions.

Article 230 (ex-Article 173 - action for annulment), Article 231 (ex-Article 174 - annulment of contested acts), Article 232 (ex-Article 175 - action for failure to act), Article 233 (ex-Article 176 - obligations arising from judgements), Article 234 (ex-Article 177 - preliminary ruling), Article 235 (ex-Article 178 - jurisdiction in actions for damages), Article 236 (ex-Article 179 - jurisdiction in disputes between the Community and its servants), Article 237 (ex-Article 180 - jurisdiction in EIB and ESCB disputes, Article 238 (ex-Article 181 - jurisdiction pursuant to an arbitration clause), Article 239 (ex-Article 182 - jurisdiction pursuant to an arbitration agreement), Article 240 (ex-Article 183 - jurisdiction of national courts), Article 241 (ex-Article 184 - invoking the inapplicability of a regulation), Article 242 (ex-Article 185 - suspensive effect of actions and suspension of contested acts), Article 243 (ex-Article 186 - interim measures) and Article 244 TEC (ex-Article 187 - enforceability of judgements) remained unaffected by the IGC. The amendments that led to the current Articles 263 to 268, 270 to 274, and 277 to 279 TFEU were essentially limited to adjustments relating to the extension of Parliament's rights.

Since the IGC 1996 at the latest, the Committee of the Regions has attempted to obtain direct access to the Court of Justice or at least to be granted the right to bring an action on its own behalf but failed with this request both in Amsterdam and in Nice, since - apart from Austria and Belgium - it found no support among the Member States, nor among the Commission and Parliament. Article 245 TEC (ex-Article 188), now Article 281 TFEU, was only amended by the IGC 2000 insofar as sub-paragraph 2 was moved from paragraph 1 to Article 223 TEC.

The ToL only interfered with some of these Articles by (i) extending the competences of the Court of Justice (Article 230 TEC, now Article 263 TFEU), and (ii) extending the plea of inapplicability to the legality of an act of general application adopted by an institution, body, office or agency of the Union (Article 241 TEC, now Article 277 TFEU).

However, the IGC 2007 added three new Articles to the Court provisions: (i) Article 269 TFEU deals with procedures in the sanctions mechanism, (ii) Article 275 TFEU contains the delimitation of the Court's competences in the framework of the Common Foreign and Security Policy, and (iii) Article 276 TFEU stipulates that in the areas of judicial cooperation in criminal matters and police cooperation, the review of the validity or proportionality of measures taken by the police or other law enforcement services of a Member State or of the exercise of the responsibilities incumbent upon Member States with regard to the maintenance of law and order and the safeguarding of internal security shall also be excluded from the jurisdiction of the ECJ de lege ferenda (as de lege lata under Article 35(5) TEU).

II.29.6. European Central Bank

Reference: Part 6 Title I Chapter 1 Section 6 Article 282 to 284 TFEU

With the introduction of the institutional status of the European Central Bank, the IGC 2007 had to include corresponding implementing provisions in primary law. It introduced a new Article 282 TFEU at the beginning of this section, which is composed of the central elements of paragraphs 1 and 2 of Article 107 TEC, which were deleted by the ToL, and considerations of the IGC 2004 and the IGC 2007. In terms of content, the article offers no surprises, as it merely establishes the context that is necessary as a legal prerequisite for the ECB to act as an institution. Articles 112 and 113 TEC, now Articles 283 and 284 TFEU, which were removed from the area of economic and monetary policy, only underwent editorial adaptations.

II.29.7. European Court of Auditors

Reference: Part 6 Title I Chapter 1 Section 7 Article 285 to 287 TFEU

Although the Court of Auditors - ECA - is the youngest institution of the Union, its de facto existence dates back to the founding of the EEC and the EAEC. On the basis of ex-Article 206 TEEC and ex-Article 180 TEAEC, provision had been made for the establishment of control committees, whose legal status was contained in a statute adopted by the Council.[399] The TECSC also had a similar institution. Article 78 paragraph 6 TECSC provided that the auditing of the ECSC's accounts was the responsibility of an auditor, whose area of control, however, was limited to the High Authority. Article 21 Merger Treaty inserted Article 78d into the TECSC, which extended the competence of the EEC/EAEC Control Committee to the ECSC's administrative budget.[400] It was not until the Treaty amending certain Financial Provisions of 22 July 1975, OJ L 359/1 of 31 December 1977, that the control units were transformed into the European Court of Auditors and the latter was given the status of a Community institution. The Member States justified this step with the need to take account of the increasing financial autonomy of the Community, but the hidden agenda was already at that time the need for increased controls in general.[401]

The Court of Auditors was only given institutional status by the ToM, when ex-Article 4 paragraph 3 TEC was repealed and the Court of Auditors was included as a community institution in ex-Article 4 paragraph 1 TEC. Articles 246 to 248 TEC (ex-Articles 188a to c) were also introduced by the ToM and deal with the task, composition, and competence of the Court of Auditors. The ToL only renumbered the provisions but did not change their content.

Article 246 TEC (ex-Article 188a), now Article 285 TFEU, states succinctly that the Court of Auditors performs the audit. The French version of the TEC, on the other hand, states that the Court of Auditors ensures the

---

399 cf. OJ 1959, p. 861.

400 The responsibility for controlling the ECSC's other revenue and expenditure remained with the ECSC auditor under Article 78d TECSC, inserted by Article 21 Merger Treaty, too.

401 At the same time as the Treaty on Financial Regulation, ex-Article 4 of the TEEC was extended by a paragraph 3, which incorporated the Court of Auditors into the institutional structure.

audit,[402] while the English version gives the Court of Auditors the task of carrying out the audit.

Article 247 TEC (ex-Article 188b), now Article 286 TFEU, which deals with the composition and appointment of members and their legal status, was adapted by the ToN to the extent that - similar to the Court of Justice - it was stipulated for the first time that the Court of Auditors consists of one national from each Member State, thus introducing an implicit system at primary law level and making an amendment of paragraph 1 unnecessary in the event of future enlargements. The amendment in paragraph 3 (electoral procedure) only concerns the transfer from unanimity to QMV, whereby the IGC 2000 justified this by pursuing its goal of transferring as many decisions as possible to QMV also with regard to the institutions.

Article 248 TEC (ex-Article 188c), now Article 287 TFEU, regulates the scope of the audit to be carried out. The IGC 1996 already felt compelled to clarify this article and to include explicitely in paragraph 2 the obligation that the ECA should comment in particular on all cases of irregularities in its audit report. With this adaptation, the IGC 1996 aimed to respond to criticism that the audit reports were not sufficiently transparent; moreover, the IGC 1996 wanted to counter allegations that the published audit reports were embellished. The IGC 2000 did not change this provision but added in paragraph 1 that the ECA should not only submit a general statement on the use of funds, but should examine all expenditure and revenue and, if necessary, make specific assessments. The IGC 2000 again faced criticism that the ECA's audit reports did not provide an overall picture of management and that the reports were therefore not sufficiently meaningful. Although some Member States were of the opinion that the ECA already had such competences on the basis of the TEC as amended by the ToA, they ultimately bowed to the argument that these competences had to be secured in primary law in order to provide a more secure basis for the requirement of comprehensive audit transparency. The changes in paragraph 3 were made at the insistence of the ECA that it should have the possibility of tracking the flow of Community funds to the Member States as well. Accordingly, the conference extended the Court's competence to natural and legal persons. Paragraph 4 was extended by the IGC 2000 in that the ECA was given the possibility of reorganising its internal structure by setting up chambers to deal with specific issues; at the same time, it was

402 *La Cour des comptes **assure** le contrôle des comptes.*

given the competence to adopt rules of procedure - subject to approval by the Council with QMV.

II.29.8. Legal acts of the Union, adoption procedures and other provisions

Reference: Part 6 Title I Chapter 2 Article 288 to 299 and Part 1 Title II Article 15 TFEU

Chapter 2 of Part 5 Title I TEC, now Part 6 Title I Chapter 2 TFEU, can be seen as the perfect mirror image of the shift in the institutional balance over the years, in particular the increase in the competences of the European Parliament and the growing complexity of the decision-making process in the Union. The TEEC comprised four, relatively short articles (ex-Articles 189 to 192 TEEC) in which the Founding States laid down the decision-making procedure of the Community. In the pre-Maastricht era, it was only the Council and the Commission that were called upon by the Treaty to legislate. The decision-making procedure was regulated even more compactly in the TECSC: Article 28 regulated the procedure for the Council's assent to proposals from the High Authority. A fundamental reorganisation of the legislative procedure was first introduced by the ToM. The ToL intervened even more dramatically in this structure by introducing an almost completely redesigned procedural order. Chapter 2 is divided into two sections, the first dealing exclusively with legislative acts per se, the second being dedicated to the procedural part.

Article 249 TEC (ex-Article 189), now Article 288 TFEU, lists the range of legal acts and was retained in its original version in the ToN.[403] The ToL intervenes here insofar as the list of possible legal acts is binding for all institutions and at the same time the instrument of decision is replaced by the instrument of resolution. The IGC 2007 clearly deviated here from the thrust of the IGC 2004, which wanted to assign state-like attributes to the Union and accordingly envisaged changing the previous legal act designations, as shown in the following table:

403 The IGC 1991 included Declaration No. 16 on the hierarchy of Community acts in the ToM, according to which the Intergovernmental Conference to be convened in 1996 would examine the extent to which it is possible to review the classification of Community acts with the aim of establishing an appropriate hierarchy of the various types of standards. The IGC 1996 dealt with this question, as did the IGC 2000, but only the IGC 2004 was able to agree to include such a hierarchy.

Article 249 TEC	***Article I-33 TCEU***	**Article 288 TFEU**
Regulation	*European Law*	Regulation
Directive	*European Framework Law*	Directive
xxxxxxxxxxxxx	*European Regulation*	xxxxxxxxxxxxx
Decision	*European Decision*	Resolution
Recommendation	*Recommendation*	Recommendation
Opinion	*Opinion*	Opinion

The IGC 2007 thus obeyed to realpolitik and the need to distance itself from the sometimes lofty wording of the failed TCEU. The wording of Article 288 TFEU prima facie indicates little change, but on closer look it becomes obvious that the IGC 2007 thereby also repealed the legal forms of the Second and Third Pillars and integrated them into the generally applicable system.[404] The IGC 2007 achieved maximum effect with this minimal adaptation of the former Treaty text and was able to reduce the possible number of legal acts from thirteen to five.

After this introductory article, the ToL adds four new articles to primary law dealing with the possible legislative procedures and their implementation. Although the IGC 2007 reverted to the basic considerations of the IGC 2004, it adapted these in the sense of a coherent new system of the TFEU.

Article 289 TFEU is an original creation of the IGC 2007, which puts a radical end to the tangle of possible legislative procedures de lege lata. De lege ferenda, there shall be only two legislative procedures: the ordinary legislative procedure and the special legislative procedure. The IGC 2007 found an extremely compact formula that covers all possible variants without leaving any gaps for interpretation. The exceptions mentioned in paragraph 4 concern (i) Criminal and Police Cooperation in the Area of Freedom, Security and Justice, where, in addition to the Commission, a quarter of the Member States may take the initiative, and (ii) cases where an institution has a right of initiative for a legislative act concerning its internal organisation.

Article 290 TFEU, which was also newly introduced into primary law, reforms the comitology procedure, which was previously regulated in the

404 The following legal instruments were enshrined in the Second Pillar: General Guideline, Common Strategy, Joint Action, Common Position. In the Third Pillar, the following legal instruments were foreseen: Common Position, Framework Decision, Decision, Agreement.

third indent of Article 202 TEC. The initiative for the new procedure for so-called delegated acts already originated from the Convention and was taken up by the IGC 2004 as well as by the IGC 2007. The aim of this reform step was to clearly regulate in primary law the implementing provisions for the Union's tertiary law that had been laid down in the Council's Comitology Decision up to then, and at the same time to establish the European Parliament as a legislator of equal rank to the Council. This also establishes a clear tiered structure by explicitly expressing the bottom-up correspondence between tertiary law, secondary law and primary law in this provision.

The new Article 291 TFEU regulates the so-called implementing acts, which had also been dealt with in Article 202 indent 3 TEC. Here too, reference is made to the Convention and the IGC 2004, but in a more compact manner.

The last newly added Article 292 TFEU deals with the issue of non-legislative acts. The IGC 2004 discussed in detail the question of whether Article I-35 TCEU should determine which body is called upon to adopt such legal acts. The Legal Service of the Council - together with the Commission and supported by a majority of Member States - was able to assert its legal opinion at the time that there should be no general authorisation of the Council to adopt recommendations. The IGC 2007 endorsed this legal opinion. According to this, the Council, the Commission and the European Central Bank can adopt recommendations, whereby the Council and the Commission can do so on their own initiative, the ECB only in the cases provided for by the TCEU. The remaining provisions of Article I-35 TCEU (i.c. paragraphs 1 and 2), which concerned the European Council and the non-adopted legal form of the European Regulation, were consequently rejected by the IGC 2007.

Article 250 TEC (ex-Article 189a), now Article 293 TFEU, was inserted by the ToM and deals with the procedure for amendments to a Commission proposal by the Council, whereby Article 250 TEC incorporates the - slightly adapted - paragraphs 1 and 3 of ex-Article 149 TEEC, as amended by Article 7 SEA. The ToL also changes little in terms of content, but inherently introduces new exceptions (i.c. conciliation procedure, multiannual financial framework, and budget).

Article 251 TEC (ex-Article 189b), now Article 294 TFEU, continues to deal with the procedure for the adoption of legal acts. The first revolutionary reorganisation of the decision-making procedure, which introduced the co-decision procedure and the Conciliation Committee, was introduced by the ToM. The IGC 1991 had decided to give in to pressure from Parliament and to raise it to the same level as the Council, i.e. to accept it as co-legislator. In doing so, the conference had not only met the demands of the Parliament, but also the pressure from outside. Criticism had been voiced in many circles that the Community - and the Union that had just come into being - was suffering from a massive democratic deficit and, as a result, had less and less acceptance among European citizens. Furthermore, it was incomprehensible why the Member States kept a parliament that could express its opinion, but nothing more. However, the codecision procedure established by the IGC 1991 was extremely complicated and - in the eyes of the Parliament - conceived rather in the sense of maintaining the Council's power. The greater - and real - weakness of the co-decision procedure as amended by the ToM, however, lay in the procedure itself, which was lengthy and complicated. It was precisely this criticism, which had been raised above all by the parties involved - Council, Parliament and Commission - on the basis of practical experience, that the IGC reacted to in 1996 by simplifying and shortening the procedure. The Parliament had recognised on the basis of practice that the co-decision procedure did not give either side - neither the Council nor the Commission - a better or even a decisive position and therefore only complained about the complexity of the procedure. The IGC 2000 had come under great pressure from the Parliament, which had demanded that the co-decision procedure be made the general procedure for decision-making and, moreover, that it always be used when the Council votes with QMV, i.e. that an automatism be introduced between QMV and co-decision procedure. The IGC 2000 did not follow any of these demands, much to the annoyance of the Parliament, which again saw itself as the loser of yet another intergovernmental conference. The IGC 2000 did, however, respond to the Parliament's requests insofar as it transferred a large number of unanimity decisions to QMV and opened up co-decision to the Parliament in several cases. The parliament had obviously under-estimated the resistance of the Heads of State and Government, who had already rejected automaticity by a clear majority in the run-up to the conference. The ToL revolutionises this procedure again after about sixteen years and regulates (in consistent implementation of the considerations of the Convention and the IGC 2004) the implementation of the ordinary legislative procedure. Although codecision is replaced by the ordinary legislative procedure, the ToL takes over the existing procedure in substance without any material changes. The new elements of this ordinary legislative procedure - compared to the codecision procedure - are:

- Article 294 TFEU explicitly refers to readings;
- The European Parliament - due to the new wording "... establishes its position ..." - also formally becomes a co-legislator in the first reading, as the Parliament's position is one of two constitutive elements required for a legal act to come into force (the second being the Council's approval);
- The new wording emphasises that the European Parliament must always be the first of the two legislative bodies to be consulted;
- Paragraph 15 regulates those cases in which the Commission does not have a monopoly on initiative and, accordingly, certain elements of the ordinary legislative procedure do not apply.

Article 252 TEC (ex-Article 189c), which had introduced the cooperation procedure through the ToM, which considerably weakened Parliament's possibility of co-decision, was repealed by the ToL. The cooperation procedure was designed - from the Parliament's point of view - as a possibility to amend legal texts, but not as a possibility to take a decision. The IGC 1996 reduced the cases of application but did not change the procedure as such. The IGC 2000 proceeded similarly with Article 252 TEC. Due to the changes made by the ToN to the individual policies, the cooperation procedure is now only applicable to the chapter on Economic and Monetary Union, but the IGC 2000 was not prepared to abolish it completely; this was left to the IGC 2007.

The repealed Article 252 TEC is replaced by Article 295 TFEU, which, however, describes a completely different subject matter. The TFEU takes up the text of Article 218 paragraph 1 TEC but places it in a new legal context. This new provision creates a legal basis for the so-called inter-institutional agreement, which had binding effect according to the case law of the ECJ, but which was not anchored in primary law prior to the ToL. The ToL takes over the already de lege lata appointed circle of those institutions that can conclude such an agreement. In this way, the IGC 2007 ensured that the two consultative bodies, the EESC and the CoR, would not be able to conclude inter-institutional agreements with the Parliament, the Council and the Commission. The IGC 2007 had taken this decision deliberately in order to avoid any tendency towards institutional status vis-à-vis the two consultative bodies.

Article 253 TEC (ex-Article 190), now Article 296 TFEU, which originally only contained the obligation for the Community legislator to give reasons, was adapted by the ToM insofar as it reacted to the new position of the Parliament as co-legislator; the change was therefore of a purely technical or editorial nature. Article 253 TEC remained unaffected by the ToA and the ToN. The ToL supplements the previous provision with a general clause for those cases in which the Treaties do not provide for a specific legal instrument, as well as with a legal interpretation of this general clause.

Article 254 TEC (ex-Article 191), now Article 297 TFEU, which regulates the publication, promulgation and entry into force of legal acts, was only editorially adapted to the new position of Parliament by the ToM. The ToN amended this article only insofar as the term Official Journal of the European *Communities* was replaced by the term Official Journal of the European *Union*. The ToL only undertook editorial adjustments.

Article 255 TEC (ex-Article 191a) was removed from its previous context in the course of the IGC 2007 and was embedded in primary law as Article 15 TFEU.

The newly added Article 298 TFEU introduces a legal definition of the Union administration into primary law. This provision provides an explicit legal basis for the self-organisation right of the Union institutions and thus closes a gap in primary law. The only comparable provision in the TEC was found in Article 199(1) TEC, according to which Parliament had the power to autonomously adopt its own rules of procedure. In any case, the right of self-organisation includes the right for the institutions to independently regulate the manner of fulfilment of the tasks assigned to them within the framework of the competences and powers assigned to them. The IGC 2007 thus closed a gap that could previously only be filled by way of interpretation.

Article 256 TEC (ex-Article 192), now Article 299 TFEU, remained in its original version, but the ToL only extended the group of institutions by including the European Central Bank.

II.29.9. The Union's Advisory Bodies

Reference: Part 6 Title I Chapter 3 Article 300 TFEU

The ToL reorganises the Union's advisory bodies by grouping them in a single chapter and replacing the previous chapters, which regulated the EESC and the CoR, with sections. To this end, a new Article 300 TFEU is introduced, which contains the general rules for the advisory bodies.

Accordingly, Article 257 TEC (composition of the EESC), Article 258(3) TEC (freedom of instructions of EESC Members), Article 261 TEC (EESC sections), Article 263 TEC paragraphs 1 (composition of the CoR) and 5 (freedom to give instructions to CoR members) are replaced by the provisions of Article 300 TFEU paragraphs 2 (composition of the EESC), 3 (composition of the CoR), and 4 (freedom to give instructions to EESC and CoR members), which remain unchanged in substance.

Article 257 TEC, now Article 300(2) TFEU, describes the tasks and the - general - composition of the EESC. This provision remained unchanged until the ToN. The IGC 2000 replaced the term "representatives of the various groups of economic and social life" with the term "representatives of the various economic and social sectors of organised civil society". At first glance, this adaptation hardly seemed to have any real effect, but the EESC had conquered a new sphere of activity with its IGC 2000 proposals, in which it had described itself as the representative of the organised civil society, because since the beginning of the 2000s the Commission has been increasingly forcing the dialogue with exactly that organised civil society.

The mandates of Article 258 paragraph 2 TEC (EESC) and Article 263 paragraph 3 TEC (CoR) were also abolished and replaced by Article 300 paragraph 4 TFEU. The IGC 2007 thus consistently followed the new regulation already adopted by Parliament to no longer anchor fixed seat allocations in primary law. However, the IGC 2007 made an eminent drafting error, as the wording of Article I-32 paragraph 5 subparagraph 2 TCEU was transferred to the TFEU. When Article 300(5) TFEU now states that "[T]he provisions of paragraphs 2 and 3 concerning the manner of their composition [i.e. EESC and CoR] shall be reviewed by the Council at regular intervals in order to take account of economic, social and demographic developments in the Union. and that [T]he Council, acting on a proposal from the Commission, [adopts] decisions to this end", it could prima facie appear that the Council could amend primary law through such decisions. This was neither meant nor intended. The only interpretation of this text that is in conformity with the Treaty is to focus on the composition of the two institutions, but not on the nature of their composition. However, this seemingly harmless provision led to massive disputes both in the two committees and at Member State level when it was first applied. In its resolution R/CdR137/2014 of 6 October 2010, after long and sometimes very robust debates, the CoR came out in favour of essentially maintaining its current distribution of mandates and, in the event of an enlargement, reallocating seats of the smaller Member States for the time being. The

German delegation to the CoR in particular had been up in arms against this proposal, insisting on a massive increase in its mandates. However, it failed due to the resistance of the medium-sized and small delegations, which was well organised by Austria of all delegations. On 12 June 2014, the Commission presented its proposal for the composition of the CoR in its VI mandate period from 1 February 2015, COM(2014)226, which was based on this resolution. Although the Commission could have simply ignored this resolution, which would have once again made the CoR aware of its position in the institutional structure and affected it accordingly, it used precisely this resolution for opportunistic reasons, as it was foreseeable that resistance was to be expected both in the CoR and in the Council after the Commission had to take away seats from certain delegations in order to be able to award mandates to Croatia on the one hand and at the same time not to exceed the maximum number of mandates of 350. During the entire procedure in the Council, the Commission argued along these lines and was ultimately successful. The German Länder were - to put it mildly - annoyed that the German government did not intend to make a casus belli out of it in the Council but could not find allies anywhere. The Member States affected by the mandate reduction (Luxembourg, Cyprus, and Estonia) finally gave up their resistance, as they too had to realise that they were isolated in the Council; all four Member States mentioned were "light years away" from a blocking minority. In the case of Luxembourg, there were also internal difficulties with the EESC due to the reduction in its mandate, as the Commission had also drafted the proposal for the EESC mutatis mutandis. On 16 December 2014, the Council decided to recompose the CoR so that the Committee could convene for its VI mandate period on 1 February 2015. The Commission's proposal for the EESC was eventually adopted, too.

II.29.9.1. The Economic and Social Committee

Reference: Part 6 Title I Chapter 3 Section 1 Article 301 to 304 TFEU

The Economic and Social Committee - in the meantime renamed the European ESC[405] - is a classic product of the post-war era. The Founding States had seen the need to integrate the socio-political forces in the

405 The decision came to the chagrin of the CoR, which felt it had once again been wronged by being denied a similar renaming. However, the renaming of the ESC

construction of post-war Europe, with the EESC as a body modelled on similar structures in the constitutions of the Benelux Countries, France and Italy. However, the EESC was never able to exert as much influence as the Parliament. Nevertheless, the EESC was able to maintain its position in the institutional structure and even strengthen it in the intergovernmental conferences since Amsterdam. There was no comparable institution in the TECSC, at best only in rudimentary form, as Article 46 TECSC granted the High Authority the possibility of consulting not only the governments but also the various parties involved (entrepreneurs, employees, consumers and traders) and their associations; these in turn had the right to submit suggestions or comments of any kind to the High Authority on the issues that concerned them; however, as explained, the TECSC did not provide for a status under primary law in the form of an independent body.

Article 257 TEC (ex-Article 193) was repealed by the ToL and essentially replaced by Article 300(2) TFEU.

Article 258 TEC (ex-Article 194), now Article 301 TFEU, described the number and manner of appointment of Committee members until the ToL and was first amended by the IGC 1991. The Member States gave the Committee a strengthened position in that they emphasised that the Committee Members carry out their activities in full independence for the general good of the Community. The nominal distribution of seats was abolished by the ToL, what remained in this provision was (i) the maximum number, (ii) the allocation of competence to the Council to decide on the distribution of seats, and (iii) the remuneration scheme.

Article 259 TEC (ex-Article 195), now Article 302 TFEU, deals with the list of candidates and the composition of the Committee. The ToN amended this article substantially. In the pre-Nice era, Member States had to submit to the Council a list of candidates containing twice as many candidates as the number of seats allocated to the Member State concerned. It was therefore up to the Council - on the basis of a unanimous decision - to make the final selection of candidates. The IGC 2000 thus ceded a competence of the Council to the Member States and - in a more radical step - relinquished the requirement that a Member State may only nominate its own nationals. Furthermore, the Council's decision to appoint

made sense for reasons of delimitation, as there is also an ESC at UN level. The CoR, though, has no equivalent outside Europe, which means that a renaming would be unwarranted. To make up for this defeat, the CoR decided to rename itself, at least informally, the European CoR, although this renaming is not reflected in any official Union text.

members only required a qualified majority, but no longer unanimity. This move away from the unanimity requirement was in line with the IGC 2000 objective of abolishing as many unanimity decisions as possible. The IGC 2007 extended the mandate period to five years and expanded the circle of relevant European organisations to include civil society. De lege lata, these organisations only had to be interested in the Union's activities; de lege ferenda, they must be affected by them. In reality, this new wording does not have any consequences.

Article 260 TEC (ex-Article 196), now Article 303 TFEU, strengthened the position of the Committee by giving it the possibility to meet not only at the request of the Council or the Commission, but also on its own decision. The ToA went a step further and relieved the EESC of the obligation to have its rules of procedure approved by the Council. The ToL also gave the Parliament the right to request that the Committee be convened. However, these convening possibilities are dead letter in the case of both the EESC and the CoR to date.

Article 261 TEC (ex-Article 197) dealt with the EESC's sections and subcommittees and was repealed by the ToL. The ToA had repealed subparagraph 2, which had provided for the establishment of a Committee on Agriculture and a Committee on Transport under primary law. This anomaly - which, moreover, had massively interfered with the EESC's right of self-organisation - was based on the view of the Founding States, which had attached particular importance to these two policy areas in the post-war era. The IGC 1996 abolished this anomaly and thus gave full responsibility for the establishment of committees to the EESC.

Article 262 TEC (ex-Article 198), now Article 304 TFEU, was adapted by the IGC 1996 and again gave the EESC an improved position by allowing it to be consulted by the Parliament. The ToL left this provision untouched.

II.29.9.2. The Committee of the Regions

Reference: Part 6 Title I Chapter 3 Section 2 Article 305 to 307 TFEU

The Committee of the Regions (CoR) is the most recent body of the Union and was established by the ToM. Its history can be described as chequered in that it was an unexpected success for the regions and municipalities to obtain independent representation, but subsequently all attempts by the CoR to gain institutional status failed; even in the course of the IGC 2004, this attempt was hopeless from the outset. The predecessor of the CoR was the so-called Advisory Council of Regional and Local Authorities, which was set up by the Commission in a decision of 24 June 1988 with the aim of advising the Commission on all questions of regional development.[406] The members of this committee had to hold an electoral mandate at regional or local level, a requirement that was not adopted when the CoR was established by the ToM and was only taken up again - in an adapted form - by the ToN. The Commission dissolved the Advisory Council - due to the establishment of the CoR - by decision of 21 April 1994.[407] The most important initiatives for the establishment of such a committee at the level of primary law came from the German Länder, which, in the so-called Munich Theses on Federalism, had already called on the German Federal Government in 1987 to work towards an appropriate consideration of federal interests in the progress of European integration.[408] These demands of the Minister Presidents of the Länder were supported and further substantiated by several resolutions of the German Bundesrat.[409]

The Commission took up the various theses circulating in the run-up to the IGC 1991 and proposed in its opinion of 21 October 1990[410] that regular concertation should take place with a body consisting of representatives of all the regions of Europe.[411] The European Council, at its summit in Rome on 27 and 28 October 1990, was - cautiously but nevertheless - inclined

406 cf. OJ. L 247/1988, p. 23.

407 cf. OJ. L 103/1994, p. 28.

408 Beschluß der Ministerpräsidentenkonferenz vom 21./23. Oktober 1987 ("10 Münchner Thesen zur Europapolitik"), in: Bauer Joachim (Hrsg.), Europa der Regionen - Aktuelle Dokumente zur Rolle und Zukunft der deutschen Länder im europäischen Integrationsprozeß, Schriften zum Europäischen Recht, Band 9, Berlin 1991, p 13-17.

409 Some of the demands made by the German Bundesrat at that time, such as (i) an obligation for the Council and the Commission to justify any deviations from the opinions of the regional council (to be established as demanded by the Bundesrat), (ii) the right of this regional council to take legal action on its own behalf, (iii) the establishment of a regional chamber at the level of the institutions, have reappeared like a ceterum censeo in the demands of the CoR since the IGC 1996, but were not granted a hearing by the Member States; it was not until the IGC 2004 that at least the second demand was met.

410 cf. COM(90)600 of 21 October 1990.

411 Although this reflected the attempt of the German Länder to ensure that only representatives of the regions would be sent to such an institution and that the representatives of the municipalities would keep the - existing - Commission Advisory Council as a platform, the German Bundesrat was nevertheless not satisfied with the Commission proposal, as it apparently did not go far enough.

to introduce provisions for taking account of the special interests of the regions, from the point of view of a general increase in the democratic legitimacy of the Community. In its resolution on the intergovernmental conferences as part of the European Parliament's strategy for the European Union, the European Parliament also spoke out in favour of a Committee of the Regions and Local Authorities.[412] The EESC was quick to recognise that there would be a need for regional representation, in whatever form, and reacted proactively by proposing two models for taking regional interests into account in its opinion on the IGC 1991, one model providing for integration into the EESC, the other for an independent body but integrated into the technical and organisational structure of the EESC.[413] The Luxembourg Presidency of the IGC 1991 presented a first draft text for the integration of the CoR in a separate document to the IGC on 21 May 1991,[414] followed by the Commission, which made a decisive contribution to the ultimate solution with another detailed text.[415] The Dutch Presidency, which brought the IGC 1991 to a conclusion, was ultimately guided in this matter by the overall draft of the Luxembourg Presidency.[416] The solution found in the ToM - independent body; equal participation of regions and municipalities; embedding in the technical and organisational structure of the EESC - led to tensions between the EESC and the CoR from the outset; moreover, the CoR has always seen itself as a political body and has regularly stated that it does not see any justification for equal treatment with the EESC. At the IGC 1996, it was once again the German and Austrian Länder, supported by the Belgian regions, who called for a clear strengthening of the CoR, but they failed, as they did at the IGC 2000.[417] Initiatives in this regard were equally futile at the IGC 2007.[418]

412 cf. OJ. C 324/1990.

413 cf. EESC, UP/45/91 of 29 April 1991.

414 cf. CONF-UP/49/91 of 21 May 1991.

415 cf. CONF-UP 1828/91 of 8 July 1991.

416 cf. CONF-UPUEM 2008/91 of 18 June 1991.

417 At the IGC level, where regions are not represented, the CoR's demands and concerns were only supported by the Austrian and Belgian delegations. The Committee was only able to achieve one success - albeit a limited one from the CoR's point of view - at the IGC 2004.

418 The legally most valid and striking argument against granting any institutional character to the CoR relates to the realm of competences. Regions and municipalities shall not be invested with more far reaching competences on EU level than they possess on national level. This would collide with the principle of non-interference in the constitutional setting of the Member States as laid down in the

Article 263 TEC (ex-Article 198a), now Article 305 TFEU, dealt with the composition and allocation of seats of the CoR. In its original version, Article 263 TEC only provided for the Committee to be composed of representatives of the regional and local authorities; a corresponding electoral mandate only became a prerequisite through the ToN. At the request of the CoR, in order to emphasise its independent position vis-à-vis the Parliament, the ToA included the provision that a dual mandate in the CoR and the European Parliament is not permitted. Otherwise, this article corresponded to the relevant provisions of the EESC, both in terms of its structure and the allocation of seats to the Member States. In the course of the IGC 2007, its paragraphs 1 and 5 were repealed and replaced by Article 300(3) and (4) TFEU (cf. above). As with the EESC, the IGC 2007 extended the mandate of the CoR to five years.

Article 264 TEC (ex-Article 198b), now Article 306 TFEU, regulates the position of the President and the Bureau as well as the rules of procedure of the CoR. These provisions are mirroring those of the EESC; the requirement for approval of the rules of procedure by the Council was only abolished by the ToA and thus brought in line with the corresponding EESC provision. The extension of the President's term of office is explained by the extended general mandate.

Article 265 TEC (ex-Article 198c), now Article 307 TFEU, describes the rights of the CoR. The provisions as amended by the ToM were adapted by the ToA in that the regional focus of the Committee was emphasised by the fact that the Council and the Commission can also consult the Committee in particular in cases concerning cross-border cooperation. Like the EESC, the CoR was also given the opportunity to be consulted by the Parliament through the ToA. The ToL left this provision untouched.

Treaty. Furthermore, such a deviation of the principle of non-interference would constitute a blatant breach of the system of legal hierarchy. Nevertheless and against better knowledge, the unimpaired will of the CoR to elevate its position within the decision making procedure sometimes results in bizzare heights, when it (i) urges to be included in the trilogue negotiations as equal partner or (ii) demands an absolute veto against decisions of Council or Parliament in matters of regional affairs.

II.29.10. European Investment Bank

Reference: Part 6 Title II Chapter 4 Article 310 to 325 TFEU

The European Investment Bank (EIB) only became an institution through the ToM, but it has a special position in the structure of the institutions in that it is characterised by relative independence, as is also claimed by the ECB, although not to such a distinctive extent as the latter.

Of the two articles concerning the EIB (Article 266 TEC (ex-Article 198d) and Article 267 TEC (ex-Article 198e)), only Article 266 subparagraph 3 TEC was adapted by the IGC 2000 by granting the Council the possibility to amend the statute of the EIB unanimously under certain conditions. This amendment was made with a view to adapting the EIB's decision-making mechanisms accordingly in the light of an extension in the statute.

Apart from editorial adaptations, the ToL left these provisions untouched.

II.30. Financial Provisions

Reference: Part 6 Title II Article 310 to 325 TFEU

Subject: Key features of the financial constitution of the Union

The financial provisions of the TEC had undergone almost no change until the ToM. The IGC 1991 adapted this title significantly. Essentially, the provisions of this title include definitions of the budget, the procedural rules, and the accounting methods; however, they do not contain the actual issues of Community financing. During all IGCs up to the year 2000, the Member States rejected a complete redrafting, and it was not until the IGC 2004 that a revised version was drawn up. The European Parliament in particular has criticised the lack of transparency of the budget provisions since the ToA and the IGC 1996 that preceded it - although the hidden agenda of the Parliament was actually aimed at gaining budgetary sovereignty.[419]

The ToL restructured the title on financial provisions for the first time since the ToM and organised it into the following chapters:

419 The Parliament had already come very close to this goal in the Convention, but literally failed in the last hours of the IGC 2004 due to the resistance of the Member States.

- Chapter 1: The Union's own resources
- Chapter 2: The multiannual financial framework
- Chapter 3: The Union's annual budget
- Chapter 4: Implementation of the budget and discharge
- Chapter 5: Common provisions
- Chapter 6: Combatting fraud

This re-structuring also goes hand in hand with a reorientation of the content, which affects almost all provisions of this title. The reorientation of budgetary provisions is characterised by the fact that the Parliament gained an extremely strong position, as it receives the right of final decision in the event that a compromise already reached with the Council in the Conciliation Committee is subsequently unilaterally rejected by the Council; the Parliament is thus granted - at least indirectly - the right of final decision.

General Provisions

Article 268 TEC (ex-Article 199), now Article 310 TFEU, which represents the basic provision on the budget, contained in its original version of the TEEC two relatively short subparagraphs which stipulated that all revenue and expenditure of the Community, including that of the European Social Fund, shall be assessed and entered in the budget for each financial year (subparagraph 1) and that the revenue and expenditure of the budget shall be in balance (subparagraph 2). As a result of the TEU and its corresponding effects, the IGC 1991 felt obliged to integrate the revenue and expenditure related to the implementation of the TEU policies into the budget of the Community. These financial provisions concerning the budget were inserted between the original - and subsequently unchanged - subparagraphs as new subparagraph 2.

The ToL assigned a clear and comprehensive programmatic function to the new Article 310 TFEU. Already at the beginning of the financial title, it is expressis verbis emphasised that the Council and the Parliament are placed on an equal footing in this area. The principle of the annuality of the budget, which was already contained in Article 271 TEC but has now been moved - as a general provision - to the introductory article, is reproduced. In addition to this principle, the introductory article also refers to the principles of budgetary discipline, sound financial management, and the need to combat fraud.

Article 200 TEC, regulating the financial contributions of the Member States, was repealed. This article laid down the percentages according to which the Member States - without prejudice to other Community revenue - had to contribute to the Community budget, i.e. how high their respective percentage contributions were to be to cover the expenditure of the ESF. This article had already been repealed twenty years prior to the IGC 1991, namely on 1 January 1971, and had been replaced by the Decision on the System of Own Resources applicable at the time. In this context, ex-Article 201 TEC, as amended by the TEEC, which had laid down the conditions under which the financial contributions of the Member States provided for in ex-Article 200 TEEC could be replaced by the Community's own resources, also became obsolete.

Chapter 1: The Union's own resources

Article 269 TEC (ex-Article 201), now Article 311 TFEU, was a classic product of the ToM and replaced (see above) the obsolete ex-Article 201 TEC. Article 269 TEC describes the Community's own resources and has been the legal basis for the own resources' decision since the ToL. The ToL intervened mainly textually, took over the original elements, and supplemented them as follows:

- Update of TEC provisions: The Council adopts the Own Resources Decision unanimously after consulting the European Parliament;
- Continuation of the TEC provisions: The consent requirement of the Member States in accordance with their respective constitutional requirements remains unaffected;
- New element: Only with this Own Resources Decision new categories of own resources may be introduced, and existing categories may be abolished.

Article 270 TEC (ex-Article 201a), which called for budgetary discipline, was incorporated into primary law by the ToM. With the inclusion of this provision, the IGC 1991 intended particularly to bind the Commission to the available budgetary resources and in doing so, accepted the restriction of the Commission's monopoly on initiative, at least with regard to the budgetary dimension. In the course of the IGC 2007, this Article was repealed and merged into the provision of the - modified - Article 310 paragraph 4 TFEU.

Chapter 2: The multiannual financial framework

The ToL introduces a new Article 312 TFEU into primary law, which puts the previous Interinstitutional Agreement between Parliament, Council, and Commission on a solid legal basis. The mention in Article 161(3) TEC, which was introduced into primary law in the course of IGC 2000, had at least placed the financial perspective in the proximity of primary law, but without having been defined in more detail. The first Interinstitutional Agreement on the budget was concluded in 1988 as Delors-I-package for the period 1988 to 1992, followed by the Delors-II-package for the period 1993 to 1999. The subsequent agreements were called - in keeping with the spirit of the times - Agenda 2000 and Agenda 2007. With this comprehensive coverage of the Multi-annual Financial Framework in only one article, the IGC 2007 showed that it had drawn the right conclusions from the mistakes of the Convention and the IGC 2004. Both had dealt with this complex matter in two articles, which, moreover, were embedded in two different titles of the TCEU.

Chapter 3: The Union's annual budget

The previous Articles 271 TEC (ex-Article 202 - Authorisation of Expenditure), 272 (ex-Article 203 - Financial Year, Draft Budget, Adoption), and 273 (ex-Article 204[420] - Emergency Budgetary Law) were taken over unchanged from the EEC Treaty and were not touched by any IGC until the ToL.[421]

The IGC 2007 intervened in this system with structural changes by adapting it to the new requirements and rewriting it.

Article 313 TFEU adopts without change the first paragraph of Article 272 TEC. The IGC 2007 thus refrained from considerations of shifting the financial year and retained the system of the uniform fiscal year, which is identical to the calendar year and is customary for states.

Article 314 TFEU basically reproduces paragraphs 2 to 10 of Article 272 TEC, although with substantial changes. In order to emphasise the equality of Council and Parliament, an introductory sentence is placed

420 ex-Article 204 TEEC had been adapted by Article 13 of the 1975 Treaty amending Certain Financial Provisions.

421 Article 203a - transitional provisions for pre-1975 budgets - which was included in the TEEC at short notice, was repealed by the IGC 1991 as having become obsolete due to the passage of time.

before the ten paragraphs of the article, which explicitly refers to this equality and also stipulates that a special legislative procedure applies and not the ordinary one. The redrafting of the original paragraphs goes back to Article III-404 TCEU, which the ToL editorially adapts and transfers to the TFEU, whereby the following essential innovations are incorporated into the budget regulations:

- Repealing the procedural differences between compulsory expenditure with the Council's right of final decision and non-compulsory expenditure with Parliament's right of final decision;
- Introduction of a uniform and compact sui generis codecision procedure for the adoption of the entire budget, in which Parliament and Council must come to an agreement. In contrast to the ordinary legislative procedure, Council and Parliament must come to a substantive result; the possibility of failure is ruled out by primary law;
- Reinforcement of the principle of budgetary discipline by anchoring the Multi-annual Financial Framework in Article 312 TFEU and the inclusion of the principle that the European Parliament, Council and Commission shall ensure that the Union has at its disposal the financial resources necessary to meet its legal obligations towards third parties, as laid down in Article 322 TFEU.

Article 315 TFEU takes over the introductory provision of Article 273 TEC and thus reproduces the system of annual twelfths and introduces deadlines for entry into force.

Article 316 TFEU reproduces Article 271 TEC with the innovation that the expenditure of the European Council, which was elevated to the status of an institution in the course of the IGC 2007, must now also be listed.

Chapter 4: Implementation of the budget and discharge

In its original version, Article 274 TEC (ex-Article 205), now Article 317 TFEU, did not contain any reference to the principle of sound financial management for the implementation of the budget, but instead entrusted its implementation to the responsibility of the Commission. The increasing Community budget, the criticism of the Parliament, and the criticism from Eurosceptic circles had prompted the IGC 1991 to anchor the principle of sound financial management, which had already been contained in Article 2 of the Financial Regulation, in primary law. However, this change not only sent a political signal, but also made the uneconomical use of budget funds a violation of primary law. The IGC 1996 went a step further and also placed the Member States under an obligation to cooperate with the Commission in order to ensure that the funds were used economically sound. As was the case in the amendment to Article 270 TEC (cf. above), both the IGC 1991 and the IGC 1996 restricted the Commission's freedom of action in this case as well, specifically in its responsibility for implementing the budget. The IGC 2007 amended the previous paragraph 2, which now specifies in detail what must be dealt with in the Financial Regulation.

Article 275 TEC (ex-Article 205a), now Article 318 TFEU, which imposes the accounting obligation on the Commission, was already incorporated into the TEEC by Article 14 of the Treaty amending certain Financial Provisions in order to ensure a more transparent budgetary procedure. The ToL adapts this provision by (i) inserting the Parliament as the first addressee of the accounts, thus at the same time pointing out the strengthened position of the Parliament, and (ii) adding a new paragraph 2 stipulating that the Commission must submit an annual financial evaluation report to both budgetary authorities. This provision was already proposed by the Convention and the IGC 2004 in order to improve transparency in the budgetary area.

Article 276 TEC (ex-Article 206), now Article 319 TFEU, deals with budget discharge. Originally, ex-Article 206 and 206a TEC dealt with the Court of Auditors and had been inserted - ex-Article 206 (with the exception of paragraph 2) - in accordance with Articles 15 and 16 respectively of the Treaty amending certain Financial Provisions; ex-Article 206b TEC - discharge - had been included by Article 17 of the Treaty amending certain Financial Provisions. The IGC 1991 completely restructured this section of the financial provisions, moved the provisions of ex-Article 206b TEEC into the new ex-Article 206 (= Article 276), repealed ex-Article 206b TEEC at the same time, and incorporated the provisions of ex-Articles 206 and 206a TEEC into the TEC as ex-Articles 188a to c (= Articles 246 to 248). The ToA supplemented Article 276 TEC in the sense of the amendment of Article 248 paragraph 1 subparagraph 2 TEC, i.e. made an editorial adjustment. The ToL only added a supplement in paragraph 1 regarding the documents to be examined.

Chapter 5: Common Provisions

Article 277 TEC (ex-Article 207 - unit of account, provision, deposit, investment of finances) and Article 278 TEC (ex-Article 208 - transfer and financial transactions) remained in their EEC Treaty version until the ToL.

Article 277 TEC, now Article 320 TFEU, is adapted insofar as the unit of account is mentioned expressis verbis. Article 278 TEC, now Article 321 TFEU, is adopted completely unchanged.

Article 279 TEC (ex Article 209), now Article 322 TFEU, governs the Financial Regulation and other budgetary provisions; it is the only article of this title to have been revised by the IGC in 2000. In the pre-Nice era, the Council had to decide unanimously on the Financial Regulation, the details, procedures, and matters of financial control. The IGC 2000 had received several proposals and demands to amend the Financial Regulation, in particular that the principle of unanimity should be abandoned in favour of QMV. Parliament had of course demanded that these decisions should also be subject to codecision. The conference was unable to overcome the opposition of some Member States but wanted to send a political signal and at least partially meet its own demand for the transfer of unanimity provisions to QMV. Among the dissenting, as was to be expected, were the net contributor countries, but surprisingly also some net recipient countries. In any case, the solution was half-hearted and even its limited application was postponed until 1 January 2007. The Parliament's criticism went as expected. It was only in the course of the Convention and the IGC 2004 that the Parliament was finally able - at least in part - to carry through its ideas. In the revision of this Article, the ToL followed the demands of the Parliament by replacing the previous paragraph 1 with the wording of Article III-412 paragraph 1 TCEU. Thereby, in future, the Financial Regulation and the control provisions will be enacted by means of regulations through the ordinary legislative procedure, thus involving Parliament by means of the codecision procedure and no longer by means of the consultation procedure. The position of the Court of Auditors is also strengthened, as the ToL grants it the right to be heard, replacing the previous right to give an opinion.

Article 323 TFEU is newly inserted and is based on Article III-413 TCEU. This provision contains new obligations for the budgetary authorities to ensure that the Union is provided with the financial resources it needs to meet its legal obligations towards third parties.

Article 324 TFEU is also a new provision introduced by the IGC 2007, incorporating elements of Article III-414 TCEU. This new article makes the so-called negotiation and conciliation procedure in the budgetary process, which had been conducted on an informal basis, subject to clear rules of primary law. The Interinstitutional Agreement between Parliament, Council, and Commission on budgetary discipline and improvement of the budgetary procedure of 17 May 2006 already provided for a trilogue on informal conciliation of positions in the budgetary procedure, which was included in Annex III of this Agreement. This trilogue, which takes place at Presidential level, is incorporated into primary law by Article 324 TFEU, while maintaining a high degree of flexibility. The division of tasks contained in the Interinstitutional Agreement, according to which the Commission convenes the trilogue when appropriate in order to make progress in the budgetary procedures, is upheld.

Chapter 6: Combatting fraud

Article 280 TEC (ex-Article 209a), now Article 325 TFEU, is devoted to combating fraud. This provision was not included in the original TEEC and was only inserted by Article 18 of the Treaty amending certain Financial Provisions. Incorporated unchanged by the ToM, the IGC 1996 fundamentally amended this article, extending it both in terms of paragraphs from two to five and in terms of content and scope of application. The tightening of the anti-fraud provisions by the ToA can be traced back to a general political tendency of the Member States, but the concrete catalogue of necessary provisions was provided by the United Kingdom. The UK successfully insisted that the conference no longer watered down any provisions. The ToL adapted this provision in two ways. On the one hand, the measures are to be applied not only vis-à-vis the Member States, but also the institutions, bodies, offices, and agencies of the Union; on the other hand, the exemption provision, according to which the application of the criminal law of the Member States and their administration of criminal justice remains unaffected by these measures, is deleted.

II.31. General and Final Provisions

II.31.1. Final Provisions in the TEU

Reference: Title VI Article 47 to 55 TEU

Subject: Technical provisions, in particular concerning entry into force, ratification formalities, denunciation, and revision

The most significant change to the final provisions of the TEU concerned Article 49 TEU (ex-Article O). The IGC 1996 amended subparagraph 1 insofar as it is no longer generally possible for every European state to apply for membership of the Union, but this invitation is only open to those states respecting the principles laid down in Article 6 (1) TEU. With this amendment, a political condition of equal importance was introduced alongside the territorial condition. This political condition may already have been implicit in the TEC preamble and its political objective, but the IGC 1996 intended to send a clear political signal, not least in view of anticipated applications for membership. The ToL continued this trend and substantially changed the Final Provisions.

Article 46 TEU was repealed by the IGC 2007, as it was rendered obsolete by the amendments made by the ToL.

Article 47 TEU is replaced by a new Article 47 TEU, which is now the only provision establishing the legal personality of the Union. This provision was necessary under international law, as the abolition of the pillar structure and the transformation of the Community into the Union means that the Union is the legal successor of the Community and has its own and uniform legal personality.

The notification of the transfer of legal personality from the - defunct - European Community to the European Union vis-à-vis the international community, as provided for under international law, took place immediately after the ToL entered into force. The distrust of the Member States with regard to the question of the distribution of competence between them and the Union is made clear by Declaration No. 24 on the legal personality of the European Union. This declaration states that the fact that the European Union has legal personality in no way authorises the Union to legislate or act beyond the competences conferred on it by the Member States in the Treaties. The relationship between the Masters of the Treaties and their distrust of the organisation they themselves have created sometimes assumes almost pathological proportions.

Article 48 TEU continues to deal with the Treaty amendment procedure, but fundamentally revises it:

- Henceforth, an Ordinary Amendment Procedure (paragraphs 2 to 5) and a Simplified Amendment Procedure (paragraphs 6 and 7) will be in place;
- The second sentence of paragraph 2 explicitly states that the renationalisation of competences is permissible. In principle, this is not a substantive innovation, since no Treaty provision has ever prohibited such renationalisation, yet this wording responds to the insistence of some Member States - not least the United Kingdom - which had difficulty digesting Article 1 TEU (... ever closer Union ...) anyway. This amendment is therefore exclusively political and declaratory, not legally relevant.
- With regard to the question of the quality of the outcome of the amendment procedures under international law, a distinction must be made between two scenarios:
  - According to prevailing theory, it is to be assumed that the result of the ordinary amendment procedure is to be classified as an international treaty qua result and is to be treated correspondingly. Accordingly, nothing changes in the previous legal situation.
  - The decision of the European Council to amend the Treaties in the simplified procedure has the same quality under international law. This results from the fact that (i) there must be a unanimous decision by all Member States to amend the Treaties, which is also a mandatory prerequisite for a treaty amendment in the ordinary amendment procedure, and (ii) the entry into force of this treaty amendment is made dependent on the consent of the Member States, which is also a prerequisite in the ordinary amendment procedure. The semantic difference between the ordinary and the simplified amendment procedure with regard to the consent clause of the Member States - in the first case the Treaty speaks of ratification, in the second case of consent - does not change the fact that the Member States remain Masters of the Treaties and thus in the simplified amendment procedure there is no final devolution of the decision-making competence to the European Council. The only substantial difference is that in the simplified procedure there is no formal intergovernmental conference.
- The Convention method becomes the standard procedure in the ordinary amendment procedure since the European Council can only dispense with a Convention with the consent of the European Parliament.

Article 49 TEU as amended by the ToL deals as de lege lata with the modalities for the accession of new Member States, but supplements the existing provisions by adding the following criteria.

- the applicant state must now respect the Union's values instead of its principles and commit itself to promoting them, which however is more of a political declaratory nature;
- the criteria for membership of the Union agreed by the European Council must be taken into account in the very decision. The inclusion of this criterion, vehemently demanded by Austria, has a legal significance in the vote on the admission of new Member States insofar as the so-called Copenhagen criteria are just as relevant to the decision as the absorption capacity of the Union itself, as described by the European Council in its relevant conclusions. Moreover, this introduces a dynamic element, as the last sentence of paragraph 1 is not limited to criteria already agreed in the past, but also allows for the inclusion of future criteria developed by the European Council.

The previous Article 50 TEU was repealed by the ToL and replaced by a new Article 50 TEU. This new article deals for the first time in primary law with the withdrawal of a Member State from the Union. This text goes back to the Convention, which insisted on anchoring such a withdrawal clause in the Treaty. Legally, this clause was by no means necessary, as withdrawal was always possible up to that point, whereby the general rules of international law (i.c. concerning the actus contrarius) and the rules under the Vienna Convention on the Law of Treaties of 23 May 1969 would have applied. The TEU and TEC were so-called perpetual treaties, which accordingly contained neither a termination date (in contrast to the ECSC Treaty) nor an explicit right of termination or withdrawal. A binding declaration of mutual agreement on termination or a declaration of withdrawal under international law were sufficient. Neither the Convention nor the IGCs 2004 and IGC 2007 were particularly innovative in the design of the withdrawal formalities but took over the general rules of the so-called actus contrarius. In doing so, both the Convention and the two IGCs, in an attempt to be particularly prudent, have inadvertently built a loophole into the withdrawal system. Withdrawal is permissible by way of two options. Under option 1, membership ends on the date of entry into force of the withdrawal agreement, but under option 2 it also ends if a period of two years has elapsed since the Member State concerned notified its intention to leave the Union. If the Member State wishing to leave the

Union or the European Council delays the negotiations on the agreement or the Parliament delays its vote of consent, membership ends without the conclusion of a withdrawal agreement. Precisely this loophole is not provided for in the procedure under international law, since in the latter membership only ends with the completion of the actus contrarius. The TEU attempts to close this self-inflicted gap by granting the possibility of an extension of the deadline by agreement between the European Council and the Member State concerned. This attempt is also unsuitable, as it could already fail due to the unwillingness of the Member State wishing to withdraw to cooperate with the Union. The sunset clause on the termination of Union membership, which is supposed to prevent protracted negotiations on withdrawal or limit them to two years, becomes even more abstruse with this ineffectual attempt to close the gap. Although the provisions of international law would have sufficed in the future, the political pressure to demonstrate that withdrawal is possible at any time was greater than the ability to formulate it in a coherent manner. In reality, Brexit is a demonstration of just how poorly Article 50 was designed.

Article 51 TEU remains unchanged as new Article 53 TEU in the Treaty and states that the TEU remains a perpetual treaty.

Likewise, Article 52 TEU remains unchanged as new Article 54 TEU in primary law.

These two provisions are preceded by two newly inserted articles.

The new Article 51 TEU takes over the text of Article 311 TEC and declares the protocols and annexes to the Treaties as integral parts thereof. The IGC 2007 has acted consistently here in implementing the requirement to anchor basic provisions in the TEU without introducing anything new in legal terms.

The same applies to the new Article 52 TEU, which takes over the text of Article 299 TEC and now regulates the scope of application in the TEU with regard to the states that are members of the Union, whereby reference is made to Article 355 TFEU with regard to the territorial scope of application. As a result of the withdrawal concluded in the meantime, the Treaties no longer apply to the United Kingdom by their very nature.

The former Article 53 TEU remains the concluding article in the recast TEU as new Article 55 TEU. This article regulates the language versions of the Treaty, the place of deposit, and - since the ToL - the possibility of providing for other official languages of the Member States as language versions. Fortunately, the IGC 2007 refrained from changing the traditional place of deposit from Rome to Brussels. This would have been difficult to explain to Italy from a political point of view and, moreover, that way the historical bridge to the Treaties of Rome remains intact.

II.31.2. General and Final Provisions in the TFEU

Reference:	Part 7 Article 335 to 358 TFEU
Subject:	Technical provisions

The General and Final Provisions of the TEC underwent a radical restructuring as a result of the ToL. These provisions will therefore be presented in two sections, the first dealing with the historical development up to the Treaty of Nice, the second presenting the changes introduced by the Treaty of Lisbon.

Development up to the Treaty of Nice

The first section of Part 6 TEC, dealing with the so-called General Provisions of the Treaty, lacks any coherence otherwise found in the TEC. Essentially, this section deals with two sets of issues: (i) the legal status of the Community and the TEC, (ii) certain aspects of the Community's external relations.

The first two articles of this section, Article 281 TEC (ex-Article 210 - legal personality of the Community) and Article 282 TEC (ex-Article 211 - legal capacity of the Community) have so far remained unchanged until the ToL. With regard to the question of legal personality, a proposal had already been submitted to the IGC 1996 to confer legal personality on the Union, whereby the Community would have had to transfer its legal personality to the Union uno actu. However, the IGC 1996 refrained from such a change, as did the subsequent IGC 2000, not least because of the opposition of the United Kingdom.

Article 283 TEC (ex-Article 212) dealing with taking over of officials and other servants of the ECSC, the EAEC, and the EEC as officials and other staff of the European Communities, remained unchanged by the IGC 1991 as amended by the Merger Treaty but shortened by the IGC 1996. The original sub-paragraph 1 had become obsolete insofar as the transfer to the Community had already taken place and could therefore be deleted.

Article 284 TEC (ex-Article 213), which gives the Commission the right to request information, remained unaffected by any IGC.

The IGC 1996 added two new articles to this provision. Article 285 TEC (ex-Article 213a), which entitles the Community to collect data for statistical purposes, provides Eurostat with a primary legal basis for its work. Article 286 TEC (ex-Article 213b) was the conference's response to the post-Maastricht criticism that the Commission could collect data without sufficient data protection having been introduced at primary law level.

Article 287 TEC (ex-Article 214 - general duty of confidentiality) and Article 288 TEC (ex-Article 215 - liability issues concerning acts of the Community and its staff) were retained unchanged.

Article 289 TEC (ex-Article 216) deals with the seat of the institutions. Although the notorious seat question is subject to constant criticism, no intergovernmental conference could bring itself to adopt a permanent solution on primary level. This provision clearly shows a reversion to intergovernmentalism, which is rather untypical for the TEC, since it is not the Council that determines the seat question, but the Member States. The seat of institutions - but of course also of offices, agencies or other bodies - is one of the most prestigious side effects of membership. The possibility of the establishment of quasi-judicial Boards of Appeal by the ToN prompted Spain to request a formal waiver from Luxembourg to ensure that Luxembourg would not claim the seat of the Board of Appeal of the Office for Harmonisation in the Internal Market (OHIM), dealing with trademarks and design, since the seat of the Court of Justice is in Luxembourg, in order to counter from the outset possible considerations of relocating the entire OHIM. Luxembourg made this declaration without hesitation as Declaration No. 1 to the ToN, which was taken note of by the conference. Although not an institution under primary law, the European Council also became the subject of the seat question. In the last hours of the IGC 2000 negotiations, a stalemate had arisen because the weighting of votes in the Council in an enlarged Union could not be resolved by consensus. In order to compensate Belgium for the fact that its weight in the redistribution of votes in the Council was increased only below average, the French Presidency proposed that the meetings of the European Council be held exclusively in Brussels once the number of Member States had reached eighteen. Accordingly, Declaration No. 22 of the conference on the venue of the European Council was included in the ToN.[422]

---

422 It will probably never be established with absolute certainty whether this proposal was ever formally submitted as a draft declaration, but sources that can be qualified as reliable deny it to this day and allow for the conclusion that this proposal was in-

Articles 290 TEC (ex-Article 217 - language regime), 291 TEC (ex-Article 218 - privileges and immunities), 292 TEC (ex-Article 219 - settlement of disputes), 293 TEC (ex-Article 220 - negotiations on equality of nationals), 294 (ex-Article 221 - equality of all nationals in the case of shareholdings), 295 TEC (ex-Article 222 - property regime), 296 TEC (ex-Article 223 - provisions not contrary to the Treaty), 297 TEC (ex-Article 224 - joint action to deal with market disturbances caused by domestic disturbances), and 298 TEC (ex-Article 225 - distortion of the conditions of competition and referral to the Court of Justice) were taken over unchanged with some editorial adaptations.

Ex-Article 226 TEC dealt with questions concerning protective measures during the transitional period of the establishment of the Common Market and had been requested by France to be included in the Treaty. Since this transitional period had expired, this article was no longer retained by the IGC 1996, but was deleted without replacement.

Article 299 TEC (ex-Article 227) deals with the scope of the Treaty. Due to the lost war in Algeria, the reference to that country in paragraph 2 was deleted by the ToM. Likewise, the ToM deleted paragraph 5, which had been inserted by the Act of Accession of Denmark, as the period provided for therein had expired on 31 December 1975.[423] The IGC 1996 modified in particular paragraph 2 by referring explicitly to the structural social and economic problems of the French overseas departments, as well as those of the Azores, Madeira, and the Canary Islands.[424]

Article 300 TEC (ex-Article 228), which governs agreements with third states or organisations, was adapted by both the IGC 1996 and the IGC 2000 by granting the European Parliament the right to information (paragraph 2 subparagraph 3 - IGC 1996) and the right to request an opinion (paragraph 6 - IGC 2000). The second amendment was made at the insistent request of the European Parliament to extend its rights in this area, putting it on an equal footing with the Council, the Commission, and the Member States.

---

deed made by Mr Chirac, but that no member of the IGC 2000 agreed to it expressis verbis, and that the chair therefore apparently regarded silence as agreement.

423 Declaration by Denmark as to whether the Treaty applies to the territory of the Faroe Islands.

424 Overall, the amendments to Article 299 TEC by the IGC 1996 are due to the desire of some Member States to prevent ECJ rulings such as in Case C-163/90 Legros [1992] ECR I-4625 and Case C-363/93 Lancry [1994] ECR I-3957 in the future.

Article 301 TEC (ex-Article 228a) was necessarily included by the ToM due to the establishment of the CFSP.

Articles 302 (ex-Article 229 - relations with international organisations), 303 (ex-Article 230 - cooperation with the Council of Europe), 304 (ex-Article 231 - cooperation with the European Economic Cooperation Organisation), 305 (ex-Article 232 - relation to the TECSC and the TEAEC), 306 (ex-Article 233 - association of the Benelux States), 307 (ex-Article 234 - relation to other international treaties), and 308 TEC (ex-Article 235 - general authorisation) were reproduced unchanged.

Ex-Article 236 TEC, dealing with the amendment of the Treaties, was repealed by the ToM and moved to Article 48 TEU (ex-Article N), ex-Article 237, which dealt with the admission of new members, was also repealed by the ToM and moved to Article 49 TEU (ex-Article O). With this transfer, the old Member States aimed to ensure that the new Member States would have to adopt the intergovernmental pillars of the TEU in particular.

Article 309 TEC was inserted by the ToA, so replacing the repealed ex-Article 236 TEC, and states that a suspension of a Member State's voting rights under Article 7(2) TEU will also apply to the TEC.

Articles 310 (ex-Article 238 - association with third states and organisations), 311 (ex-Article 239 - protocols as an integral part of the Treaty), and 312 TEC (ex-Article 240 - period of validity) have been taken over unchanged, apart from editorial adjustments of ex-Article 238 TEC.

The ex-Articles 241 to 246 TEC dealt with the establishment of the institutions and were repealed without replacement in the course of the IGC 1996.

The New Design introduced by the Treaty of Lisbon

The ToL made lasting changes to primary law, which naturally also made it necessary to adapt the General and Final Provisions. The ToL provided for repeals and repositioning for this concluding part of the agreement, as listed below:

Repeals

- Article 281 TEC is essentially replaced by Article 47 TEU as the Community merges into the Union;
- Article 286 TEC on data protection is replaced by Article 16 TFEU;

- Article 293 TEC on subsidiary conventions is obsolete due to the Union's autonomy in the area of civil law and other legal developments and is repealed without replacement;
- Article 299 (1) TEC is essentially replaced by Article 49 TEU;
- Article 305 ex-TEC is repealed as obsolete, since it regulated the relationship of the Community to the ECSC Treaty, which has expired in the meantime, and to the Euratom Treaty;
- Article 311 ex-TEC is essentially replaced by Article 51 TEU;
- Article 314 ex-TEC is essentially replaced by Article 55 TEU.

Repositioning

- Article 294 ex-TEC becomes Article 55 TEU;
- Article 299(2), first subparagraph, and (3) to (6) ex-TEC becomes Article 355 TFEU;
- Article 300 and 302 to 304 ex-TEC become Articles 218 and 220 TFEU;
- Article 301 ex-TEC becomes Article 215 TFEU;
- Article 310 ex-TEC becomes Article 217 TFEU.

Redesign of the Individual Provisions

Article 335 TFEU is the new opening provision of the General and Final Provisions,[425] reproduces the text of Article 282 TEC, but adds a second sentence to it, which legalises an established practice whereby the Union is represented by the institution concerned in matters relating to the functioning of the individual institutions. This addition had already been provided for in Article III-426 TCEU.

Article 336 TFEU reproduces Article 283 TEC but stipulates that the staff regulations must be adopted jointly by Parliament and Council in accordance with the ordinary legislative procedure.

Articles 337 to 351 TFEU basically reproduce the previous provisions of Articles 284, 285, 287 to 292, 295 to 299, as well as 306 and 307 TEC. The amendments are of editorial nature or serve the purpose of clarification (as particularly in the case of Articles 340 and 349 TFEU).

Article 352 TFEU deals with the flexibility clause, which was already enshrined in Article 308 TEC, containing a supplementary competence

425 The previous Article 282 TEC, which stated that the Community has legal personality, has been repealed as the Community has ceased to exist and has been replaced uno actu by the Union (cf. above).

clause. This supplementary legislative power was considered unavoidable both in the Convention and in the IGC 2004 but triggered heated debates about its permissible scope. The IGC 2007 could not avoid renewed debates but found an adequate solution in particular for the question of applicability with regard to the Common Foreign and Security Policy. The amendment in paragraph 1 (assent procedure as a special legislative procedure) gives Parliament a far stronger position and can clearly be seen as a success. The newly added paragraph 4 clarifies that the flexibility clause cannot be used in the area of the Common Foreign and Security Policy. Some Member States, especially those with a more robust view of security policy, asked for this addition, which re-emphasises the hidden intergovernmental nature of foreign and security policy. Even this safeguard was not sufficient, as also those Member States with a less prominent external profile wanted to prevent this policy area from being completely communitarised. Accordingly, the two declarations No. 41 and 42 on Article 352 TFEU are of particular importance, as they reflect the fears of the Member States that this policy could, through whatever back door, establish itself as an equally regular Union policy. Declaration No. 41 states that the reference in Article 352(1) TFEU to the objectives of the Union concerns the objectives set out in Article 2(2) and (3) TEU and the objectives of Article 2(5) of that Treaty concerning external action under Part Five of the Treaty on the Functioning of the European Union. It is therefore excluded that measures based on Article 352 TFEU exclusively pursue objectives under Article 2(1) TEU. In this context, the conference also notes that, in accordance with Article 31(1) TEU, no legislative acts may be adopted in the field of the Common Foreign and Security Policy. Declaration No. 42 underlines that, according to the established case-law of the European Court of Justice, Article 352 TFEU is an integral part of an institutional system based on the principle of conferral and cannot therefore provide a basis for extending the scope of the Union's powers beyond the general framework resulting from the provisions of the Treaties as a whole, in particular those defining the tasks and activities of the Union. In any event, this article cannot serve as a legal basis for the adoption of provisions which, in terms of their substance and consequences, would amount to an amendment of the Treaties without complying with the procedure laid down in the Treaties for that purpose.

Article 353 TFEU is an original insertion by the ToL and excludes that the following matters can be adapted by a simplified Treaty amendment procedure:

- own resources decision
- multiannual financial framework
- flexibility clause
- votes in the sanctions procedure

These exceptional provisions emphasise the special status of these topics and underline their constitutive character. This article has been of eminent political importance, as national prerogatives are affected.

Article 354 TFEU regulates the voting modalities already contained in Article 309 TEC for the sanctions procedure according to Article 7 TEU.

Article 355 TFEU reproduces Article 299 (2) and (3) to (6) TEC and further regulates territorial jurisdiction in implementation of Article 52 TEU. As a result of the withdrawal concluded in the meantime, the Treaties no longer apply to the United Kingdom and thus the references to the United Kingdom in this article have also become obsolete.

The last three provisions of the TFEU, Articles 356 to 358, reproduce the provisions of Articles 312 (perpetual treaty), 313 (ratification and deposit), and 314 TEC (language regime), the latter provision being repealed and replaced by a terse reference to Article 55 TEU.

III. Annex

Non in actis, non in mundo.
Latin proverb

III.1. Overview of the Reforms of the European Treaties[426]

III.1.1. General Remarks[427]

The Founding Treaties establishing the Communities and subsequently the Union provided for the possibility of further development from the outset; they were thus never designed to be static, but rather to adapt to the circumstances of the time and the challenges in question. With regard to the Founding Treaties, however, it should be pointed out that there is a substantial difference between the Treaty establishing the European Coal and Steel Community (= TECSC) and the two other Founding Treaties on the European Economic Community (= TEEC) and the European Atomic Energy Community (= TEAEC). The TECSC provided for a simplified procedure for amending the provisions of the Treaties, in contrast to the TEEC and TEAEC, which provided for the classical procedure of unanimity combined with compulsory ratification by all Member States.

Until the 1980s, Member States rarely made use of the possibility to amend the Treaties with the exception of the Merger Treaty, OJ 152 of 13 July 1967, and the Treaty on Budgetary Provisions, OJ L 2 of 2 January 1971.

This category of the pre-Single European Act era also includes the various accession treaties and the Act concerning the Election of the Representatives of the Assembly by Direct Universal Suffrage (OJ. C 77 of 19

---

426 This chapter has been taken from: Fischer, Klemens H. Der Vertrag von Lissabon, 2nd edition, Baden-Baden - Wien - Bern 2010, p. 605 to 611 and amended by the section concerning the Treaty of Lisbon. For detailed information on all Treaty changes since the founding Treaties, cf. also http://europa.eu/scadplus/leg/de/s90001.htm.

427 The IGC 2004, which resulted in the proposal for the TCEU, is also dealt with in this annex. The failure of the ratification process did not constitute a corresponding Treaty modification, but the IGC 2007 took the draft TCEU as the basis for its work.

March 1984, p 53). The latter has been dealt with in detail in the relevant chapter on the provisions concerning the European Parliament. However, the various accession treaties do not bring about any actual changes to the Treaties but are essentially limited to extending the applicability of the Treaties to the respective new Member States. Accordingly, they have not been included in the following overview.

The lasting effect of the United Kingdom's withdrawal requires the inclusion of an overview of the provisions of the Withdrawal Agreement as well as the Windsor Framework and the decision of the ECJ of 15 June 2023 concerning the definitive dismissal of the actions brought by British citizens challenging the loss of their rights as EU citizens as a result of Brexit (Judgement of the Court in Case C-499/21 P | Silver and Others v Council C-501/21 P | Shindler and Others v Council, and C-502/21 P | Price v Council).

III.1.2. Single European Act

The first major revision of the Treaties was the Single European Act (= SEA) of 1986. The aim of the IGC on the SEA was to revise the following issues:

- Decision-making process in the Council
- Competences of the Commission
- Competences of the Parliament
- Extension of the competences of the Communities

The changes that were eventually made to the Treaty can be divided into an institutional and a political category.

Institutional changes

- Extension of the scope of qualified majority voting in the Council to facilitate the implementation of the Common Market. However, the provisions on taxation, free movement of persons,, workers' rights, and interests are excluded from this simplification.
- Introduction of the European Council, which institutionalised the conferences or summits of Heads of State and Government.
- Strengthening of the rights of the European Parliament (its assent is from then on required for Community association agreements).

- Introduction of the cooperation procedure (possibility of a double reading of legislative proposals). However, the scope of this procedure is limited to cases where the Council acts by qualified majority, with the exception of environment policy.
- Introduction of the comitology procedure.
- Creation of the basis for the establishment of the Court of First Instance.

Political changes

- Inclusion of the target date for the completion of the Common Market (31 December 1992).
- Extension of already existing competences in the field of social policy:
  - Empowering the Council, acting by qualified majority under the co-operation procedure, to adopt minimum requirements to encourage improvements in the working environment and to protect the safety and health of workers;
  - Entrusting the Commission with the task of developing the dialogue between the social partners at European level;
- Establishing a common policy on economic and social cohesion.
- Introduction of a research and technological development policy.
- Extending competence in environmental policy to enable the Community to preserve, protect, and improve the quality of the environment, to contribute to the protection of human health, and to ensure prudent and rational utilisation of natural resources, subject to the principle of subsidiarity according to which Community action in the field of the environment shall be taken only where the objectives can be better achieved by the Community than by individual Member States.
- Establishing the foundations for the development of a future European foreign policy.

III.1.3. Treaty of Maastricht – Treaty on European Union[428]

The Treaty on European Union, signed in Maastricht on 7 February 1992, entered into force on 1 November 1993 and was the result of a double intergovernmental conference, the first part of which dealt with the subject of Economic and Monetary Union, the second with Political Union.

---

428 cf. Fischer, Vertragsrecht, p 51 ff.

The ToM/TEU has the following five main objectives:

- Strengthening the democratic legitimacy of the institutions
- Improving the functioning of the institutions
- Establishing an Economic and Monetary Union
- Developing a social dimension of the Community
- Introducing of a Common Foreign and Security Policy
  The key innovations of the ToM/TEU relate to the following areas:
- Establishing the European Union
- Introducing a pillar structure, namely one supranational EC pillar and two intergovernmental pillars on (i) the Common Foreign and Security Policy and (ii) Cooperation in the Fields of Justice and Home Affairs
- Further extension of the cases of application of qualified majority voting in the Council
- Strengthening the position of the European Parliament by introducing the codecision procedure
- Introducing the Economic and Monetary Union
  - The Economic Policy comprises the following three aspects: (i) coordination of the economic policies of the Member States, (ii) introduction of multilateral surveillance of this coordination, (iii) subjection to a certain fiscal and budgetary discipline.
  - The Monetary Policy is based on the European System of Central Banks, of which the ECB and the central banks of the Member States are members. These institutions are independent of the political authorities of the Member States and of the Community.[429] The aim of this monetary policy is to introduce a single currency and to ensure the stability of this currency by maintaining price stability and a market economy.
- Introducing a protocol on social policy
- Introducing the citizenship of the Union
- Establishing the Committee of the Regions as an additional advisory body alongside the Economic and Social Committee
- Introducing the following new policy areas:
  - Trans-European Networks
  - Industrial policy

429 The United Kingdom did not commit to joining the third stage of EMU. Denmark was granted a protocol making participation in the third stage conditional on the outcome of a referendum.

- Consumer protection
- Education and Training
- Youth
- Culture

III.1.4. Treaty of Amsterdam[430]

The Treaty of Amsterdam is the result of the IGC 1997, which was concluded - politically - on 17 June 1997. The Treaty was signed on 2 October 1997 and entered into force on 1 May 1999.

The aim of the IGC 1997 was to pave the way politically and institutionally for the European Union to be ready to meet the future challenges posed by the rapid evolution of the international situation, the globalisation of the economy and its impact on employment, the fight against terrorism, international crime and illicit drug trafficking, environmental imbalances, and threats to human health. In addition, issues related to the functioning of the institutions were also included, in particular the composition of the Commission and the weighting of votes in the Council.

The IGC 1997 failed on the key issues of (i) the size and composition of the Commission, (ii) the weighting of votes in the Council, and (iii) the extension of the application of qualified majority voting in the Council, the three so-called Amsterdam-left-overs.

The key innovations of the ToA concern the following areas:

- Establishing the Area of Freedom, Security and Justice, in particular through guarantees concerning the protection of fundamental rights in the European Union, especially with regard to equality between men and women, non-discrimination, and the processing of personal data
- Introducing provisions concerning visa, asylum, immigration, and other policies relating to the free movement of persons
- Introducing provisions on police and judicial cooperation in criminal matters and the integration of the Schengen acquis into the legal framework of the European Union
- Broadening the concept of citizenship of the Union with a view to completing the list of citizenship rights of Union citizens and clarifying the link between nationality of a Member State and citizenship of the Union

430 cf. Fischer: Vertragsrecht, p 57 ff.

- Including a new title on employment (definition of common policies for employment and coordination of national policies)
- Incorporating the Agreement on Social Policy into the Treaty, in particular to combat social exclusion and to ensure equal treatment of men and women
- Strengthening European environmental policy by (i) emphasising sustainable development, (ii) integrating environmental protection into all sectoral policies, (iii) simplifying Community decision-making
- Improving health and consumer protection policies
- Ensuring citizens' right of access to the institutions' documents and the use of their own language in their dealings with them
- Strengthening the EU's external policy by (i) introducing the new instrument of the common strategy, (ii) improving decision-making in the Council through more qualified majority voting, (iii) introducing the function of High Representative for the CFSP, (iv) creating a policy planning and early warning unit for joint analysis of international events and their consequences, (v) including the so-called "Petersberg tasks", (vi) simplifying procedures concerning the financing of the CFSP, and (vii) extending the scope of the common trade policy to international agreements on services and intellectual property rights
- Introducing enhanced cooperation
- Strengthening the role of the Court of Justice in areas such as fundamental rights and certain issues directly related to the internal security of the European Union
- Strengthening the role of the Court of Auditors, the Economic and Social Committee and the Committee of the Regions
- Ensuring better information and greater involvement of national parliaments in the activities of the European Union
- Consolidating the principle of subsidiarity by adding a protocol with legally binding guidelines

III.1.5. Treaty of Nice[431]

The Treaty of Nice is the result of the IGC 2000, which was politically concluded on 11 December 2000. The Treaty was signed on 26 February 2001 and entered into force on 1 February 2003.

The aim of the IGC 2000 was to overcome the above-mentioned Amsterdam-left-overs and to achieve an improvement in enhanced cooperation.

The key innovations of the ToN concern the following areas:

- Establishing a new weighting of votes in the Council by bringing about a new balance between the Member States in favour of the more populous ones and dividing the votes between first 25 and then 27 Member States, in order to be able to react already to the upcoming enlargement negotiations
- Changing the composition of the Commission and strengthening the powers of the President, as well as changing the appointment procedure
- Reallocating competences to the two court instances (Court of Justice and Court of First Instance) and the possibility of setting up special judicial chambers
- Strengthening of the European Parliament through a comprehensive extension of the scope of qualified majority voting and simultaneous application of the codecision procedure
- Modifying the number of Members of the European Parliament allocated to each Member State and each candidate country
- Modifying the composition and appointment of the members of the Court of Auditors, the European Economic and Social Committee, and the Committee of the Regions
- Improving the application of enhanced cooperation by making the conditions more flexible, abolishing the right of veto and extending the scope of application
- Adapting further policy areas, in particular fundamental rights, security and defence, as well as judicial cooperation in criminal matters
- Introducing regulations for political parties at European level
- Introducing a more precise division of competences between the European Union and the Member States
- Clarifying the status of the Charter of Fundamental Rights of the European Union

431 cf. Fischer: Nizza, and: Vertragsrecht, p 65 ff.

- Simplifying the Treaties
- Clarifying the role of national parliaments in the architecture of Europe
- Adopting the so-called Declaration on the Future of the Union, in which the IGC called for a broader and more in-depth debate on the future of the European Union to be launched. This debate should involve national parliaments and the public as well as the applicant states. Subsequently, a new IGC should convene in 2004. In the course of this process, the following four key issues should be addressed:
  - Clarifying the division of competences between the European Union and the Member States.
  - Clarifying the status of the Charter of Fundamental Rights of the European Union
  - Simplifying of the Treaties
  - Clarifying the role of national parliaments in the architecture of Europe

III.1.6. Treaty establishing a Constitution for Europe (draft)[432]

The Convention met from 28 February 2002 to July 2003. The Convention's draft for a Constitutional Treaty contained in part almost unexpected innovations, but in part it adhered closely to the established setting. The Convention showed a spirit of innovation and the courage to embrace new ideas particularly in Parts I (Fundamental Provisions) and IV (General and Final Provisions) of its draft. Part III remained conservative, and the adoption of the Charter of Fundamental Rights in Part II merely represents the autonomous implementation of the demands made since Nice.

The following aspects can be regarded as key points of the draft:
European Principles
The preamble of the draft describes the values on which the future Union, which is a union of the citizens and states of Europe, shall be established. These values lie in the cultural, religious, and humanistic traditions. The citizens of this Union will in future have a dual citizenship - both national and European.

432 Cf. Fischer: Konvent, pp 96-98.

Competences

The distribution of competences provides for exclusive Union competences and shared competences between the Union and the Member States. Those areas of competence which are not expressly mentioned in the Constitution remain - within the framework of the principle of subsidiarity - the exclusive competence of the Member States.

Institutions

- The institutions of the Union are the European Parliament, the European Council, the Council of Ministers, the European Commission, and the European Court of Justice.
- A dual presidency is provided for, consisting of the President of the European Commission, elected for five years, and the President of the European Council, elected for two and a half years with the option of a one-off extension for a further two and a half years.
- The President of the Commission will in future be elected by the Parliament on the proposal of the Council.
- The Commission will be reduced to fifteen members with voting rights as of 2009. The non-participating Member States will be able to send members to the Commission without voting rights.
- One of the two Vice-Presidents of the Commission will be the European Minister for Foreign Affairs, who will also chair the External Relations Council.

Parliament and Citizens

- The European Parliament's rights of participation will be drastically extended, and it will accordingly act as co-legislator for most EU acts. A decisive contribution to the strengthening of the Parliament will be made by the decision-making process in the budgetary procedure, in whose new form the Parliament would have the final decision-making power.
- In future, citizens will have the possibility of a plebiscite in the form of a citizens' referendum. If the initiative in question has at least one million signatures, the Commission will have to deal with the issue in question.

Qualified majority

The application of QMV is extended, but does not relate to the area foreign and security policy.

Entitlement to sue

The right to take legal action is extended to national parliaments.

Withdrawal clause
In future, withdrawal from the Union will no longer be possible according to the rules of general international law, but according to detailed clauses in the Constitutional Treaty.

III.1.7. Treaty establishing a Constitution for Europe[433]

The IGC 2004 lasted from 4 October 2003 to 18 June 2004 and adopted the Constitutional Treaty, that never entered into force as it failed in the referenda in the Netherlands and France. Nevertheless, it must retain its place in the evolution of treaty law, as it pointed the way to the following intergovernmental conference and thus to the Treaty of Lisbon. The result of the IGC 2004 was a complex set of provisions that would have placed the European Union on a fundamentally new footing in some respects. In the following, the key features of the Constitutional Treaty are presented in so far as they differed from the outcome of the Convention.

The cornerstones of the Convention's draft, such as the dissolution of the pillar structure and the merging of the TEU and TEC into a single Treaty, were essentially retained and so was the structure.

The key features of the European Constitutional Treaty are:
Single Treaty
The TCEU is a single Treaty and replaces the previous Treaties (i.e. TEU and TEC). The Euratom Treaty will continue to exist due to the lack of agreement in the IGC 2004.

Legal personality
The TCEU confers on the European Union - also as the legal successor to the European Community - an independent legal personality.

Dissolution of the pillar structure
The TEU had placed the European Union on three pillars, of which the EC pillar was supranational, while the CFSP and the CJHA pillars were intergovernmental. The TCEU dissolves these three pillars and transfers them to the single Treaty. At the same time, the intergovernmental elements are - formally – abolished, as the Treaty setting is completely supranational.

433 Cf. Fischer: Verfassung, pp 97-102.

Structure of the Treaty

Part I: Institutional Issues

Part II: The Charter of Fundamental Rights of the Union

Part III: The policies and functioning of the Union

Part IV: General and final provisions

Simplification of legislative instruments
The TCEU provides the Union with six legislative instruments, significantly reducing the number from the previous fifteen

Institutional framework

- *European Council*
  - Acquires the status of an institution
  - Presidency to be held by a President elected for two and a half years
- *EU Foreign Minister*
  - Is a member of the Commission and presides over the Foreign Affairs Council
  - As such, he or she performs the combined functions of High Representative for the CFSP and EU Commissioner for Foreign Affairs
- *Council of Ministers*
  - Rotates the Presidency of the Council formations (except Foreign Affairs Council) under the team presidency system
  - The rotation is based on a system to be decided by the European Council
- *European Parliament*
  - Maximum number of seats: 750
  - Minimum number of seats per Member State: 6
  - Maximum number of seats per Member State: 96
  - The European Council shall decide unanimously on the composition of the Parliament before the EP elections in 2009 based on a proposal from the European Parliament
  - Approximately 95% of EU legislative acts will be subject to the co-decision procedure, which will become the standard procedure

- *Commission*
  - One Commissioner per Member State until 2014
  - From 2014, the number of Commissioners will be reduced to two-thirds of the number of Member States with equal rotation (unless the European Council decides until 2014 to continue the system de lege lata)

Division of competences
The competences of the Union and those of the Member States are divided into

- *Exclusive Union competences*
  - Customs union; definition of the competition rules necessary for the functioning of the Internal Market; monetary policy for those Member States which have adopted the euro as their currency; conservation of marine biological resources under the common fisheries policy; common commercial policy
  - The Union is also responsible for defining and implementing the CFSP, including the progressive framing of a defence policy
- *Shared competences*
  - Internal Market; certain aspects of social policy; economic, social and territorial cohesion; agriculture and fisheries, with the exception of the conservation of marine biological resources; environment; consumer protection; transport; trans-European networks; energy supply; area of freedom, security and justice; certain aspects of common safety concerns in the field of public health; certain competences in the fields of research, technological development and space: certain competences in the fields of development cooperation and humanitarian aid
  - In the field of economic and monetary policy, the Union has the competence to coordinate national policies
- *Supporting competences*
  Protection and improvement of human health; industry; culture; tourism; education, youth, sport and vocational training; disaster prevention; administrative cooperation.

Definition of qualified majority

- A qualified majority is reached when a majority of 55% - but at least fifteen - Member States representing at least 65% of the European population vote in favour of a decision.

- A blocking minority occurs when at least four Member States oppose a decision.
- Until 2014, members of the Council can block a decision if they represent at least three quarters of the blocking minority, be it on the level of Member States or population. However, this blocking minority only has a suspensive effect, as these Member States can demand from the Council that the proposal in question be discussed again. If the Council does not decide otherwise, this regulation will expire in 2014.
- If the Council acts (i) on its own initiative, or (ii) on the initiative of a Member State, or (iii) on a recommendation from the Commission, or (iv) from the European Central Bank, a qualified majority shall be defined as 72% of the Member States, representing 65% of the European population, voting in favour of the decision. The main cases in which this special qualified majority is required are in the areas of justice and home affairs, CFSP, economic and monetary policy, and the possible exclusion of a Member State.
- In those cases where not all Member States are entitled to vote (e.g. Eurozone, enhanced cooperation), the basic percentages apply, but only in relation to the Member States entitled to vote. Whether the normal qualified majority or the special qualified majority is applied depends on the respective issue.
- This system should enter into force on 1 November 2009.

Unanimity
In the following cases, the Council will also have to reach unanimity in the future, whereby this system should enter into force on 1 November 2009:

- Fiscal matters
- Social policy (partly)
- Foreign, security, and defence policy (partly)
- Own resources decisions
- Financial perspectives
- Treaty revisions

Enhanced cooperation

- So-called permanent enhanced cooperation will be allowed in the field of defence
- Normal enhanced cooperation will be permitted for the areas of foreign policy and security policy

- In all other cases, Member States wishing to establish enhanced cooperation may request the Commission to submit a proposal to the Council, which may establish such cooperation by means of a European decision after obtaining the consent of the European Parliament

Economic and Monetary Union

- The members of the Eurogroup are granted more legislative rights in this area.
- The decision-making power will lie with the Euro-ECOFIN, in which only the members of the Eurozone meet. This Council formation can decide on legal acts concerning the Eurozone on the one hand, and excessive deficits on the other.

Area of Freedom, Security and Justice

- In future, the Community method will apply to all decisions in this area.
- QMV will apply to almost all decisions, in particular asylum, immigration, and judicial cooperation in criminal matters.
- Emergency clauses are introduced for those cases in which Member States are convinced that their respective national interests are at stake. In this case, they can refer the matter to the European Council.
- The Council may establish a European Public Prosecutor, whose competence will initially be limited to matters of crime against the Union's financial interests.

Transparency

- The Commission can be prompted by one million signatures from a significant number of Member States to draw up a legislative proposal to this effect.
- When the Council acts as a legislative body, such meetings must be held in public.
- An early warning system involving national parliaments will be introduced to ensure compliance with the subsidiarity principle.

Fundamental rights
The incorporation of the EU Charter of Fundamental Rights will improve the protection of fundamental rights at Union level.

III.1.8. Treaty of Lisbon[434]

The Treaty of Lisbon, a classic covering agreement, amends the existing Treaties, but does not replace them, as would have been the case with the TCEU. The fundamental changes to the Treaties are presented below.[435]

Amendments concerning the Title of the Treaties

The ToL amends the TEU and the TEC. Accordingly, the Treaties shall be renamed as follows:

Treaty	**Title**	**Abbreviation**
Covering Treaty	Treaty of Lisbon	ToL
EU Treaty	Treaty on European Union	TEU
(ex-)EC Treaty	Treaty on the Functioning of the European Union	TFEU

Institutional Amendments

Above all, the institutional amendments introduced into primary law by the ToL take account of the fact that in a Union with almost 30 Member States, the voting processes in the Council on the one hand and between it and the other institutions on the other hand have become increasingly complex. Accordingly, the amendments in the institutional field aim to remedy this situation and to optimise the efficiency of the decision-making process.

- *Presidential System [TCEU]*
  Introduction of Troika Presidencies for 18 months.
- *European Council [TCEU]*
  The European Council is assigned the status of an institution, the - new - permanent President is elected by the European Council for a period of two and a half years.
- *European Parliament [TCEU/ToL]*
  The European Parliament is given a strengthened role by extending the scope of the codecision procedure (renamed the ordinary legislative procedure) and the assent procedure (to the detriment of the consultation procedure). The Parliament is also strengthened by increased possibilities of control vis-à-vis the Commission. The improved position in the

434 Cf. Fischer: Lissabon, 93 bis 98.

435 The respective heading indicates whether it is (i) a simple adoption of the TCEU [= TCEU], (ii) an innovation by the ToL [= ToL], (iii) a hybrid form [= TCEU/ToL], or (iv) a further development of the ToN (= [ToN]+[TCEU]).

budgetary procedure is particularly important for the Parliament. The European Parliament will comprise a maximum of 750 members plus the President. In contrast to earlier Treaty versions, the exact distribution of seats will no longer be part of the Treaty but will be determined by the European Council on a proposal of the European Parliament.

- *European Commission [ToN] + [TCEU]*
  The Commission is to be reduced in size from 2014 and thus no longer comprises one college member per Member State;[436] furthermore, the role of the EC President is strengthened.
- *High Representative of the Union for Foreign Affairs and Security Policy and the European External Action Service [RoN]+[TCEU]*
  The EU Minister for Foreign Affairs of the TCEU is given the title High Representative of the Union for Foreign Affairs and Security Policy under the ToL. On the one hand, the High Representative is a Member of the Commission and its Vice-President, on the other hand, he/she chairs the Foreign Affairs Council, which means that this Council formation is no longer subject to the rotation of the Presidency. The High Representative is assisted by a so-called European External Action Service, which, however, does not replace the external services of the Member States and their representative authorities, but acts alongside them.
- *Qualified Majority Voting [TCEU/ToL]*
  Qualified majority voting will henceforth be referred to as the ordinary legislative procedure and shall be the standard procedure. The cases of application of qualified majority voting will be extended, notably in the field of Justice and Home Affairs. However, not all Member States will participate fully, as the United Kingdom and Ireland have extensive opt-out provisions. As far as the jurisdiction of the ECJ for existing 3rd pillar acts (Justice and Home Affairs) is concerned, a five-year transitional period applies. Moreover, the UK negotiated to be able to announce six months before the end of the transitional period whether she opts out of this existing body of law, too.
- *European Court of Justice [TCEU/ToL]*
  In addition to its existing competences, the ECJ will have jurisdiction over (i) actions brought by non-privileged claimants and the Committee of the Regions and (ii) actions for failure to act against the European Council and institutions of the Union. A committee will be set up to evaluate candidates for the selection of judges and advocates-general.

436 Due to the concessions made to Ireland, this reform step was reversed.

- *European Economic and Social Committee [TCEU/ToL]*
  The EESC will be entitled to advise the Parliament as well. Its term of office will be extended from four to five years and its composition will no longer be determined by primary law but will be decided by the Council.
- *Committee of the Regions [TCEU/ToL]*
  The CoR is given the right to bring actions before the ECJ against legislative acts for infringement of the subsidiarity principle. Its term of office is extended from four to five years and its composition is no longer determined by primary law but is decided by the Council.
- *Weighting of votes in the Council [TCEU/ToL].*
  The changeover to the double majority system took place under the following timeline:
  - Until 1 November 2014, the ToN system (qualified majority voting) continues to apply.
  - Between 1 November 2014 and 31 March 2017, the double majority voting system comes into force in principle. However, if a Member State requests the application of the Nice regime for a decision to be taken by qualified majority, this request must be granted.
  - Until 31 March 2017, the so-called Ioannina Clause applied, the content of which was laid down in a Council decision and which was attached to the ToL as a document in the form of a declaration; as a special safeguard, a protocol also stipulated that the Ioannina Mechanism could only be amended by consensus, i.e. unanimously.

  The double majority came into force on 1 April 2017. In addition, a - modified - Ioannina clause will continue to apply.
- *External representation [TCEU/ToL]*
  Introduction of the position of High Representative of the Union for Foreign Affairs and Security Policy. The High Representative will be supported by a European External Action Service (EEAS) and was appointed for the first time on 1 January 2009. The High Representative will chair the Foreign Affairs Council - whereby this Council formation will no longer be subject to a presidency rotation. Furthermore, this Council formation will be separated from the General Affairs Council.[437] The High Representative will at the same time be Vice-President of the EC,

437 The Council meets in the following formations until further notice: 1. General Affairs; 2. External Relations [including European Security and Defence Policy and Development Cooperation]; 3. Economic and Financial Affairs [including Budget]; 4. Justice and Home Affairs [including Civil Protection]; 5. Employment, Social Policy, Health and Consumer Affairs; 6. Competitiveness (Internal Market, Industry

thus introducing the so-called double-hatted model. The High Representative thus combines the previous functions of the High Representative (Council) and the Commissioner responsible for Foreign Affairs; in future, he or she will represent the Union externally.

- *Legal personality [TCEU]*
  The Union will have its own legal personality and will thus be able to act as a subject of international law. It is thereby concurrently the successor to the European Community, whose legal personality will be transferred to it uno actu.
- *Security and Defence Policy [TCEU/ToL]*
  The Common Security and Defence Policy will be strengthened by the following elements:
  - The new solidarity clause [ToL] substantiates the obligation of Member States to support each other in the event of a terrorist attack, a natural disaster or a man-made disaster.
  - The mutual assistance guarantee [TCEU] of all EU Member States, already contained in Article I-41 paragraph 7 TCEU (Article 27 TEU as amended by the ToL), provides that a Member State which has been the victim of an armed attack on its territory shall be granted assistance and support in accordance with Article 51 UN Charter, whereby the specific character of the security and defence policy of certain Member States (e.g. neutrality obligations) remains unaffected, as do the assistance obligations of the Member States that are members of NATO. It is up to the neutral and non-aligned Member States to decide on a case-by-case basis on the merits, nature, and scope of any assistance to be provided.
  - The already existing broad range of missions [ToN] conducted by the Union within the framework of the CSDP - in the civilian, military, and humanitarian fields, in conflict prevention, and in the post-conflict area - is upheld.
  - Structured cooperation [TCEU] in CSDP is envisaged.
  - The European Defence Agency [ToN] + [ToL] is mentioned in the Treaty and supposed to better coordinate and make more efficient the

---

and Research) [including Tourism]; 7. Transport, Telecommunications and Energy; 8. Agriculture and Fisheries; 9. Environment; 10. Education, Youth and Culture [including Audiovisual].

procurement processes of the national armies as well as the field of research.

Changes related to democracy and proximity issues

- *Improved involvement of national parliaments [TCEU/ToL]*
  The ToL provides that national parliaments should actively contribute to the functioning of the Union. This is not a mandatory provision, but rather an invitation. Moreover, Protocols 1 and 2 provide for increased rights of participation of national parliaments in the context of subsidiarity control, above all - in contrast to the TCEU - the pre-clearance period for opinions of national parliaments was increased to eight weeks.
- *Charter of Fundamental Rights [ToL]*
  The Charter becomes legally binding through a reference in the TEU. However, under Protocol 7, the courts of the United Kingdom and Poland are exempt from the obligation to apply the Charter.
- *Participatory Democracy [TCEU/ToL]*
  Article 8b (now Article 11) TEU as amended by the ToL stipulates that the EU institutions must maintain an open, transparent, and regular dialogue with representative associations and civil society. Furthermore, the Commission must consult widely on legislative proposals. In addition, there is a right of initiative for EU citizens, whereby 1 million EU citizens from a significant number of Member States can invite the Commission to submit a legislative proposal on a specific topic.
- *Set of values [TCEU/ToL]*
  The ToL sets out the values of the Union, including direct reference to security, prosperity and protection of citizens.
- *European Convention on Human Rights [TCEU]*
  The EU is entitled to accede to the European Convention on Human Rights.
- *Division of Competences between the Union and the Member States [TCEU/ ToL]*
  The EU can only act within the competences explicitly granted to it by the Member States. Moreover, the final provisions of the TEU stipulate that the Union's competences can be extended as well as restricted by future Treaty revisions.
- *Pillar structure [TCEU/ToL]*
  The previous pillar structure (one supranational [EC] and two intergovernmental [CFSP, CJHA] pillars) is abandoned in favour of a (more)

supranational concept (two supranational [EC, JHA] areas and one quasi-supranational [CFSP] area).

- *Enlargement [ToL]*
  The enlargement provisions now stipulate that enlargement must take into account the criteria agreed by the European Council; this includes consideration of the Union's reception capacity (integration capacity as well as absorption capacity).
- *Withdrawal from the Union [TCEU]*
  Introduction of a special procedure governing voluntary withdrawal from the Union.
- *Efficiency and transparency in the Council [TCEU/ToL]*
  A large number of areas where unanimity was previously required in the Council are transferred to qualified majority voting. The Council will also be required to hold its meetings in public when adopting or deliberating on legal acts, which will be broadcast on the internet.
- *Social policy [TCEU/ToL]*
  A new horizontal social clause gives a prominent position to the Union's obligation to protect employment and social security. The role of the social partners is confirmed as part of the political, economic, and social fabric of the European Union.
- *Role of the regions [TCEU/ToL].*
  The role of the regions is confirmed as part of the political, economic, and social fabric of the European Union.

Amendments to key policies of the European Union

- *General Provisions [TCEU/ToL]*
  The ToL introduces a new and stronger legal basis in priority areas for the European Union such as energy, health, civil protection, climate policy, services of general interest, research and technological development, territorial cohesion, trade policy, space, humanitarian aid, sport, tourism, and administrative cooperation.
- *Energy [TCEU/ToL]*
  The ToL introduces a solidarity clause in the event of energy supply shortages.
- *Environment [ToL]*
  In the area of environmental policy, the specific need to combat climate change at international level is added.

III.1.9. Conference on the Future of Europe[438]

The Conference on the Future of Europe (CFEU) took place from April 2021 to May 2022 and was a series of conferences, citizen-led debates, and plenary sessions. The aim of the conference, which brought together representatives of European citizens, EU institutions and bodies, Member State governments, and European civil society, was to formulate non-binding ideas for the future development of Europe. The conference resulted in 49 proposals and 326 specific measures in nine thematic clusters:

- Climate change and the environment
- Health
- A stronger economy, social justice, and jobs
- EU in the world
- Values and rights, rule of law, security
- Digital transformation
- European democracy
- Migration
- Education, culture, youth, and sport.

III.2. Brexit

III.2.1. Agreement on the Withdrawal of the United Kingdom of Great Britain and Northern Ireland from the European Union and the European Atomic Energy Community[439]

The Brexit Withdrawal Agreement (= WA) was finally drafted in November 2018 and revised in October 2019. It was signed on 24 January 2020 and became effective on 1 February 2020.

The Withdrawal Agreement addresses the following elements:

- *Common provisions*
  Set of classic standard clauses for the proper understanding, functioning, and operation of the agreement.

438 Detailed results cf.: https://commission.europa.eu/system/files/2022-06/communication_1.pdf. On the CFEU cf.: https://futureu.europa.eu/en/?locale=en.

439 https://www.legislation.gov.uk/eut/withdrawal-agreement/contents/adopted and https://commission.europa.eu/strategy-and-policy/relations-non-eu-countries/relations-united-kingdom/eu-uk-withdrawal-agreement_en.

- *Citizens' rights*
  Protecting the life choices of over 5 million EU citizens in the UK and over 1 million UK nationals in EU countries, securing their right to remain, and ensuring they can continue to contribute to their community.
- *Separation issues*
  Ensuring a smooth transition and enabling an orderly withdrawal of the UK, including inter alia:
  - Goods placed on the market before the end of the transition period under EU rules can continue to reach their destination
  - Protection of existing intellectual property rights, including geographical indications
  - Completion of ongoing procedures related to police and judicial cooperation in criminal matters and other administrative and judicial procedures.
  - Use and protection of data and information exchanged before the end of the transitional period
  - Issues related to Euratom
- *Transitional provisions*
  During a transitional period (1 February - 31 December 2020) the EU treats the UK as a Member State, except for participation in EU institutions and administrative structures.[440]
- *Financial settlement*
  Ensuring that the UK and the EU meet all financial commitments made during the UK's membership of the EU.
- *Governance structure*
  Providing for the effective administration, implementation, and enforcement of the Agreement, including appropriate dispute settlement mechanisms.
- *Ireland*
  A legally enforceable solution that avoids a hard border on the island of Ireland, protecting the economy on all islands and the Good Friday Agreement in all its dimensions, and safeguarding the integrity of the EU's Internal Market.

---

440 The EU and the UK made use of these months to negotiate the EU-UK Trade and Cooperation Agreement.

- *Cyprus*
  A Protocol on the Sovereign Base Areas (SBA) in Cyprus to protect the interests of Cypriots living and working in the SBAs following the UK's withdrawal from the EU.
- *Gibraltar*
  A Protocol on Gibraltar facilitating close cooperation between Spain and the UK in relation to Gibraltar in the implementation of citizens' rights under the Withdrawal Agreement. The Protocol also covers administrative cooperation between appropriate authorities in a number of policy areas.
- *Annexes*
  The following annexes are attached to and form part of the agreement:
  - Annex 1: Social security coordination
  - Annex 2: Provisions of union law referred to in Article 41(4) WA
  - Annex 3: Time limits for situations or customs procedures referred to in Article 49(1) WA
  - Annex 4: List of networks, information systems, and databases referred in Articles 50, 53, 99 and 100 WA
  - Annex 5: Euratom
  - Annex 6: List of administrative cooperation procedures referred to in Article 98 WA
  - Annex 7: List of acts/provisions referred to in Article 128(6) WA
  - Annex 8: Rules of procedures of the joint committee and specialized committees
  - Annex 9: Rules of procedures for dispute settlement and code of conduct for members of arbitration panels

The WA is accompanied by a Political Declaration, which was revised in 2019 as the agreement itself, replacing the word "adequate" with "appropriate" in regard to labour standards. Furthermore, the level playing field mechanism was moved from the legally binding WA to the Political Declaration as part of the 2019 revision. At the insistence of the UK, the line that "the UK will consider aligning with Union rules in relevant areas" was removed from the Political Declaration.

Article 164 establishes a Joint Committee for the implementation, co-chaired by the EU and the UK, comprising six specialised committees. The WA entrusted the Joint Committee with the decision on some arrangements related to the separation of the UK from the EU.

There is equal representation from both sides with no casting vote and the option to go to an international arbitration panel if there is no agreement. There are a number of special subcommittees that report to the main committee, of which the 'Northern Ireland subcommittee' (dealing with the Northern Ireland Protocol) attracted most news-media attention in Spring 2021, because of the controversy over what became known as the Irish Sea border. Both sides are equally represented, with no casting vote and the option of recourse to international arbitration if agreement cannot be reached.

III.2.2. The Windsor Framework[441]

The Windsor Framework is a follow-up legal agreement between the EU and the United Kingdom that addresses certain aspects of the Northern Ireland Protocol annexed to the WA, in particular on the issue of movement of goods between the European Single Market and the United Kingdom, while the issue mainly relates to imports from the United Kingdom into Northern Ireland. The Windsor Framework was formally adopted by both parties on 24 March 2023.

The Windsor Framework is not a stand-alone agreement but an integral part of the WA as it was concluded in accordance with Articles 16 and 17 of the Northern Ireland Protocol.

The Windsor Agreement deals exclusively with goods crossing the Irish Sea from Great Britain to Northern Ireland and introduces so-called green and red lanes, with green lanes allowing direct import into Northern Ireland and red lanes for import into the Republic of Ireland and the European Single Market respectively. That way, checks and paperwork on goods destined for Northern Ireland shall be reduced. At the same time, these goods will be physically separated from those destined for transport to the EU.

In addition, the Windsor Framework includes arrangements on medicine control, VAT, and alcohol duty.

One of the key elements is the so-called "Stormont brake". Under this emergency brake, the Northern Ireland Assembly can temporarily prevent changes to EU goods regulations from applying in Northern Ireland if the Assembly considers that these changes have "significant and lasting

441 https://www.gov.uk/government/publications/the-windsor-framework.

effects on daily life". The threshold for triggering this brake on any new "significantly different" rule is 30 Members of the Legislative Assembly from two or more parties. If this threshold is reached, there is a 14-day consultation period before the matter can be referred to the UK government for consideration.

III.2.3. The Judgement of the European Court of Justice in Case C-499/21 P | Silver and Others v Council C-501/21 P | Shindler and Others v Council, and C-502/21 P | Price v Council Definitive dismissal of the actions brought by British citizens challenging the loss of their rights as EU citizens as a result of Brexit[442]

Since the entry into force of the withdrawal of the UK from the EU, several British citizens have tried to claim their rights as EU citizens. In Case C-673/20 (EP v Préfet du Gers, Institut national de la statistique et des études économiques (INSEE)), the ECJ had ruled on 9 June 2022 that "as of the withdrawal of the United Kingdom of Great Britain and Northern Ireland from the European Union, on 1 February 2020, nationals of that State who exercised their right to reside in a Member State before the end of the transition period no longer enjoy the status of citizen of the Union". The Court had "pointed out that citizenship of the Union requires possession of the nationality of a Member State". Some commentators stated that it is not often that the Court is confronted with a case where the legal position is so clear and contradicts the applicant's claims as clearly as in this case.[443]

However, the question in the joined cases C-499/21 P, C-501/21 P and C-502/21 P was aimed at a different issue and moved the claim to a higher level. The complainants had brought an action before the General Court challenging the Brexit withdrawal agreement and the Council's decision, claiming, inter alia, that those acts had deprived them of rights that they had exercised and acquired as EU citizens.[444] The applicants challenged the dismissal of their claims by the General Court at the ECJ.

---

442 https://curia.europa.eu/juris/document/document.jsf;jsessionid=90CB1FAF7BAFC8BB68542B759DC0DD69?text=&docid=274657&pageIndex=0&doclang=EN&mode=req&dir=&occ=first&part=1&cid=140645.

443 Cf. https://verfassungsblog.de/claiming-we-are-out-but-i-am-in-post-brexit/.

444 https://curia.europa.eu/jcms/upload/docs/application/pdf/2023-06/cp230101en.pdf.

On 15 June 2023, the ECJ dismissed the actions brought by British citizens challenging the loss of their rights as EU citizens as a result of Brexit.[445] The Court ruled that "the loss of the status of citizen of the European Union, and consequently the loss of the rights attached to that status, is an automatic consequence of the sole sovereign decision taken by the United Kingdom to withdraw from the European Union, by virtue of Article 50(1) TEU". The ECJ had thus made it perfectly clear that neither the WA nor the Council Decision, but only the sovereign decision taken by the United Kingdom to withdraw was the constitutive act of withdrawal. The ECJ has thus definitively established that it is only this decision by the United Kingdom that is responsible for the deprivation of rights as an EU citizen.

The ECJ highlights some noteworthy aspects:

- The action of the appellants is directed against the WA or the Council's decision at issue on the ground that those acts allegedly entailed the loss for the appellants of the status of EU citizen and of the rights attaching to that status;
- An action for annulment brought by a natural or legal person is admissible only in so far as that person has an interest in the annulment of the contested act. Such an interest presupposes that the annulment of the act is likely, in itself, to have legal consequences and that the action may thus, by its result, procure a benefit for the party that brought it.
- Neither the Council's decision at issue nor the WA was addressed to individual citizens;
- The decision to withdraw is for that Member State alone to take, in accordance with its constitutional requirements, and therefore depends solely on its sovereign choice;
- The annulment of the decision at issue could not procure an advantage for the appellants capable of justifying an interest in bringing proceedings, since that loss would not, in any event, be called into question by that annulment, as the loss of the status of citizen of the European Union, and consequently the loss of the rights attached to that status, is an automatic consequence of the sole sovereign decision taken by the United Kingdom to withdraw from the European Union.

445 https://eur-lex.europa.eu/legal-content/EN/TXT/HTML/?uri=CELEX:62020CJ0673.

At the same time, this ruling emphasised the UK's sovereignty under international law, as withdrawal under Article 50(4) TEU (in conjunction with Article 54 Vienna Convention on the Law of Treaties (= VCLT)) is a voluntary and unilateral act and will take effect two years after notification of withdrawal if no agreement can be reached. Should there be a withdrawal without an agreement, the rules of general international law will apply, in this case a roll-back. This so-called "hard Brexit" could be avoided through the WA. However, the UK is irrevocably responsible for the withdrawal and its consequences.

Sources and Literature

If you cannot read all your books,
at any rate handle, or as it were, fondle them.
Winston Churchill

ACEMOGLU, Daron/ ROBINSON, James A.: Why Nations Fail – Then Origins of Power, Prosperity, and Poverty, New York 2012

ARBLASTER, Anthony: Democracy, Third Edition, Buckingham 2002

BACH, Maurizio (Hrsg.): Die Europäisierung nationaler Gesellschaften, Köln 2000

BARNIER, Michel: My Secret Brexit Diary, Cambridge 2021

BARROSO, José Manuel Durão: Die Europäische Kommission 2004-2014 – Eine Bilanz des Präsidenten, Luxemburg 2014

BAUER, Joachim (Ed): Europa der Regionen - Aktuelle Dokumente zur Rolle und Zukunft der deutschen Länder im europäischen Integrationsprozeß, Schriften zum Europäischen Recht, Band 9, Berlin 1991, p 13-17

BAUM, Wilhem (Hrsg.): Kaiser Manuel II. Palaiologos: Dialog über den Islam und Erziehungsratschläge

BENEDIKT XVI.: Glaube und Vernunft – Die Regensburger Vorlesung, Freiburg – Basel – Wien2006

BERGMANN (Hrsg): Handlexikon der Europäischen Unionm, 4. Auflage, Baden-Baden – Wien – Basel 2012

BERMAN, Harold J.: Recht und Revolution – Die Bildung der westlichen Rechtstradition, Frankfurt 1995

BIEBER, Roland/ EPINEY, Astrid/ HAAG, Marcel: Die Europäische Union – Europarecht und Politik, 10. Auflage, Baden-Baden – Basel 2013

BIERMAN, Scott H./ FERNANDEZ, Luis: Game Theory with Economic Applications, Second Edition, New York 1998

BISCOP, Sven: Peace Without Money, War without Americans – Can European Strategy Cope?, Farnhem – Burlington 2015

BLAIR, Tony: A Journey, London 2010

BLUMENTHAL, Sidney: The Clinton Wars, New York 2003

BOGDANDY, Armin von/ VENZKE, Ingo: In wessen Namen? Internationale Gerichte in Zeiten globalen Regierens, Berlin 2014

BOTTCHER, Winfried (Hrsg): Klassiker des europäischen Denkens, Baden-Baden 2014

BRADFORD, Anu: The Brussels Effect – How the European Union Rules the World, Oxford 2020

BRANDSTETTER, Gerfried: Chronologisches Lexikon der europäischen Integration 1945 - 1995, Wien 1996

BRZEZINSKI, Zbigniew: The Grand Chessboard: American Primacy And Its Geostrategic Imperatives, New York 1998

BROOK-SHEPERD, Gordon: The Austrians: A Thousand-Year Odyssey, New York 2003

BRUNN, Gerhard: Die Europäische Einigung. Von 1945 bis heute, Stuttgart 2009

BUCHWALD, Wolfgang/ Hohlweg, Armin/ PRINZ, Otto (Hrsg.): Tusculum Lexikon griechischer und lateinischer Autoren des Altertums und des Mittelalters, völlig neu bearbeitete Auflage, Reinbek 1974

BUNDESKANZLERAMT ÖSTERREICH (Hrsg): Europa fängt zu Hause an – Subsidiaritätskonferenz St. Pölten, Wien 2006

BURCHILL, Scott/ LINKLATER, Andrew/ DEVETAK, Richard/ DONNELLY, Jack/ NARDIN, Terry/ PATERSON, Matthew/ REUS-SMIT, Christian/ TRUE, Jacqui: Theories of International Relations, Fifth Edition, New York 2013

CAMERON, David: For the Record, London 2019

CAMPBELL, Alastair/ SCOTT, Richard: The Blair Years, London 2008

CAMPBELL, John: Margaret Thatcher, Volume Two: The Iron Lady, London 2003

CASSEL, Dieter (1988): Wirtschaftspolitik als Ordnungspolitik. In: Cassel, Dieter/ Ramb, Bernd-Thomas /Thieme, H.J Jörg (Hrsg.): Ordnungspolitik, München 1988

CHALMERS, Damian/ DAVIES, Gareth/ MONTI, Giorgio: European Union Law, 3rd Edition, Cambridge 2014

CHURCH, Clive H./ PHINNEMORE, David: The Penguin Guide to the European Treaties, From Rome to Maastricht, Amsterdam, Nice and beyond, London 2002

CHURCHILL, Winston S.: The Second World War, London 1989

COGGAN, Philip: The Last Vote – The Threats to Western Democracy, London 2013

COOPER, Robert: The Breaking of Nations – Order and Chaos in the Twenty-First Century, London 2003

CRAIG, Paul/de BÚRCA, Gráinne: EU Law, Text, Cases and Materials, Seventh Edition, Oxford 2020

CRAIG, Paul/de BÚRCA, Gráinne (Eds): The Evolution of EU Law, Third Edition, Oxford 2021

CROUCH, Colin: Post-Democracy, Cambridge 2004

– The Strange Non-Death of Neoliberalism, Cambridge 2011

DAVIS, Norman: Europe – A History, Oxford 1996

DEMURO, Gianmario: A EU Constitutional Identity? An Inquiry into the Legal and Extra-Legal Elemets of Legitimation of the EU Process of Integration, in: PICHLER, Johannes W./ BALTHASAR, Alexander (Eds.): The Report on the Future of Europe – Striking the Balance between "Unity" and "Diversity", Proceedings of the Conference on European Democracy 2013, Wien – Graz 2014, S. 19-23

DÖRR, Oliver/ Schmalenbach, Kirsten (Eds): Vienna Convention on the Law of Treaties – A Commentary, 2nd Edition, Berlin 2018

DUFF, Andrew: The Treaty of Amsterdam, Text and Commentary, London 1997

ECCLESHALL et al. (Eds.): Political Ideologies, Third Edition, London 2003

EUCKEN, Walter: Über die Gesamtausrichtung der Wirtschaftspolitik (1946), in: OSWALT, Walter (Hrsg.): Ordnungspolitik von Walter Eucken, Münster - Hamburg – London 1999, S 1-24

FERDOWSI, Mir A. (Hrsg): Internationale Politik im 21. Jahrhundert, München 2002

FISCHER, Joschka: Die rot-grünen Jahre. Deutsche Außenpolitik vom Kosovo bis zum 11. September, Köln 2007

– "I am not convinced": Der Irak-Krieg und die rot-grünen Jahre, Köln 2011

– Scheitert Europa?, Köln 2014

– Vom Staatenbund zur Föderation. Gedanken übder die Finalität der europäischen Integration, Frankfurt 2000

FISCHER, Klemens H.: Der Europäische Verfassungsvertrag, Texte und Kommentar, 1. Auflage, Baden-Baden – Wien – Zürich 2004 [Verfassung]

– Der Konvent zur Zukunft Europas, Text und Kommentar, 1. Auflage, Baden-Baden – Wien – Zürich 2003 [Konvent]

– Der Vertrag von Lissabon, Text und Kommentar, 2. aktualisierte Auflage, Baden-Baden 2010 [Lissabon]

– Der Vertrag von Nizza, Text und Kommentar, 2. aktualisierte Auflage, Baden-Baden 2003 [Nizza]

– Der Vertrag von Lissabon: Die neue außen- und sicherheitspolitische Dimension der Europäischen Union - Ein politischer Stresstest, in: ALGIERI, Franco/ KAMMEL, Arnold H./ REHRL, Jochen: Integrationsprojekt Sicherheit – Aspekte europäischer Sicherheitspolitik im Vertrag von Lissabon, Baden-Baden 2011, pp 25-52

– EU Geopolitics: A Means to an End or an End in Itself – When the Exception becomes the Rule, the Crisis becomes Permanent, in: FISCHER, Klemens H. (Ed): European Security Put to the Test – Volume II: Geopolitics in Times of Permanent Crisis, Baden-Baden 2022, pp 243-297

– Lost in Implementation – The Political Dilemma of Enforcing the Rule of Law and its Impact on Foreign and Security Policy, in: FISCHER, Klemens H. (Ed): European Security Put to the Test – Volume I: Perspectives and Challenges for the Next Decade, Baden-Baden 2021, pp 195-220

– The European Union – A compact guide for business-government-relations, Baden-Baden 2001

– The Quest for Intermediate Europe – Politics based on Values, the Rule of Law, Good Governance, and the Triple-M-Approach – Providing Stability in Ukraine by Decentralization – The Comprehensive Approach, in: BALTHASAR, Alexander/ FISCHER, Klemens H. (Eds): Good Governance based on a Common Bedrock of Values – Providing Stability in Times of Crisis? Proceedings of the Conference on European Democracy 2015 (EuDEM 2015) 27 and 28 April 2015 (Vienna), pp. 61-104

FISCHER, Peter/ KÖCK, Heribert Franz/ KAROLLUS, Margit Maria: Europarecht, 4. Auflage, Wien 2002

FISHMAN, Ben (Ed): North Africa in Transition – The Struggle for Democracies and Institutions, London 2015

FLINT, Colin: Introduction to Geopolitics, Second Edition, Oxon – New York 2012

FOSTER, Peter: Facing Facts – Is Britain's Power Diminishing? Wrocław 2015

– *What went wrong with BREXIT and what can we do about it, London 2023*

FUKUYAMA, Francis: Political Order and Political Decay – From the Industrial Revolution to the Globalization of Democracy, New York 2014

GADDIS, John Lewis: The Cold War. A new History, New York 2007

GEHLER, Michael: Europa – Ideen, Institutionen, Vereinigungen, München 2010

GILLINGHAM, John: European Integration – 1950-2003, Cambridge 2003

GROEBEN, Hans von der: Legitimationsprobleme der Europäischen Gemeinschaft, Baden-Baden 1987

GROEBEN, Hans von der/ THIESING, Jochen/ EHLERMANN, Claus-Dieter (Hrsg): Kommentar zum EU-/ EG-Vertrag, Fünfte neu bearbeitete Auflage, Baden-Baden 1997

HABERMAS, Jürgen: Zur Verfassung Europas – Ein Essay, Berlin 2011

HABERMAS, Jürgen/ DERRIDA, Jacques: Unsere Erneuerung, Feuilleton, Frankfurter Allgemeine Zeitung, 31. Mai 2003, S 33 f

HEISBOURG, François : The EU Without the Euro, Survival, Volume 56 Number 2, April-May 2014, 27-48

HOBSBAWM, Eric: The Age of Extremes, New York 1996

– Nations and Nationalism since 1780, 2nd Ed, Cambridge 2012

HOYER, Werner/ KALDRACK, Gerd F. (Hrsg.): Europäische Sicherheits- und Verteidungspolitik (ESVP), Baden-Baden 2002

JONES, Erik/ KELEMAN, R. Daniel: The Euro Goes to Court, Survival, Volume 56 Number 2, April-May 2014, 15-22

KAGAN, Robert: Paradise and Power – America and Europe in the new World Order, London 2003

KAGAN, Robert: The Return of History and the End of Dreams, New York 2008

KAHN, Robert/ KUPCHAN, Charles: Europe's Make or Break Moment, Survival, Volume 55 Number 6, December 2013-January 2014, 29-48

KARNOW, Stanley: Vietnam – A History, London 1994

KISSINGER, Henry A.: Diplomacy, New York 1993

– Does America need a Foreign Policy? – Towards a Diplomacy for the 21st Century, New York 2001

– World Order, *New York 2014*

KOHL, Helmut: Aus Sorge um Europa – Ein Appell, München 2014

KUCHARSKI, Adam: The Rules of Contagion, London 2020

LARRES, Klaus: Churchill's Cold War – The Politics of Personal Diplomacy, New Haven – London 2002

LEITL, Christoph/ VERHEUGEN, Günter (Hrsg): Europa? Europa! – Wo liegt die Zukunft unseres Kontinents, Baden-Baden 2011

LUKIN, Alexander: Eurasian Integration and the Clash of Values, Survival, Volume 56 Number 3, June-July 2014, 43-60

MACMILLAN, Margaret: Peacemakers, London 2002

MAURER, Andreas/ NEISSER, Heinrich/ POLLAK, Johannes (Hrsg): 20 Jahre EU-Mitgliedschaft Österrreichs, Wien 2015

McCOURT, David M.: Has Britain Found its Role?, Survival, Volume 56 Number 2, April-May 2014, 159-178

McNAMARA, Robert S.: In Retrospect – The Tragedy and Lessons of Vietnam, New York 1995

MERRIT, Giles: Slippery Slope – Europe's Troubled Future, Oxford 2016

MIDDELAAR, Luuk van: The Passage to Europe – How a Continent became a Union, London 2013

MONNET, Jean: Mémoires, Paris 1976

MORDAUNT, Penny/ LEWIS, Chris: Greater Britain after the Storm, London 2021

NASSMACHER, Karl-Heinz (Ed): Foundations or Democracy, Baden-Baden 2001

NIXON, Richard: Beyond Peace, New York 1995

OLIVER, Craig: Unleashing Demons – The Inside Story of Brexit, London 2016

PICHLER, Johannes W. (Hrsg): Rechtswertestiftung und Rechtswertebewahrung in Europa, Schriften zur Rechtspolitik 37, Wien – Graz 2015

PIRIS, Jean-Claude: The Lisbon Treaty – A Legal and Political Analysis, Cambridge 2010

PORTER, Roy: Enlightenment, London 2000

RAT DER EUROPÄISCHEN UNION (Hrsg): Europa – Eine Idee nimmt Gestalt an, Baden-Baden – Luxemburg 2009

REICHENBACH, Horst/ EMMERLING, Eva/ STAUDENMAYER, Dirk/ SCHMIDT, Sönke: Integration: Wanderung über europäische Gipfel, Baden-Baden 1999

REUS-SMIT, Christian/ Snidal, Duncan (Eds): The Oxford Handbook of International Relations, Oxford 2010

REYNOLDS, David: Summits – Six Meetings that shaped the Twentieth Century, New York

OMP, Graham: Game Theory – Introduction and Applications, Oxford 1977

SCHEICH, Manfred: Tabubruch – Österreichs Entscheidung für die Europäische Union, Wien – Köln – Weimar 2005

SCHMIDT, Helmut: Ausser Dienst, München 2008

– Die Selbstbehauptung Europas – Perspektiven für das 21. Jahrhundert, München 2002

– *Weizsäcker, Richard von (Hrsg.):* Innenansichten aus Europa, München 2007

SCHWARZE, Jürgen (Hrsg.): EU-Kommentar, 3. Auflage, Baden-Baden – Basel – Wien 2012

SCHÜSSEL, Wolfgang: Offengelegt, Salzburg 2009

SEBESTYEN, Victor: 1946: The Making of the Modern World, London 2015

SHAW, Malcolm N.: International Law, Fourth Edition, Cambridge 1997

SIEDENTOP, Larry: Democracy in Europe, London 2001

SPINNEY, Laura: Pale Rider – The Spanish Flu of 1918 and how it changed the World, London 2017

STORA, Benjamin: Histoire de la Guerre d'Algérie, 1954-1962, 4e édition, Paris 2004

TAYLOR, Charles: A Secular Age, London 2007

TECHAU, Jan (Ed): Strategic Europe, Washington, DC – Brussels 2012

THATCHER, Margaret: The Downing Street Years, London 1993

THATCHER, Margaret: Statecraft – Strategies for a Changing World, London 2003

TUNSJØ, Oystein: Europe's Favourable Isolation, Survival, Volume 55 Number 6, December 2013-January 2014, 91-106

VEDDER, Christoph/ von HEINEGG, Wolff Heintschel (Hrsg.): Europäischer Verfassungsvertrag, Baden-Baden 2007

WARLEIGH, Alex: Democracy in the European Union, London 2003

WEIDENFELD, Werner (Hrsg): Die Europäische Verfassung in der Analyse, Gütersloh 2005

WEILER, Joseph H. H.: The Constitution of Europe, Cambridge 1999

Wheatcroft, Andrew: Infidels. The Conflict between Christendom and Islam 638-2002, London 2003

WIESSALA, Georg: The European Union and the Asian Countries, London 2002

WINDROW, Martin: The Last Valley – Dien Bien Phu and the French Defeat in Vietnam, London 2004

WRIGHT, Thomas: Europe's Lost Decade, Survival, Volume 55 Number 6, December 2013-January 2014, 7-28

WOSCHNAGG, Gregor/ MÜCK, Werner/ PAYRLEITNER, Alfred: Hinter den Kulissen – Österreichs EU-Vorsitz und die Zukunft Europas, Wien – Graz - Klagenfurt 2007

YOUNGS, Richard: The Uncertain Legacy of Crisis – European Foreign Policy Faces the Future, Washington D.C. 2014

ZERVAKIS, Peter A./ CULLEN, Peter J. (Eds): The Post-Nice-Process: Towards a European Constitution, Baden-Baden 2002

ZIEGERHOFER, Anita/ PICHLER, Johannes W./ LIKAR, Reinhard (Hrsg.): Die „Vereinigten Staaten von Europa" – Dokumente eines Werdens, Wien 1999

ZUCKERMAN, Gregory: A Shot to Safe the World, New York 2021

Register

D

F

G

H

I

N

O

S

T

U

V

W

X

Y

Z